Sentiment Analysis
in Social Networks

Sentiment Analysis in Social Networks

Edited by

Federico Alberto Pozzi

Elisabetta Fersini

Enza Messina

Bing Liu

AMSTERDAM • BOSTON • HEIDELBERG • LONDON
NEW YORK • OXFORD • PARIS • SAN DIEGO
SAN FRANCISCO • SINGAPORE • SYDNEY • TOKYO

Morgan Kaufmann is an imprint of Elsevier

Morgan Kaufmann is an imprint of Elsevier
50 Hampshire Street, 5th Floor, Cambridge, MA 02139, United States

Library of Congress Cataloging-in-Publication Data
A catalog record for this book is available from the Library of Congress

British Library Cataloguing-in-Publication Data
A catalogue record for this book is available from the British Library

ISBN: 978-0-12-804412-4

For information on all Morgan Kaufmann publications
visit our website at https://www.elsevier.com/

Working together
to grow libraries in
developing countries

www.elsevier.com • www.bookaid.org

Publisher: Todd Green
Acquisition Editor: Brian Romer
Editorial Project Manager: Amy Invernizzi
Production Project Manager: Priya Kumaraguruparan
Cover Designer: Victoria Pearson

Typeset by SPi Global, India

Contents

Contributors

F. Bisio
University of Genoa, Genoa, Italy

A. Bittar
Holmes Semantic Solutions, Gières, France

P. Buitelaar
National University of Ireland, Galway, Ireland

E. Cambria
Nanyang Technological University, Singapore, Singapore

G. Carenini
University of British Columbia, Vancouver, BC, Canada

P. Cipresso
Applied Technology for Neuro-Psychology Lab, IRCCS Istituto Auxologico Italiano, Milan, Italy

L. Dini
Holmes Semantic Solutions, Gières, France

M. Dinsoreanu
Technical University of Cluj-Napoca, Cluj-Napoca, Romania

G. Fei
University of Illinois at Chicago, Chicago, IL, United States

E. Fersini
University of Milano-Bicocca, Milan, Italy

D.I. Hernández Farias
Technical University of Valencia, Valencia, Spain; University of Turin, Turin, Italy

B.H.B. Honan
KRC Research, New York, NY, United States

E. Hoque
University of British Columbia, Vancouver, BC, Canada

I. Iennaco
Engineering Ingegneria Informatica, Turin, Italy

C.A. Iglesias
Technical University of Madrid, Madrid, Spain

C. Lemnaru
Technical University of Cluj-Napoca, Cluj-Napoca, Romania

H. Li
University of Illinois at Chicago, Chicago, IL, United States

B. Liu
University of Illinois at Chicago, Chicago, IL, United States

F. Mantovani
University of Milano-Bicocca, Milan, Italy

E. Messina
University of Milano-Bicocca, Milan, Italy

K. Moilanen
TheySay Ltd., London; University of Oxford, Oxford, United Kingdom

M. Montaner
Strategic Attention Management, Girona, Spain

G. Murray
University of the Fraser Valley, Abbotsford, BC, Canada

S. Negi
National University of Ireland, Galway, Ireland

M. Nissim
University of Groningen, Groningen, The Netherlands

L. Oneto
University of Genoa, Genoa, Italy

F. Pallavicini
University of Milano-Bicocca, Milan, Italy

P. Parau
Technical University of Cluj-Napoca, Cluj-Napoca, Romania

V. Patti
University of Turin, Torino, Italy

L. Pernigotti
Engineering Ingegneria Informatica, Bologna, Italy

R. Potolea
Technical University of Cluj-Napoca, Cluj-Napoca, Romania

F.A. Pozzi
SAS Institute Srl, Milan, Italy

S. Pulman
TheySay Ltd., London; University of Oxford, Oxford, United Kingdom

D. Richer
KRC Research, New York, NY, United States

C. Robin
Holmes Semantic Solutions, Gières, France

P. Rosso
Technical University of Valencia, Valencia, Spain

J.F. Sánchez-Rada
Technical University of Madrid, Madrid, Spain

S. Scamuzzo
Engineering Ingegneria Informatica, Assago (MI), Italy

F. Segond
Viseo Technologies, Grenoble, France

G. Vulcu
National University of Ireland, Galway, Ireland

Editors' Biographies

Dr. Federico Alberto Pozzi received his PhD degree in computer science from the University of Milano-Bicocca (Milan, Italy). His PhD thesis focused on probabilistic relational models for sentiment analysis in social networks. His research interests primarily focus on data mining, text mining, machine learning, natural language processing, and social network analysis, in particular applied to sentiment analysis and community discovery in social networks. He currently works at SAS Institute (Italy) as a senior solutions specialist in the area of integrated marketing management and analytics.

Dr. Elisabetta Fersini is currently a postdoctoral research fellow at the University of Milano-Bicocca. Her research activity is mainly focused on statistical relational learning, with particular interest in supervised and unsupervised classification. The research activity finds application in web/text mining, sentiment analysis, social network analysis, e-justice, and bioinformatics. She has actively participated in several national and international research projects. She has been an evaluator for international research projects and a member of several scientific committees. She cofounded an academic spin-off specialized in sentiment analysis and community discovery in social networks.

Dr. Enza Messina is a professor in operations research in the Department of Informatics, Systems, and Communication of the University of Milano-Bicocca, where she leads the research laboratory MIND ("Models in Decision Making and Data Analysis"). She holds a PhD degree in computational mathematics and operations research from the University of Milano. Her research activity is mainly focused on decision models under uncertainty and more recently on statistical relational models for data analysis and knowledge extraction. In particular, she has developed relational classification and clustering models that find application in domains such as systems biology, e-justice, text mining, and social network analysis.

Dr. Bing Liu is a professor of computer science at the University of Illinois at Chicago. He received his PhD degree in artificial intelligence from the University of Edinburgh. His current research interests include sentiment analysis and opinion mining, data mining, machine learning, and natural language processing. He has published extensively at top conferences and in journals, and is the author of three books: *Sentiment Analysis and Opinion Mining* (2012), *Web Data Mining: Exploring Hyperlinks, Contents, and Usage Data* (first edition, 2007; second edition, 2011), and *Sentiment Analysis: Mining Opinions, Sentiments and Emotions* (2015). Two of his articles received 10-year test-of-time awards from KDD, the premier conference of data mining and big data. His research has also been cited on the front page of the *New York Times*. He currently serves as Chair of the Association for Computing Machinery's Special Interest Group on Knowledge Discovery, and is a fellow of the Association for Computing Machinery, the Association for the Advancement of Artificial Intelligence, and the Institute of Electrical and Electronics Engineers.

Preface

The great diffusion of social networks and their role in modern society are among the more interesting novelties in recent years, capturing the interest of researchers, journalists, companies, and governments. The dense interconnection that often arises among active users generates a discussion space that is able to motivate and involve individuals, linking people with common objectives and facilitating diverse forms of collective action. This gives rise to what is called "individualism on the net": instead of always counting on a single reference community, thanks to the social networks it becomes possible to be stimulated by moving among more people and resources, which are often heterogeneous. Social networks are therefore creating a digital revolution. The most interesting aspect of this change is not solely related to the possibility of promoting political participation and activism. This social revolution influences the lives of every individual. It is the freedom to express ourselves, to have our own space in which we can be ourselves, or to be who we would like to be, with few limits and barriers.

The social network revolution enables us to talk about our emotions and opinions not only to ourselves but especially to those around us, interacting with them, opening a window on the worlds of others, and snooping into their lives. Paradoxically, all this happens while we are living in a society where it is even more difficult to know the names of our neighbors, and where the right to privacy becomes an imperative to which we submit. Because of social media, we effectively end up telling the whole (or most) of our life: happiness at the birth of a child, anger at a train delay, pre-Christmas shopping, or the choice made in the secrecy of the voting booth. It is then not surprising that researchers started to discuss the methods to capture this vast sea of information. The data on the net, if properly collected and analyzed, allows us not only to understand and explain many complex social phenomena but also to predict them. In this context, sentiment analysis tries to make evident *what people think* by providing representations, models, and algorithms able to move from "simple unstructured text" to "complex insight." In this book we want to provide a comprehensive understanding of this topic, with a particular emphasis on its role in social networks.

Sentiment Analysis in Social Networks is first of all directed at researchers with computer science, mathematics, and statistics skills both in academia and in industry. Researchers in academia can benefit from a consolidated knowledge background to create innovative solutions tuned in the challenging environment of social networks. On the other hand, companies and organizations can take advantage of the most recent state of the art to innovate processes, products, and services and therefore increase their competitiveness.

The book is organized as follows: Chapter 1 is intended to make the reader aware of the challenges related to sentiment analysis in social networks and prepare the reader for a full and precise understanding of the problems and solutions presented in the next chapters.

Chapter 2 introduces the psychological and sociological processes underlying social network interactions. The chapter starts by highlighting the differences and specific features that characterize online social network dynamics and finally points out how this understanding can be effectively exploited by sentiment analysis methodological approaches.

Chapter 3 describes the role of semantics in sentiment analysis by analyzing two main perspectives: the way semantics is encoded in sentiment resources, such as lexica, corpora, and ontologies, and the way it is used by automatic systems that perform sentiment analysis on social network data.

Chapter 4 highlights the main issues related to the interoperability of language resources for sentiment analysis. After an introduction to the linked data perspective for semantic modeling of sentiment and emotions, the chapter presents a linked data model based on two vocabularies: Marl and Onyx.

Chapter 5 presents the most recent state of the art with regard to the affective characterization of sentiment in social networks, then highlighting how affective reasoning can be employed for the development of applications in the context of big social data analysis.

Chapter 6 discusses a machine learning approach to sentiment analysis in social networks, by distinguishing between supervised, unsupervised, and semisupervised models and highlighting the potential leverage that the network structure can have.

Chapter 7 introduces irony and sarcasm when dealing with informal text on the network, underlining the difficulties that these figures of speech can cause for understanding the real sentiment of everyday communications.

Chapter 8 presents a comprehensive overview of a novel task related to suggestion mining from opinionated text. Various aspects are discussed, including the analysis of suggestions appearing in reviews, the relation between sentiments and suggestions, and the most recent methods for addressing the problem.

Chapter 9 introduces the problem of opinion spam detection. After an overview of the problem, different techniques to leverage the relationships between different entities in the network are presented for the detection of both opinion spam and opinion spammers.

Chapter 10 presents a comprehensive analysis of the state of the art related to opinion leader detection strategies and the associated challenges. A critical discussion of the advantages, limitations, and suitability of the approaches is provided, illustrating the potential for generating added value in different scenarios.

Chapter 11 surveys the techniques for both extractive and abstractive summarization of opinion-filled text, including a discussion of summarization evaluation. Then approaches to show opinion summaries to the users in the form of visualizations are discussed, including several interactive solutions.

In the following chapters, contributions from small- and medium-sized enterprises related to their solutions to sentiment analysis in social networks are presented. A comprehensive review of software tools and environments (both proprietary and open source) is presented and some case studies are outlined.

Chapter 12 presets SpagoBI, which is an entirely open source business intelligence suite. It offers a wide range of analytical tools to perform reporting, multidimensional analysis, key performance indicator management, visualization through charts, dashboards and cockpits, ad hoc querying and reporting, location intelligence, and network analysis.

Chapter 13 details SOMA, which is a smart social customer relationship management tool for companies aimed at monitoring and dealing with consumers' complaints and interactions in social networks, with a particular focus on both sentiment and emotions.

Chapter 14 describes KRC's proprietary social and digital media analytics suite, which is able to combine human intelligence with advanced predictive models.

Chapter 15 presents TheySay, which is a multidimensional opinion streaming architecture, powered by a large-scale custom natural language processing pipeline for sentiment, affect, and irrealis analysis used to monitor, quantify, and estimate the impact of corporate announcements to provide rich price-sensitive feedback and insights.

Finally, Chapter 16 presents a final discussion, concluding with some thoughts and opinions about future directions.

Acknowledgments

The completion of this book would not have been possible without the contribution of many individuals, to whom we express our appreciation and gratitude. Without their help the book might never have become a reality. First of all, we thank all the prestigious authors who accepted our offer to be part of this book. We are very grateful for their praiseworthy work and for the professionalism and seriousness they demonstrated during the preparation of this book. In particular, we thank Giuseppe Carenini, Erik Cambria, Stephen Pulman, Paolo Rosso, Delia Irazú Hernández Faria, Huayi Li, Sapna Negi, Carlos A. Iglesias, Viviana Patti, Malvina Nissim, Stefano Scamuzzo, Fabrizia Mantovani, Bradley Honan, Luca Dini, Karo Moilanen, Paul Parau, Paul Buitelaar, J. Fernando Sánchez-Rada, Gabi Vulcu, Letizia Pernigotti, Isabella Iennaco, Pietro Cipresso, Federica Pallavicini, Derek Richer, Gabriel Murray, Enamul Hoque, Geli Fei, Miquel Montaner, André Bittar, Cécile Robin, Frédérique Segond, Camelia Lemnaru, Mihaela Dinsoreanu, Rodica Potolea, Federica Bisio, and Luca Oneto.

We also express our gratitude to the companies which agreed to provide important contributions and to write about their good practices. On the publication side, it was a pleasure working with the helpful staff of Morgan Kaufmann, an imprint of Elsevier. We thank our editorial project manager, Amy Invernizzi, who has been very helpful for the success of this book. It has been a wonderful experience working with her. Finally, we thank all researchers, scientists and industries operating in this field for their important contributions in the literature regarding sentiment analysis.

CHALLENGES OF SENTIMENT ANALYSIS IN SOCIAL NETWORKS: AN OVERVIEW

1

F.A. Pozzi[a], E. Fersini[b], E. Messina[b], B. Liu[c]

SAS Institute Srl, Milan, Italy[a] University of Milano-Bicocca, Milan, Italy[b] University of Illinois at Chicago, Chicago, IL, United States[c]

1 BACKGROUND

Sentiment analysis, which is also called *opinion mining*, has been one of the most active research areas in natural language processing since early 2000 [1]. The aim of sentiment analysis is to define automatic tools able to extract subjective information from texts in natural language, such as opinions and sentiments, so as to create structured and actionable knowledge to be used by either a decision support system or a decision maker.

Unsurprisingly, there has been some confusion among researchers about the difference between *sentiment* and *opinion*, thus debating whether the field should be called *sentiment analysis* or *opinion mining*. In *Merriam-Webster's Collegiate Dictionary*, *sentiment* is defined as an attitude, thought, or judgment prompted by feeling, whereas *opinion* is defined as a view, judgment, or appraisal formed in the mind about a particular matter. The difference is quite subtle, and each of them contains some elements of the other. The definitions indicate that an opinion is more of a person's concrete view about something, whereas a sentiment is more of a feeling. For example, the sentence "*I am concerned about the current political situation*" expresses a sentiment, whereas the sentence "*I think politics is not doing well*" expresses an opinion. If someone says the first sentence in a conversation, we can respond by saying "*I share your sentiment,*" but for the second sentence we would normally say "*I agree/disagree with you.*" However, the underlying meanings of the two sentences are strictly related because the sentiment depicted in the first sentence is likely to be a feeling caused by the opinion in the second sentence. Conversely, the first sentiment sentence implies a negative opinion about politics, which is what the second sentence is saying. Although in most cases opinions imply positive or negative sentiments, some opinions do not, such as "*I think he will win at the next presidential election.*"

More formally, as defined in [1], an *opinion* is a quintuple,

$$(e_i, a_{ij}, s_{ijkl}, h_k, t_l), \tag{1.1}$$

where e_i is the name of an entity, a_{ij} is an aspect of e_i, s_{ijkl} is the sentiment on aspect a_{ij} of entity e_i, h_k denotes the opinion holder, and t_l is the time when the opinion is expressed by h_k.

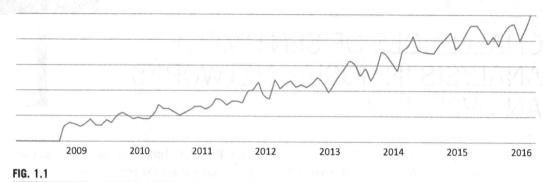

FIG. 1.1

Google Trends data related to the keywords *sentiment analysis*.

The sentiment s_{ijkl} is positive, negative, or neutral, or expressed with different strength/intensity levels, such as the 1–5 stars system used by most review websites (eg, Amazon[1]).

For example, consider that yesterday **John** bought an iPhone. He tested it during the whole day and when he went home from work (at **19:00** on **2-15-2014**) he wrote on his favorite social network the message "*The iPhone is very good, but they still need to work on battery life and security issues.*" Let us index "iPhone," "battery life," and "security" as 1, 2, and 3 respectively. John is indexed as 4 and the time when he wrote the sentence is indexed as 5. Then John is the opinion holder h_4 and t_5 ("19:00 2-15-2014") is the time when the opinion is expressed by h_4 (John). The term "iPhone" is the entity e_1, "battery life" and "security issues" are aspects a_{12} and a_{13} of entity e_1 ("iPhone"), $s_{1245} = neg$ is the sentiment on aspect a_{12} ("battery life") of entity e_1 ("iPhone"). and $s_{1345} = neg$ is the sentiment on aspect a_{13} ("security issues") of entity e_1 ("iPhone'). When an opinion is on the entity itself as a whole, the special aspect "GENERAL" is used to denote it.

From the definition of sentiment analysis reported above, "*the aim of sentiment analysis is therefore to define automatic tools able to extract subjective information in order to create structured and actionable knowledge.*" In line with this, the quintuple-based definition provides a framework to transform unstructured text to structured data (eg, a database table). Then a rich set of qualitative, quantitative, and trend analyses can be performed with traditional database management systems and online analytical processing tools.

Because of the importance of sentiment analysis to business and society, it has spread from computer science to management science and the social sciences. In recent years industrial activities surrounding sentiment analysis have also thrived: numerous start-ups have emerged, and many large corporations have built their own in-house capabilities (eg, Microsoft, Google, Hewlett-Packard, IBM, SAP, and SAS Global Communications).

Thanks to its strong applicability and interest in both the academic field and the industrial field, sentiment analysis is nowadays a trending topic. Fig. 1.1 represents the Google Trends data related to the keywords *sentiment analysis*, clearly demonstrating the continuous and increasing interest in this field.

Nowadays, sentiment analysis has gained even more value with the advent of social networks. Their great diffusion and their role in modern society represent one of the most interesting novelties

[1]http://www.amazon.com

in recent years, capturing the interest of researchers, journalists, companies, and governments. The dense interconnection that often arises among active users generates a discussion space that is able to motivate and involve individuals of a larger agora, linking people with common objectives and facilitating diverse forms of collective action. Social networks are therefore creating a digital revolution, enabling the expression and spread of emotions and opinions through the network, opening a window on others' respective worlds, and snooping into their lives. Opinionated data on the net, if properly collected and analyzed, allow one not only to understand and explain many complex social phenomena but also to predict them.

Considering that nowadays the current technological progress enables the efficient storing and retrieval of a huge amount of data, the current focus is now on methods for extracting information and creating knowledge from raw sources. Social networks represent an emerging challenging sector in the context of big data: the natural language expressions of people can be easily reported through short text messages, rapidly creating unique content of huge dimensions that must be efficiently and effectively analyzed to create actionable knowledge for decision making processes.

The massive quantity of continuously contributing texts in social networks, which should be processed in real time so as to make informed decisions, calls for two main types of radical progress: (1) a change of direction in the research through the transition from a data-constrained to data-enabled paradigm and (2) the convergence to a multidisciplinary area that mainly takes advantage of psychology, sociology, natural language processing, and machine learning. The knowledge embedded in social network content has been shown to be of paramount importance from both user and company/organization points of view: while people express opinions on any kind of topic in an unconstrained and unbiased environment, corporations and institutions can gauge valuable information from raw sources. To make qualitative textual data effectively functional for decision processes, the quantification of "what people think" becomes a mandatory step.

However, *sentiment analysis* is often improperly used when one is referring to *polarity classification*, which instead is a subtask aimed at extracting positive, negative, or neutral sentiments (also called *polarities*) from texts. Although an opinion could also have a neutral polarity (eg, "*I don't know if I liked the movie or not. I should watch it quietly.*"), most work in sentiment analysis usually assumes only positive and negative sentiments for simplicity. Depending on the field of application, several names are used for *sentiment analysis* (eg, *opinion mining*, *opinion extraction*, *sentiment mining*, *subjectivity analysis*, *affect analysis*, *emotion analysis*, and *review mining*). A taxonomy of the most popular sentiment analysis tasks is reported in Fig. 1.2.

Sentiment Analysis in Social Networks tries to overcome this limitation by (1) collecting and proposing new relevant research work from experts in the field, (2) debating the advantages and disadvantages when one is applying sentiment analysis in social networks, and (3) discussing the progress of sentiment analysis in social networks and future directions.

This book will accurately investigate the above-mentioned needs by providing advanced and specific solutions to address sentiment analysis in social networks. In particular, it presents the latest work by some of the most relevant experts in the field. At the end, a detailed conclusive discussion is provided and the personal and valuable thoughts and opinions of these researchers on future directions are presented. Although polarity classification is usually considered a core task because of its direct utility and applicability in working systems, all the chapters aspire to be relevant with respect to the needs outlined above. This is not a mere protocol declaration: the book has been thought about and designed

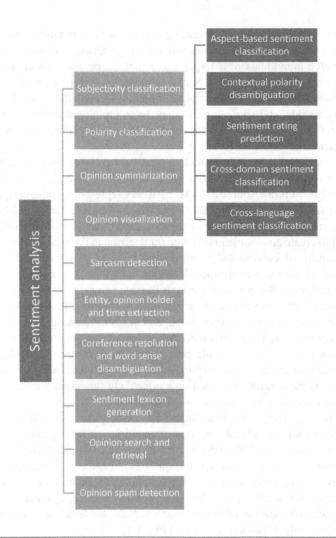

FIG. 1.2

Sentiment analysis tasks.

as a whole, as an indivisible gold mine, which intends to provide contributions highly connected to each other.

2 SENTIMENT ANALYSIS IN SOCIAL NETWORKS: A NEW RESEARCH APPROACH

The general trend in research regarding sentiment analysis in social networks is to apply the techniques inherited from traditional sentiment analysis studied since early 2000. However, considering the evolution of the sources where opinions are voiced, the strategies available in the current state of the art are no longer effective for mining opinions in this new and challenging environment. In fact, social network sentiment analysis, in addition to inheriting a multitude of issues from traditional sentiment analysis and natural language processing, introduces further complexities (short messages, noisy content, metadata such as gender, location, and age) and new sources of information not leveraged in traditional approaches.

In particular, given that social networks are clearly having an impact on *language*, the daily challenges regarding sentiment analysis mainly focus on the constant evolution of the language used online in user-generated content: the words that surround us every day influence the words we use. Since much of the written language we see is now on the screens of our computers, tablets, and smartphones, language now evolves partly through our interaction with technology. And because the language used in social networks for us to communicate with each other tends to be more malleable than formal writing, the combination of informal, personal communication, and the mass audience afforded by social networks is a recipe for rapid change. Taking into serious consideration the continuous language revolution, we believe sentiment analysis systems should be able to natively adapt to it, or alternatively be adapted by researchers. Being able to juggle these problems requires strong natural language processing and linguistics skills. As a side effect, this language evolution strongly influences the way in which irony and sarcasm is uttered.

A further daily challenge relates to the nature of social networks, which by definition are dynamic and heterogeneous and the entities involved are connected to each other. Conversely, a representation of real-world data where instances are considered as homogeneous, independent, and identically distributed leads us to a substantial loss of information and to the introduction of a statistical bias. Dealing with *relational* environments by our taking advantage of social network analysis becomes a mandatory step to go beyond the current state of the art, where only textual content is tackled. For this reason, the combination of content and relationships is a core task of the recent literature on sentiment analysis.

A final crucial issue, which is usually overlooked, is concerned with visualization and summarization of opinions. This issue becomes more important when opinions need to be concisely presented over large networked environments. Traditional visual analytic tools need to be redesigned according to this novel necessity.

3 SENTIMENT ANALYSIS CHARACTERISTICS

Sentiment analysis is a broad and complex field of research. In the following, the main characteristics that constitute sentiment analysis are described and discussed in detail.

3.1 SENTIMENT CATEGORIZATION: OBJECTIVE VERSUS SUBJECTIVE SENTENCES

The first aim when one is dealing with sentiment analysis usually consists in distinguishing between subjective and objective sentences. If a given sentence is classified as objective, no other fundamental tasks are required, while if the sentence is classified as subjective, its polarity (positive, negative, or neutral) needs to be estimated (see Fig. 1.3). Subjectivity classification [2] is the task that distinguishes

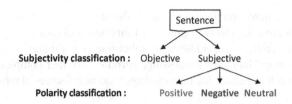

FIG. 1.3

Sentiment analysis workflow.

sentences that express objective (or factual) information (**objective sentences**) from sentences that express subjective views and opinions (**subjective sentences**).

An example of an objective sentence is "*The iPhone is a smartphone*," while an example of a subjective sentence is "*The iPhone is awesome*." Polarity classification is the task that distinguishes sentences that express positive, negative, or neutral polarities. Note that a subjective sentence may not express any positive or negative sentiment (eg, "*I guess he has arrived*"). For this reason, it should be classified as "neutral."

3.2 LEVELS OF ANALYSIS

As mentioned earlier, the aim of sentiment analysis is to "*define automatic tools able to extract subjective information from texts in natural language*." The first choice when one is applying sentiment analysis is to define what *text* (ie, the analyzed object) means in the case of study considered.

In general, sentiment analysis in social networks can be investigated mainly at three levels (represented graphically in Fig. 1.4):

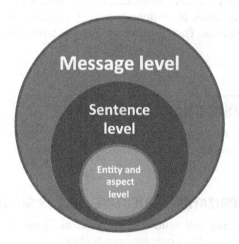

FIG. 1.4

Different levels of analysis.

- **Message level**: The aim is to classify the polarity of a whole opinionated message. For example, given a product review, the system determines whether the text message expresses an overall positive, negative, or neutral opinion about the product. The assumption is that the entire message expresses only one opinion on a single entity (eg, a single product).
- **Sentence level**: The aim is to determine the polarity of each sentence contained in a text message. The assumption is that each sentence, in a given message, denotes a single opinion on a single entity.
- **Entity and aspect level**: Performs a finer-grained analysis than message and sentence level. It is based on the idea that an opinion consists of a *sentiment* and a *target* (of opinion). For example, the sentence "*The iPhone is very good, but they still need to work on battery life and security issues*" evaluates three aspects: iPhone (positive), battery life (negative), and security (negative).

3.3 REGULAR VERSUS COMPARATIVE OPINION

An opinion can assume different shades and can be assigned to one of the following groups:

- **Regular opinion**: A regular opinion is often referred to in the literature as a *standard opinion* and it has two main subtypes:
  - **Direct opinion**: A direct opinion refers to an opinion expressed directly on an entity (eg, "*The screen brightness of the iPhone is awesome*").
  - **Indirect opinion**: An indirect opinion is an opinion that is expressed indirectly on an entity on the basis of its effects on some other entities. For example, the sentence "*After I switched to the iPhone, I lost all my data!*" describes an undesirable effect of the switch on "my data," which indirectly gives a negative sentiment to the iPhone.
- **Comparative opinion**: A comparative opinion expresses a relation of similarities or differences between two or more entities and/or a preference of the opinion holder based on some shared aspects of the entities [3]. For example, the sentences, "*iOS is better performing than Android*" and "*iOS is the best performing operating system*" express two comparative opinions. A comparative opinion is usually expressed with use of the comparative or superlative form of an adjective or adverb.

3.4 EXPLICIT VERSUS IMPLICIT OPINIONS

Among the different shades that an opinion can assume, we have to distinguish explicit and implicit opinions:

- **Explicit opinion**: An explicit opinion is a subjective statement that gives a regular or comparative opinion (eg, "*The screen brightness of the iPhone is awesome*").
- **Implicit opinion**: An implicit opinion is an objective statement that implies a regular or comparative opinion that usually expresses a desirable or undesirable fact (eg, "*Saturday night I'll go to the movie theater to watch 'Lone Survivor.' I cannot wait to watch it!*" and "*'Saving Private Ryan' is more violent than 'Lone Survivor'*"). The first example suggests that there is some good expectation about the movie, although it is not explicated in words, while understanding the hidden opinion in the second example is difficult even for humans. For some people, violence in war

movies could be a good characteristic that makes the movie more realistic, whereas it could be a negative feature for others.

Clearly, explicit opinions are easier to detect and to classify than implicit opinions. Much of the current research has focused on explicit opinions. Relatively less work has been done on implicit opinions.

3.5 THE ROLE OF SEMANTICS

The semantics of the language used in social networks is fundamental to accurately analyze user expressions. The context of a textual expression is therefore a crucial element that should be taken into account to properly deal with the underlying sentiment. A sentence "taken as it is" can appear as negative or positive, but if it is properly analyzed from a semantic point of view it can be completely different. For instance, the sentences *"I watched the most terrific horror movie. It was like a real nightmare! PAAAANIIIICCC"* can be initially interpreted as negative, but taking into account the context where these kinds of opinions are expressed (ie, a community of horror-movie lovers) and some lexical cues that are typical of the social network language, we should derive a (real) positive judgment. Lexica, corpora, and ontologies need to be properly constructed and used for us to have a deep understanding of the semantics of the natural language in online social networks.

3.6 DEALING WITH FIGURES OF SPEECH

A figure of speech is any artful deviation from the ordinary mode of speaking or writing [4]. In the tradition of Aristotle, figures of speech can be divided into two groups: *schemes* and *tropes*. The function of schemes and tropes is to carry out a transference of some kind; schemes are characterized by a transference in order, while tropes are characterized by a transference in meaning.

For example, the most problematic figures of speech in natural language processing are **irony** and **sarcasm**, which are collocated under the tropes group. While irony is often used to emphasize occurrences that deviate from the expected, such as twists of fate, sarcasm is commonly used to convey implicit criticism with a particular victim as its target [5]. Examples of sarcastic and ironic sentences are:

1. **Sarcasm** (*Note: Alice hates Bill's travel books*)
   - Alice: Yeah, I like, really dig your travel books, Bill. You're a really skillful author.
   - Bill: Oh.
2. **Irony** (*Note: Bill and Alice have just seen a really appalling play at the theater. Both Bill and Alice are disappointed.*)
   - Bill: Well! What a worthwhile use of an evening!
   - Alice : Yeah.

In the irony example, there was no sarcasm because Bill was not intending to wound Alice with his comment. He was using irony to remark that he felt he had wasted his evening at the theater. In the sarcasm example, Alice used sarcasm to show Bill that she did not like his books and thought that he is not a good writer. There is irony too, but the tone of the delivery that conveys implicit criticism makes it sarcastic.

One inherent characteristic of the sarcastic and irony speech acts is that they are sometimes hard to recognize, first for humans and then for machines. The difficulty in the recognition of sarcasm and irony causes misunderstanding in everyday communication and poses problems to many natural language processing systems because of the poor results obtained by state-of-the-art work. In the context of sentiment analysis (where *sarcasm* and *irony* are usually considered as synonyms) when a sarcastic/ironic sentence is detected as positive, it likely means negative, and vice versa.

3.7 RELATIONSHIPS IN SOCIAL NETWORKS

Sentiment analysis in social networks is generally based on the assumption that the texts provided by the users are independent and identically distributed. Although much effort has been expended on handling the complex characteristics of the language in social networking environments, consideration of user-generated content as networked text is still an open issue. A first tentative approach to deal with the real nature of social network content is related to the principle of homophily [6]. In this context, "friendship" relationships can be used to infer that connected users may be likelier to hold similar opinions. However, a sentiment analysis system should take into account that the assumption about the friendship relations does not properly reflect the real world, where two connected users could have different opinions about the same topic. According to this remark, several other pieces of relational information can be extracted from the social network itself for better representation of user and post connections. Relationships based on sharing activities or that represent an appreciation can be more informative than a simple friendship.

4 APPLICATIONS

One of the most important needs of businesses and organizations in the real world is to find and analyze consumer or public opinions about their products and services (eg, "Why aren't consumers buying our laptop?"). Knowing the opinions of existing users regarding a specific product is also interesting for individual consumers. This information could be useful to decide whether to buy the product or not. This shows that decision making processes are also common in everyday lives. However, with the advent of sentiment analysis, an individual is no longer strictly limited to asking friends and family for their opinions or an organization is no longer limited to conducting surveys, opinion polls, and focus groups to sound out public or consumer opinions. Sentiment analysis paves the way to several and interesting applications, in almost every possible domain.

For example, summarizing user reviews is a relevant task. In addition, errors in user ratings could be fixed [7]: it is possible that users accidentally select a low rating when their review indicates a positive evaluation. Moreover, opinions matter a great deal in politics. Some work has focused on understanding what voters are thinking [8,9]. For instance, the US president Barack Obama used sentiment analysis to gauge the feelings of core voters during the 2008 presidential election. Other projects have as a long-term goal the clarification of politicians' positions, such as what public figures support or oppose, to enhance the quality of information that voters have access to [10,11]. A further task is the augmentation of recommendation systems, where the system might not recommend items that receive negative feedback several times.

Moreover, ads are displayed in sidebars in some online systems. It could be useful to detect webpages that contain inappropriate content for the placement of ads [12]. The system could highlight product ads when relevant positive sentiments are detected, and hide the ads when negative statements are discovered.

Opinionated documents could also have the form of organizations' internal data (eg, customer feedback). Sentiment analysis applications have spread to several domains, from services and health care to financial services and political elections. However, sentiment analysis can also be applied to more ethical principles. For example, on the basis of observations of Twitter's role in civilian response during the 2009 Jakarta and Mumbai terrorist attacks, Cheong and Lee [13] proposed a structured framework to harvest civilian sentiment and response on Twitter during terrorism scenarios. Coupled with intelligent data mining, visualization, and filtering methods, these data can be collated into a knowledge base that would be of great utility to decision makers and the authorities for rapid response and monitoring during such scenarios. Sentiment analysis is also applied to the medical field. Cobb et al. [14] applied sentiment analysis to examine how exposure to messages about the smoking-cessation drug varenicline (used to treat nicotine addiction) affects smokers' decision making regarding its use.

REFERENCES

[1] B. Liu, Sentiment Analysis and Opinion Mining, Morgan & Claypool, San Rafael, CA, 2012.
[2] J.M. Wiebe, R.F. Bruce, T.P. O'Hara, Development and use of a gold-standard data set for subjectivity classifications, in: Proceedings of the 37th Annual Meeting of the Association for Computational Linguistics on Computational Linguistics, ACL '99, Association for Computational Linguistics, 1999, pp. 246–253.
[3] N. Jindal, B. Liu, Identifying comparative sentences in text documents, in: Proceedings of the 29th Annual International ACM SIGIR Conference on Research and Development in Information Retrieval, SIGIR '06, ACM, 2006, pp. 244–251.
[4] E.P.J. Corbett, Classical Rhetoric for the Modern Student, second ed., Oxford University Press, Oxford, UK, 1971.
[5] S. McDonald, Exploring the process of inference generation in sarcasm: a review of normal and clinical studies, Brain Lang. 68 (3) (1999) 486–506.
[6] P.F. Lazarsfeld, R.K. Merton, Friendship as a social process: a substantive and methodological analysis, in: M. Berger, T. Abel, C.H. Page (Eds.), Freedom and Control in Modern Society, Van Nostrand, New York, 1954, pp. 8–66.
[7] B. Pang, L. Lee, Opinion Mining and Sentiment Analysis, Found. Trends Inf. Retr. 2 (1–2) (2008) 1–135.
[8] A.B. Goldberg, X. Zhu, S.J. Wright, Dissimilarity in graph-based semi-supervised classification, in: AISTATS, vol. 2, 2007, pp. 155–162.
[9] D. Hopkins, G. King, Extracting systematic social science meaning from text, Manuscript available at http:// gking.harvard.edu/files/words.pdf, (2007).
[10] M. Bansal, C. Cardie, L. Lee, The power of negative thinking: exploiting label disagreement in the min-cut classification framework, in: COLING (Posters), 2008, pp. 15–18.
[11] S.C. Greene, Spin: Lexical Semantics, Transitivity, and the Identification of Implicit Sentiment, ProQuest, Ann Arbor, MI, 2007.

[12] X. Jin,Y. Li, T. Mah, J. Tong, Sensitive webpage classification for content advertising, in: Proceedings of the First International Workshop on Data Mining and Audience Intelligence for Advertising, ADKDD '07, ACM, 2007, pp. 28–33.

[13] M. Cheong, V.C.S. Lee, A microblogging-based approach to terrorism informatics: exploration and chronicling civilian sentiment and response to terrorism events via Twitter, Inform. Syst. Front. 13 (1) (2011) 45–59.

[14] N.K. Cobb, D. Mays, A.L. Graham, Sentiment analysis to determine the impact of online messages on smokers' choices to use varenicline, J. Natl. Cancer Inst. Monogr. 47 (2013) 224–230.

BEYOND SENTIMENT: HOW SOCIAL NETWORK ANALYTICS CAN ENHANCE OPINION MINING AND SENTIMENT ANALYSIS

F. Pallavicini[a], P. Cipresso[b], F. Mantovani[a]

*University of Milano-Bicocca, Milan, Italy[a] Applied Technology for Neuro-Psychology Lab,
IRCCS Istituto Auxologico Italiano, Milan, Italy[b]*

1 INTRODUCTION

The exponential growth in the use of digital devices, together with ubiquitous online access, provides unprecedented ground for the constant connectivity of people and offers tremendous capabilities for publicly expressing opinions, attitudes, or reactions regarding many aspects of everyday human activities [1]. Social media, such as blogs, forums, and social network platforms (eg, Facebook, LinkedIn, Twitter, Instagram, YouTube) are quickly becoming an integral part of people's lives, the virtual spaces where daily individuals share opinions and information and maintain and/or expand their relational network. The massive use of online social networks and the abundance of data collected through them has raised exponentially the attention of the scientific and business community toward them [2–4]. Nowadays, the constant refinement of analytical tools is offering a richer array of opportunities to analyze these data for many different purposes [5]. Differences in features and characteristics of online social networks are reflected in the huge amount of different statistics and metrics that it is possible to track and analyze. The most adopted metrics are numeric, relatively easy to obtain, and freely available, such as engagement and influence metrics [6]. However, metrics of this types are often defined as "vanity metrics," since they do not interpret or contextualize the data collected.[1,2] For this reason, other types of methods of analysis has been introduced. Among them, one of the most used is sentiment analysis (SA) [7], which is the analysis of the feelings (ie, opinions, emotions and attitudes) behind the words using natural language processing tools. SA is considered a quality metric, which looks behind numbers to understand how information about emotion and attitudes is conveyed in language [7]. Given the rising interest in the application of SA to data from online social networks, the research in this area has acknowledged the limitations

---

[1]http://www.socialmediatoday.com/social-business/2015-04-09/social-vanity-metrics-top-4-worst-offenders
[2]https://www.socialmediaexplorer.com/social-media-measurement/in-praise-of-vanity-metrics/

Sentiment Analysis in Social Networks. http://dx.doi.org/10.1016/B978-0-12-804412-4.00002-4

coming from handling the complex characteristics of natural language (and related inferences) without considering the data collected through social networks as "networked data." Most of the work in SA [8,9] is based merely on textual information expressed in online posts and comments. Early approaches to overcome this important limitation are emerging in recent literature, trying, for example, to leverage information on friendship relationships between individuals, since connected users may be likelier to hold similar opinions[3] [10,11]. However, these features only approximate the rich relation structure encoded in an online social network. Among possible complementary analytical methods that are starting to be introduced in the analysis of data collected through online social networks, one of the most interesting is social network analysis (SNA), which, through a quantitative-relational approach, makes it possible to consider relational data (ie, existing connections and links between users on social networks). Within this context this chapter will first define online social networks and briefly describe their history, highlighting the differences and specific features that characterize them. Then the psychological and sociological processes underlying online social network interactions will be discussed within the framework of relevant theoretical constructs and methods of analysis (with special focus on SNA). Finally, the chapter will point out how this understanding can be effectively integrated into SA methodological approaches to empower their reliability and validity.

2 DEFINITIONS AND HISTORY OF ONLINE SOCIAL NETWORKS

When analyzing the communication that takes place through online social networks, one must consider that communication follows specific rules and expectations of computer-mediated communication environments [12]. Different levels of virtuality and differences in terms of available repertoire of signaling systems significantly affect the ways that interlocutors communicate with each other across different media [13,14]. In addition, depending on the specific online social networks, there are different possibilities for users to communicate with each other and to express themselves. On each social network platform, people have several possibilities to interact, and there are very different types of data that can be collected through them (eg, texts, videos, photos). There are some key differences among these sources, and an accurate understanding of what they are can help us to define more efficient ways to analyze the rich information they contain.

2.1 WHAT EXACTLY IS AN ONLINE SOCIAL NETWORK?

Digital media are defined as the set of media based on digital technologies that have common characteristics that differentiate them from the media that preceded them (radio, press, television, etc.) [15]. Among digital media, the use of social media (ie, the part of the services and online communication platforms based on the exploitation of social dynamics) has risen especially. The terms *online social networks* and *social media* are often confused with each other. However, there are several differences between them.[4,5] The main one is that the term *social media* refers only to the web, while *social network* does not. The concept of a social network is much older than the advent of

---

[3] http://firstmonday.org/ojs/index.php/fm/article/view/4944/3863
[4] http://lonscohen.com/blog/2009/04/difference-between-social-media-and-social-networking/
[5] http://www.socialmediatoday.com/content/5-differences-between-social-media-and-social-networking

the World Wide Web and advanced technological devices; it results from historical studies conducted within sociology, and, in particular, sociometry; that is, the science that studies relationships between people from a quantitative point of view [16,17]. However, when the term *social network* is considered referring to the features identified by Boyd and Ellison [13], the history of social networks, as will be discussed in the following paragraph, is much more recent.

An online social network could be considered the prototypical form of social media, and it can be defined as "a platform based on new media" that allows users to manage both their social network (organization, extension, exploration, and comparison) and their social identity (description and definition) [18]. According to Boyd and Ellison [13], there are three constitutive elements of a social network:

- the presence of a virtual space (forum) in which users can make and present their own profile; the profile must be accessible, at least in partial form, to all the users of the network;
- the possibility to create a network with other users with whom they can communicate;
- the possibility to analyze the characteristics of an individual own network, in particular the connections with other users [16,17].

Social networks sites, in particular, are defined as web services where people can (1) construct a public or semipublic profile within a bounded system, (2) define a list of users with whom they establish a connection, and (3) view their list of connections and those made by the others within the system [13].

2.2 BRIEF HISTORY OF ONLINE SOCIAL NETWORKS

Most of the functions of online social networks have been available separately in the different tools that preceded them: the creation of networks was possible even with newsgroups, and the creation and sharing of personal content online was possible through websites and blogs. However, with reference to the presence of all the features identified by Boyd and Ellison [13], the first social network site was SixDegrees.com, designed in 1997 by Andrew Weinreich, born as an online dating website. SixDegrees.com allowed its users to create relationships only with people who were "friends of friends" (ie, who had a certain degree of connection between them). This innovative feature was aimed at preventing the sharing of false information and the presence of users with bad intentions, as happened on similar dating sites. The goal of this strategy was threefold:

- to give the possibility to verify the user's profile information by asking one's own friends;
- to obtain indirect information about people through the analysis of their social network;
- to increase the possibility that individuals engage with each other.

SixDegrees.com had more than 1 million users, and was active until 2001. Starting in the first decade of this century, many social networking sites were born, trying to capitalize on the winning ideas of SixDegrees.com. In these years, popular names, including Friendster, MySpace, Facebook, and YouTube, were created [19].

Facebook, which in a few years has become the most famous and most used online social network worldwide, was initially created by Mark Zuckerberg in 2004 as a tool to connect students at Harvard University. The idea was to develop a social network to support a closed community, creating the online version of the university yearbook. Then Facebook was expanded to connect all US universities, and was eventually opened to all, until its spread as a mass phenomenon in 2006, when it had 12 million users. From a strategic point of view, the winning move that allowed the rise of Facebook was primarily to progressively increase the relational and expressive opportunities of the service, through the introduction of applications including the profile page, groups, photos, notes, and events. Another important decision was to make the Facebook system able to fully cover the needs of the user, becoming an aggregator of information and services. This was possible thanks to the development of Facebook Platform, consisting of a set of procedures (application programming interface) used to create a usable app inside Facebook. Another milestone in the history of online social networks is February 14, 2005: Chad Hurley, Steve Chen, and Jawked Karim, three young PayPal employees, registered the domain name YouTube and on April 23 of the same year the first video - Me at the Zoo - was uploaded. Just 10 months after the official launch, this platform had already set a record: in 2006 YouTube had an average of 65,000 video uploads per day and 20 million unique accesses. The success did not go unnoticed, and in October 2009 YouTube was sold to Google for US$1.65 billion. Just 1 year after the founding of YouTube, in 2006 Twitter was created. Its creators Jack Dorsey, Evan Williams, and Biz Stone wanted to create a system able to allow people to communicate via SMS with a small number of friends. So Twitter was developed as a microblogging system, a service for exchange of information, which allows users to send messages (ie, a tweet) of 140 characters. As stated by its creators, Twitter can be defined as "a real-time information network that connects you to the latest information about what you find interesting" [20]. Since the main reason for the publication of a tweet is sharing, Twitter has developed a system to expand the target audience: the hashtag. This feature facilitates the ability to follow topics and threads of interest: if a word is preceded by the # (in English "hash") symbol, then clicking on it leads to the result.

3 ARE ONLINE SOCIAL NETWORKS ALL THE SAME? FEATURES AND METRICS

Beyond the shared features identified by Boyd and Ellison [13], online social networks are very different in their features and in the expressive possibilities they offer to their users. According to this general definition, there are different types of online social networks that need to be distinguished further. There is currently no systematic and exhaustive categorization of the different social networks that is unanimously agreed on. However, it is possible to group them and organize their complexity according to their different features, including the types of user-generated content and the types of relationships that are allowed between users.

After having explored the differences between online social networks on the basis of these characteristics, we will present the most used statistics and metrics so as to provide an overview on methods of analysis and interpretation of data collected through them.

3.1 TYPES OF USER-GENERATED CONTENT

According to the types of user-generated content, online social networks can be divided into several categories [21], including:

- profile-based social networks: focused on the users and on their desire to express themselves and communicate with their contacts (eg, Facebook, MySpace); among social networks of this type, Facebook is the first resource concerning the social sphere of people (friends, family, etc.), where individuals share content especially about their private lives, personal interests, and activities;

- microblogging social networks: focused on the shared message, which has to be short and clear (eg, Twitter). Twitter is the most famous one, and is often described as a site of "amateur journalism" [20] where people share content especially about specific and current events and situations;
- content-based social networks: focused on the content posted by users (eg, YouTube, Flickr, Instagram).

3.2 TYPES OF RELATIONSHIPS BETWEEN USERS

Online social networks represent virtual places where people can meet and communicate with each other. On these platforms people tend to shape their contacts as they do offline [22,23]. However, the possibilities of interaction between people in online social networks are linked to the specific characteristics of the platform used and, in particular, to the ways through which they allow contact between users. In particular, the type of relationship that people can have on a social network can be divided as follows [18]:

- Two way, or "friendship" (eg, Facebook): this allows users who are friends with each other to their access friends' profiles, contact them directly through a private chat (ie, Messenger), read new messages on their bulletin board, explore their social network, and know the actions within the social network (ie, membership in groups, places visited, etc.). This mechanism allows the creation of a closed social network: only people accepted as friends can access it, no one is a total stranger, and anyone can be identified as a friend of someone else.
- "Star" (eg, Twitter): this clearly distinguishes between sender and receiver. The message issuer can be general (ie, shared with all the receivers on the social network) or individual (ie, directed to a specific receiver). Through this mechanism a user can be both a sender and a receiver depending on the social network to which the user is connected. The mode of connection in a star relationship is open: most receivers (followers) have no other contact with the sender, apart from that in the social network. The model of communication is "from one to many": individuals share content that could arouse interest, or, better, could be retweeted. Tweeting is not mandatory, and people can follow others according to their shared interests.

3.3 INDEXES AND METRICS TO ANALYZE DATA COLLECTED THROUGH ONLINE SOCIAL NETWORKS

Differences in the features and characteristics of online social networks are reflected by the huge amount of different statistics and metrics that can be tracked and analyzed. Although the following list is not meant to be exhaustive, it provides the most relevant metrics and statistics adopted in research on online social networks, described according to specific data application and objects:

1. Engagement metrics: numerically quantify a phenomenon and the features that led to its spread. They include:

   - Amplification metrics: computed counting of the number of shares for Facebook and retweets for Twitter. An analysis over time of metrics of this type allows feedback to assess the content shared by a user within that user's social network.
   - Applause metrics: represent an approval rating from the audience of a particular content; it is expressed on Twitter, Facebook, and YouTube as "like."

- Conversation rate: number of the conversations per post. On Facebook, YouTube, and LinkedIn they consist of comments, and on Twitter they consist of replies.

2. Influence metrics: analyze quantitatively users who participated in the conversations, and they include content per time (ie, a fundamental measure to define a phenomenon). This is defined as the ability to generate a multitude of content in a limited period of time.
3. Reach: number of unique individuals (account) that have been exposed to the content analyzed and who have had the opportunity to engage with it. If the same content is presented several times (shared by multiple friends or displayed on more social network platforms, the reach will give a value for each unique user. It is considered a measurement of potential impact: a significant increase of the value of impression (see below), with equal reach, means that people involved have had more opportunities to be exposed to the content and therefore to notice exposure.
4. Impression: the number of times that some content has had the opportunity to be seen within the social network platform, without taking into consideration the duplication of users (each user has the possibility to be exposed to the content multiple times on multiple devices and by multiple shares on the platform).

- Total audience: Total of people who have participated in a post regardless of the specific social network platform used.
- Number of unique users: one of the metrics most used to assess the efficacy of action on social networks. It is considered an index of users' real engagement since it represents the ability of some online content to "activate" the social network. The actions that are examined are the number of tweets and retweets on Twitter, and Facebook the number users who have commented on or "liked" posts on Facebook.
- Number of active/passive users: this is used primarily to understand phenomena related to specific events (eg, political elections, sport events). The number of active users on Twitter is defined as the number of users who tweet, while passive ones are users who limit themselves to mere retweets; on Facebook active users are considered individuals who comment on posts, while passive ones are users who only "like" posts.

4 PSYCHOLOGICAL AND MOTIVATIONAL FACTORS FOR PEOPLE TO SHARE OPINIONS AND TO EXPRESS THEMSELVES ON SOCIAL NETWORKS

From the point of view of psychology, the success of social networks is linked to their ability to meet basic and very different needs of people. As we will discuss in the following paragraphs, in particular, online social networks allow people to receive social support, to engage in and enjoy thinking, and to define identity [14,24,25]. On the one hand, people can use social networks to ask for and to offer social support; on the other hand, they can use social networks to describe themselves and to compare themselves with others, defining their social identity.

4.1 NEED TO BELONG

One of the main needs that social networks are able to satisfy is "the need to belong": people need to be appreciated and to be socially accepted [26–28]. Social networks offer, virtual places where individuals can present themselves, interact with others, and share and express opinions [29]. The need to belong can be understood on the basis of three basic needs that underlie an individual's group seeking behavior: (1) inclusion (ie, the need to belong to or include others in a circle of acquaintances), (2) affection (the need to love or be loved by others), and (3) control (the need to exert power over others or give power over the self to others) [30].

4.2 NEED FOR COGNITION

From a psychological point of view, another important reason that drives people to use social networks is the "need for cognition"; that is, the "individual's tendency to engage in and enjoy effortful cognitive endeavors" [31]. The need for cognition is strongly linked to information seeking behavior and varies among individuals. It is related to an individual's tendency to engage in and enjoy thinking [31], and it has a moderating effect on variables such as attitudes and purchase intentions, and also on the web [32].

4.3 SELF-PRESENTATION AND IMPRESSION MANAGEMENT

By means of web communities, personal blogs, and especially social networks, every individual can easily create a space on the web to present himself or herself [33,34], which means managing personal information, expressing attitudes and opinions, uploading private content, and taking and sharing photos. Through social network sites, people can shape and change their representation, reconstructing how they see themselves and others. Social networks allow individuals to decide how to present themselves to the people who make up their network (impression management). The main instrument for self-presentation is the personal profile, where individuals can describe themselves according to a number of characteristics (eg, interests, music) and share multimedia content as photos and videos.

In this context, many studies have been conducted to understand the personality traits and the motivational factors associated with self-presentation activities on social networking sites such as Facebook, Twitter, or Instagram [13,33,35,36]. For example, extraversion (such as sociable, energetic, and enthusiastic people) was often found to predict high social network use, a high number of friends, and high engagement in networking activities [37,38]; differently, neuroticism (such as tense, irritable, and moody people) has been found to be associated with use of social networks for self-disclosure and belongingness-related motivations, since neurotic individuals tend to perceive social networks as safe and controllable places for self-expression [39–41]. Some recent approaches focused on precise features of the phenomenon, such as personality correlates of preferences among different social networks [42], link creation [43], content of profile pictures [44], and status update [45].

5 FROM SOCIOLOGY PRINCIPLES TO SOCIAL NETWORKS ANALYTICS

The study of social networks, as privileged places of exchange and activators of social processes, is intrinsically linked to sociology, the academic field that studies the nature of human communication, the effects of mass communication, and the connections between the social system and the mass [46,47].

An interesting key to understanding the phenomena that take place on social networks is represented by the sociological theory of constructuralism [48].

The process by which people interact, exchange information, and consequently learn is the central component of Carley's theory [49,50], which describes how shared knowledge, representative of cultural forms, develops between individuals through social interaction. Constructuralism argues that through interaction and individual learning, the social network (who interacts with whom) and the knowledge network (who knows what) coevolve. This approach to the coevolution of knowledge and social relationships has considerable explanatory power over the dynamics of social networks [51,52], and has proved to be an effective tool for social simulation [53,54]. Three important concepts to understand interactions between people on social networks are tie strengths, homophily, and source credibility, and will be discussed next.

5.1 TIE STRENGTHS

The properties of the linkage between individuals on social networks are critical to an understanding of the process of social influence through them. Online, as in real life, all the communications between people take place within a social relationship that may be categorized according to the closeness of the relationship between individuals [55,56]. This concept is well represented by the sociological construct of tie strength; that is, "a multidimensional construct that represents the strength of the dyadic interpersonal relationships in the context of social networks" [55] and includes closeness, intimacy, support, and association [57]. The strength of the tie may range from strong to weak depending on the number and types of resources that are exchanged, the frequency of exchanges, and the intimacy of the exchanges between them [58]. Research suggests that tie strength affects information flows. Individuals in a strong tie relationship tend to interact more frequently and exchange more information than those in a weak tie relationship [59]. In addition, strong ties have greater influence than weaker ties on the behavior of receivers because of the frequency and perceived importance of social contact among strong-tie individuals [60].

5.2 HOMOPHILY OR SIMILARITY BREEDS CONNECTION

Related to, but conceptually distinct from tie strengths, is the construct of homophily [59]. Homophily can be defined as the extent to which pairs of individuals are similar in terms of certain attributes, such as age, gender, education, or lifestyle [61], and it explains group composition in terms of the similarity of members' characteristics. The main homophily principle is that the similarity of individuals predisposes individuals to a greater level of interpersonal attraction, trust, and understanding than would be expected among dissimilar individuals [62]. Thus individuals tend to affiliate with others who share similar interests or who are in a similar situation [63]. The stronger the social tie connecting two individuals, the more similar they tend to be [64,65]. Tie strength, therefore, increases with homophily [61].

5.3 SOURCE CREDIBILITY

Source credibility theory identifies source expertise and source bias as elements that affect the credibility of an information source [66,67]. Source expertise refers to the perceived competence of the source providing the information. A source should be perceived as more credible when it (1) possesses greater expertise and (2) is less prone to bias. Source bias, also conceptualized as source trustworthiness, refers to the possible bias/incentives that may be reflected in the source's information [68]. Whether or not a message sender is perceived as an "expert" (and thus of high credibility) is determined from an evaluation of the knowledge that person holds [69], as well as if—by virtue of his or her occupation, social training, or experience—that person is in a unique position. Reputation is thus key to allocation of a value to information [70]. In the online environment, such evaluations must be made from the relatively impersonal text-based resource exchange provided by actors in the site network. Knowledge of the individuals' attributes and background is limited, and evaluation will take place in a reduced-cues or altered-cues environment.

6 HOW CAN SOCIAL NETWORK ANALYTICS IMPROVE SENTIMENT ANALYSIS ON ONLINE SOCIAL NETWORKS?

As already pointed out, SA is one of the most used methods adopted to analyze data collected through online social networks [4,71,72]. This method, unlike purely numeric metrics, offers the possibility to investigate the opinions and attitudes expressed online by means of natural language processing tools [7]. However, one of the main problems with the interpretation of SA is that it does not allow one to consider data within the online network in which they have been collected. This is an important limitation since online social networks are characterized by definition by a highly relational nature [52].

Not considering the "network context" can lead to important misunderstandings in reading and interpreting collected data. For example, during the 2012 US presidential election, *USA Today* published in May and November a "sentiment score" of Obama and Romney, the candidates in the US presidential election of that year, based on Twitter data.[6] The newspaper reported a major change in the sentiment index in both candidates, commenting on the data in the light of presidential results. However, after a more careful look at the data reported, it appeared that while the May survey had been made on a sample made especially by Obama supporters, the November survey had involved mainly Romney supporters. The difference in the sentiment scores was therefore not due to a change in public opinion toward the candidates but was simply due to differences in the sample selected for the survey. This mistake would not have occurred if the data had been considered within the context in which they had been collected.

Among alternative analytical methods, or rather complementary analytical methods, that are being introduced in the analysis of data obtained through social networks, one of the most interesting is SNA [64,73,74]. SNA, through a quantitative-relational approach, makes it possible to consider data as "networked" (ie, considering existing connections and links between users). Models of SA and SNA have been successfully applied in various fields. However, what is still missing and has been little explored is a deep understanding of the ways in which the two can interact so as to increase the validity and the significance of the collected data thought online social networks. We will now briefly

---

[6]http://www.fastcompany.com/3037915/the-problem-with-sentiment-analysis

introduce the main characteristics of SNA so as to discuss in the final part of this section how it could be effectively integrated in traditional SA approaches.

6.1 WHAT IS SOCIAL NETWORK ANALYSIS?

SNA basically consists of a series of mathematical and computational techniques that, using network and graph theories, can be used to understand the structure and the dynamics of real or artificial networks [64,73,74]. Most of the early work was conducted on data collected from individuals in particular social settings to study a specific phenomenon [16,75]. Nowadays, the huge computational capacity of personal computers and the fact that people increasingly entertain relations on online social networks [23] have made SNA an important tool for psychologists and other social scientists to study interactions between people. SNA adopts a quantitative-relational approach, rather than relying on characteristics and attributes of individuals (eg, number of messages sent and received), and is based on relational data (or links, contacts, or ties) that characterize a group of people or a set of organizations of varying complexity (eg, families, groups of friends, associations). Relationships are represented by interactions of various kinds (friendship, money, flows of information). The potentiality of SNA is essentially twofold: the application of the theory of graphs to data relationships and, consequently, the description of the structure of the interaction though mathematical-algebraic indices [72,76].

Social networks are generally represented through graphs, which have the advantage of making a clear and immediate picture of the social structure. Graphs are the mathematical structure of a sociogram, visually expressed as a network composed of connected nodes. Therefore graphs are the spatial representation of social relationships among individuals. Graphs are useful because they represent graphically the social relationships and above all provide a formal representation of them (see Fig. 2.1). Moreover, it is possible to calculate an index to describe specific structural dimensions, such as density, inclusion, and cohesion.

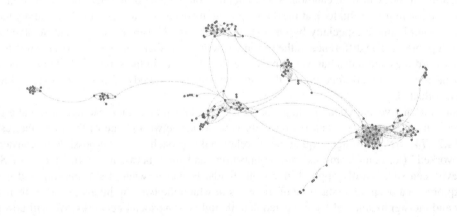

FIG. 2.1

A graph reporting the Facebook connections of an individual and his relationships. A set of subcomponents is clearly observable.

6.2 HOW TO INTEGRATE SOCIAL NETWORK ANALYTICS IN SENTIMENT ANALYSIS: SOME EXAMPLES

The properties of the linkage between individuals on online social networks are critical to an understanding of the process of social influence through them. This concept is well represented by the sociological construct of tie strength [55], as discussed earlier, that represents the strength of the dyadic interpersonal relationships in the context of social networks [55], and that has been found to affect information flows [59,60]. Interestingly, studies conducted on SNA suggest one path forward: how one person will evaluate another can often be predicted from the network in which they are embedded. In online social network scenarios, specific features are associated with edges between two people, such as comments they made about each other or messages they exchanged. Such behavioral features may contain a strong sentiment signal, which is useful for predicting edge signs and may be used to fit a conventional sentiment model. A purely edge feature–based sentiment model cannot account for the network structure since it reasons about edges as independent of each other.

Starting from these premises, recent studies have tried to jointly consider SA and social network analytics so as to give better predictions than either one can on its own [71,72,77–82]. West et al. [72], in particular, have developed a graphical model that synthesizes network and linguistic information to make more and better predictions about both. To capture such interactions, they developed a model that provides an example of how joint models of text and network structure can excel where their components parts cannot.

On the basis of another fundamental sociological principle, that of homophily [59], recent work has been trying to include features of user connections to predict attitudes about political and social events using SNA methods and indexes

Thomas et al. [82], in particular, used party affiliation and mentions in speeches to predict voting patterns from the transcripts of US Congress floor debates. They showed that the integration of even very limited information regarding interdocument relationships can significantly increase the accuracy of support/opposition classification. Incorporating agreement information provides additional benefit only when the input documents are relatively difficult to classify individually.

Tan et al. [71] used information about relationships between users of Twitter (eg, follows and mentions) to improve SA to predict attitudes about political and social events. Working within a semisupervised framework, they proposed models that are induced either from the Twitter follower/followee network or from the network in Twitter formed by users referring to each other using @- mentions. Their results revealed that incorporating social network information can indeed lead to statistically significant sentiment-classification improvements over the performance of an approach based on support vector machines having access to only textual features. In more detail, they found that (1) the probability that two users share the same opinion is indeed correlated with whether they are connected in the social network and (2) use of graphical models incorporating social network information can lead to statistically significant improvements in user-level sentiment polarity classification with respect to an approach using only textual information.

Bermingham et al. [77] tried to combine SA and SNA to explore the potential for online violent radicalization. In particular, through a detailed analysis of a real YouTube dataset, they developed a model that synthesizes textual and social network information to jointly predict the polarity (positive or negative) of person-to-person evaluations. More specifically, they incorporated in their model both intranet work measures (ie, centrality and betweenness) and whole-network (density and average communication speed) analytics. Adopting their dictionary-based polarity scoring method to assign positivity and negativity scores to YouTube profiles and comments, they were able to characterize users and groups of users by their sentiment toward a set of concepts that were of particular interest to jihadists.

Pozzi et al. [80] stated that considering friendship connections is a weak assumption for modeling homophily: online, as offline, two friends might not share the same opinion about a given topic. Starting from this criticism, they proposed an alternative method to represent homophily; that is, a user who approves of something (eg, by "likes" or a retweet). A semisupervised framework was used to estimate user polarities about a given topic by combining post content and weighted approval relations on microblogs (Twitter). The study showed that incorporation of approval relations significantly outperformed the text-only based approach, leading to significant improvements over the performance of complex supervised classifiers based only on textual features.

Related ideas were pursued by Ma et al. [79] and Hu et al. [78], who added terms to their models enforcing homophily between friends with regard to their preferences.

Ma et al. [79], proposed two social recommendation methods that use social information to improve the prediction accuracy of traditional recommender systems. More specifically, the social network information was used in the design of two social regularization terms to constrain the matrix factorization objective function. In addition, friends with dissimilar tastes were treated differently in the social regularization terms so as to represent the taste diversity of each user's friends. The experimental analysis on two large datasets (one dataset contained a social friend network, while the other dataset contained a social trust network) showed that these proposed methods outperform other state-of-the-art algorithms.

Similarly, Hu et al. [78] proposed a mathematical optimization formulation that incorporates the sentiment consistency and sociological theories of emotional contagion for sentiment classification. They used a method called a "sociological approach to handling noisy and short texts" (SANT), which extracted sentiment relations between tweets on the basis of social theories, and modeled the relations using a graph Laplacian matrix. They reported that the proposed method can utilize sentiment relations between messages to facilitate sentiment classification and effectively handle noisy Twitter data. An empirical study of two real-world Twitter datasets showed the superior performance of the adopted framework in handling noisy and short tweets, and SANT achieves consistent performance for different sizes of training data.

Finally, Sperious et al. [81] explored the possibility of exploiting the Twitter follower graph to improve polarity classification, under the assumption that people influence one another or have shared affinities with regard to topics. More specifically, they proposed incorporating labels from a maximum entropy classifier, in combination with the Twitter follower graph. The user's followers were used as separate features and combined with the content matrix. They constructed a graph that has users, tweets, word unigrams, word bigrams, hashtags, and emoticons as its nodes; users are connected on the basis of the Twitter follower graph to the tweets they created, and tweets are connected to the unigrams, bigrams, hashtags, and emoticons they contain. Sperious et al. compared the label propagation approach with the noisily supervised classifier itself and with a standard lexicon-based method using positive/negative ratios on several datasets of tweets that had been annotated for polarity. They showed that a maximum entropy classifier trained with distant supervision works better than a lexicon-based ratio predictor, improving the accuracy for polarity classification on from 58.1% to 62.9%. By using the predictions of that classifier in combination with a graph that incorporates tweets and lexical features, they obtained even better accuracy of 71.2%.

7 CONCLUSION AND FUTURE DIRECTIONS

The increasing use of online social networks and the consequent large amount of available data have rapidly increased attention on the problem of how to analyze data of this type. As pointed out in this chapter, SNA is one of the most interesting methods that are starting to be introduced in the analysis of data collected through online social networks. This method, unlike other methods such as SA, allow one to consider data as "networked," increasing their explanatory and predictive value. Recent studies on this issue have provided some interesting evidence for the benefits of using SNA combined with other methods in analyzing online social network data [71,72,77–82]. These can be summarized as follows:

- Use of social networks analytics allows one to consider structure interactions and the roles that individual users play. Considering the specific online social networks context, SNA makes it virtually possible to compare different types of online communities or to monitor over time the structure of interactions and the roles that users have within the social platform.
- SNA permits the reduction of the quantitative data resulting from automatic tracking for assessment of the quality (eg, the frequency with which individuals use social networks and their types of interests). Social network analytics (as centrality and neighborhood) allows one to go beyond mere numerical data and to assess the role and function of the users in the process of collaborative construction of knowledge on online social networks.
- Use of SNA combined with SA support to disambiguate sentences. For example, a statement such as *"I really hate beer but I love Heineken"* is very difficult to interpret correctly unless the network where it was expressed is considered [72].

REFERENCES

[1] D. Meshi, D.I. Tamir, H.R. Heekeren, The emerging neuroscience of social media, Trends Cogn. Sci. 19 (12) (2015) 771–782.
[2] A.M. Kaplan, M. Haenlein, Users of the world, unite! The challenges and opportunities of social media, Bus. Horizons 53 (1) (2010) 59–68.
[3] G. Merchant, Unravelling the social network: theory and research, Learn. Media Technol. 37 (1) (2012) 4–19.
[4] M. Salampasis, G. Paltoglou, A. Giachanou, Using social media for continuous monitoring and mining of consumer behaviour, Int. J. Electron. Bus. 11 (1) (2013) 85–96.
[5] S. Edosomwan, S.K. Prakasan, D. Kouame, J. Watson, T. Seymour, The history of social media and its impact on business, J. Appl. Manage. Entrep. 16 (3) (2011) 79.
[6] S. Ye, S.F. Wu, Measuring message propagation and social influence on Twitter.com, in: Proceedings of Social Informatics: Second International Conference, SocInfo 2010, Laxenburg, Austria, October 27–29, 2010, Springer, Berlin, Heidelberg, 2010, pp. 216–231.

[7] B. Pang, L. Lee, Opinion mining and sentiment analysis, Found. Trends Inform. Retr. 2 (1–2) (2008) 1–135.

[8] A.L. Maas, R.E. Daly, P.T. Pham, D. Huang, A.Y. Ng, C. Potts, Learning word vectors for sentiment analysis, in: Proceedings of the 49th Annual Meeting of the Association for Computational Linguistics: Human Language Technologies—Volume 1, Association for Computational Linguistics, 2011, pp. 142–150.

[9] S. Wang, C.D. Manning, Baselines and bigrams: simple, good sentiment and topic classification, in: Proceedings of the 50th Annual Meeting of the Association for Computational Linguistics: Short Papers-Volume 2, Association for Computational Linguistics, 2012, pp. 90–94.

[10] J. Blitzer, M. Dredze, F. Pereira, et al., Biographies, bollywood, boom-boxes and blenders: domain adaptation for sentiment classification, in: ACL, vol. 7, 2007, pp. 440–447.

[11] T. Wilson, J. Wiebe, P. Hoffmann, Recognizing contextual polarity in phrase-level sentiment analysis, in: Proceedings of the Conference on Human Language Technology and Empirical Methods in Natural Language Processing, Association for Computational Linguistics, 2005, pp. 347–354.

[12] C. Thurlow, L. Lengel, A. Tomic, Computer Mediated Communication, Sage, London, UK, 2004.

[13] N.B. Ellison, Social network sites: definition, history, and scholarship, J. Comput. Mediat. Commun. 13 (1) (2007) 210–230.

[14] A. Ramirez, J.B. Walther, J.K. Burgoon, M. Sunnafrank, Information-seeking strategies, uncertainty, and computer-mediated communication, Hum. Commun. Res. 28 (2) (2002) 213–228.

[15] A. Arvidsson, A. Delfanti, Introduzione ai Media Digitali, Il Mulino, Italy, 2013.

[16] J.L. Moreno, Who Shall Survive, vol. 58, JSTOR, 1934.

[17] J.L. Moreno, Sociometry, Experimental Method and the Science of Society, Beacon House, Oxford, England, 1951.

[18] G. Riva, I Social Network, Il Mulino, Italy, 2010.

[19] R. Junco, G. Heiberger, E. Loken, The effect of Twitter on college student engagement and grades, J. Comput. Assist. Learn. 27 (2) (2011) 119–132.

[20] N. Bilton, Hatching Twitter: A True Story of Money, Power, Friendship, and Betrayal, Portfolio, London, UK, 2014.

[21] A. Ferrandina, R. Zarriello, Social Media Marketing. Una Guida per i Nuovi Comunicatori Digitali, vol. 120, FrancoAngeli, Milan, Italy, 2014.

[22] N.B. Ellison, C. Steinfield, C. Lampe, The benefits of Facebook friends: social capital and college students use of online social network sites, J. Comput. Mediat. Commun. 12 (4) (2007) 1143–1168.

[23] K. Subrahmanyam, S.M. Reich, N. Waechter, G. Espinoza, Online and offline social networks: use of social networking sites by emerging adults, J. Appl. Dev. Psychol. 29 (6) (2008) 420–433.

[24] J. Van Dijck, The Culture of Connectivity: A Critical History of Social Media, Oxford University Press, Oxford, UK, 2013.

[25] G. Riva, The sociocognitive psychology of computer-mediated communication: the present and future of technology-based interactions, Cyberpsychol. Behav. 5 (6) (2002) 581–598.

[26] R.F. Baumeister, M.R. Leary, The need to belong: desire for interpersonal attachments as a fundamental human motivation, Psychol. Bull. 117 (3) (1995) 497.

[27] M.R. Leary, K.M. Kelly, C.A. Cottrell, L.S. Schreindorfer, Individual differences in the need to belong, Unpublished, 2001.

[28] A.H. Maslow, A theory of human motivation, Psychol. Rev. 50 (4) (1943) 370.

[29] H. Gangadharbatla, Facebook me: collective self-esteem, need to belong, and internet self-efficacy as predictors of the iGenerations attitudes toward social networking sites, J. Interact. Advertising 8 (2) (2008) 5–15.

[30] W. Schutz, The Interpersonal Underworld, Science & Behavior Books, Palo Alto, CA, 1966.

[31] J.T. Cacioppo, R.E. Petty, The need for cognition, J. Pers. Soc. Psychol. 42 (1) (1982) 116.

[32] S. Das, R. Echambadi, M. McCardle, M. Luckett, The effect of interpersonal trust, need for cognition, and social loneliness on shopping, information seeking and surfing on the web, Market. Lett. 14 (3) (2003) 185–202.

[33] N. Krämer, S. Winter, Impression management 2.0, J. Media Psychol. 20 (2008) 106–116.

[34] P.M. Valkenburg, J. Peter, A.P. Schouten, Friend networking sites and their relationship to adolescents' well-being and social self-esteem, CyberPsychol. Behav. 9 (5) (2006) 584–590.

[35] T. Jung, H. Youn, S. McClung, Motivations and self-presentation strategies on Korean-based "Cyworld" weblog format personal homepages, CyberPsychol. Behav. 10 (1) (2007) 24–31.

[36] T.A. Pempek, Y.A. Yermolayeva, S.L. Calvert, College students' social networking experiences on Facebook, J. Appl. Dev. Psychol. 30 (3) (2009) 227–238.

[37] T. Correa, A.W. Hinsley, H.G. De Zuniga, Who interacts on the Web?: the intersection of users personality and social media use, Comput. Hum. Behav. 26 (2) (2010) 247–253.

[38] S.D. Gosling, A.A. Augustine, S. Vazire, N. Holtzman, S. Gaddis, Manifestations of personality in online social networks: self-reported Facebook-related behaviors and observable profile information, Cyberpsychol. Behav. Soc. Netw. 14 (9) (2011) 483–488.

[39] Y. Amichai-Hamburger, G. Vinitzky, Social network use and personality, Comput. Hum. Behav. 26 (6) (2010) 1289–1295.

[40] Y. Amichai-Hamburger, G. Wainapel, S. Fox, "On the Internet no one knows I'm an introvert": extroversion, neuroticism, and Internet interaction, CyberPsychol. Behav. 5 (2) (2002) 125–128.

[41] G. Seidman, Self-presentation and belonging on Facebook: how personality influences social media use and motivations, Pers. Ind. Dif. 54 (3) (2013) 402–407.

[42] D.J. Hughes, M. Rowe, M. Batey, A. Lee, A tale of two sites: Twitter vs. Facebook and the personality predictors of social media usage, Comput. Hum. Behav. 28 (2) (2012) 561–569.

[43] L.M. Aiello, A. Barrat, C. Cattuto, G. Ruffo, R. Schifanella, Link creation and profile alignment in the aNobii social network, in: Proceedings of the 2010 IEEE Second International Conference on Social Computing (SocialCom), IEEE, 2010, pp. 249–256.

[44] N.J. Hum, P.E. Chamberlin, B.L. Hambright, A.C. Portwood, A.C. Schat, J.L. Bevan, A picture is worth a thousand words: a content analysis of Facebook profile photographs, Comput. Hum. Behav. 27 (5) (2011) 1828–1833.

[45] S. Winter, G. Neubaum, S.C. Eimler, V. Gordon, J. Theil, J. Herrmann, J. Meinert, N.C. Krämer, Another brick in the Facebook wall-How personality traits relate to the content of status updates, Comput. Hum. Behav. 34 (2014) 194–202.

[46] O.D.M. Ashley, Sociological Theory: Classical Statements, Pearson Education, Upper Saddle River, NJ, 2005.

[47] A. Giddens, M. Duneier, R.P. Appelbaum, Introduction to Sociology, Norton, New York, NY, 2003.

[48] P.L. Berger, T. Luckmann, The Social Construction of Reality, Penguin Books, London, UK, 1991.

[49] K. Carley, Coordinating the success: trading information redundancy for task simplicity, in: Proceedings of the Twenty-Third Annual Hawaii International Conference on System Sciences, vol. 4, IEEE, 1990, pp. 261–270.

[50] K. Carley, A theory of group stability, Am. Sociol. Rev. 56 (3) (1991) 331–354.

[51] O. Lizardo, How cultural tastes shape personal networks, Am. Soc. Rev. 71 (5) (2006) 778–807.

[52] M.A. Pachucki, R.L. Breiger, Cultural holes: beyond relationality in social networks and culture, Ann. Rev. Sociol. 36 (2010) 205–224.

[53] K.M. Carley, V. Hill, Structural change and learning within organizations, in: Dynamics of Organizations: Computational Modeling and Organizational Theories, MIT Press, Cambridge, MA, 2001, pp. 63–92.

[54] B.R. Hirshman, J.S. Charles, K.M. Carley, Leaving us in tiers: can homophily be used to generate tiering effects? Comput. Math. Organ. Theory 17 (4) (2011) 318–343.

[55] R.B. Money, M.C. Gilly, J.L. Graham, Explorations of national culture and word-of-mouth referral behavior in the purchase of industrial services in the United States and Japan, J. Market. 62 (4) (1998) 76–87.

[56] D.F. Duhan, S.D. Johnson, J.B. Wilcox, G.D. Harrell, Influences on consumer use of word-of-mouth recommendation sources, J. Acad. Market. Sci. 25 (4) (1997) 283–295.

[57] J.K. Frenzen, H.L. Davis, Purchasing behavior in embedded markets, J. Consum. Res. 17 (1) (1990) 1–12.

[58] P.V. Marsden, K.E. Campbell, Measuring tie strength, Soc Forces 63 (2) (1984) 482–501.

[59] J.J. Brown, P.H. Reingen, Social ties and word-of-mouth referral behavior, J. Consum. Res. 14 (3) (1987) 350–362.

[60] H.S. Bansal, P.A. Voyer, Word-of-mouth processes within a services purchase decision context, J. Serv. Res. 3 (2) (2000) 166–177.

[61] E. Rogers, Diffusion of Innovations, Free Press, New York, NY, 1983.

[62] M. Ruef, H.E. Aldrich, N.M. Carter, The structure of founding teams: homophily, strong ties, and isolation among US entrepreneurs, Am. Sociol. Rev. 68 (2) (2003) 195–222.

[63] S. Schachter, The Psychology of Affiliation: Experimental Studies of the Sources of Gregariousness, no. 1, Stanford University Press, Stanford, CA, 1959.

[64] M.S. Granovetter, The strength of weak ties, Am. J. Sociol. 78 (6) (1973) 1360–1380.

[65] J.M. McPherson, L. Smith-Lovin, Homophily in voluntary organizations: status distance and the composition of face-to-face groups, Am. Sociol. Rev. 52 (1987) 370–379.

[66] R. Buda, Y. Zhang, Consumer product evaluation: the interactive effect of message framing, presentation order, and source credibility, J. Prod. Brand Manage. 9 (4) (2000) 229–242.

[67] M.H. Birnbaum, S.E. Stegner, Source credibility in social judgment: bias, expertise, and the judge's point of view, J. Pers. Soc. Psychol. 37 (1) (1979) 48.

[68] A.H. Eagly, S. Chaiken, The Psychology of Attitudes, Harcourt Brace Jovanovich College Publishers, New York, NY, 1993.

[69] J.B. Gotlieb, D. Sarel, Comparative advertising effectiveness: the role of involvement and source credibility, J. Advertising 20 (1) (1991) 38–45.

[70] S. Tadelis, The market for reputations as an incentive mechanism, J. Polit. Econ. 110 (4) (2002) 854–882.

[71] C. Tan, L. Lee, J. Tang, L. Jiang, M. Zhou, P. Li, User-level sentiment analysis incorporating social networks, in: Proceedings of the 17th ACM SIGKDD International Conference on Knowledge Discovery and Data Mining, ACM, 2011, pp. 1397–1405.

[72] R. West, H.S. Paskov, J. Leskovec, C. Potts, Exploiting social network structure for person-to-person sentiment analysis, Trans. Assoc. Comput. Linguist. 2 (2014) 297–310.

[73] J.G. Anderson, S.J. Jay, Computers and clinical judgment: the role of physician networks, in: Use and Impact of Computers in Clinical Medicine, Springer, New York, NY, 1985, pp. 161–184.

[74] B. Wellman, Structural analysis: from method and metaphor to theory and substance, Contemp. Stud. Sociol. 15 (1997) 19–61.

[75] F. Heider, Attitudes and cognitive organization, J. Psychol. 21 (1) (1946) 107–112.

[76] F. Bonchi, C. Castillo, A. Gionis, A. Jaimes, Social network analysis and mining for business applications, ACM Trans. Intell. Syst. Technol. 2 (3) (2011) 22.

[77] A. Bermingham, M. Conway, L. McInerney, N. O'Hare, A.F. Smeaton, Combining social network analysis and sentiment analysis to explore the potential for online radicalisation, in: Proceedings of the International Conference on Advances in Social Network Analysis and Mining, 2009, ASONAM'09, IEEE, 2009, pp. 231–236.

[78] X. Hu, L. Tang, J. Tang, H. Liu, Exploiting social relations for sentiment analysis in microblogging, in: Proceedings of the Sixth ACM International Conference on Web Search and Data Mining, ACM, 2013, pp. 537–546.

[79] H. Ma, D. Zhou, C. Liu, M.R. Lyu, I. King, Recommender systems with social regularization, in: Proceedings of the Fourth ACM International Conference on Web Search and Data Mining, ACM, 2011, pp. 287–296.

[80] F.A. Pozzi, D. Maccagnola, E. Fersini, E. Messina, Enhance user-level sentiment analysis on microblogs with approval relations, in: AI*IA 2013: Advances in Artificial Intelligence, Springer, New York, NY, 2013, pp. 133–144.

[81] M. Sperious, N. Sudan, S. Upadhyay, J. Baldridge, Twitter polarity classification with label propagation over lexical links and the follower graph, in: Proceedings of the First Workshop on Unsupervised Learning in NLP, Association for Computational Linguistics, 2011, pp. 53–63.

[82] M. Thomas, B. Pang, L. Lee, Get out the vote: determining support or opposition from congressional floor-debate transcripts, in: Proceedings of the 2006 Conference on Empirical Methods in Natural Language Processing, Association for Computational Linguistics, 2006, pp. 327–335.

SEMANTIC ASPECTS IN SENTIMENT ANALYSIS

3

M. Nissim[a], V. Patti[b]

University of Groningen, Groningen, The Netherlands[a] University of Turin, Torino, Italy[b]

1 INTRODUCTION

The fact that semantics must play a crucial role in the sentiment interpretation of text is rather obvious, as even just considering the plain meaning of words can be very indicative (*"I liked it"* vs. *"I hated it"*). However, things are not that simple or straightforward for at least two reasons: (1) *meaning* is not so easy to define, detect, and extract automatically, and (2) sentiment analysis is often not just a matter of distinguishing positive from negative opinions, especially in recent developments.

In the 2015 SemEval campaign, four shared tasks were organized within the *Sentiment Analysis* track: a rather general task on *sentiment analysis in Twitter* (task 10 [1], with four subtasks), a task focused on figurative language, entitled *"Sentiment Analysis of Figurative Language in Twitter"* (task 11 [2]), an *aspect-based sentiment analysis* task (task 12 [3]), where systems had to identify aspects of entities and the sentiment expressed for each aspect, and a rather different task focused on events' polarity, entitled *"CLIPEval Implicit Polarity of Events"* (task 9 [4]). Within the ongoing SemEval 2016, there is also a task on detecting *stance* in tweets (task 6[1])—that is, detecting the position of the author with respect to a given target (against/in favor/neutral)—and one on determining sentiment intensity (task 7[2]). Some of these tasks provide datasets in more than one language. Additionally, a shared task on concept-level sentiment analysis has been organized recently in the context of the European Semantic Web Conference [5]. This fervent, current action on stimulating research, resources, and tools in this field by organizing more numerous and more complex tasks tells us not only that interest in sentiment analysis is growing but also that sentiment analysis is no longer just about detecting whether a given review or tweet is objective or subjective, and in the latter case it is whether positive or negative. Rather, it requires a more complex analysis and interpretation of messages that in turn must rely on deeper processing and understanding. Thus although it is true that semantics and semantic processing play a crucial role in this, we must see *how* this happens, from several points of view.

First, and following intuition, words are sentiment informative at a plain lexical semantics level ("good" is positive, "bad" is negative). This is reflected in the creation of sentiment and emotion lexica

---

[1] http://alt.qcri.org/semeval2016/task6/
[2] http://alt.qcri.org/semeval2016/task7/

Sentiment Analysis in Social Networks. http://dx.doi.org/10.1016/B978-0-12-804412-4.00003-6

31

and corpora that can be used in system development, also for languages other than English. Second, deeper linguistic processing is required to perform finer-grained tasks. For instance, in aspect-based sentiment analysis, entities and aspects must be identified, as well as relations among them, and one cannot rely on lexical semantics only; also, in irony detection, systems must incorporate some module that deals with figurative language. Third, even deeper text processing might not suffice for the level of analysis required, and might need to be complemented by *reasoning* over concepts, which could be done by exploitation of semantic resources that the Semantic Web community has to offer in this sense, such as web ontologies and semantic networks. Fourth, sentiment analysis stretches out to, and intersects with, other related areas, such as emotion and personality detection, so the semantics of words and text has to be determined at different levels of affect interpretation.

In this chapter, we review a large collection of semantic resources for sentiment analysis and show how semantics plays various roles in the development of sentiment-aware tools and resources. Specifically, we discuss how state-of-the-art semantic processing is used and adapted to fit the requirements of progressively finer-grained tasks; for example, how semantic information is exploited in statistical models, how advances in semantic similarity models can be ported to sentiment analysis, and how automated reasoning and semantic metadata processing can be used in this field. Through this review we highlight the interaction of sentiment analysis with related affect resources and processing.

2 SEMANTIC RESOURCES FOR SENTIMENT ANALYSIS

Affective information expressed in our texts is multifaceted. Both sentiment and emotion lexicons, and psycholinguistic resources available for English, refer to various affective models and capture different nuances of affect, such as sentiment polarity, emotional categories, and emotional dimensions. Such lexica are usually lists of words with which a positive or negative or emotion-related label (or score) is associated. Besides flat vocabularies of affective words, other resources include and model semantic, conceptual, and affective information associated with multiword natural language expressions, by enabling concept-level analysis of sentiment and emotions conveyed in texts. In our view all such resources represent a rich and varied lexical knowledge of affect, under different perspectives. Therefore we offer here a comprehensive description of such different resources and of their use in the context of sentiment analysis to distinguish between different opinions and sentiment.

2.1 CLASSICAL RESOURCES ON SENTIMENT

One of the first and most widely used resources is the Subjectivity Lexicon [6],[3] which is a list of subjectivity clues compiled from several sources, annotated both manually and automatically. This lexicon is the core of OpinionFinder, one of the first systems for the automatic detection of polarity. Another widely used resource is the Opinion Lexicon[4] compiled by Bing Liu. The list contains approximately 6800 English words that are classified as either positive or negative. Both resources were compiled manually and are thus quite accurate. However, they make two simplifications: first, they encode sentiment information in terms of a sharp division between a positive and negative sentiment

---

[3]http://mpqa.cs.pitt.edu/lexicons/subj_lexicon/
[4]https://www.cs.uic.edu/~liub/FBS/sentiment-analysis.html

value rather than providing a scale of positivity/negativity; second, they associate sentiment with words rather than with their *senses*. We will discuss the latter issue first, and the former later.

The lack of sense distinctions is quite a limitation from a semantic perspective. Indeed, lexical entries are often polysemous, so the same string might actually have a completely opposite sentiment depending on the context in which it is used. For example, "crazy" can be used in a negative as well as a positive way, which is strictly context dependent. Creating a flat list where words are assigned a binary polarity value will not account for the complexity of such semantic aspects.

One step further in creating sentiment resources is thus assigning polarity values at the *sense* level rather than the *word* level. This is the principle behind the annotation scheme developed in [7], which gave rise to the Subjectivity Sense Annotations,[5] a sense-aware lexicon. This resource actually addresses sentiment at one level up with respect to polarity, as it classifies a given word sense as objective or subjective, without specifying, in the latter case, its polarity value. As a plus, though, this lexicon includes part-of-speech information. Apart from sense distinctions of exactly the same lexical entries, there can also be ambiguities related to parts of speech, as a given word could be, for example, a noun and also an adjective, and could exhibit different polarity features accordingly. A good example is "novel," which has a neutral polarity when used as a noun but a rather positive one when used as an adjective.

The creation of SentiWordNet [8] addresses ambiguities both within and across parts of speech. SentiWordNet is an extension of WordNet [9], where three sentiment scores are assigned to *each synset*, thus to word senses: positivity, negativity, and objectivity. In addition to the assigning of sentiment to senses, one nice feature of SentiWordNet is that sentiment is a *gradual* concept rather than a categorical one, thus addressing the first limitation of the simplest resources highlighted above. The same synset can exhibit the three values (positivity, negativity, neutrality) with different degrees, summing up to 1. The main drawback of SentiWordNet is that its sentiment scores are for the most part automatically assigned, so the presence of noise is not trivial. It is also known to have a *positive bias* [10], and so is not so good for detecting negative opinions.

The very first sentiment-aware resource we know of—namely, General Inquirer[6] [11], whose compilation was started in 1966—accounted for sense distinctions, although polarity was conceived as a binary value rather than a gradual concept.

Another way to indirectly address word sense disambiguation is to have *domain-dependent lexica*. Often a given word will exhibit only one sense in a specific domain (the classic example of "bank" is indicative here, as in a financial context it is unlikely this term would be used in its "river bank" sense). There are two large lexica that are built around very specific domains, exploiting contributors' reviews: the Yelp Lexicon, with a focus on restaurant reviews, derived from the very large Yelp challenge dataset,[7] and the Amazon Lexicon, built on laptop reviews posted on *Amazon* from June 1995 to March 2013 [12,13]. Additionally, there are sentiment lists tailored for the financial domain, developed chiefly by Loughran and McDonald [14] after they noted that three quarters of the words with a negative polarity contained in standard, domain-independent resources did not actually have a negative connotation in the financial domain.

---

[5]http://mpqa.cs.pitt.edu/lexicons/subj_sense_annotations/
[6]http://www.wjh.harvard.edu/~inquirer/
[7]http://www.yelp.com/dataset_challenge

Among the resources that conceive polarity as a gradual rather than categorical value, we mention AFINN, which is a manually compiled list of 2477 English words and phrases rated with an integer between −5 (very negative) and +5 (very positive),[8] and the Sentiment140 lexicon, which contains about 60,000 unigrams and 10 times more bigrams. Differently from the AFINN lexicon, Sentiment140 is compiled automatically by exploiting tweets with emoticons. This resource is part of a suite of lexica all automatically compiled by Said Mohammad and coworkers,[9] under the NRC general label [15,16], which also includes the NRC Hashtag Sentiment Lexicon, built by exploiting the sentiment of hashtags, and two more "double" resources built on the previous ones; namely, the NRC Hashtag Affirmative Context Sentiment Lexicon (and NRC Hashtag Negated Context Sentiment Lexicon), and the Sentiment140 Affirmative Context Lexicon (and Sentiment140 Negated Context Lexicon), where the average sentiment of a term occurring in an affirmative context is separate from the average sentiment of the same term occurring in a negated context.

Within the NRC tools there is also a small manually (crowdsourced) produced lexicon of about 1500 entries, the MaxDiff Twitter Sentiment Lexicon [17]. Handmade resources are always smaller than automatically built ones, as they are costly to create, but they are obviously more reliable. The ways of reducing noise in the automatic acquisition of resources have been explored by, for instance, the use of sentiment proxies such as emoticons [18] or, usually, the adoption of a semiautomatic approach, bootstrapping manually annotated sets of seeds [19,20]. This is also the approach behind the original creation of SentiWordNet. Finally, using seeds, Chen and Skien [21] automatically produced sentiment lexica for more than 130 languages, reporting an overlap with existing resources of more than 90%.

For the same economical reasons we have just mentioned, and because tools for basic text processing are more advanced for English than for other languages, the creation of lexica for other languages can benefit from the automatic porting of data and techniques from already existing English resources [22]. An example is the transfer of SentiWordNet to other languages. Because English Wordnet is easily aligned to WordNets in other languages, porting SentiWordNet becomes rather straightforward, and it has been shown that sense transfer is robust across languages in about 90% of cases [23] (see also [24] for a WordNet-based, almost unsupervised approach for generating polarity lexica in multiple languages). Transfer of resources can be done in two ways: to create a stable, reusable resource, or "on the fly." An example of the former is Sentix for Italian (via SentiWordNet), which is currently the most commonly used resource for this language in sentiment analysis systems [25,26]. As for the latter, resources are translated and used in the context of a sentiment analysis system, but are not necessarily stabilized and distributed for further use; for example, Hernández Farías et al. [27] use a large number of English lexica/resources automatically translated into Italian to exploit information as features in their supervised system, but no specific evaluation or refining of such resources is performed.

2.2 BEYOND THE POLARITY VALENCE: EMOTION LEXICA, ONTOLOGIES, AND PSYCHOLINGUISTIC RESOURCES

Recently, a variety of affective lexica have been proposed to offer information about affect expressed in text according to finer levels of granularity (eg, referring not simply to positive or negative

---

[8]https://github.com/abromberg/sentiment_analysis/blob/master/AFINN/AFINN-111.txt
[9]http://saifmohammad.com/WebPages/lexicons.html

sentiment polarity but to emotional categories such as joy, sadness, and fear). Moreover, a variety of psycholinguistic resources are available that can give some additional measure about the emotional disclosure in social media texts, according to different theoretical perspectives on emotions. All such affect-related resources could be useful with the purpose to increase the coverage of different aspects of affect in textual content. We organize the description of such resources into three groups: the first group is related to information about emotions by referring to a finer-grained categorization model; the second group includes *psycholinguistic* resources and other resources that refer to different perspectives on affect, according to dimensional approaches to emotion modeling; the third group includes *knowledge-based* resources and ontologies, which have been developed with the twofold aim to help sentiment analysis systems to grasp the conceptual and affective information associated with natural language opinions, and to use Semantic Web and linked data technologies to provide structured, reusable, and meaningful sentiment analysis results.

2.2.1 Emotion lexica: finer-grained affective lexica based on emotional categories

Theories in the nature of emotion suggest the existence of basic or fundamental emotions such as anger, fear, joy, sadness, and disgust. Different approaches propose different basic or fundamental sets, each having its own specific eliciting conditions and its own specific physiological, expressive, and behavioral reaction patterns. Accordingly, available resources refer to different models of emotions well grounded in psychology, such as the ones proposed by Plutchik [28] and Ekman [29].

One of the first resources referring to a finer-grained model of affect is WordNet-Affect,[10] which was developed through the selection and labeling of WordNet synsets representing affective concepts [30]. A number of WordNet synsets are assigned to one or more affective labels (called a-labels). In particular, the affective concepts representing emotional states are individuated by synsets marked with the a-label emotion. There are also other a-labels for those concepts representing moods, traits, situations eliciting emotions, and so on. The newer version, WordNet-Affect 1.1, includes more than 900 synsets and proposes also a taxonomy of emotions, where the hierarchical structure is modeled on the WordNet hyperonym relation. Starting from WordNet-Affect, for task 14 at SemEval 2007, a new version of the resource has been provided [31]. This resource includes only a portion of WordNet-Affect, as it was reannotated at a finer-grained level with use of the six emotional category labels from [29]: joy, fear, anger, sadness, disgust, and surprise. The resource EmoLex[11] has been developed as part of the NRC suite of lexica. It is a word-emotion association lexicon [32] built via crowdsourcing; the annotations were manually done through Amazon's Mechanical Turk. It contains 14,182 words labeled according to Plutchik's eight primary emotions [28]—joy, sadness, anger, fear, trust, surprise, disgust, and anticipation—and also annotations for negative and positive sentiments. Emolex was originally annotated at a word-sense level. Then the word-level lexicon was created by the taking of the union of emotions associated with all the senses of a word. Very recently, NRC Emolex has been provided also in more than 20 languages as a result of translation of the English terms with use of Google Translate. The underlying assumption is that, despite some cultural differences, affective norms are stable across languages.

---

[10]http://wndomains.fbk.eu/wnaffect.html
[11]http://www.saifmohammad.com/WebPages/lexicons.html

Another sense-level affective lexicon is SentiSense,[12] which attaches emotional meanings to concepts from the WordNet lexical database [33]. It is composed by a list of 2190 synsets tagged with emotional labels from a set of 14 emotional categories, which refer to a merger of models by Arnold [34], Plutchik, and Parrot [35]: joy, fear, surprise, anger, disgust, love, anticipation, hope, despair, sadness, calmness, like, hate, and ambiguous. Such emotional categories are also related via an antonym relationship. SentiSense has been developed semiautomatically with use of several semantic relations between synsets in WordNet.

2.2.2 Psycholinguistic resources and other accounts of affect

Psycholinguistic resources can be also helpful for capturing the emotional content of the text, allowing the mapping of words onto psychologically valid dimensions. One of the most well-known psycholinguistic resources is the Linguistic Inquiry and Word Count (LIWC)[13] dictionary [36], which assigns one or more psychological categories, such as <u>positive emotion</u> and <u>negative emotion</u>, to individual words. The 2007 version of LIWC comprises almost 4500 words and word stems distributed in categories for analysis of psycholinguistic features in texts. For example, the word "happy" would be labeled with the categories <u>positive emotion</u> and <u>affect</u>. The most recent evolution, LIWC2015, is composed of almost 6400 words, word stems, and selected emoticons, distributed in a wider set of categories arranged hierarchically. The dictionary has been extended and new categories have been added. The new additions allow the user to better tackle with social media language.

Moreover, some psychological theories propose that the nature of an emotional state is determined by its position in a space of independent dimensions. According to such an approach, emotions can be defined as a coincidence of values on a number of different strategic dimensions. Therefore they are described not by marking a small set of discrete categories but rather by scoring properties such as valence (positive/negative) and arousal (active/passive) in a continuous range of values. Accordingly, some lexical resources have been built by reference to models with a dimensional view on affect-related phenomena.

For instance, the Dictionary of Affect in Language[14] developed by Whissell [37] includes 8742 English words rated on a three-point scale along three dimensions: activation (degree of response that humans have under an emotional state); imagery (how difficult it is to form a mental picture of a given word); pleasantness (degree of pleasure produced by words). Instead, the Affective Norms for English Words[15] [38] is a database developed by the rating of 1034 English words in terms of the Osgood, Suci, and Tannenbaum dimensional theory of emotions along three dimensions of the valence-arousal-dominance model [39]: valence or pleasure (the polarity of the emotional activation ranging from positive to negative); arousal or intensity (the degree of excitement or activation an individual feels toward a given stimulus, ranging from calm to exciting); dominance or control (the degree of control an individual feels over a specific stimulus, ranging from out of control to in control).

---

[12]http://nlp.uned.es/~jcalbornoz/SentiSense.html
[13]http://www.liwc.net
[14]ftp://perceptmx.com/wdalman.pdf
[15]http://csea.phhp.ufl.edu/media/anewmessage.html

2.2.3 Concept-based resources and ontologies: toward a knowledge-based approach to sentiment analysis

Many researchers are currently devoting efforts to develop ontologies of emotions, in some cases also referring to the Semantic Web initiative [40–43]. The use of structured knowledge via ontologies or semantic networks in the sentiment analysis tasks opens new opportunities for understanding opinions expressed in texts. In particular, such knowledge bases can include semantic information both on the sentiment domain and the emotion domain, or on the concepts and the context related to words used for expressing opinions, enabling interesting possibilities of reasoning on such knowledge (see Section 3.4). Again, these ontologies typically try to mirror models of emotions well established in psychology. However, as a difference from emotion lexica such as Emolex, where emotions are taken as a flat list of concepts, here a more sophisticated knowledge can be encoded. For instance, in ontologies the taxonomic relationships among the emotions can be represented, or other interesting relations such as intensity, similarity, or oppositions. The representation of such relationships between concepts in the ontology enables also interesting possibility to automatically reason on such knowledge about emotions. As we will see, Plutchik's circumplex model [28], which inspired the development of the Emolex lexicon, has also been exploited as a reference of concept-level resources and ontology of emotions with important differences that we will highlight.

Concept-level resources use ontologies or semantic networks to enable semantic text analysis. One of the most used resources in this category is SenticNet[16] [40], which aims to create a collection of commonly used polarity concepts (ie, commonsense concepts with relatively strong positive or negative polarity). Differently from other resources such as SentiWordNet, which also contains null-polarity terms, SenticNet does not contain concepts with neutral or almost neutral polarity. The current version includes 30,000 natural language concepts collected from the Open Mind corpus, and the resource is distributed in Resource Description Framework (RDF) XML format. Each concept is associated with emotion categorization values expressed in terms of the hourglass of emotions model [44], which organizes and blends 24 emotional categories from Plutchik's model into four affective dimensions (pleasantness, attention, sensitivity, and aptitude). Moreover, in SenticNet a polarity value that lies in the interval $[-1, 1]$ is associated with each concept. This value is calculated in terms of the four dimensions of the hourglass of emotions model, and specifies if (and to what extent) the input concept is positive or negative (eg, concepts such as "make a good impression" will have a polarity value close to 1, whereas concepts such as "being fired," "leave behind," or "lose control" will have a polarity value close to -1. In this case the emotion categorization model supports comparison and aggregation among results of an emotional analysis of concepts into polarity values.

EmoSenticNet[17] is another concept-based lexical resource [45] and was automatically built by the merging of WordNet-Affect and SenticNet, with the main aim to have a more complete resource containing not only quantitative polarity scores associated with each SenticNet concept but also qualitative affective labels. In particular, it assigns WordNet-Affect emotion labels related to the six Ekman basic emotions mentioned before (disgust, sadness, anger, joy, fear, and surprise) to SenticNet concepts. The whole list currently includes 13189 annotated entries.

---

[16]http://sentic.net
[17]http://www.gelbukh.com/emosenticnet/

In [46], an ontology of emotional categories based Plutchik's circumplex model [28] was developed (ArsEmotica Ontology of Emotions), encoded in OWL 2 QL. The ontology has been defined in the context of the ArsEmotica project (see Section 3.4) but it is so generic that it might be used to analyze emotions in running text in any domain. It encodes the emotional categories of Plutchik's model and links them with semantic relationships, which can be represented as a wheel of emotions. In particular, it accounts for various levels of intensity, the similarity and opposite relationships, and compositions of basic emotions (primary dyads). Overall, it distinguishes the 32 emotional concepts of the wheel of emotions. The emotional concepts have been semiautomatically linked to synsets from WordNet-Affect 1.1, and then to Italian lexical entries, by exploitation of MultiWordNet, an Italian WordNet strictly aligned with Princeton WordNet 1.6. The linkage between the language level (lexicon based) and the conceptual level representing the emotional concepts has been formalized by integration of the ontology framework Lexicon Model for Ontologies [47].

Finally, we mention a set of affect-related ontologies in the Semantic Web field that are not lexical resources but were created as a response to a more foundational need to represent all the main features of an emotion, and to standardize the knowledge of emotions, so as to support very broad semantic interoperability among affective computing applications, by allowing the mapping of concepts and properties belonging to different emotion representation models.

The Human Emotion Ontology [41] has been developed in this direction, as has the semantic vocabulary Onyx,[18] which has been proposed to describe emotion analysis processes and results [43].

2.3 SOCIAL MEDIA CORPORA ANNOTATED FOR SENTIMENT AND FINE EMOTION CATEGORIES

The growing interest in the development of automatic systems for sentiment analysis has also prompted the production of annotated corpora that could be exploited for the development of such systems in a learning fashion (see also Section 3).

The design of schemes for the annotation of corpora is always a task in the field of data classification, which leads to theoretical assumptions about the concepts to be annotated. It defines what kind of information must be annotated, the inventory of markers to be used, and the annotation's granularity. As highlighted in [48], in annotated corpora for sentiment analysis this is especially challenging. Research in psychology outlines three main approaches to the modeling of emotions and sentiments: the categorical, the dimensional, and the appraisal-based approach. The most widespread are the categorical and the dimensional ones, which describe emotions by marking a small set of discrete categories and scoring properties in a continuous range of values. Accordingly, the kinds of knowledge usually annotated are the sentiment's polarity (positive vs. negative), category (happiness vs. sadness), the source and target of the sentiment, and its intensity. Annotations can be based on simple broad polarity labels, possibly equipped with intensity ratings, which also helps us to classify texts where mixed sentiments are expressed. They can also be based on labels representing different emotions.

The resources developed within the SemEval evaluation campaigns (regularly since 2013) comprise tweet collections annotated for subjectivity, polarity, emotions, irony, and aspects/properties, and are

---

[18]https://www.gsi.dit.upm.es/ontologies/onyx/

not restricted to English [25,26,48,49]. In addition to the SemEval related data, other collections have been constructed, especially on news and events or product reviews, which are obviously a very good source of opinionated texts, and a field of interest for any business-related application that works with users' opinions. For example, a widely used dataset is the Movie Review Data,[19] a collection of movie reviews [50]. Sentiment labels (positive vs. negative) are assigned to the global review, while in an extension of this corpus, annotation is done at the sentence level [51]. Another classic resource is the MPQA corpus,[20] based on [52], which contains news articles from a wide variety of sources and which was manually annotated for opinions and other private states. This corpus has been expanded very recently with finer-grained information, and now includes entity and event target annotations [53], in line with the increasing interest in aspect-based sentiment analysis. A pioneer work in this sense is [54]: given a product, Hu and Liu [54] mine and summarize reviews related to specific features of that product, on which customers have expressed their positive or negative opinion, so that sentiment is associated with aspects of rather than the whole product. Extraction of opinions on aspects (specifically service, location, and rooms of hotels) is also the focus in [55], where the authors collected and processed 10,000 TripAdvisor reviews.

Interest in properties and aspect-based sentiment analysis is increasing also in Twitter-based work, as shown by recently organized evaluation campaigns on this [3]. Indeed, even if a lot shorter in characters than a product review, the same tweet can contain both positive and negative information, possibly relating to different entities that are mentioned. Niek Sanders's Twitter dataset[21] is not aspect annotated but a specific topic is assigned to each tweet, and this topic can be possibly used as a proxy for the entity with which the sentiment is associated, as is also done in [25], where specific hashtags are used as proxies.

Still in term of proxies, it is interesting to note that to save annotation effort in the creation of sentiment datasets, there have been experiments with *distant learning*, where class labels are not assigned manually but are rather derived from other information available. Performing sentiment analysis on tweets, Go et al. [56] trained a few classifiers using emoticons as noisy labels, and achieved an accuracy of about 80%. Recently, a new Twitter corpus was released by Mohammad et al. [57], where a multilayer scheme is applied. It contains a set of tweets with annotations concerning different aspects: sentiment (positive or negative), but also finer-grained annotation of emotions (anger, anticipation, disgust, fear, joy, sadness, surprise, and trust), and in addition purpose (to point out a mistake, to support, to ridicule, etc.) and style (simple statement, sarcasm, hyperbole, understatement). The corpus is not generic but focused on the political domain. Mohammad et al. collected tweets labeled with a set of hashtags pertaining to the 2012 US presidential election. The tweets were annotated manually by reliance on crowdsourcing platforms. This is the first dataset including a fine-grained annotation concerning stylistic features related to irony, and also a multilayer annotation concerning affect, since both annotations on sentiment polarity and on emotions are provided. For style, only 23% of the tweets were labeled with a style tag pertinent to the expression of irony, whereas most of them were annotated with the label <u>simple statement</u>, which can be interpreted as a tag for marking nonironic expressions.

---

[19]http://www.cs.cornell.edu/people/pabo/movie-review-data/
[20]http://mpqa.cs.pitt.edu/corpora/mpqa_corpus/
[21]http://www.sananalytics.com/lab/twitter-sentiment/

Previous corpora annotated for fine-grained emotion categories, such as the one proposed for SemEval 2007 task14 [31], were not focused on social media data. The availability of such a new kind of datasets opens the way to the possibility of building machine learning systems that predict emotion and purpose labels in unseen tweets, as proposed by Mohammad et al. [57], who also presented the first results and a baseline for such new sentiment-related tasks on Twitter.

3 USING SEMANTICS IN SENTIMENT ANALYSIS

Because of the task's nature, semantics is obviously a crucial ingredient of any sentiment analysis system. However, depending on the system's complexity, and depending also on the specific task that is undertaken (see Section 1), semantic information of different types can be accessed and incorporated in various different ways. In Section 3.1 we discuss how lexical information mostly derived by the resources discussed in Section 2 is used, while in Section 3.2 we briefly review how current semantic similarity models are adapted to sentiment processing. In Section 3.3 we explore the deeper semantic processing that is required by finer-grained tasks such as aspect-based sentiment analysis. Finally, in Section 3.4 we review systems that perform sentiment analysis by *reasoning* over semantic resources.

3.1 LEXICAL INFORMATION

Independently of the approach (rule based or statistical), virtually all systems for sentiment analysis rely on information derived from lexical resources. In machine learning such information is used as features, normally in combination with other features, too. The best performing system for subtask B of SemEval 2015's task 10, which is the most standard message-level polarity task, is an ensemble classifier that builds on three well-performing classifiers at SemEval 2013 and one at SemEval 2014 [58]. Although the classifiers were handpicked with attention not only to performance but also to significant differences in feature combinations, all four classifiers employ polarity dictionaries of some sort and in some way. Some systems rely on one resource only; for example, Günther and Furrer [59] only use SentiWordNet, while other systems will try to use and combine information from all available sources [15,60].

As a general strategy, lexical information is collected at the word level (eg, the categorical or gradual polarity of a given token) for each word of the whole tweet, and is then propagated via different combinations at the sentence/message level. Such combinations yield values that are then used as different features. For example, feature values can be the number of tokens in the text with a positive score or the number of those with a negative score, but also derived values such as the global polarity score of a tweet obtained as the average of the tokens' polarities. Also, maximum and minimum scores, when available, are used as features.

Most statistical approaches are support vector machine models that implement such features and similar features, and Taboada et al. [10] highlight that information from basic unigrams appears to be the most useful. Although this shows that words in themselves are very informative for this task, the intrinsic limitations in the use of information from a plain dictionary lookup are quite evident if one thinks that words are used in a specific (syntactic) context, and their polarity can change substantially according to how they relate to other words in the text. Mainly because of the lack of tools that can deal with Twitter, few systems perform word sense disambiguation, so the richer sense-annotated lexica cannot be exploited to their full potential. A way of addressing polysemy without disambiguation was suggested by Basile and Nissim [25], who introduced the concept of *polypathy* (calculated as the standard deviation of the polarity scores of the possible senses of a lemma) as an indicator of variance of polarity scores across a lemma's synsets, which can then be used as a feature or threshold value (tokens that have a too high polypathy could, for example, be ignored, as they provide conflicting information).

Another crucial limitation of not taking context into account is *negation* [61] (recall also the separate lexica for negated and affirmative contexts reviewed earlier). To cope with this aspect, Taboada et al. [10] incorporate information from what they call *contextual valence shifters*, showing an increase in performance. This is a first step toward deeper language processing, which is considered more and more necessary, even for short texts such as tweets.

3.2 DISTRIBUTIONAL SEMANTICS

In the context of sentiment analysis the idea of exploiting the distributional hypothesis—namely, the assumption that words that occur in the same contexts tend to have similar meanings [62,63]— simply boils down to the fact that similarity models that predict, for example, that "amazing" and "wonderful" are similar could be extended to predict that if "amazing" has a positive value, so too will "wonderful," and will be at the opposite end of spectrum to, say, "terrible" and "awful." However, general similarity models usually take into account the lexical and morphosyntactic context of a word but not necessarily the text's polarity. Therefore similarity is potentially accurate at a syntactic and more general semantic level but not necessarily in a sentiment-aware way, so "good" and "bad" end up being very similar. This is true for classic distributional similarity models as well as for the more recent and successful distributed vector representations known as *word embeddings*, at least in their standard formulation [64,65].

As a first attempt at directly incorporating sentiment in learning the distributional context of a word, so that words expressing similar sentiment do indeed end up having similar vector representations, Maas et al. [66] developed a model where they give a sentiment predictor function to each word. On the positive/negative classification of tweets, their system is shown to perform better than models that incorporate embeddings trained in a nonsentiment-aware fashion. An even more powerful and recent model, which outperforms that of Maas et al. [66], was proposed by Tang et al. [67], who train a neural network by associating each n-gram with the polarity of a sentence (thus beyond the word level, as in [66]), and show that sentiment-specific word embeddings effectively distinguish words with opposite sentiment polarity. This model performs better than other models that use generally learned embeddings.

3.3 ENTITIES, PROPERTIES, AND RELATIONS

Interest in finer-grained sentiment analysis has also necessarily prompted the need for finer-grained semantic analysis, and therefore deeper language processing. For example, aspect-based sentiment analysis must rely on the identification of specific entities and/or properties of entities in reviews or tweets. To do this, standard techniques for entity detection and classification are employed, such as sequential taggers, possibly retrained for specific domains. Particular attention to (named) entities in sentiment analysis is also shown by the OpeNER EU-funded project,[22] which focuses on named entity recognition within sentiment analysis.

---

[22]http://www.opener-project.eu/

Further, relations between the entities and events involved must be identified, so as to know what is said of which entity. An obvious way to do this is to exploit dependency relations, although deeper processing of tweets is not so simple because of the idiosyncratic and often ungrammatical language such short texts contain (although recent work based on learning neural knowledge graph embeddings shows an error reduction of more than 26% in semantic parsing of tweets [68]). Similar issues arise when one is developing systems to detect stance, as in order to assess the opinion of someone toward a given target, all relations between the entities involved must be correctly identified and associated with the sentiment expressed. However, a deeper linguistic analysis of text is also beneficial, if not necessary, for standard message- or text-level sentiment analysis, as it helps to treat the issue of *contextual valence shifters* mentioned in Section 3.1 by also accounting for word order and sentence structure. To this end, the Natural Language Processing Group at Stanford University developed a *sentiment treebank*.[23] This treebank has been used to train a recursive neural network built on top of grammatical structures [69], achieving an increase of 5 percentage points on sentence polarity classification. On fine-grained sentiment level they obtained a 9.7% improvement over a bag-of-words baseline, and overall showed the ability to accurately capture the effects of negation and its scope at various levels in the tree structures.

3.4 CONCEPT-LEVEL SENTIMENT ANALYSIS: REASONING WITH SEMANTICS

Approaches enabling concept- and context-based analysis can lead to a better understanding of opinions expressed in textual data, therefore reducing the gap between unstructured information and structured machine-processable data. Concept-level sentiment analysis exploits large semantic knowledge bases (eg, ontologies and semantic networks), together with natural language processing tools and techniques, thus stepping away from blind use of keywords and word co-occurrence counts. Rather, it relies on the implicit features associated with natural language concepts. Unlike purely syntactic techniques, concept-based approaches are able to detect also sentiments that are expressed in a subtle manner (eg, through the analysis of concepts that do not explicitly convey any emotion) but that are implicitly linked to other concepts that do so.

The accent on concept-level sentiment analysis is recent. We can observe different knowledge representations of the concepts related to words and of their affective load, as well as different ways in which systems that embrace this perspective on sentiment analysis exploit and reason about such knowledge, depending also on the specific task they address.

Also, this perspective on sentiment analysis offers a challenge to the Semantic Web community. A periodic shared task on concept-level sentiment analysis has been launched recently [5], and some of the systems described below explicitly rely on the use of Semantic Web and linked data resources and tools to enable automated reasoning (eg, ontological reasoning on the taxonomic structure of an ontology of affect) and semantic metadata processing.

Let us start with Sentilo,[24] an unsupervised, domain-independent system that relies on a knowledge-based approach where existing tools for natural language processing and publicly available lexical/affective resources are combined with Semantic Web techniques for representing and reasoning about knowledge involved in opinion sentences. Sentilo exploits the semantic graph representation

[23]http://nlp.stanford.edu/sentiment/treebank.html
[24]http://wit.istc.cnr.it/stlab-tools/sentilo/

of a sentence enriched with opinion-related information (eg, opinion holder, topics, sentiment scores). Such a semantic representation allows Sentilo to address the finer-grained tasks of detecting holders and topics of an opinion, and additionally to identify and distinguish both main topics and subtopics. Specifically, given an input opinion sentence (natural language text), the system returns the corresponding semantic representation as a FRED graph (RDF/OWL graph) annotated with concepts from a semantic model of opinions. Annotations concerning the opinion holder, opinion features, and opinion topics are produced on the basis of a set of heuristic rules exploiting the FRED semantic representation and by use of lexical and affective resources, such as SentiWordNet and SenticNet. An evaluation of Sentilo as the opinion holder and main/subtopic detection tool has been presented [70]. The system is able to achieve good performance compared with the other tools, highlighting promising results on opinion holder (F1: 95%), subtopic (F1: 78%), and topic (F1: 68%) detection. Sentilo is also available as a REST service that returns RDF as output. This is important to make the output of the system machine processable and reusable.

In other systems the accent is on the use of conceptual and affective knowledge of words, the focus being on sophisticated representations of the affective space that can enable commonsense or ontological reasoning on networks or taxonomies of concepts. This is, for instance, the case for many systems exploiting the resources of the SenticNet suite of resources [71]. Another system that can be placed in this category is ArsEmotica,[25] which is an example of a domain-dependent system focused on cultural heritage. It applies sentiment analysis to resources from online art collections, and exploits tags given by the visitors on social platforms as an additional source of information [46]. The extraction of the emotional semantics from social tags is driven by an ontology-based representation of the emotional categories presented in the previous section. Methods and tools from the Semantic Web and natural language processing provide the building blocks for the creation of a semantic social space to organize artworks according to the ontology of emotions. The output is encoded into World Wide Web Consortium ontology languages. The semantic representation is not limited to affect but concerns also aspects of the specific art domain. This gives the twofold advantage of enabling tractable reasoning on the relationships between emotions and other interesting dimensions of the domain (eg, artists and artworks), and fostering the interoperability and integration of tools developed in the Semantic Web and linked data community. The system has been evaluated against a dataset of tagged multimedia artworks from the ArsMeteo Italian art portal.[26] A SPARQL end point has been implemented to explore the collection and to extract information about the relationships among emotions, artworks and authors by posing queries such as: *"Give me the artworks stirring emotions similar to sadness and belonging to the music genre."* In some systems the focus on conceptual semantics, not limited to affect, is also combined with issues related to the contextual semantics of words. Such approaches do not offer fixed sentiment polarities but assign context-specific sentiment orientation to words. An interesting proposal in this line is SentiCircles, a lexicon-based approach for the detection of sentiment in Twitter posts at both entity level and tweet level [72]. SentiCircle builds a dynamic representation of context to tune the preassigned strength and polarity of words in the lexicon, and incorporates both contextual semantics (ie, semantics inferred from the co-occurrence of words) and conceptual semantics (ie, semantics extracted from background ontologies).

---

[25]http://di.unito.it/arsemotica
[26]http://www.arsmeteo.org

4 CONCLUSIONS

We started this contribution by pointing out how much interest and research in sentiment analysis have grown in the past few years. We have highlighted that in the recent SemEval campaigns tasks more complex than basic polarity classification have been proposed. And complexity here means finer-grained interpretations of sentiment, be it related to figurative uses such as irony or be it related to singling out which entities or entity properties are actually in focus in an opinionated statement. This is also reflected in resource creation, where we have seen that corpora have been extended in their annotation to include polarity at the sentence level, where before this was done at the global document level, or at the entity level, where before it was done at the message level.

Accordingly, sentiment analysis systems are required to be ever more accurate and more sophisticated at the same time, thus attempting to perform deeper semantic processing that is rather successful on language data cleaner than that from Twitter and for other natural language processing tasks but is still experimental with regard to noisy social media data, with all the subjectivity that sentiment analysis carries. We have provided a survey of the state-of-the-art approaches and resources in this sense, highlighting how semantics is being coded and used in this emerging and growing field. From what we see, sentiment analysis in social media appears to be expanding in a variety of directions, incorporating and adapting processing tools from natural language processing and reasoning tools from the Semantic Web community, as well as including possibly orthogonal aspects such as a whole range of affect-related concepts. What we also see is that semantics necessarily remains the core of this, in the use, coding, and processing of the meaning of words and larger phrases, so we can only hope that this survey serves as a starting point for much more to come.

Our expectations do not concern only the development of sentiment analysis per se, since related tasks, such as personality and irony detection [73–75], or author profiling [76], also have interest in exploiting the lexical knowledge of affect encoded in the resources we have described.

REFERENCES

[1] S. Rosenthal, P. Nakov, S. Kiritchenko, S. Mohammad, A. Ritter, V. Stoyanov, SemEval-2015 task 10: sentiment analysis in Twitter, in: Proceedings of the Ninth International Workshop on Semantic Evaluation (SemEval 2015), Association for Computational Linguistics, Denver, CO, 2015, pp. 451–463.

[2] A. Ghosh, G. Li, T. Veale, P. Rosso, E. Shutova, J. Barnden, A. Reyes, SemEval-2015 task 11: sentiment analysis of figurative language in Twitter, in: Proceedings of the Ninth International Workshop on Semantic Evaluation (SemEval 2015), Association for Computational Linguistics, Denver, CO, 2015, pp. 470–478.

[3] M. Pontiki, D. Galanis, H. Papageorgiou, S. Manandhar, I. Androutsopoulos, SemEval-2015 task 12: aspect based sentiment analysis, in: Proceedings of the Ninth International Workshop on Semantic Evaluation (SemEval 2015), Association for Computational Linguistics, Denver, CO, 2015, pp. 486–495.

[4] I. Russo, T. Caselli, C. Strapparava, SemEval-2015 task 9: CLIPEval implicit polarity of events, in: Proceedings of the Ninth International Workshop on Semantic Evaluation (SemEval 2015), Association for Computational Linguistics, Denver, CO, 2015, pp. 443–450.

[5] D.R. Recupero, E. Cambria, ESWC'14 challenge on concept-level sentiment analysis, in: Semantic Web Evaluation Challenge—SemWebEval 2014 at ESWC 2014, Anissaras, Crete, Greece, May 25–29, 2014, Revised Selected Papers, Communications in Computer and Information Science, vol. 475, Springer, 2014, pp. 3–20.

[6] T. Wilson, J. Wiebe, P. Hoffmann, Recognizing contextual polarity in phrase-level sentiment analysis, in: Proceedings of the conference on Human Language Technology and Empirical Methods in Natural Language Processing, HLT '05, Vancouver, Canada, 2005, pp. 347–354.

[7] J. Wiebe, R. Mihalcea, Word sense and subjectivity, in: Proceedings of the 21st International Conference on Computational Linguistics and the 44th Annual Meeting of the Association for Computational Linguistics, 2006, pp. 1065–1072.

[8] S. Baccianella, A. Esuli, F. Sebastiani, SentiWordNet 3.0: an enhanced lexical resource for sentiment analysis and opinion mining, in: Proceedings of the Seventh International Conference on Language Resources and Evaluation (LREC'10), European Language Resources Association (ELRA), Valletta, Malta, 2010, pp. 2200–2204.

[9] C. Fellbaum, WordNet: An Electronic Lexical Database, Bradford Books, Cambridge, MA, 1998.

[10] M. Taboada, J. Brooke, M. Tofiloski, K. Voll, M. Stede, Lexicon-based methods for sentiment analysis, Comput. Linguist. 37 (2) (2011) 267–307.

[11] P.J. Stone, D.C. Dunphy, M.S. Smith, D.M. Ogilvie, The general inquirer: a computer approach to content analysis, Am. J. Sociol. 73 (5) (1966) 634–635.

[12] J. J. McAuley, J. Leskovec, Hidden factors and hidden topics: understanding rating dimensions with review text, in: Proceedings of the 7th ACM Conference on Recommender Systems, 2013, pp. 165–172.

[13] S. Kiritchenko, X. Zhu, C. Cherry, S. Mohammad, NRC-Canada-2014: detecting aspects and sentiment in customer reviews, in: Proceedings of the Eighth International Workshop on Semantic Evaluation (SemEval 2014), Association for Computational Linguistics and Dublin City University, Dublin, Ireland, 2014, pp. 437–442.

[14] T. Loughran, B. McDonald, When is a liability not a liability? Textual analysis, dictionaries, and 10-ks, J. Financ. 66 (1) (2011) 35–65.

[15] S. Mohammad, S. Kiritchenko, X. Zhu, NRC-Canada: building the state-of-the art in sentiment analysis of tweets, in: Proceedings of the Seventh International Workshop on Semantic Evaluation Exercises (SemEval-2013), Atlanta, GA, 2013, pp. 321–327.

[16] X. Zhu, S. Kiritchenko, S. Mohammad, NRC-Canada-2014: recent improvements in the sentiment analysis of tweets, in: Proceedings of the Eighth International Workshop on Semantic Evaluation (SemEval 2014), Association for Computational Linguistics and Dublin City University, Dublin, Ireland, 2014, pp. 443–447.

[17] S. Kiritchenko, X. Zhu, S.M. Mohammad, Sentiment analysis of short informal texts, J. Artif. Intell. Res. 50 (2014) 723–762.

[18] A. Pak, P. Paroubek, Twitter for sentiment analysis: when language resources are not available, in: Proceedings of the 23rd International Workshop on Database and Expert Systems Applications, 2011, pp. 111–115.

[19] G. Pitel, G. Grefenstette, Semi-automatic building method for a multidimensional affect dictionary for a new language, in: Proceedings of the Sixth International Conference on Language Resources and Evaluation (LREC'08), European Language Resources Association (ELRA), Marrakech, Morocco, 2008.

[20] T.D. Smedt, W. Daelemans, "Vreselijk mooi!" (terribly beautiful): a subjectivity lexicon for Dutch adjectives, in: N. Calzolari, K. Choukri, T. Declerck, M.U. Dogan, B. Maegaard, J. Mariani, J. Odijk, S. Piperidis (Eds.), Proceedings of LREC 2012, European Language Resources Association (ELRA), 2012, pp. 3568–3572.

[21] Y. Chen, S. Skiena, Building sentiment lexicons for all major languages, in: Proceedings of the 52nd Annual Meeting of the Association for Computational Linguistics (Volume 2: Short Papers), Association for Computational Linguistics, Baltimore, Maryland, 2014, pp. 383–389.

[22] C. Banea, R. Mihalcea, J. Wiebe, Porting multilingual subjectivity resources across languages, Trans. Affect. Comput. 4 (2) (2013) 211–225.

[23] C. Banea, R. Mihalcea, J. Wiebe, Sense-level subjectivity in a multilingual setting, Comput. Speech Lang. 28 (1) (2014) 7–19.

[24] I. San Vicente, R. Agerri, G. Rigau, Simple, robust and (almost) unsupervised generation of polarity lexicons for multiple languages, in: Proceedings of the 14th Conference of the European Chapter of the Association for Computational Linguistics (EACL2014), Gothenburg, Sweden, 2014, pp. 88–97.

[25] V. Basile, M. Nissim, Sentiment analysis on Italian tweets, in: Proceedings of the Fourth Workshop on Computational Approaches to Subjectivity, Sentiment and Social Media Analysis, ACL, Atlanta, GA, 2013, pp. 100–107.

[26] V. Basile, A. Bolioli, M. Nissim, V. Patti, P. Rosso, Overview of the Evalita 2014 SENTIment POLarity classification task, in: Proceedings of the Fourth Evaluation Campaign of Natural Language Processing and Speech Tools for Italian (EVALITA 2014), Pisa, Italy, 2014.

[27] D.I. Hernández Farías, D. Buscaldi, B. Priego-Sánchez, IRADABE: adapting English lexicons to the Italian sentiment polarity classification task, in: First Italian Conference on Computational Linguistics (CLiC-it 2014) and the Fourth International Workshop EVALITA 2014, 2014, pp. 75–81.

[28] R. Plutchik, The nature of emotions, Am. Sci. 89 (4) (2001) 344–350.

[29] P. Ekman, An argument for basic emotions, Cogn. Emot. 6 (3–4) (1992) 169–200.

[30] C. Strapparava, A. Valitutti, WordNet-Affect: an affective extension of WordNet, in: Proceedings of the International Conference on Language Resources and Evaluation (LREC'04), vol. 4, European Language Resources Association (ELRA), 2004, pp. 1083–1086.

[31] C. Strapparava, R. Mihalcea, SemEval-2007 task 14: affective text, in: Proceedings of the Fourth International Workshop on Semantic Evaluations, SemEval '07, Association for Computational Linguistics, Stroudsburg, PA, 2007, pp. 70–74.

[32] S.M. Mohammad, P.D. Turney, Crowdsourcing a word-emotion association lexicon, Comput. Intell. 29 (3) (2013) 436–465.

[33] J. Carrillo de Albornoz, L. Plaza, P. Gervás, SentiSense: an easily scalable concept-based affective lexicon for sentiment analysis, in: Proceedings of the Eight International Conference on Language Resources and Evaluation (LREC'12), European Language Resources Association (ELRA), Istanbul, Turkey, 2012, pp. 3562–3567.

[34] M.B. Arnold, Emotion and Personality, vol. 1, Columbia University Press, New York, NY, 1960.

[35] W.G. Parrot, Emotions in Social Psychology: Essential Readings, Psychology Press, Philadelphia, 2001.

[36] J.W. Pennebaker, M.E. Francis, R.J. Booth, Linguistic Inquiry and Word Count: LIWC 2001, Lawrence Erlbaum Associates, Mahwah, NJ, 2001.

[37] C. Whissell, Using the revised dictionary of affect in language to quantify the emotional undertones of samples of natural languages, Psychol. Rep. 2 (105) (2009) 509–521.

[38] M.M. Bradley, P.J. Lang, Affective norms for English words (ANEW): instruction manual and affective ratings, tech. rep., Center for Research in Psychophysiology, University of Florida, Gainesville, FL, 1999.

[39] J.A. Russell, A. Mehrabian, Evidence for a three-factor theory of emotions, J. Res. Pers. 11 (3) (1977) 273–294.

[40] E. Cambria, D. Olsher, D. Rajagopal, SenticNet 3: a common and common-sense knowledge base for cognition-driven sentiment analysis, in: Proceedings of AAAI Conference on Artificial Intelligence, 2014, pp. 1515–1521.

[41] M. Grassi, Developing HEO human emotions ontology, in: Proceedings of the 2009 Joint COST 2101 and 2102 International Conference on Biometric ID Management and Multimodal Communication, Springer-Verlag, Berlin, Heidelberg, 2009, pp. 244–251.

[42] V. Francisco, P. Gervas, F. Peinado, Ontological reasoning for improving the treatment of emotions in text, Knowl. Inform. Syst. 25 (2010) 421–443.

[43] J.F. Sánchez-Rada, C.A. Iglesias, Onyx: a linked data approach to emotion representation, Inform. Process. Manage. 52 (1) (2016) 99–114.

[44] E. Cambria, A. Livingstone, A. Hussain, The hourglass of emotions, in: COST 2102 Training School, Revised Selected Papers, Lecture Notes in Computer Science, vol. 7403, Springer, 2011, pp. 144–157.

[45] S. Poria, A. Gelbukh, A. Hussain, N. Howard, D. Das, S. Bandyopadhyay, Enhanced SenticNet with affective labels for concept-based opinion mining, IEEE Intell. Syst. 28 (2) (2013) 31–38.

[46] F. Bertola, V. Patti, Ontology-based affective models to organize artworks in the social semantic web, Inform. Process. Manage. 52 (1) (2016) 139–162.

[47] J. McCrae, D. Spohr, P. Cimiano, Linking lexical resources and ontologies on the semantic web with LEMON, in: The Semantic Web: Research and Applications, Springer, New York, NY, 2011, pp. 245–259.

[48] C. Bosco, V. Patti, A. Bolioli, Developing corpora for sentiment analysis: the case of Irony and Senti-TUT, IEEE Intell. Syst. 28 (2) (2013) 55–63.

[49] J. Steinberger, T. Brychcın, M. Konkol, Aspect-level sentiment analysis in czech, in: Proceedings of the 52nd Annual Meeting of the Association for Computational Linguistics (ACL 2014), 2014, pp. 24.

[50] B. Pang, L. Lee, A sentimental education: sentiment analysis using subjectivity, in: Proceedings of the 42nd Annual Meeting of the Association for Computational Linguistics (ACL 2004), 2004, pp. 271–278.

[51] B. Pang, L. Lee, Seeing stars: exploiting class relationships for sentiment categorization with respect to rating scales, in: Proceedings of the 43rd Annual Meeting of the Association for Computational Linguistics (ACL 2005), 2005, pp. 115–124.

[52] J. Wiebe, T. Wilson, C. Cardie, Annotating expressions of opinions and emotions in language, Lang. Resour. Eval. 39 (2–3) (2005) 165–210.

[53] L. Deng, J. Wiebe, MPQA 3.0: an entity/event-level sentiment corpus, in: R. Mihalcea, J.Y. Chai, A. Sarkar (Eds.), Proceedings of HLT-NAACL 2015, The Association for Computational Linguistics, 2015, pp. 1323–1328.

[54] M. Hu, B. Liu, Mining and summarizing customer reviews, in: Proceedings of the Tenth ACM SIGKDD International Conference on Knowledge Discovery and Data Mining, KDD '04, ACM, New York, NY, 2004, pp. 168–177.

[55] I. Titov, R.T. McDonald, A joint model of text and aspect ratings for sentiment summarization, in: Proceedings of the 46th Annual Meeting of the Association for Computational Linguistics (ACL 2008), vol. 8, 2008, pp. 308–316.

[56] A. Go, R. Bhayani, L. Huang, Twitter sentiment classification using distant supervision, CS224N Project Report, Stanford 1 (2009) 12.

[57] S.M. Mohammad, X. Zhu, S. Kiritchenko, J. Martin, Sentiment, emotion, purpose, and style in electoral tweets, Inform. Process. Manage. 51 (4) (2015) 480–499.

[58] M. Hagen, M. Potthast, M. Büchner, B. Stein, Webis: an ensemble for Twitter sentiment detection, in: Proceedings of the Ninth International Workshop on Semantic Evaluation (SemEval 2015), Association for Computational Linguistics, Denver, CO, 2015, pp. 582–589.

[59] T. Günther, L. Furrer, GU-MLT-LT: sentiment analysis of short messages using linguistic features and stochastic gradient descent, in: Proceedings of the Second Joint Conference on Lexical and Computational Semantics (*SEM), Volume 2: Proceedings of the Seventh International Workshop on Semantic Evaluation (SemEval 2013), Association for Computational Linguistics, Atlanta, GA, 2013, pp. 328–332.

[60] Y. Miura, S. Sakaki, K. Hattori, T. Ohkuma, Teamx: a sentiment analyzer with enhanced lexicon mapping and weighting scheme for unbalanced data, in: Proceedings of the Eighth International Workshop on Semantic Evaluation (SemEval 2014), 2014, pp. 628–632.

[61] R. Saurí, A Factuality Profiler for Eventualities in Text, ProQuest, Ann Arbor, MI, 2008.

[62] Z. Harris, Distributional structure, Word 10 (23) (1954) 146–162.

[63] M. Sahlgren, The distributional hypothesis, Ital. J. Linguist. 20 (1) (2008) 33–54.

[64] T. Mikolov, K. Chen, G. Corrado, J. Dean, Efficient estimation of word representations in vector space, in: Proceedings of the ICLR Workshop, 2013, pp. 1–12.

[65] T. Mikolov, I. Sutskever, K. Chen, G.S. Corrado, J. Dean, Distributed representations of words and phrases and their compositionality, in: Advances in Neural Information Processing Systems (NIPS), 2013, pp. 3111–3119.

[66] A.L. Maas, R.E. Daly, P.T. Pham, D. Huang, A.Y. Ng, C. Potts, Learning word vectors for sentiment analysis, in: Proceedings of the 49th Annual Meeting of the Association for Computational Linguistics: Human Language Technologies—Volume 1, HLT '11, Association for Computational Linguistics, Stroudsburg, PA, 2011, pp. 142–150.

[67] D. Tang, F. Wei, N. Yang, M. Zhou, T. Liu, B. Qin, Learning sentiment-specific word embedding for Twitter sentiment classification, in: Proceedings of the 52nd Annual Meeting of the Association for Computational Linguistics, vol. 1, 2014, pp. 1555–1565.

[68] L. Heck, H. Huang, Deep learning of knowledge graph embeddings for semantic parsing of Twitter dialogs, in: Proceedings of the Second IEEE Global Conference on Signal and Information Processing (DRAFT), IEEE Institute of Electrical and Electronics Engineers, 2014, pp. 597–601.

[69] R. Socher, A. Perelygin, J. Wu, J. Chuang, C.D. Manning, A. Ng, C. Potts, Recursive deep models for semantic compositionality over a sentiment treebank, in: Proceedings of the 2013 Conference on Empirical Methods in Natural Language Processing, Association for Computational Linguistics, Seattle, WA, 2013, pp. 1631–1642.

[70] A. Gangemi, V. Presutti, D. Reforgiato Recupero, Frame-based detection of opinion holders and topics: a model and a tool, IEEE Comp. Int. Mag. 9 (1) (2014) 20–30.

[71] E. Cambria, B.W. Schuller, B. Liu, H. Wang, C. Havasi, Knowledge-based approaches to concept-level sentiment analysis, IEEE Intell. Syst. 28 (2) (2013) 12–14.

[72] H. Saif, Y. He, M. Fernandez, H. Alani, Contextual semantics for sentiment analysis of Twitter, Inform. Process. Manage. 52 (1) (2016) 5–19.

[73] S. Poria, A.F. Gelbukh, B. Agarwal, E. Cambria, N. Howard, Common sense knowledge based personality recognition from text, in: Advances in Soft Computing and Its Applications, Proceedings of the 12th Mexican International Conference on Artificial Intelligence, MICAI 2013, Part II, Springer, 2013, pp. 484–496.

[74] D.I. Hernández Farías, J. Benedí, P. Rosso, Applying basic features from sentiment analysis for automatic irony detection, in: Pattern Recognition and Image Analysis, Proceedings of IbPRIA 2015, Lecture Notes in Computer Science, vol. 9117, Springer, 2015, pp. 337–344.

[75] E. Sulis, D.I.H. Farías, P. Rosso, V. Patti, G. Ruffo, Figurative messages and affect in Twitter: Differences between #irony, #sarcasm and #not, Knowledge-Based Systems, Elsevier, 2016, In Press. http://dx.doi.org/10.1016/j.knosys.2016.05.035

[76] F.M. Rangel, P. Rosso, On the impact of emotions on author profiling, Inform. Process. Manage. 52 (1) (2016) 73–92.

LINKED DATA MODELS FOR SENTIMENT AND EMOTION ANALYSIS IN SOCIAL NETWORKS

4

C.A. Iglesias[a], J.F. Sánchez-Rada[a], G. Vulcu[b], P. Buitelaar[b]

Technical University of Madrid, Madrid, Spain[a] National University of Ireland, Galway, Ireland[b]

1 INTRODUCTION

Sentiment analysis is now an established field of research and a growing industry [1]. However, language resources for sentiment analysis are being developed by individual companies or research organizations and are normally not shared, with the exception of a few publicly available resources such as WordNet-Affect [2] and SentiWordNet [3].

Domain-specific resources for multiple languages are potentially valuable but not shared, sometimes because of intellectual property and license considerations, but often because of technical reasons, including interoperability. Several initiatives have addressed interoperability of language resources since the late 1980s, such as Text Encoding Initiative [4], but there is not yet a widely accepted global solution for integrating and combining heterogeneous linguistic resources from different sources [5]. In this respect the data interoperability problem has been addressed by linked data technologies, which have gained wide acceptance. *Linked data* [6] refers to best practices and technologies for publishing, sharing, and connecting structured data on the web. This approach has been followed by the linking open data (LOD) project, a grassroots community effort supported by the World Wide Web Consortium (W3C) whose aim is to bootstrap the Web of Data by identifying existing datasets available under open licenses, converting them to Resource Description Framework (RDF) format following the linked data principles, and publishing them on the web. The data cloud that originated from this initiative is known as the *LOD cloud*. Several communities such as the Open Linguistics Working Group [5] proposed the idea of adopting linked data principles for representing, sharing, and publishing open linguistic resources with the aim of developing a subcloud of the LOD cloud of linguistic resources, known as the *linguistic linked open data (LLOD) cloud* [7].

In addition, the use of linked data for modeling linguistic resources provides a clear path to their semantic annotation and linking with semantic resources of the Web of Data. This is especially important for making sense of social media streams, whose semantic interpretation is particularly challenging because they are strongly interconnected, temporal, noisy, short, and full of slang [8]. Moreover, several authors [9] have shown that the use of semantics in sentiment analysis outperforms semantics-free methods. Thus the availability of semantically annotated linguistic resources is crucial to the development of the field of sentiment analysis.

This chapter presents our contribution to the development of the sentiment LLOD cloud through a linked data model for sentiment and emotion analysis in social networks that is based on two vocabularies: Marl and Onyx for sentiment and emotion modeling respectively as described in Sections 2 and 3. The rest of the chapter illustrates how these vocabularies are used for annotation of sentiment language resources as well as services (Fig. 4.1). Section 4 describes the generation of a sentiment-linked data corpus based on the use of Marl, Onyx, and Natural Language Processing Interchange Format (NIF), which allows the representation of text with unique URLs. Section 5 describes how sentiment lexicons can be expressed with Marl, Onyx, and the Lexicon Model for Ontologies (lemon), which provides lexical information and differentiates between different domains and senses of a word. Section 6 introduces sentiment analysis interoperability through the use of a Representational State Transfer NIF application programming interface in combination with Marl and Onyx. Section 7 illustrates the benefits of this linguistic linked data approach in the generation of a domain-specific sentiment lexicon on a big linked data platform. Finally, we present our conclusions in Section 8.

2 MARL: A VOCABULARY FOR SENTIMENT ANNOTATION

The Marl ontology [10,11] is a vocabulary designed for annotation and description of subjective opinions expressed in text. The goals of the Marl ontology are to (1) enable the publishing of raw data on opinions and the sentiments, (2) deliver schema that will allow opinions coming from different systems (polarity, topics, and features) to be compared, and (3) interconnect opinions by linking them to contextual information expressed from other popular ontologies or specialized domain ontologies.

The Marl ontology is aligned with the W3C PROV Ontology (PROV-O) [12] to support provenance modeling. Provenance is information about the entities, activities, and people involved in producing a piece of data or thing, which can be used to form an assessment of its quality, reliability, and trustworthiness. The main concepts of PROV-O are entities, activities, and agents. Entities are physical or digital assets, such as web pages, spell checkers or, in our case, dictionaries or analysis services. Provenance records describe the provenance of entities, and an entity's provenance can refer to other entities. For example, a dictionary is an entity whose provenance refers to other entities such as lexical entries. Activities are how entities come into existence. For example, starting from a webpage, a sentiment analysis activity creates an opinion entity describing the opinions extracted from that webpage. Finally, agents are responsible for the activities and can be a person, a piece of software, an organization, or other entities. The Marl ontology has been aligned with the PROV-O so that provenance of language resources can be tracked and shared.

The Marl ontology consists of four main classes as shown in Fig. 4.2: <u>SentimentAnalysis</u>, <u>Opinion</u>, <u>AggregatedOpinion</u>, and <u>Polarity</u>. They are related as follows: a <u>SentimentAnalysis</u> instance is an <u>Activity</u> that analyzes a source text to detect the <u>Polarity</u> of the <u>Opinion</u> expressed in that text. The main features of the extracted opinion are the polarity (<u>hasPolarity</u>), the polarity value (<u>polarityValue</u>) or strength, whose range is defined between minimum (<u>minPolarityValue</u>) and maximum (<u>maxPolarityValue</u>) values, and the described entity (<u>describesObject</u>) and feature (<u>describesFeature</u>) of that opinion. When several opinions are equivalent, we can opt to aggregate them

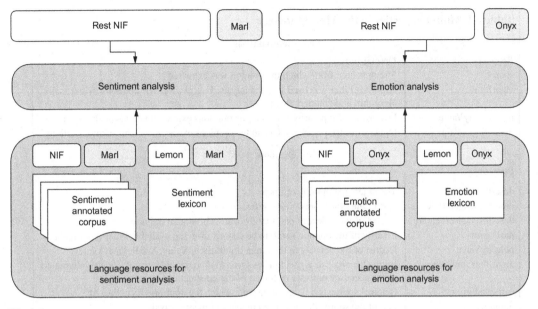

FIG. 4.1

Overview of the vocabularies used for modeling affective language resources and services. *NIF*, Natural Language Processing Interchange Format; *REST*, Representational State Transfer.

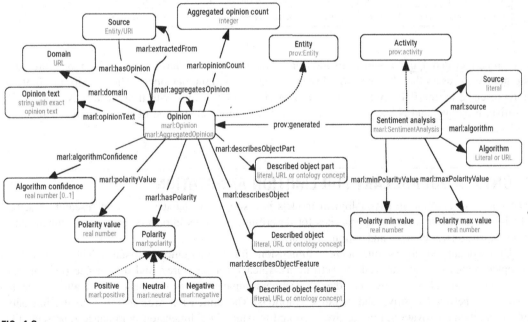

FIG. 4.2

Class diagram of the Marl ontology.

Table 4.1 Main Properties in the Marl Ontology	
SentimentAnalysis	
Property	**Description**
source	Site or source from which the opinion was extracted
algorithm	Algorithm that was used in the analysis. Useful to group opinions by extraction algorithm and compare them
minPolarityValue	Lower limit for polarity values in the opinions extracted via this analysis activity
maxPolarityValue	Upper limit for polarity values in the opinions extracted via this analysis activity
Opinion	
Property	**Description**
describesObject	The object the opinion refers to
describesObjectPart	Part of the object the opinion refers to
describesObjectFeature	Aspect of the object or part that the user is giving an opinion of
hasPolarity	Polarity of the opinion itself, to be chosen from the available Polarity individuals
polarityValue	Degree of the polarity in the range [minPolarityValue, maxPolarityValue]
algorithmConfidence	Rating the analysis algorithm has given to this particular result. Can be interpreted as the accuracy or trustworthiness of the information
extractedFrom	Original source text or resource from which the opinion was extracted
opinionText	Part of the source that was used in the sentiment analysis
domain	Context domain of the result
AggregatedOpinion	
Property	**Description**
opinionCount	The number of individual opinions this AggregatedOpinion represents

The specification contains the full description of all properties: http://www.gsi.dit.upm.es/ontologies/marl.

into an AggregatedOpinion, which, in addition to the properties we have already mentioned, provides the number of users that the aggregated opinion represents (opinionCount). The polarity of opinions is represented by the Polarity base class. The Marl ontology comes with three instances of Polarity: Positive, Negative, and Neutral. Table 4.1 contains a comprehensive list of the properties associated with each of these classes.

3 ONYX: A VOCABULARY FOR EMOTION ANNOTATION

The notion of emotion in psychological models is a subject of debate in current research. Scherer [13,14] classifies the existing approaches for describing emotions into three categories: dimensional models, categorical models, and appraisal theories.

Dimensional models use one or more dimensions for distinct emotional states. The most widely accepted dimensions are arousal (or activation), valence (or pleasure), and dominance (or control). The dimension valence represents the pleasantness-unpleasantness dimension, and allows one to distinguish between positive and negative emotions. The dimension arousal refers to the intensity of the emotional activation, ranging from excited to calm. The dimension dominance represents the controlling and dominant nature of the emotion, ranging from dominant to submissive. Unidimensional models use the arousal or valence dimension. Multidimensional models use more than one dimension to characterize emotional states. There are several popular multidimensional models: two-dimensional models (valence, arousal) by Plutchick and Russell and three-dimensional models, such as the valence, arousal, and dominance model.

Categorical models, also known as discrete emotion models, suggest that there exists an innate set of basic emotions. The best known model is Ekman's "big six": anger, disgust, fear, happiness, sadness, and surprise.

Appraisal theories assume that emotions are elicited by a cognitive evaluation (appraisal) of situations and events that cause specific reactions in people, allowing for a large number of highly differentiated emotions. The result of the appraisal will generally have an impact on motivation, which changes the tendency for action.

Onyx [15] is a vocabulary that models emotions and the emotion analysis process itself. It can be used to represent the results of an emotion analysis service or the lexical resources involved (eg, corpora and lexicons). This vocabulary can be used to connect results from different providers and applications, even when different models of emotions are used.

At its core, the ontology has three main classes as shown in Fig. 4.3: *EmotionAnalysis*, *EmotionSet*, and *Emotion*. In a standard emotion analysis these three classes are related as follows: an *EmotionAnalysis* is run on a source (generally text, eg, a status update), and the result is represented as one or more *EmotionSet* instances that each contain one or more *Emotion* instances. The model of emotions in Onyx is very generic to reflect the lack of consensus on modeling and categorizing emotions. An advantage of this approach is that the representation and psychological emotion models are decoupled. Emotions have been described in a number of different ways, by means of categories (eg, "happiness").

The *EmotionAnalysis* instance contains information about the source (eg, dataset) from which the information was taken, the algorithm used to process it, and the emotion model followed (eg, Plutchik's categories). Additionally, it can make use of provenance to specify the agent in charge of the analysis, the resources used (eg, dictionaries), and other useful information.

An *EmotionSet* contains a group of emotions found in the text or one of its parts. As such, it contains information about the original text (*extractedFrom*), the exact excerpt that contains the emotion or emotions (*emotionText*), the person who showed the emotions (*sioc:has_creator*), the entity that the emotion is related to (*describesObject*), the concrete part of that object it refers to (*describesObjectPart*), the feature about that part or object that triggers the emotion (*describesFeature*), and the domain detected. All these properties are straightforward, but a comment about the domain property is necessary. Different emotions could have different interpretations in different contexts (eg, fear is positive when referred to a thriller but negative when it comes to cars and safety). When several *EmotionSet* instances are related, an *AggregatedEmotionSet* can be created that links to all of them. *AggregatedEmotionSet* is a subclass of *EmotionSet* that contains additional information about the original *EmotionSet* instances it aggregates. For instance, we could aggregate all the emotions related to a particular movie, or all the emotions shown by a particular user, and still be able to trace back to the original individual emotions.

Onyx's *Emotion* model includes *EmotionCategory*, which is a specific category of emotion (eg, "sadness," although more than one could be specified), linked through the *hasEmotionCategory* property; the emotion intensity via *hasEmotionIntensity*; action tendencies related to this emotion, or actions that are triggered by the emotion; appraisals and dimensions. Lastly, specific appraisals, dimensions, and action tendencies can be defined by extending *Appraisal*, *Dimension*, and *ActionTendency*, whose value should be a float number.

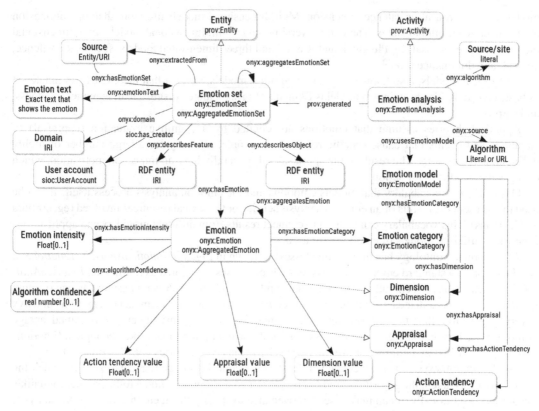

FIG. 4.3

Class diagram of the Onyx ontology. *IRI*, Internationalized Resource Identifier; *RDF*, Resource Description Framework.

On top of that generic model we have included two different models: the WordNet-Affect taxonomy, and the Emotion Markup Language (EmotionML) vocabularies for categories, dimensions, and appraisals, which are detailed in Section 3.1.

Although emotional models and categories differ in how they classify or quantify emotions, they describe different aspects of the same complex emotion phenomenon [16]. Hence there are equivalence relationships between different categories or emotions in different models. To state such equivalence between emotion categories in Onyx one can use the properties defined in SKOS [17] such as *skos:exactMatch* or *skos:closeMatch*. This approach falls short when one is dealing with dimensional emotional theories or complex category theories.

Within a single model it is also possible that two separate emotions, when found simultaneously, imply a third one. For instance, "thinking of the awful things I've done makes me want to cry" might reveal sadness and disgust, which together might be interpreted as remorse. Some representations would refer to remorse as a complex emotion. Onyx purposely does not include the notion of complex emotions. It follows the same approach as EmotionML in this respect, as the Human-Machine

Interaction Network on Emotion Annotation and Representation Language [18] included this distinction between simple and complex emotions but it was not included in the EmotionML specification. This simplifies the ontology and avoids discussion about the definition of complex emotions, since there are several possible definitions of a complex emotion, and different levels of emotions (eg, the hourglass of emotions model). One possible way to deal with such a situation is to add an *AggregatedEmotion* that represents remorse to the *EmotionSet*, linking it to the primary emotions with the *aggregatesEmotion* property.

Table 4.2 contains a comprehensive list of the properties associated with each of these classes. To group all the attributes that correspond to a specific emotion model, we created the *EmotionModel* class. Each *EmotionModel* will be linked to the different categories it contains (*hasEmotionCategory*), the *Appraisal* or *Dimension* instances it introduces (through *hasAppraisal* and *hasDimension*), etc. Having a formal representation of the categories and dimensions proves very useful when one is dealing with heterogeneous datasets in emotion analysis. In addition to being necessary to interpret the results, this information can be used to filter out results and for automation.

3.1 ONYX EXTENSIBILITY: VOCABULARIES

Annotators can define their own ad hoc models and categories, but the linked data approach dictates that vocabularies and entities should be reused when appropriate. To remedy this, we offer several

Table 4.2 Main Properties in the Onyx Ontology

EmotionAnalysis	
Property	**Description**
source	Identifies the source of the user-generated content
algorithm	Emotion analysis algorithm that was used
usesEmotionModel	Link to the emotion model used, which defines the categories, dimensions, appraisals, etc.

EmotionSet	
Property	**Description**
domain	The specific domain in which the emotion analysis was carried out
algorithmConfidence	Numeric value that represents the predicted accuracy of the result, as given by the algorithm in use
extractedFrom	Text or resource that was subject to the analysis
hasEmotion	An emotion that is shown by the EmotionSet. An EmotionExpression may contain several emotions

Emotion	
Property	**Description**
hasEmotionCategory	The type of emotion, defined by an instance of the emotion ontology as specified in the corresponding EmotionAnalysis
hasEmotionIntensity	Degree of intensity of the emotion
emotionText	Fragment of the EmotionSet's source that contained emotion information

The specification contains the full description of all properties: http://www.gsi.dit.upm.es/ontologies/onyx.

EmotionModel vocabularies that can be used with Onyx. As of this writing, we have modeled the quite extensive WordNet-Affect taxonomy as an *EmotionModel*, to be used as the reference for categorical representation. We also ported the main vocabularies defined for EmotionML [19], and created a model based on the hourglass of emotions model [20]. A list of vocabularies with a detailed explanation is publicly available [21].

3.2 EMOTION MARKUP LANGUAGE

EmotionML does not include any emotion vocabulary in itself. However, the Multimodal Interaction Working Group released a series of vocabularies that cover the most frequently used models of emotions [19]. Users have to define their own vocabularies or reuse one of the existing ones. We have developed a tool that generates an *EmotionModel* model from a vocabulary definition, including all its dimension, category, appraisal, or action tendency entries. Using this tool, we have processed the vocabularies released by the Multimodal Interaction Working Group. EmotionML has four types of vocabularies, according to the type of characteristic of the emotion phenomenon they represent: emotion categories, emotion dimensions, appraisals, and action tendencies. If an emotion model addresses several of these characteristics, there will be an independent vocabulary for each of them. In Onyx, instead of following this approach, we opted for adding all characteristics in the same model. This results in cleaner uniform resource identifiers (URIs) and helps represent the emotion model as a whole (Listing 1).

```
emoml:big6 a onyx:EmotionModel ;
    onyx:hasEmotionCategory emoml:big6_anger , emoml:big6_disgust ,
                            emoml:big6_fear , emoml:big6_happiness ,
                            emoml:big6_sadness , emoml:big6_surprise .
emoml:pad a onyx:EmotionModel ;
    onyx:hasDimension emoml:pad_arousal , emoml:pad_dominance ,
                      emoml:pad_pleasure .
```

LISTING 1

Excerpt of a number of models from Emotion Markup Language in Onyx

4 LINKED DATA CORPUS CREATION FOR SENTIMENT ANALYSIS

Some of the most valuable linguistic resources for sentiment analysis are labeled corpora for subjectivity, sentiment, and emotion analysis. Labeled corpora are used in a number of sentiment analysis tasks, such as polarity detection or sentiment lexicon generation. Nevertheless, there is not yet a widely accepted format for annotating sentiment corpora as illustrated in the following samples of a sentiment corpus (Listings 2 and 3) and an emotion corpus (Listing 4). Some additional problems we face are the different range of polarities in different datasets, as well as the use of different emotion models depending on the application field.

```
<review id="1'' item="Sennheiser RS 120 Consumer Wireless Headphones'' rating="4"><title>
        <sentence id="6">The(1) sound(2) quality(3) is(4) not(5) bad(6) ,(7) but(8) the(9)
            bass(10) sounds(11) a(12) little(13) muffled(14) .(15)
                <opinion polarity="+'' feature="sound quality'' featWords="2,3'' opWords="
                    5,6"/>
                <opinion polarity="-'' feature="bass'' featWords="10'' opWords="14''
                    potency="13"/>
        </sentence>
</review>
```

LISTING 2

Example of a labeled review in the electronics domain [22]

```
<sentence id="813">
 <text>All the appetizers and salads were fabulous</text>
        <aspectTerms>
                <aspectTerm term="appetizers'' polarity="positive'' from="8'' to="18"/>
                <aspectTerm term="salads'' polarity="positive'' from="23'' to="29"/>
        </aspectTerms>
    <aspectCategories>
                <aspectCategory category="food'' polarity="positive"/>
        </aspectCategories>
</sentence>
```

LISTING 3

Example of a labeled review in the restaurants domain [23]

```
# emotion id sentence
happy 1 This was the best summer I have ever experienced
neutral 5 I've found it but I've also found other tunnels

# tweet id, tweet text, emotion
145353048817012736:    Thinks that @melbahughes had a great 50th birthday party
    :)    :: surprise
144279638024257536:    Como una expresión tan simple, puede llegar a dañarte
    tanto.    :: sadness
```

LISTING 4

Example of emotion-labeled tweets with use of two different annotation schemes [24,25]

In this chapter we present how a sentiment corpus and an emotion corpus can be annotated through the use of NIF together with Marl and Onyx respectively. NIF 2.0 [26] is an RDF/OWL-based format that aims to achieve interoperability between natural language processing tools, language resources, and annotations. NIF provides a way to identify strings using URIs and annotate them with an ontology [27]. Strings are identified by URIs following a URI scheme based on RFC5147 [28], which standardizes fragment ids for texts. For a given document we want to annotate with NIF, the URI scheme consists of the URI of the document itself, a separator (#), and the character at the beginning and end of the string we want to annotate. Character indices in NIF are counted offset based, starting at zero before the first character and with the gaps between the characters counted until after the last character of the referenced string. After URIs have been assigned to meaningful strings of the corpus, these URIs can be annotated with the NIF core ontology, which provides classes and properties to describe the relationships between substrings, text, documents, and their URI schemes. NIF can be extended with vocabularies, such as Marl or Onyx, for specific purposes.

4.1 SENTIMENT CORPUS

In this section we illustrate how a sentiment corpus can be annotated with Marl and NIF. We will annotate a review corpus following the sentiment tasks identified in the aspect-based sentiment analysis task of the challenge at SemEval 2004 [23], which was originally annotated as shown in Listing 3. The first step for annotating a corpus is to publish the corpus in a public URI. On the basis of NIF, offset-based URIs are assigned to every meaningful string of the corpus. Let us start by annotating the review *"I love their fajitas, their pico de gallo is not bad, and the service is correct"* as given in Listing 5. First, we annotate that the review has an opinion (opinion/1) in the offset (0,80), which in this case matches the full review. Then we annotate that this opinion is positive as is the provenance of the sentiment analysis task (analysis/1). Finally, we annotate and link two meaningful terms with entities of the DBpedia knowledge base. Since NIF follows an offset-based URI fragment scheme, single-word terms (eg, *fajitas*) as well as multiword terms (eg, *pico de gallo*) can be annotated. Since these two aspect terms have an associated polarity, we annotate that the opinion opinion/1 is an AggregatedOpinion that includes two opinions (opinion/2 and opinion/3) about the two aspect terms previously annotated.

```
<http://semeval2014.org/myrestaurant#char=0,80>
  rdf:type nif:RDF5147String , nif:Context;
  nif:beginIndex "0";
  nif:endIndex "53";
  nif:sourceURL <http://tripadvisor.com/myrestaurant.txt>;
  nif:isString "I love their fajitas,  their pico de gallo is not bad and the
      service is correct.";
  marl:hasOpinion <http:///semeval2014.org/myrestaurant/opinion/1>.

<http://semeval2014.org/myrestaurant/opinion/1>
  rdf:type marl:AggregatedOpinion;
  prov:wasGeneratedBy <http://mixedemotions.eu/analysis/1;
  marl:describesObject dbp:Restaurant;
  marl:polarityValue "0.4";
  marl:hasPolarity <http://purl.org/marl/ns#Positive>;
  marl:aggregatesOpinion <http://semeval2014.org/myrestaurant/opinion/2>;
  marl:aggregatesOpinion <http://semeval2014.org/myrestaurant/opinion/3>.

<http://mixedemotions.eu/analysis/1>
  rdf:type marl:SentimentAnalysis;
  marl:maxPolarityValue "1";
  marl:minPolarityValue "-1";
  marl:algorithm "dictionary-based";
  prov:used le:restaurant_en;
  prov:wasAssociatedWith <http://dbpedia.org/resource/UPM>.

<http://semeval2014.org/myrestaurant#char=14,21>
  rdf:type nif:RDF5147String;
  nif:anchorOf "fajitas";
  nif:beginIndex "14";
  nif:endIndex "21";
  sso:oen dbp:Fajita;
  marl:hasOpinion <http://semeval2014.org/myrestaurant/opinion/2>.

<http://semeval2014.org/myrestaurant#char=31,43>
  rdf:type nif:RDF5147String;
  nif:anchorOf "pico de gallo";
  nif:beginIndex "31";
```

```
    nif:endIndex "43";
    sso:oen dbpedia:Pico_de_gallo;
    <http://semeval2014.org/myrestaurant/opinion/3>.

<http://semeval2014.org/myrestaurant/opinion/2>
    rdf:type marl:Opinion;
    prov:wasGeneratedBy <http://mixedemotions.eu/analysis/1;
    marl:describesObject dbpedia:Fajita;
    marl:polarityValue "0.8";
    marl:hasPolarity <http://purl.org/marl/ns#Positive>;

<http://semeval2014.org/myrestaurant/opinion/3>
    rdf:type marl:Opinion;
    prov:wasGeneratedBy <http://mixedemotions.eu/analysis/1;
    marl:describesObject dbpedia:Pico_de_gallo;
    marl:polarityValue "0.2";
    marl:hasPolarity <http://purl.org/marl/ns#Positive>;
```

LISTING 5

Example of aspect term extraction and aspect term polarity detection

Aspect-based sentiment analysis identifies the aspects of a given target entity and the sentiment expressed toward each aspect. Aspect categories (eg, food, price) identify coarser features than aspect terms, and they do not necessarily occur as terms in a given sentence. In our example, the terms fajitas and pico de gallo refer to the same aspect category food, while the term service refers to the aspect category service. In Listing 6 we annotate aspect categories and introduce the use of the property marl:describesFeature for this purpose.

```
<http://semeval2014.org/myrestaurant#char=0,80>
    rdf:type nif:RDF5147String , nif:Context;
    nif:beginIndex "0";
    nif:endIndex "53";
    nif:sourceURL <http://tripadvisor.com/myrestaurant.txt>;
    nif:isString "I love their fajitas,  their pico de gallo is not bad and the
        service is correct.";
    marl:hasOpinion <http:///semeval2014.org/myrestaurant/opinion/4>.

<http://mixedemotions.eu/analysis/2>
    rdf:type marl:SentimentAnalysis;
    marl:maxPolarityValue "1";
    marl:minPolarityValue "-1";
    marl:algorithm "aspect-based";
    prov:used le:restaurant_en;
    prov:wasAssociatedWith <http://dbpedia.org/resource/UPM>.

<http://semeval2014.org/myrestaurant/opinion/4>
    rdf:type marl:AggregatedOpinion;
    prov:wasGeneratedBy <http://mixedemotions.eu/analysis/2;
    marl:polarityValue "0.4";
    marl:hasPolarity <http://purl.org/marl/ns#Positive>
    marl:aggregatesOpinion <http:///semeval2014.org/myrestaurant/opinion/5>;
    marl:aggregatesOpinion <http:///semeval2014.org/myrestaurant/opinion/6>.

<http://semeval2014.org/myrestaurant/opinion/5>
    rdf:type marl:Opinion;
    prov:wasGeneratedBy <http://mixedemotions.eu/analysis/2;
    marl:describesObject dbp:Restaurant;
    marl:describesFeature dbp:Food;
    marl:polarityValue "0.6";
    marl:hasPolarity: http://purl.org/marl/ns#Positive.
```

```
<http://semeval2014.org/myrestaurant/opinion/6>
  rdf:type marl:Opinion;
  prov:wasGeneratedBy <http://mixedemotions.eu/analysis/2;
  marl:describesObject dbp:Restaurant;
  marl:describesFeature dbp:Service;
  marl:polarityValue "0.0";
  marl:hasPolarity: http://purl.org/marl/ns#Neutral.
```

LISTING 6

Annotation of aspect categories and their polarity

4.2 EMOTION CORPUS

An emotion corpus can be annotated in the same way as a sentiment corpus but with use of the Onyx vocabulary instead of the Marl vocabulary. There are two main differences for annotating an emotion corpus. First, a sentiment analysis provides a certain polarity for a given string, while an emotion analysis can identify several emotions with different intensities. Second, the same corpus can be annotated on the basis of different emotion models. In Listing 4.7 we illustrate how the previous example can be annotated as a result of an emotion analysis.

```
<http://semeval2014.org/myrestaurant#char=0,80>
  rdf:type nif:RDF5147String , nif:Context;
  nif:beginIndex "0";
  nif:endIndex "80";
  nif:sourceURL <http://tripadvisor.com/myrestaurant.txt>;
  nif:isString "I loved their fajitas and their pico de gallo is not bad and
  the service is correct.";
  onyx:hasEmotionSet <http:///semeval2014.org/myrestaurant/emotion/1>.

<http://semeval2014.org/myrestaurant/emotion/1>
  rdf:type onyx:EmotionSet;
  prov:wasGeneratedBy <http://mixedemotions.eu/analysis/2;
  onyx:describesObject dbp:Restaurant;
  onyx:describesFeature dbp:Food;
  onyx:hasEmotion [:Emo1, :Emo2].

:Emo1 a onyx:Emotion;
  onyx:hasEmotionCategory emoml:happiness;
  onyx:hasEmotionIntensity 0.7.

:Emo2 a onyx: Emotion;
  onyx:hasEmotionCategory emoml:disgust;
  onyx:hasEmotionIntensity 0.1.

<http://mixedemotions.eu/analysis/2>
  rdf:type onyx:EmotionAnalysis;
  onyx:usesEmotionModel emoml:big6;
  onyx:algorithm "dictionary-based";
  prov:used le:restaurant_en;
  prov:wasAssociatedWith <http://dbpedia.org/resource/UPM>.
```

LISTING 7

Example of an annotated emotion corpus

5 LINKED DATA LEXICON CREATION FOR SENTIMENT ANALYSIS

Sentiment lexicons are lists of words with an associated a priori polarity or emotion. Some of the most popular sentiment lexicons are the NRC Emotion Lexicon [29], the MPQA Subjectivity lexicon [30], SentiWordNet [31], the Sentiment140 NRC Twitter Sentiment Lexicon [32], and Affective Norms for English Words (ANEW) [33], which are shown in Listing 8.

```
#NRC disgust (0), fear (1), joy (0) negative (1) positive (0) sadness (1)
# surprise (0) trust (0)
abandon  0  1  0  1  0  1  0  0
#MPQA
type=weaksubj len=1 word1=abandon pos1=verb stemmed1=y priorpolarity=negative
#SentiWordNet (positive (0.5) and negative (0) scores)
01317231   0.5    0   abandoned#2  free from constraint;  "an abandoned sadness"
#NRC Sentiment140 (sentiment score (-1.049), number of times the term
#co-occurred with a positive (15) and a negative marker (45)
abandon -1.049  15   45
#ANEW Word number (1591) valence Mean (3.19),
# valence standard deviation (sd) (1.41) arousal mean (5.77),
# arousal sd (1.99), dominance mean (4.12), dominance sd(1.73)
fright 1591 3.19  1.41 5.77 1.99 4.12 1.73
```

LISTING 8

Example of sentiment lexicons [29–33]. *ANEW,* Affective Norms for English Words

As shown, the available lexicons follow different formats, have different properties, and their values are not normalized. In addition to the interoperability problem, a major shortcoming of the available representations is that the polarity is assigned to a term, independently of its context. For example, the adjective cold will have a certain polarity (eg, positive) for cold beer but also for cold pizza. In this section we illustrate how the lemon lexicon model can be used together with Marl and Onyx to publish and interlink sentiment and emotion lexicons. Lemon builds on previous work on standards for the representation of lexical resources—that is, the Lexical Markup Framework [34]—but extends the underlying formal model and provides a native integration of lexicons with domain ontologies. The lemon model is described in detail in the lemon cookbook [35] and supports the linking of a computational lexical resource with the semantic information defined in an ontology. Lemon defines a set of basic aspects of lexical entries, including morphosyntactic variants and normalizations. Lexical entries can be linked to semantic information through lexical sense objects. In addition, lemon has a number of modules that allow further modeling. Currently defined modules are linguistic description, phrase structure, morphology, syntax and mapping, and variation.

5.1 SENTIMENT LEXICON

Sentiment lexicons can be expressed with lemon, which has been extended with two properties of Marl, marl:polarityValue and marl:hasPolarity. Polarities can be defined within a particular context of the lexical entry. For example, for the Spanish word susto (meaning "fright"), we can assign a positive polarity in horror movies but a negative polarity in children's movies, as illustrated in Listing 4.9.

```
:susto a lemon:Lexicalentry ;
  lemon:canonicalForm [ lemon:writtenRep "susto"@es ] ;
  lemon:sense [ lemon:reference wn:synset-fear-noun-1;
  marl:polarityValue 0.375 ;
  marl:hasPolarity marl:positive ;
```

```
lemon:context wd:horror_movies ] ;
lemon:sense [ lemon:reference wn:synset-fear-noun-1;
marl:polarityValue 0.375 ;
marl:hasPolarity marl:negative ;
lemon:context wd:children_movies ];
lexinfo:partOfSpeech lexinfo:noun .
```

LISTING 9

Example of a sentiment lexicon entry

5.2 EMOTION LEXICON

Lexical entries expressed with lemon can also be annotated with Onyx. Suitable emotion models should be selected depending on the application domain. An annotated example of the Affective Norms for English Words lexicon is shown in Listing 4,10, with use of the emotion model emoml:pad.

```
:susto a lemon:Lexicalentry ;
  lemon:canonicalForm [ lemon:writtenRep "susto"@es ] ;
  lemon:sense [ lemon:reference wn:synset-fear-noun-1 ;
  onyx:usesEmotionModel emoml:pad ;
  emoml:pad_dominance 4.12 ;
  emoml:pad_arousal 5.77 ;
  emoml:pad_pleasure 3.19 ;
  lexinfo:partOfSpeech lexinfo:noun .
```

LISTING 10

Example of a sentiment lexicon entry

6 SENTIMENT AND EMOTION ANALYSIS SERVICES

NIF defines an input and output format for Representational State Transfer web services in the NIF 2.0 public application programming interface specification [36]. In this way, natural language processing tools and services can interoperate seamlessly. This specification defines a set of parameters that should be supported by NIF-compliant services, which have been extended for sentiment and emotion services as shown in Table 4.3.

The open source project Senpy [37] provides a reference implementation for sentiment and emotion services that is extendable through plugins. A number of wrappers have been developed for popular services such as Sentiment140 [38] test service interoperability. In addition, in the context of the European projects EuroSentiment and MixedEmotions, this application programming interface has been implemented by several vendors.

The example in Listing 11 shows how a sentiment service is invoked and how the output of that service is annotated with use of NIF together with Marl and Onyx.

Table 4.3 Parameters of an Emotion or Sentiment Analysis Service Compliant With Natural Language Processing Interchange Format

Parameter	Description
input(i)	Serialized data (ie, the text or other formats, depends on the format)
informat(f)	Format in which the input is provided: turtle (default), text, or json-ld
outformat(o)	Format in which the output is serialized: turtle (default), text, or json-ld
prefix(f)	Prefix used to create and parse URIs
emodel(e)	Emotion model in which the output is serialized (eg, WordNet-Affect, PAD)
minpolarity (min)	Minimum polarity value of the sentiment analysis
maxpolarity (max)	Maximum polarity value of the sentiment analysis
language(l)	Language of the sentiment or emotion analysis
domain(d)	Domain of the sentiment or emotion analysis

PAD: Pleasure, Arousal, Dominance Emotion Model, ; URI, uniform resource identifier.

```
Service Call: curl --data-urlencode input="My iPad is an awesome device"
          -d informat=text -prefix="http://mixedemotions.eu/example/ipad\#"
          -emodel="wna" "http://www.gsi.dit.upm.es/sa-nif-ws.py"}
Service Output:
<http://mixedemotions.eu/example/ipad#char=0,28>
  rdf:type nif:RDF5147String ;
  nif:beginIndex "0'' ;
  nif:endIndex "28'' ;
  nif:sourceURL < http://mixedemotions.eu/example/ipad>;
  onyx:hasEmotionSet :emotionSet1.

:customAnalysis
  a onyx:EmotionAnalysis;
  onyx:algorithm "SVM";
  onyx:usesEmotionModel wna:WNAModel.

:emotionSet1
  a onyx:EmotionSet;
  prov:wasGenerated :customAnalysis;
  sioc:has_creator [
      sioc:UserAccount <http://www.gsi.dit.upm.es/jfernando>. ];
  onyx:hasEmotion [ :emotion1; emotion2 ]
  onyx:emotionText: "My iPad is an awesome device".

:emotion1
  a onyx:Emotion
  onyx:hasEmotionCategory wna:dislike;
  onyx:hasEmotionIntensity 0.7.

:emotion2
  a onyx:Emotion
  onyx:hasEmotionCategory wna:despair;
  onyx:hasEmotionIntensity 0.1.

<http://mixedemotions.eu/example/ipad#3,6>
  nif:anchorOf "iPad";
  itsrdf:taIdentRef: <http://dbpedia.org/iPad>.
```

LISTING 11

Example of an emotion service output

7 CASE STUDY: GENERATION OF A DOMAIN-SPECIFIC SENTIMENT LEXICON

This section presents a practical case study [39] of the use of the previously introduced technologies for the generation of a domain-specific sentiment lexicon from legacy language resources and enrichment with semantics and additional linguistic information from resources such as DBpedia and BabelNet. The language resources adaptation pipeline consists of four main steps highlighted by dark boxes in Fig. 4.4: (1) the corpus conversion step normalizes the different language resources to a common schema based on Marl and NIF; (2) the semantic analysis step extracts the domain-specific entity classes and named entities and identifies links between these entities and concepts from the LLOD cloud; (3) the sentiment analysis step extracts contextual sentiments and identifies SentiWordNet synsets corresponding to these contextual sentiment words; and (4) the lexicon generator step uses the results of the previous steps, enhances them with multilingual and morphosyntactic information, and converts the results into a lexicon based on the lemon and Marl formats. Different language resources are processed with variations of the given adaptation pipeline. For example, the domain-specific English

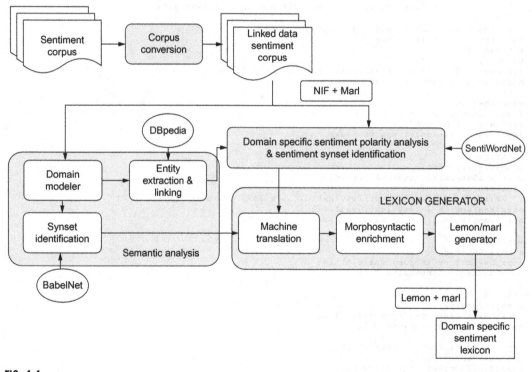

FIG. 4.4

Pipeline for domain-specific sentiment lexicon generation. *NIF,* Natural Language Processing Interchange Format.

review corpora are processed with the pipeline described in Fig. 4.4, while the sentiment annotated dictionaries are converted to the lemon/Marl format in the lexicon generator step.

Once the sentiment corpora have been converted and the domain-specific sentiment lexicon has been generated, we can use SPARQL to explore it as shown in Listing 12.

```
# Query Get most used sentiment words in the 'hotel' domain
PREFIX lemon: <http://lemon-model.net/lemon#>
PREFIX marl: <http://purl.org/marl/ns/>
SELECT ?sentiment (count(distinct ?cx) as ?occurrences)
WHERE {GRAPH <http://www.eurosentiment.eu/dataset/hotel/en/paradigma/0008/
    lexicon> {
    ?sentimentURI lemon:sense ?sense .
    ?sentimentURI lemon:canonicalForm ?cf.
    ?cf lemon:writtenRep ?sentiment.
    ?sense lemon:context ?cx.
    ?sense marl:polarityValue ?polarityValue .
    ?sense marl:hasPolarity <http://purl.org/marl/ns/positive> .
}}
GROUP BY ?sentimentURI ?sentiment
ORDER BY DESC(?occurences) limit 10

#Get domain aspects and their sentiments
PREFIX lemon: <http://lemon-model.net/lemon#>
PREFIX marl: <http://purl.org/marl/ns/>
SELECT DISTINCT ?domainAspect ?sentiment ?polarityValue ?polarity
WHERE { GRAPH <http://www.eurosentiment.eu/dataset/hotel/en/paradigma/0008/
    lexicon> {
    ?entryWithSentiment lemon:sense ?context .
    ?entryWithSentiment lemon:canonicalForm ?cf .
    ?cf lemon:writtenRep ?domainAspect .
    ?sentimentEntry lemon:sense ?sense .
    ?sentimentEntry lemon:canonicalForm ?senseCf .
    ?senseCf lemon:writtenRep ?sentiment .
    ?sense marl:polarityValue ?polarityValue .
    ?sense marl:hasPolarity ?polarity .
    ?sense lemon:reference ?reference .
    ?sense lemon:context ?context .
  } }
LIMIT 50
```

LISTING 12

Example of SPARQL queries for sentiment lexicons

8 CONCLUSIONS

This chapter has provided an introduction to the potential and advantages of the use of a linked data approach for sentiment linguistic resources to overcome the interoperability problem and take advantage of the distributed annotation nature of the linked data cloud. The chapter has introduced the main concepts and technologies to annotate sentiment and emotion corpora, lexicons, and services, and how we can link lexical and semantic resources.

The technologies presented in this chapter have been evaluated in a number of research projects. The research projects TrendMiner [40] and FinancialTwitterTracker [41] have used Marl to annotate the opinion detected in financial news and the social network Twitter. Both projects allow users to visualize time-based sentiment and activity on a particular topic of interest and to compare them visually with the time series of a financial instrument. The research project MixedEmotions [42] is applying both Marl and Onyx for annotation of sentiment and emotion in three business cases: (1) annotation of phone calls in a call center for quality assurance; (2) annotation of emotion and sentiment in news and social networks for a brand monitoring system; and (3) annotation of emotion and sentiment social networks for a social TV system.

All that said, much remains to be done. On the one hand, linked data technologies are still not widely used by the computational linguistic and natural language processing communities. On the other hand, there is an increasing number of available datasets in the LLOD, and an ongoing community effort that supports this approach, such as the W3C Community Group on Linked Data Models for Sentiment and Emotion Analysis, the W3C Best Practices on Multilingual Linked Open Data Community Group, the W3C Ontology-Lexica Community Group, the W3C Linked Data for Language Technology Community Group, and the Open Linguistics Working Group of the Open Knowledge Foundation.

Despite these concerns, the increasing popularity of linked data technology and the availability of tools and resources are tremendous incentives for its adoption. Regarding the sentiment analysis community, the W3C Community Group on Linked Data Models for Sentiment and Emotion Analysis provides a suitable forum for fostering the adoption of linked data practices and the generation of interoperable sentiment language resources and services.

This chapter has presented the current directions in the publication of language resources for sentiment analysis as linked data. One of the future directions is the harmonization of metadata of existing language resources, as proposed by the Linghub project [43], which collects and harmonizes metadata from some of the existing language resources and publishes the records as linked data. In addition, one important aspect is the development of business models for sentiment language resources. One of the initial initiatives in this respect is the Eurosentiment project [44], which proposed a multilingual resource pool supported by a subscription business model. Moreover, given the scarcity of sentiment language resources for many languages, it is necessary to investigate automatic machine translation of these resources [45] and avoid the negative effect of low quality in these translations [46]. Finally, since the content shared in social networks is not only textual, multimodal sentiment analysis [47] aims at alleviating the ambiguity of text with the fusion of sentiment analysis of textual, visual, and audio modalities. This requires research on semantic models for annotating sentiment and emotion in multimodal resources [42].

ACKNOWLEDGMENTS

This work was funded by the European Union Horizon 2020 program under grant agreement no. 644632 MixedEmotions, by Science Foundation Ireland under Grant No. SFI/12/RC/2289 (Insight Centre for Data Analytics) and by the Spanish Ministry of Economy under the Project SEMOLA (Grant TEC2015-68284-R).

REFERENCES

[1] B. Liu, Sentiment analysis and opinion mining, Synth. Lect. Hum. Lang. Technol. 5 (1) (2012) 1–167.
[2] C. Strapparava, A. Valitutti, WordNet-Affect: an affective extension of WordNet, in: Proceedings of LREC, vol. 4, 2004, pp. 1083–1086.

[3] A. Esuli, F. Sebastiani, Sentiwordnet: a publicly available lexical resource for opinion mining, in: Proceedings of LREC, vol. 6, 2006, pp. 417–422.

[4] N. Ide, J. Veronis, Text Encoding Initiative: Background and Contexts, vol. 29, Springer Science & Business Media, New York, NY, 1995.

[5] C. Chiarcos, Linguistic linked open data (LLOD)-building the cloud, in: Proceedings of the Joint Workshop on NLP&LOD and SWAIE: Semantic Web, Linked Open Data and Information Extraction, 2013, pp. 1.

[6] C. Bizer, T. Heath, T. Berners-Lee, Linked data-the story so far, Semant. Serv. Interop. Web Appl. Emerg. Concepts (2009) 205–227.

[7] C. Chiarcos, S. Hellmann, S. Nordhoff, Towards a linguistic linked open data cloud: the open linguistics working group, TAL 52 (3) (2011) 245–275.

[8] K. Bontcheva, D. Rout, Making sense of social media streams through semantics: a survey, Semant. Web 1 (2012) 1–31.

[9] H. Saif, Y. He, H. Alani, Alleviating data sparsity for twitter sentiment analysis, in: MSM2012 Workshop Proceedings, 2012, pp. 2–9.

[10] A. Westerski, C.A. Iglesias, F. Tapia, Linked opinions: describing sentiments on the structured web of data, in: Proceedings of the Fourth International Workshop on Social Data on the Web (SDoW2011), 2011, pp. 21–32.

[11] J.F. Sánchez-Rada, A. Westerski, Marl ontology specification, tech. rep. 1.3, Grupo de Sistemas Inteligentes, Universidad Politécnica de Madrid 2013, Available at http://www.gsi.dit.upm.es/ontologies/marl/.

[12] T. Lebo, S. Sahoo, D. McGuinness, K. Belhajjame, J. Cheney, D. Corsar, D. Garijo, S. Soiland-Reyes, S. Zednik, J. Zhao, Prov-o: the prov ontology, tech. rep., W3C Recommendation, 2013.

[13] K.R. Scherer, Psychological models of emotion, Neuropsychol. Emot. 137 (3) (2000) 137–162.

[14] K.R. Scherer, On the rationality of emotions: or, When are emotions rational? Soc. Sci. Inform. 50 (3–4) (2011) 330–350.

[15] J.F. Sánchez-Rada, C.A. Iglesias, Onyx: a linked data approach to emotion representation, Inform. Process. Manage. 52 (1) (2016) 99–114.

[16] M. Schröder, The SEMAINE API: towards a standards-based framework for building emotion-oriented systems, Adv. Hum. Comput. Interact. 2010 (319406) (2010) 21.

[17] A. Miles, S. Bechhofer, SKOS simple knowledge organization system reference, W3C Recommendation, W3C, 2009.

[18] HUMAINE Association, et al., HUMAINE Emotion Annotation and Representation Language (EARL): Proposal, HUMAINE Association, 2006.

[19] K. Ashimura, P. Baggia, F. Burkhardt, A. Oltramari, C. Peter, E. Zovato, EmotionML vocabularies, tech. rep., W3C, 2012.

[20] E. Cambria, A. Livingstone, A. Hussain, The hourglass of emotions, in: Cognitive Behavioural Systems, vol. 7403, Springer, 2012, pp. 144–157.

[21] J.F. Sánchez-Rada, C.A. Iglesias, Onyx specification, tech. rep., Unversidad Politécnica de Madrid, 2013.

[22] F.L. Cruz, J.A. Troyano, F. EnríQuez, F.J. Ortega, C.G. Vallejo, 'Long autonomy or long delay?' The importance of domain in opinion mining, Expert Syst. Appl. 40 (8) (2013) 3174–3184.

[23] M. Pontiki, H. Papageorgiou, D. Galanis, I. Androutsopoulos, J. Pavlopoulos, S. Manandhar, Semeval-2014 task 4: aspect based sentiment analysis, in: Proceedings of the Eighth International Workshop on Semantic Evaluation (SemEval 2014), 2014, pp. 27–35.

[24] R. Balabantaray, M. Mohammad, N. Sharma, Multi-class twitter emotion classification: a new approach, Int. J. Appl. Inform. Syst. 4 (1) (2012) 48–53.

[25] S.M. Mohammad, # Emotional tweets, in: Proceedings of the First Joint Conference on Lexical and Computational Semantics (SEM*), Association for Computational Linguistics, 2012, pp. 246–255.

[26] S. Hellmann, Integrating natural language processing (NLP) and language resources using linked data, PhD thesis, Universität Leipzig, 2013.

[27] M. Brümmer, M. Ackermann, M. Dojchinovski, Guidelines for linked data corpus creation using NIF. Draft Community Group Report, September 29, 2015, tech. rep., W3C Community Group, 2015.

[28] E. Wilde, M. Duerst, URI fragment identifiers for the text/plain media type, Internet Engineering Task Force, 2008.

[29] S.M. Mohammad, S. Kiritchenko, X. Zhu, NRC-Canada: building the state-of-the-art in sentiment analysis of tweets, in: Proceedings of the Second Joint Conference on Lexical and Computational Semantics Joint Conference on Lexical and Computational Semantics, vol. 2, 2013, pp. 321–327.

[30] T. Wilson, J. Wiebe, P. Hoffmann, Recognizing contextual polarity in phrase-level sentiment analysis, in: Proceedings of the Conference on Human Language Technology and Empirical Methods in Natural Language Processing, Association for Computational Linguistics, 2005, pp. 347–354.

[31] S. Baccianella, A. Esuli, F. Sebastiani, SentiWordNet 3.0: an enhanced lexical resource for sentiment analysis and opinion mining, in: LREC, vol. 10, 2010, pp. 2200–2204.

[32] S. Kiritchenko, X. Zhu, S.M. Mohammad, Sentiment analysis of short informal texts, J. Artif. Intell. Res. (JAIR) 50 (2014) 723–762.

[33] M.M. Bradley, P.J. Lang, Affective norms for English words (ANEW): instruction manual and affective ratings, tech. rep., Technical report C-1, The Center for Research in Psychophysiology, University of Florida, 1999.

[34] G. Francopoulo, LMF Lexical Markup Framework, John Wiley & Sons, New York, 2013.

[35] J. McCrae, G. Aguado-de Cea, P. Buitelaar, P. Cimiano, T. Declerck, A. Gómez-Pérez, J. Gracia, L. Hollink, E. Montiel-Ponsoda, D. Spohr, et al., Interchanging lexical resources on the Semantic Web, Lang. Resour. Eval. 46 (4) (2012) 701–719.

[36] S. Hellmann, J. Lehmann, S. Auer, M. Brümmer, Integrating NLP using linked data, in: The Semantic Web-ISWC 2013, Springer, New York, 2013, pp. 98–113.

[37] M. Coronado, F. Sánchez-Rada, C.A. Iglesias, D7.5 evaluation and assessment of language resource pool, tech. rep., Eurosentiment Project, 2014.

[38] A. Go, R. Bhayani, L. Huang, Twitter sentiment classification using distant supervision, in: CS224N Project Report, Stanford 1 (2009) 12.

[39] G. Vulcu, P. Buitelaar, S. Negi, B. Pereira, M. Arcan, B. Coughlan, J.F. Sánchez-Rada, C.A. Iglesias, Generating linked-data based domain-specific sentiment lexicons from legacy language and semantic resources, in: Proceedings of the Fifth International Workshop on Emotion, Social Signals, Sentiment and Linked Open Data, co-located with LREC 2014, LREC2014, Reykjavik, Iceland, 2014, pp. 6–9.

[40] H.-U. Krieger, T. Declerck, TMO—The Federated Ontology of the TrendMiner Project, in: Proceedings of the Ninth International Conference on Language Resources and Evaluation (LREC-2014), European Language Resources Association, 2014, pp. 4164–4171.

[41] J.F. Sánchez-Rada, M. Torres, C.A. Iglesias, R. Maestre, R. Peinado, A Linked data approach to sentiment and emotion analysis of twitter in the financial domain, in: Proceedings of the Second International Workshop on Finance and Economics on the Semantic Web, vol. 1240, 2014, pp. 51–62.

[42] J.F. Sánchez-Rada, C.A. Iglesias, R. Gil, A linked data model for multimodal sentiment and emotion analysis, in: Proceedings of the Fourth Workshop on Linked Data in Linguistics: Resources and Applications, Association for Computational Linguistics, Beijing, China, 2015, pp. 11–19.

[43] J.P. McCrae, P. Cimiano, Linghub: a linked data based portal supporting the discovery of language resources, in: A. Filipowska, R. Verborgh, A. Polleres (Eds.), SEMANTiCS (Posters & Demos), vol. 1481, 2015, pp. 88–91.

[44] J.F. Sánchez-Rada, G. Vulcu, C.A. Iglesias, P. Buitelaar, EUROSENTIMENT: linked data sentiment analysis, in: Proceedings of the 13th International Semantic Web Conference ISWC, 2014, pp. 145–148.

[45] V. Gabriela, B. Paul, N. Sapna, P. Bianca, A. Mihael, C. Barry, S.J. Fernando, C.A. Iglesias, Generating linked-data based domain-specific sentiment lexicons from legacy language and semantic resources, in: Proceedings of the Fifth International Workshop on Emotion, Social Signals, Sentiment and Linked Open Data (ES3LOD), co-located with LREC 2014, Reykjavik, Iceland, 2014, pp. 6–9.

[46] R. Klinger, P. Cimiano, Instance selection improves cross-lingual model training for fine-grained sentiment analysis, in: Proceedings of the Nineteenth Conference on Computational Natural Language Learning, Association for Computational Linguistics, Beijing, China, 2015, pp. 153–163.

[47] L.-P. Morency, R. Mihalcea, P. Doshi, Towards multimodal sentiment analysis: harvesting opinions from the web, in: Proceedings of the 13th International Conference on Multimodal Interfaces, ACM, New York, NY, 2011, pp. 169–176.

SENTIC COMPUTING FOR SOCIAL NETWORK ANALYSIS

5

F. Bisio[a], L. Oneto[a], E. Cambria[b]

University of Genoa, Genoa, Italy[a] Nanyang Technological University, Singapore, Singapore[b]

1 INTRODUCTION

Sentiment analysis or opinion mining can be defined as a particular application of data mining, which aims to aggregate and extract emotions and feelings from different types of documents [1]. The amount of data available on the web is growing exponentially; these data, however, are mainly in an unstructured format and hence are not machine processable and machine interpretable. Therefore graph-mining and natural language processing (NLP) techniques may contribute to the distillation of knowledge and opinions from the huge amount of information present in the web.

Sentiment analysis can enhance the capabilities of customer relationship management and recommendation systems by allowing one, for example, to find out which features customers are particularly interested in or to exclude from ads items that have received unfavorable feedback. Likewise, it can be used in social communication to enhance antispam systems.

Business intelligence can also benefit from sentiment analysis. Since predicting the attitude of the public toward a brand or a product has become of crucial importance for companies, an increasing amount of money has been invested in marketing strategies involving opinion and sentiment mining.

That scenario led to sentic computing [2], which tackles those crucial issues by exploiting affective commonsense reasoning (ie, the intrinsically human capacity to interpret the cognitive and affective information associated with natural language). In particular, sentic computing leverages a commonsense knowledge base built through crowdsourcing [3,4]. Common sense is useful in many different computer science applications, including data visualization [5], text recognition [6], and human-computer interaction [7]. In this context, common sense is used to bridge the semantic gap between word-level natural language data and the concept-level opinions conveyed by these [8].

To perform affective commonsense reasoning [9], a knowledge database is required for storage and extraction of the affective and emotional information associated with word and multiword expressions. Graph-mining [10] and dimensionality reduction [11] techniques have been employed on a knowledge base obtained by the blending of ConceptNet [12], a directed graph representation of commonsense knowledge, with WordNet-Affect [13], a linguistic resource for the lexical representation of feelings. Unlike WordNet-Affect, SenticNet [14] and its extended versions [15,16] exploit an ensemble of

Sentiment Analysis in Social Networks. http://dx.doi.org/10.1016/B978-0-12-804412-4.00005-X

common and commonsense knowledge to go beyond word-level opinion mining, and hence to associate semantics and sentics with a set of natural language concepts.

With the rise of the Social Web, there are now millions of humans offering their knowledge online, which means that the information is stored, searchable, and easily shared. This trend has created and maintained an ecosystem of participation, where the value is created by the aggregation of many individual user contributions. Such contributions, however, are meant for human consumption and hence are hardly accessible and processable by computers. Making sense of the huge amount of social data available on the web requires the adoption of novel approaches to natural language understanding that can give a structure to such data in a way that they can be more easily aggregated and analyzed [17,18].

Social networks are indeed a popular means of sharing data and ideas, and have witnessed an ever-increasing diffusion. The amount of data generated in 30 seconds on the Internet is about 600 GB of traffic[1]: this fact confirms that online information, with a particular focus on social networks, has become a source of big data. For example, considering the specific case of the Twitter community, every minute more than 320 new accounts are created and more than 98,000 tweets are posted. This makes the analysis of Twitter microblogging a topmost and significant domain for business intelligence and marketing strategies. A multiplicity of users populate this social network, sharing different types of information. The average age of users on Twitter ranges from 14 to 60 years, equally distributed among individuals of both genders. Hence among the multitude of tweets, one may want to retrieve information associated with specific relevant topics and identify the related polarity and affective characterization. Therefore one of the most interesting applications of sentiment analysis in recent years has involved social networks, so as to be able to analyze opinions on Twitter, Facebook, or other digital communities in real time [19–21]. In this context, sentic computing can be exploited for NLP tasks requiring the inference of semantic and/or affective information associated with both text (eg, for the analysis of social network interaction dynamics) [22] and online multimodal data [23].

This chapter presents an overview of the most recent and advanced technologies of sentiment analysis, with particular focus on the applications related to social networks. The main result consists of a review of the most interesting methods employed to compare, classify, and visualize messages on social media platforms. The chapter is organized as follows: Section 2 provides a description of state-of-the-art sentiment analysis techniques, with particular regard to the affective characterization of the data; Section 3 describes an affective characterization of emotions and sentiments; Section 4 describes several applications that employ sentiment analysis methods; Section 5 discusses some future trends and directions; and Section 6 presents our conclusions and final remarks.

2 RELATED WORK

The Social Web has provided people with new content-sharing services that allow them to create and share personal content, ideas, and opinions, in a time-and cost-efficient way, with virtually millions of other people connected to the World Wide Web. Since this amount of information is mainly unstructured, research has so far focused on online information retrieval, aggregation, and processing.

---

[1] http://pennystocks.la/internet-in-real-time/

The potential applications of concept-level sentiment analysis are countless and span interdisciplinary areas, such as stock market prediction, political forecasting, social network analysis, social stream mining, and man-machine interactions.

Today, most of the existing approaches still rely on word co-occurrence frequencies (ie, the syntactic representation of text). Therefore computational models aim to bridge the cognitive gap by emulating the way the human brain processes natural language. For instance, by leveraging semantic features that are not explicitly expressed in text, one may accomplish complex NLP tasks such as word-sense disambiguation, textual entailment, and semantic role labeling. Computational models are useful for both scientific purposes (such as exploring the nature of linguistic communication),and practical purposes (such as enabling effective human-machine communication [24]).

Most existing approaches to sentiment analysis rely on the extraction of a vector representing the most salient and important text features, which is later used for classification purposes [25,26]. Commonly used features include term frequency and the presence and the position of a token in a text. An extension of this feature is the presence of *n*-grams, typically bigrams and trigrams. Other methods rely on the distance between terms or on the part-of-speech information: for example, certain adjectives may be good indicators of sentiment orientation. A drawback of these approaches is the strict dependency on the domain of application considered and the related topics.

Sentiment analysis systems aim to classify entire documents by associating content with some overall positive or negative polarity or rating scores (eg, 1–5 stars) [27–31]. These approaches are typically supervised and rely on manually labeled samples [32,33]. We can distinguish between knowledge-based systems [34], based on approaches such as keyword spotting and lexical affinity, and statistics-based systems [35]. At first, the identification of emotions and polarity was performed mainly by means of knowledge-based methods; recently, sentiment analysis researchers have been increasingly using statistics-based approaches, with a special focus on supervised statistical methods.

Keyword spotting is the most straightforward, and possibly also the most popular, approach thanks to its accessibility and economy. Text is classified into affect categories on the basis of the presence of fairly unambiguous "affect words" such as "happy," "sad," "afraid," and "bored." Elliott's Affective Reasoner [36], for example, looks for 198 affect keywords plus affect intensity modifiers and a handful of cue phrases. Other popular sources of affect words are Ortony's Affective Lexicon [37], which groups terms into affective categories, and Wiebe's linguistic annotation scheme [38]. The crucial issue of these approaches lies in the ineffectiveness at handling negations and in the structure based on the presence of obvious affect words.

Rather than simply detecting affect words, lexical affinity assigns each word a probabilistic "affinity" for a particular emotion. These probabilities are usually learned from linguistic corpora [39–41]. Even if this method often outperforms pure keyword spotting, it still works at word level and can be easily tricked by negations and different senses of the same word. Besides, lexical affinity probabilities are often biased by the linguistic corpora adopted, which makes it difficult to develop a reusable, domain-independent model.

Statistical-based approaches, such as Bayesian inference and support vector machines (SVMs), have been used in several projects [27,42–44]. By feeding a machine learning algorithm [45] a large training corpus of affectively annotated texts, one can learn not only the affective valence of affect keywords (as in the keyword spotting approach), but also the affective valence of other arbitrary keywords (like lexical affinity), punctuation, and word co-occurrence frequencies. Anyway, it is worth noting that statistical classifiers work well only when a sufficiently large text dataset is given as input. This is because, with the exception of affect keywords, other lexical or co-occurrence elements possess little predictive value individually.

For example, Pang et al. [27] used a movie review dataset to compare the performance of different machine learning algorithms: in particular, they obtained 82.90% accuracy when they used a large number of textual features. Socher et al. [46] proposed a recursive neural tensor network and improved the accuracy (85%). Yu and Hatzivassiloglou [47] identified polarity at sentence level using semantic orientation of words. Melville et al. [48] developed a framework exploiting word-class association information for domain-dependent sentiment analysis. Bisio et al. [49] tackled a particular aspect of the sentiment classification problem: the ability of the framework itself to operate effectively in heterogeneous commercial domains. The approach adopts a distance-based predictive model to combine computational efficiency and modularity.

Some approaches are based on the following assumption: many short n-grams are usually neutral, while longer phrases are well distributed among positive and negative subjective sentence classes. Therefore matrix representations for long phrases and matrix multiplication to model composition can also be used to evaluate sentiment. In such models, sentence composition is modeled with use of deep neural networks such as recursive auto-associated memories. Recursive neural networks predict the sentiment class at each node in the parse tree and try to capture the negation and its scope in the entire sentence.

Several unsupervised learning approaches have also been proposed, and rely on the creation of the lexicon via the unsupervised labeling of words or phrases with their sentiment polarity or subjectivity [50]. To this aim, early work was mainly based on linguistic heuristics. For example, Hatzivassiloglou and McKeown [51] built a system based on "opposition constraints" to help label decisions in the case of polarity classification.

Other work exploited the seed words, defined as terms for which the polarity is known, and propagated them to terms that co-occur with them in general text, or in specific WordNet-defined relations. Popescu and Etzioni [52] proposed an algorithm that, starting from a global word label computed over a large collection of generic topic text, gradually tried to redefine such a label for a more and more specific corpus, until the one that is specific to the particular context in which the word occurs. Snyder and Barzilay [53] exploited the idea of utilizing discourse information to aid in the inference of relationships between product attributes.

Concept-based approaches [54–57] focus on a semantic analysis of text through the use of web ontologies or semantic networks, which allow the handling of conceptual and affective information associated with natural language opinions. By relying on large semantic knowledge bases, such approaches step away from blind use of keywords and word co-occurrence counts, and rather rely on the implicit meaning/features associated with natural language concepts. Unlike purely syntactical techniques, concept-based approaches are also able to detect sentiments that are expressed in a subtle manner (eg, through the analysis of concepts that do not explicitly convey any emotion but are implicitly linked to other concepts that do so).

More recent studies [58–61] tackled the problem of sentiment analysis in social networks: for example, by enhancing sentiment analysis of tweets by exploiting microblogging text or Twitter-specific features such as emoticons, hashtags, URLs, @ symbols, capitalization, and elongations. Tang et al. [62] developed a convolutional neural network–based approach to obtain word embeddings for the words mostly used in tweets. These word vectors were then fed to a convolutional neural network for sentiment analysis. A deep convolutional neural network for sentiment detection in short text was also proposed by dos Santos and Gatti [63]. The approach based on sentiment-specific word embeddings [64] considers word embeddings based on a sentiment corpus: this means the inclusion of more affective clues than regular word vectors and the production of a better result.

3 AFFECTIVE CHARACTERIZATION

Emotions and affective information can be represented through the hourglass of emotions model [65], an affective categorization model that allows emotions to be deconstructed into independent but concomitant affective dimensions, whose different levels of activation compose the total emotional state of the mind. Such a reinterpretation is inspired by Minsky's theory of the mind, according to which brain activity consists of different independent resources and that emotional states result from turning some set of these resources on and turning another set of them off.

The model can potentially synthesize the full range of emotional experiences in terms of four affective dimensions—pleasantness, attention, sensitivity, and aptitude—which define the intensity of the expressed/perceived emotion in the interval $\in [-1, +1]$. Each affective dimension is characterized by six levels of activation, termed "sentic levels," which are also labeled as a set of 24 basic emotions (six for each affective dimension) (see Table 5.1). In the model the vertical dimension represents the intensity of the different affective dimensions (ie, their level of activation). The model follows the pattern used in color theory and research to obtain judgments about combinations (ie, the emotions that result when two or more fundamental emotions are combined).

The transition between different emotional states is modeled, within the same affective dimension, by means of the function $G(x) = -\frac{1}{\sigma\sqrt{2\pi}}e^{-x^2/2\sigma^2}$, for its symmetric inverted bell curve shape that quickly rises up toward 1. In particular, the function models how the valence or intensity of an affective dimension varies according to different values of arousal or activation, ranging from 0 (emotional void) to 1 (heightened emotionality). Mapping this space of possible emotions leads to a hourglass shape (see Fig. 5.1). The justification for assuming that the Gaussian function (rather than a step or simple linear function) is appropriate for modeling the variation of emotion intensity is based on research into the neural and behavioral correlates of emotion, which are assumed to indicate emotional intensity in some sense.

It is worth noting that, in the model, the state of "emotional void" is adimensional, which contributes to the creation of the hourglass shape. Total absence of emotion can be associated with the total absence

Table 5.1 The Sentic Levels of the Hourglass Model

Interval	Pleasantness	Attention	Sensitivity	Aptitude
$G(1), G(2/3)$	Ecstasy	Vigilance	Rage	Admiration
$[G(2/3), G(1/3))$	Joy	Anticipation	Anger	Trust
$[G(1/3), G(0))$	Serenity	Interest	Annoyance	Acceptance
$(G(0), G(-1/3)]$	Pensiveness	Distraction	Apprehension	Boredom
$(G(-1/3), G(-2/3)]$	Sadness	Surprise	Fear	Disgust
$(G(-2/3), G(-1)]$	Grief	Amazement	Terror	Loathing

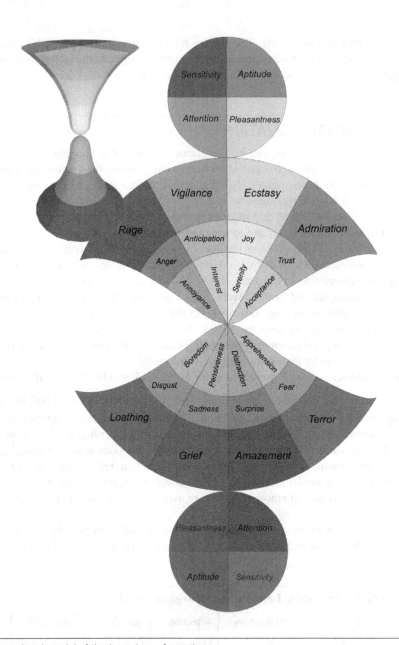

FIG. 5.1

The three-dimensional model of the hourglass of emotions.

Table 5.2 The Emotions Generated by Pairwise Combination of the Sentic Levels of the Hourglass Model

	Attention >0	Attention <0	Aptitude >0	Aptitude <0
Pleasantness >0	Optimism	Frivolity	Love	Gloat
Pleasantness <0	Frustration	Disapproval	Envy	Remorse
Sensitivity >0	Aggressiveness	Rejection	Rivalry	Contempt
Sensitivity <0	Anxiety	Awe	Submission	Coercion

of reasoning (or, at least, consciousness), which is not an envisaged mental state as, in the human mind, there is never nothing going on.

Complex emotions can be synthesized by use of different sentic levels, as shown in Table 5.2, which represent the intensity thresholds of the expressed or perceived emotion.

4 APPLICATIONS

This section describes how sentic computing tools and techniques can be employed for the development of applications in the context of big social data analysis.

4.1 TROLL FILTERING

The democracy of the web has allowed a high degree of freedom of expression, which also gave birth to negative side effects: in the Social Web context the possibility of anonymity often results in the posting of inflammatory, extraneous, or off-topic messages in an online community, with the primary intent of provoking other users into making a desired emotional response or of otherwise disrupting normal on-topic discussion.

Such practice is usually referred to as "trolling," and the generator of such messages is called a "troll." Trolling appears to have spread a lot recently and it is alarming most of the biggest social networking sites since, in extreme cases such as abuse, it has led some teenagers to commit suicide. These attacks usually address not only individuals but also entire communities.

At present, users cannot do much other than to manually delete abusive messages. Current antitrolling methods mainly consist in identifying additional accounts that use the same IP address and blocking fake accounts on the basis of the name and anomalous site activity (eg, users who send lots of messages to nonfriends or whose friend requests are rejected at a high rate). Even though there is the possibility of reporting trouble, social networking websites usually cannot react instantly to these alarms.

A prior analysis of the trustworthiness of statements published on the web was presented by Rowe and Butters [66]. Their approach adopts a contextual trust value determined for the person who asserted a statement as the trustworthiness of the statement itself. Their study, however, focuses not on the problem of trolling but rather on defining a contextual accountability for the detection of web, email, and opinion spam.

The main aim of the troll filter [67] is to identify malicious content in natural language text with a certain confidence level and hence to automatically block trolls. To train the system, the concepts most commonly used by trolls are first identified by use of the concept frequency–inverted opinion frequency technique [2], and then this set is expanded through spectral association. In particular, after a set of 1000 offensive phrases extracted from Wordnik[2] had been analyzed, it was found that, statistically, a post is likely to be edited by a troll when its average sentic vector has a high absolute value of sensitivity (one of the dimensions of the hourglass of emotions [65]) and a very low polarity. Hence the *trollness* t_i associated with a concept $c_i \in [0, 1]$ is

$$t_i(c_i) = \frac{s_i(c_i) + |sensitivity(c_i)| - p_i(c_i)}{3},\tag{5.1}$$

where $s_i \in [0, 1]$ is the semantic similarity of c_i with any of the concept frequency–inverted opinion frequency seed concepts, $p_i \in [-1, 1]$ is the polarity associated with the concept c_i, and 3 is the normalization factor. Hence the total *trollness* of a post containing N concepts is defined as

$$t = \sum_{i=1}^{N} \frac{3\, s_i(c_i) + 4\, |Se(c_i)| - Pl(c_i) - |At(c_i)| - Ap(c_i)}{9N},\tag{5.2}$$

where Se is the sensitivity, Pl the pleasantness, At the attention, and Ap the aptitude. This information is stored, together with the post type and content plus the sender ID and the receiver ID, in an interaction database that keeps track of all the messages and comments interchanged between users within the same social network.

Posts with a high level of *trollness* (with a threshold set, by means of a trial-and-error approach, to 60%) are labeled as troll posts and, whenever a specific user addresses more than two troll posts to the same person or community, his/her sender ID is labeled as a troll for that particular receiver ID. All the past troll posts sent to that particular receiver ID by that specific sender ID are then automatically deleted from the website. Moreover, any new post with a high level of *trollness* edited by a user labeled as a troll for that specific receiver is automatically blocked.

The evaluation of this approach [67] was performed by consideration of a set of 500 tweets manually annotated as troll and nontroll posts, most of which were fetched from Wordnik.

In Table 5.3 a comparison of three different vector space representations for commonsense concepts is presented. AnalogySpace [68] forms the analogical closure of a semantic network through dimensionality reduction. IsaCore [69] is a strongly connected core of hyponym-hypernym common knowledge. AffectNet is a semantic network in which commonsense concepts are linked to a hierarchy of affective domain labels (eg, "joy," "amazement," "fear," "admiration"). To enable affective analogical reasoning on natural language concepts, AffectiveSpace [70] is obtained as the vector space representation of such a semantic network.

The results show that, by use of the troll filtering process, inflammatory and outrageous messages can be identified with good precision (82.5%) and a good recall rate (75.1%). In particular, the F score (78.6%) is significantly high compared with the corresponding F scores obtained by use of IsaCore and AnalogySpace in place of the AffectiveSpace process (Table 5.3).

---

[2]https://www.wordnik.com/

Table 5.3 Precision, Recall, and *F* Score for the Troll Filter Evaluation

Metric	IsaCore (%)	AnalogySpace (%)	AffectiveSpace (%)
Precision	57.1	69.1	82.5
Recall	40.0	56.6	75.1
F score	47.0	62.2	78.6

4.2 SOCIAL MEDIA MARKETING

The online review of commercial services and products allows users to share their opinions about services they have received or products they have bought, and it constitutes an immeasurable value for other potential buyers. This trend opened new doors to enterprises that want to reinforce their brand and product presence in the market by investing in online advertising and positioning. Given the growing interest in social media marketing, several commercial tools have been developed recently to provide companies with the possibility to analyze the blogosphere on a large scale so they can extract information about the trend of the opinions relative to their products. Nevertheless, most of the existing tools and research efforts are limited to a polarity evaluation or a mood classification according to a very limited set of emotions. In addition, such methods mainly rely on parts of text in which emotional states are explicitly expressed, and hence they are unable to capture opinions and sentiments that are expressed implicitly.

To this end, a novel social media marketing tool has been proposed [71] to provide marketers with a tool for the management of social media information at the semantic level, able to capture both opinion polarity and affective information.

In particular, YouTube was selected as a social media source since, with its more than 2 billion views per day, 24 hours of video uploaded every minute, and 15 minutes a day spent by the average user, it represents more than 40% of the online video market.[3] Specifically, the focus was on video reviews of cell phones because of the quantity and the quality of the comments usually associated with them.

The social media analysis was performed through three main steps: firstly, comments are analyzed with an opinion mining engine; secondly, the extracted information is encoded on the basis of different web ontologies; finally, the resulting knowledge base is made available for browsing through a multifaceted classification website.

To make the tool applicable to most online resources (videos, images, text), the information relative to multimedia resources and people is encoded with use of the descriptors provided by the Ontology for Media Resources (OMR)[4] and Friend of a Friend (FOAF) ontology[5] respectively.

OMR offers a core vocabulary to describe media resources on the web, introducing descriptors such as "title," "creator," "publisher," "createDate," and "rating," and it defines semantic-preserving mappings between elements from existing formats to foster interoperability among them.

---

[3]http://www.viralblog.com/research-cases/youtube-statistics
[4]https://www.w3.org/TR/mediaont-10
[5]http://www.foaf-project.org/

FOAF represents a recognized standard in describing people, providing information such as their names, birthdays, pictures, blogs, and especially other people they know, which makes it particularly suitable for representing data that appear in social networks and communities.

OMR and FOAF together supply most of the vocabulary needed to describe media and people; other descriptors are added only when necessary. For example, OMR does not currently supply vocabulary for describing comments, which are hereby analyzed to extract the affective information relative to media. Hence the ontology is extended by the introduction of the "Comment" class and by defining for it the "author," "text," and "publicationDate" properties.

In the human emotion ontology (HEO) [72], properties to link emotions to multimedia resources and people are introduced (see Fig. 5.2). Additionally, WordNet-Affect [13] is exploited as an ontology to improve the hierarchical organization of emotions in HEO. Thus the combination of HEO and WordNet-Affect, OMR, and FOAF provides a complete framework to describe not only multimedia content and the users that have created, uploaded, or interacted with it but also the opinions and the affective content carried by the media and the way they are perceived by web users. To make this information visualizable, the multifaceted categorization paradigm is exploited (see Fig. 5.3). Faceted

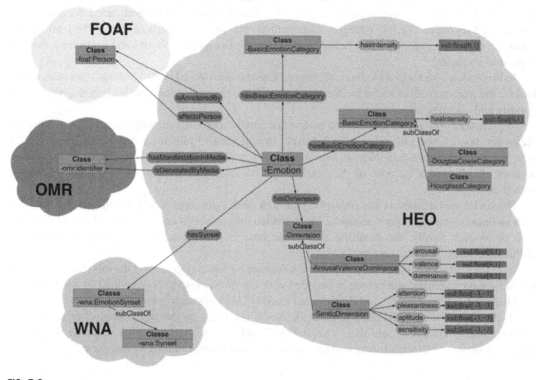

FIG. 5.2

Merging different ontologies. *FOAF*, Friend of a Friend; *HEO*, Human Emotion Ontology; *OMR*, Ontology for Media Resources; *WNA*, WordNet-Affect.

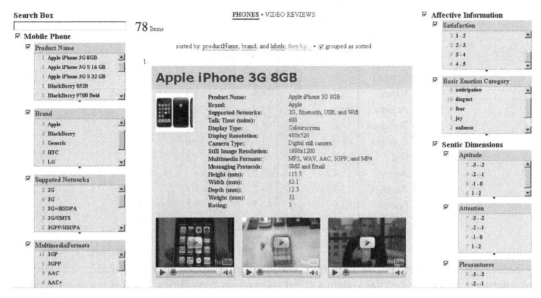

FIG. 5.3

A screenshot of the social media marketing tool.

classification allows the assignment of multiple categories to an object, enabling the classifications to be ordered in multiple ways, rather than in a single, pre-determined, and taxonomic order. This makes it possible to perform searches combining the textual approach with the navigational one.

To evaluate the proposed system on the level of both opinion mining and sentiment analysis, its polarity detection accuracy was separately tested with a set of like/dislike-rated video reviews from YouTube and its affect recognition capabilities were evaluated with a corpus of mood-tagged blogs from LiveJournal.

To evaluate the system in terms of polarity detection accuracy, the YouTube data application programming interface was used to retrieve from the YouTube database the ratings relative to 220 video reviews of cell phones. On YouTube, users can express their opinions about videos either by adding comments or by simply rating them using a like/dislike button. The YouTube data application programming interface makes this kind of information available by providing, for each video, the number of raters and the average rating (ie, the sum of likes and dislikes divided by the number of raters).

This takes a value in the range $[1, 5]$ and indicates if a video is generally considered bad (values in the range $[1, 3]$) or good (values in the range $[3, 5]$). This information was compared with the polarity values previously extracted by use of sentic computing on the comments relative to each of the 220 videos. True positives were identified as videos with both an average rating $r \in [3, 5]$ and a polarity $p \in [0, 1]$ (for positively rated videos), or videos with both an average rating $r \in [1, 3]$ and a polarity $p \in [-1, 0]$ (for negatively rated videos). The evaluation showed that, by use of the system to perform polarity detection, negatively and positively rated videos (37.7% and 62.3% of the total respectively) can be identified with a precision of 97.1% and recall of 86.3% (F score of 91.3%).

Table 5.4 Evaluation Results of the Sentics Extraction Process

Mood	Precision (%)	Recall (%)	F score (%)
Ecstatic	73.1	61.3	66.6
Happy	89.2	76.5	82.3
Pensive	69.6	52.9	60.1
Surprised	81.2	65.8	72.6
Enraged	68.9	51.6	59.0
Sad	81.8	68.4	74.5
Angry	81.4	53.3	64.4
Annoyed	77.3	58.7	66.7
Scared	82.6	63.5	71.8
Bored	70.3	55.1	61.7

Since no mood-labeled dataset regarding commercial products is currently available, the LiveJournal database was used to test the system's affect recognition capabilities. For this test, a reduced set of 10 moods was considered: ecstatic, happy, pensive, surprised, enraged, sad, angry, annoyed, scared, and bored. After relevant data and metadata for 5000 posts had been had been retrieved and stored, the sentics extraction process was conducted on each of these and the outputs were compared with the relative LiveJournal mood tags to compute recall and precision rates as evaluation metrics.

On average, each post contained around 140 words and, from this about 4 affective valence indicators and 60 sentic vectors were extracted. According to this information, mood labels were assigned to each post and compared with the corresponding LiveJournal mood tags, resulting in very good accuracy for each of the 10 selected moods (Table 5.4). Among these, "happy" and "sad" posts were identified with particularly high precision (89.2% and 81.8% respectively) and good recall rates (76.5% and 68.4%). The F scores obtained were also good (82.3% and 74.5% respectively), especially when compared with the corresponding F scores for a standard keyword spotting system based on a set of 500 affect words (65.7% and 58.6%).

4.3 A MODEL FOR SENTIMENT CLASSIFICATION IN TWITTER

This section describes a Twitter sentiment analysis system able to classify a tweet as positive or negative on the basis of its overall tweet-level polarity. The need for such a tool comes from the following consideration: supervised learning classifiers often misclassify tweets containing conjunctions such as "but" and conditionals such as "if" because of their special linguistic characteristics. Moreover, tweets often contain misspelled words, slang, URLs, elongations, repeated punctuation, emoticons, abbreviations, and hashtags. To counter these challenges, a system that enhances supervised learning for polarity classification by leveraging linguistic rules and sentic computing resources is proposed [61]. The general scheme of the system is presented in Fig. 5.4.

First all tweets are preprocessed to change all the @*<username>* references to *@USER* and all the *URLs* to *http://URL.com*. Then tweets are tokenized and a part-of-speech tag is assigned to each token. Then all the emoticons are identified. Since people often repeat certain punctuation to

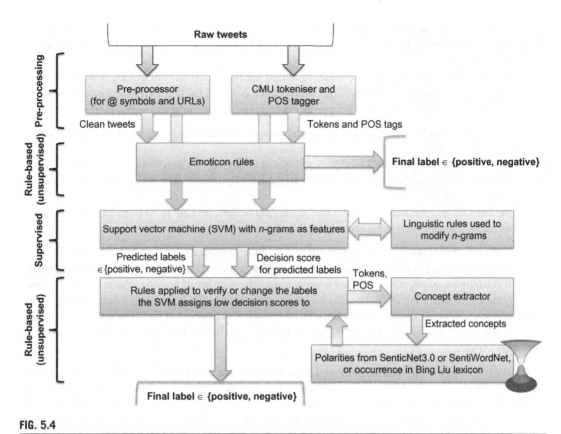

FIG. 5.4

Flowchart of the Twitter sentiment analysis system. *CMU,* Carnegie Mellon University; *POS,* part of speech.

emphasize emoticons, all repeated characters from every emoticon string are removed to obtain the bag of emoticons present in the tweet.

The number of positive and negative emoticons in the tweet are counted and the following rules are applied:

- If a tweet contains one or more positive emoticons and no negative emoticons, it is labeled as *positive.*
- If a tweet contains one or more negative emoticons and no positive emoticons, it is labeled as *negative.*
- If neither of the two rules above can be applied, the tweet is labeled as *unknown.*

If these emoticon-based rules label a tweet as *positive* or *negative,* this is considered the final label outputted by the system. Otherwise all tweets labeled as *unknown* are passed into a supervised learning classifier. In this case, each tweet is represented as a feature vector of case-sensitive *n*-grams (unigrams, bigrams, and trigrams). These *n*-grams are frequencies of sequences of one, two, or three contiguous tokens in a tweet. Besides, negation is taken into consideration. Moreover, all tweets containing the conjunction "but" and the conditionals "if," "unless," "until," and "in case" are considered, and specific linguistic rules are formulated to enable removal of irrelevant or oppositely oriented n-grams from the tweet's feature vector.

Finally, a SVM classifier is trained so as to obtain the tweet's label. For tweets with an absolute decision score or confidence below 0.5, the class labels assigned by the SVM are discarded and an unsupervised classifier is employed. This unsupervised classification process works as follows:

1. Single-word and multiword concepts are extracted from the tweets so as to fetch their polarities from SenticNet [14].
2. If a single-word concept is not found in SenticNet, it is queried in SentiWordNet [73], and if it is not found in SentiWordNet, it is searched for in the list of positive and negative words from the Bing Liu lexicon [74].
3. On the basis of the number of positive and negative concepts, and the most polar value occurring in the tweet, the following rules are applied:

   - If the number of positive concepts is greater than the number of negative concepts and the most polar value occurring in the tweet is greater than or equal to 0.6, the tweet is labeled as positive.
   - If the number of negative concepts is greater than the number of positive concepts and the most polar value occurring in the tweet is less than or equal to −0.6, the tweet is labeled as negative.
   - If neither of the two rules stated above can be applied, the tweet is labeled as unknown by the rule-based classifier, and the SVM's low confidence prediction is taken as the final output of the system.

An SVM classifier [75] was trained on 1.6 million positive and negative tweets provided by Go et al. [76]. After a standard 10 cross-validation procedure to set the model parameters [77,78], the method was evaluated on two publicly available datasets: SemEval 2013 [79] and SemEval 2014 [80]. Tables 5.5 and 5.6 show the results obtained on these two datasets. In these tables, each row shows the

Table 5.5 Results Obtained on 1794 Positive/Negative Tweets From the SemEval 2013 Dataset

Method	Positive			Negative			Average		
	P	R	F	P	R	F	P	R	F
n-grams	90.48	82.67	86.40	61.98	76.45	68.46	76.23	79.56	77.43
n-grams and emoticon rules	90.62	83.36	86.84	62.99	76.65	69.15	76.80	80.00	78.00
Modified *n*-grams	89.95	84.05	86.90	63.33	74.59	68.50	76.64	79.32	77.70
Modified *n*-grams and emoticon rules	90.10	84.73	87.33	64.41	74.79	69.22	77.26	79.76	78.27
Modified *n*-grams, emoticon rules, and word-level unsupervised rules	91.40	86.79	89.04	68.55	77.89	72.92	79.97	82.34	80.98
Modified *n*-grams, emoticon rules, and concept-level unsupervised rules	92.42	86.56	89.40	68.96	80.79	74.41	80.69	83.68	81.90

F, F score; P, precision; R, recall.

Table 5.6 Results Obtained on 3584 Positive/Negative Tweets From the SemEval 2014 Dataset

Method	Positive			Negative			Average		
	P	R	F	P	R	F	P	R	F
n-grams	89.92	81.90	85.72	61.20	75.66	67.67	75.56	78.78	76.69
n-grams and emoticon rules	89.74	83.05	86.27	62.50	74.85	68.11	76.12	78.95	77.19
Modified *n*-grams	89.39	82.90	86.02	62.00	73.93	67.44	75.69	78.41	76.73
Modified *n*-grams and emoticon eules	89.25	83.97	86.53	63.29	73.22	67.89	76.27	78.60	77.21
Modified *n*-grams, emoticon rules, and word-level unsupervised rules	90.22	86.24	88.19	67.37	75.25	71.09	78.80	80.75	79.64
Modified *n*-grams, emoticon rules, and concept-level unsupervised rules	90.41	86.20	88.25	67.45	75.76	71.37	78.93	80.98	79.81

F, F score; P, precision; R, recall.

precision, recall, and *F* score for the positive and negative classes, followed by the average positive and negative precision, recall, and *F* score. In the tables we indicate as modified *n*-grams the method that takes into account the linguistic rules employed on conjunctions and conditionals.

When comparing the standard *n*-grams model with the *n*-grams and emoticon rules model, one may notice that emoticon rules increase the average *F* by 0.57 and 0.50 in the 2013 and 2014 datasets respectively. A comparison between the modified *n*-grams model and the modified *n*-grams and emoticon rules model also shows that emoticon rules increase the average *F* by 0.57 and 0.48 in the two datasets respectively. This confirms that emoticon rules may significantly improve the classification. Moreover, modification of *n*-grams with use of linguistic rules for conjunctions and conditionals increases the average *F* by 0.27 and 0.04 in the two datasets respectively. Even if the increase is not very significant for the 2014 dataset, modified *n*-grams are still useful since a typical Twitter corpus usually contains a very small percentage of tweets with such conjunctions and conditionals.

A further comparison involves the analysis of the unsupervised rules: the results obtained by use of a bag-of-concepts model are compared with the ones obtained by use of a bag-of-words (or single-word concepts only) model. The average *F* for the bag-of-concepts model is 0.92 greater than for the bag-of-words model for the 2013 dataset, and 0.17 greater than the bag-of-words model for the 2014 dataset, thus confirming the effectiveness of the concept-level sentiment features. Overall, the final sentiment analysis system achieves an average *F* score that is greater by 4.47 and 3.12 than for the standard *n*-grams model.

5 FUTURE TRENDS AND DIRECTIONS

The research work carried out so far has formed a solid base for the development of a variety of emotion-sensitive systems and applications in the fields of opinion mining and sentiment analysis. This chapter has presented an overview of approaches to the analysis of opinions and sentiments in social networks, which go beyond keyword-based methods by using commonsense reasoning tools and affective ontologies. The techniques developed, however, are still far from perfect as the common and commonsense knowledge bases need to be further expanded and the reasoning tools built on top of them adjusted accordingly.

To overcome these limitations, current research work is focusing on expanding the affective knowledge by employing external resources (eg, Cyc, Freebase, and Yago). New graph-mining and multidimensionality reduction techniques are also being explored to perform reasoning on the commonsense knowledge bases. Moreover, new classification techniques are being tested, together with the ensemble application of dimensionality reduction and neural networks techniques for emulation of fast affective learning. Therefore, looking ahead, we believe the combined use of different knowledge bases and affective commonsense reasoning techniques will, eventually, pave the way for the development of more bio-inspired approaches to the design of intelligent systems capable of handling knowledge, making analogies, learning from experience, and perceiving and expressing affect.

6 CONCLUSION

With the advent of the Social Web, the way people express their views and opinions has dramatically changed. Social networks now represent huge sources of information with many practical applications. However, finding opinion sources and monitoring them can be a formidable task because there are a large number of diverse sources and each source may also have a huge volume of opinionated text. Thus automated opinion discovery and summarization systems are needed. Because of their tremendous value for practical applications, there has been an explosive growth of sentiment analysis techniques in both research in academia and applications in industry. However, most of the existing approaches still rely on syntactical structure of text, which is far from the way the human mind processes natural language.

In this chapter we have presented an overview of the most recent state-of-the-art sentiment-based techniques applied to social networks applications and tools. To assess the capability of sentiment analysis to tackle real-world NLP tasks, we considered several applications in different domains. Specifically, sentiment analysis tools and techniques were used for the design of Social Web applications (ie, a troll filtering system, a social media marketing tool, and a Twitter sentiment analysis system).

All these applications demonstrate how sentiment analysis can be a useful resource for the analysis of affective information in social platforms, relying not on domain-dependent keywords but rather on commonsense knowledge bases that allow one to extrapolate the cognitive and affective information associated with natural language text.

REFERENCES

[1] E. Cambria, Affective computing and sentiment analysis, IEEE Intell. Syst. 31 (2) (2016) 102–107.
[2] E. Cambria, A. Hussain, Sentic Computing: A Common-Sense-Based Framework for Concept-Level Sentiment Analysis, Springer, Cham, Switzerland, 2015.

[3] E. Cambria, Y. Xia, A. Hussain, Affective common sense knowledge acquisition for sentiment analysis, in: LREC, Istanbul, 2012, pp. 3580–3585.

[4] E. Cambria, D. Rajagopal, K. Kwok, J. Sepulveda, GECKA: game engine for commonsense knowledge acquisition, in: FLAIRS, 2015, pp. 282–287.

[5] E. Cambria, A. Hussain, C. Havasi, C. Eckl, SenticSpace: visualizing opinions and sentiments in a multi-dimensional vector space, in: R. Setchi, I. Jordanov, R. Howlett, L. Jain (Eds.), Knowledge-Based and Intelligent Information and Engineering Systems, Lecture Notes in Artificial Intelligence, vol. 6279, Springer, Berlin, 2010, pp. 385–393.

[6] Q. Wang, E. Cambria, C. Liu, A. Hussain, Common sense knowledge for handwritten Chinese recognition, Cogn. Comput. 5 (2) (2013) 234–242.

[7] S. Poria, E. Cambria, N. Howard, G.-B. Huang, A. Hussain, Fusing audio, visual and textual clues for sentiment analysis from multimodal content, Neurocomputing 174 (2016) 50–59.

[8] E. Cambria, S. Poria, F. Bisio, R. Bajpai, I. Chaturvedi, The CLSA model: a novel framework for concept-level sentiment analysis, in: LNCS, vol. 9042, Springer, Berlin, 2015, pp. 3–22.

[9] F. Bisio, P. Gastaldo, R. Zunino, E. Cambria, A learning scheme based on similarity functions for affective common-sense reasoning, in: IJCNN, 2015, pp. 2476–2481.

[10] E. Cambria, D. Olsher, K. Kwok, Sentic activation: a two-level affective common sense reasoning framework, in: AAAI, Toronto, 2012, pp. 186–192.

[11] E. Cambria, J. Fu, F. Bisio, S. Poria, AffectiveSpace 2: enabling affective intuition for concept-level sentiment analysis, in: AAAI, Austin, 2015, pp. 508–514.

[12] R. Speer, C. Havasi, ConceptNet 5: a large semantic network for relational knowledge, in: Theory and Applications of Natural Language Processing, 2012.

[13] C. Strapparava, A. Valitutti, WordNet-Affect: an Affective Extension of WordNet, in: Proceedings of the 4th International Conference on Language Resources and Evaluation (LREC 2004), Lisbon, May 2004, pp. 1083–1086.

[14] E. Cambria, D. Olsher, D. Rajagopal, SenticNet 3: a common and common-sense knowledge base for cognition-driven sentiment analysis, in: AAAI, Quebec City, 2014, pp. 1515–1521.

[15] S. Poria, A. Gelbukh, E. Cambria, D. Das, S. Bandyopadhyay, Enriching SenticNet polarity scores through semi-supervised fuzzy clustering, in: IEEE ICDM, Brussels, 2012, pp. 709–716.

[16] S. Poria, A. Gelbukh, E. Cambria, P. Yang, A. Hussain, T. Durrani, Merging SenticNet and WordNet-Affect emotion lists for sentiment analysis, in: 2012 IEEE 11th International Conference on Signal Processing (ICSP), vol. 2, IEEE, 2012, pp. 1251–1255.

[17] E. Cambria, H. Wang, B. White, Guest editorial: big social data analysis, Knowl. Based Syst. 69 (2014) 1–2.

[18] S. Poria, E. Cambria, A. Gelbukh, F. Bisio, A. Hussain, Sentiment data flow analysis by means of dynamic linguistic patterns, IEEE Comput. Intell. Mag. 10 (4) (2015) 26–36.

[19] S. Chinthala, R. Mande, S. Manne, S. Vemuri, Sentiment analysis on twitter streaming data, in: Annual Convention of the Computer Society of India, 2015.

[20] S. Rosenthal, P. Nakov, S. Kiritchenko, S.M. Mohammad, A. Ritter, V. Stoyanov, Semeval-2015 task 10: sentiment analysis in twitter, in: International Workshop on Semantic Evaluation, 2015.

[21] A. Ortigosa, J.M. Martín, R.M. Carro, Sentiment analysis in Facebook and its application to e-learning, Comput. Hum. Behav. 31 (2014) 527–541.

[22] P. Chandra, E. Cambria, A. Hussain, Clustering social networks using interaction semantics and sentics, in: J. Wang, G. Yen, M. Polycarpou (Eds.), Advances in Neural Networks, Lecture Notes in Computer Science, vol. 7367, Springer, Heidelberg, 2012, pp. 379–385.

[23] S. Poria, E. Cambria, A. Hussain, G.-B. Huang, Towards an intelligent framework for multimodal affective data analysis, Neural Netw. 63 (2015) 104–116.

[24] J.L. Reyes-Ortiz, L. Oneto, A. Samá, X. Parra, D. Anguita, Transition-aware human activity recognition using smartphones, Neurocomputing 171 (2016) 754–767.

[25] E. Fersini, E. Messina, F. Pozzi, Expressive signals in social media languages to improve polarity detection, Inform. Process. Manage. 52 (1) (2016) 20–35.

[26] D. Tang, B. Qin, F. Wei, L. Dong, T. Liu, M. Zhou, A joint segmentation and classification framework for sentence level sentiment classification, IEEE/ACM Trans. Audio Speech Lang. Process. 23 (11) (2015) 1750–1761.

[27] B. Pang, L. Lee, S. Vaithyanathan, Thumbs up? Sentiment classification using machine learning techniques, in: Conference on Empirical Methods on Natural Language Processing, 2002.

[28] B. Pang, L. Lee, Seeing stars: exploiting class relationships for sentiment categorization with respect to rating scales, in: Annual Meeting on Association for Computational Linguistics, 2005.

[29] K.L. Devi, P. Subathra, P. Kumar, Tweet sentiment classification using an ensemble of machine learning supervised classifiers employing statistical feature selection methods, in: International Conference on Fuzzy and Neuro Computing, 2015.

[30] G. Wang, J. Sun, J. Ma, K. Xu, J. Gu, Sentiment classification: the contribution of ensemble learning, Decis. Support Syst. 57 (2014) 77–93.

[31] E. Fersini, E. Messina, F. Pozzi, Sentiment analysis: Bayesian ensemble learning, Decis. Support Syst. 68 (2014) 26–38.

[32] A. Cernian, V. Sgarciu, B. Martin, Sentiment analysis from product reviews using SentiWordNet as lexical resource, in: International Conference on Electronics, Computers and Artificial Intelligence, 2015.

[33] D. Tang, B. Qin, T. Liu, Y. Yang, User modeling with neural network for review rating prediction, in: International Joint Conferences on Artificial Intelligence, 2015.

[34] E. Cambria, B. Schuller, B. Liu, H. Wang, C. Havasi, Knowledge-based approaches to concept-level sentiment analysis, IEEE Intell. Syst. 28 (2) (2013) 12–14.

[35] E. Cambria, B. Schuller, B. Liu, H. Wang, C. Havasi, Statistical approaches to concept-level sentiment analysis, IEEE Intell. Syst. 28 (3) (2013) 6–9.

[36] C.D. Elliott, The Affective Reasoner: A Process Model of Emotions in a Multi-Agent System, Northwestern University, Evanston, IL, 1992.

[37] A. Ortony, G. Clore, A. Collins, The Cognitive Structure of Emotions, Cambridge University Press, Cambridge, UK, 1988.

[38] J. Wiebe, T. Wilson, C. Cardie, Annotating expressions of opinions and emotions in language, Lang. Resour. Eval. 39 (2) (2005) 165–210.

[39] R. Stevenson, J. Mikels, T. James, Characterization of the affective norms for English words by discrete emotional categories, Behav. Res. Methods 39 (2007) 1020–1024.

[40] S. Somasundaran, J. Wiebe, J. Ruppenhofer, Discourse level opinion interpretation, in: International Conference on Computational Linguistics, 2008.

[41] D. Rao, D. Ravichandran, Semi-supervised polarity lexicon induction, in: Conference of the European Chapter of the Association for Computational Linguistics, 2009.

[42] A. Weichselbraun, S. Gindl, A. Scharl, Extracting and grounding context-aware sentiment lexicons, IEEE Intell. Syst. 28 (2) (2013) 39–46.

[43] L. García-Moya, H. Anaya-Sanchez, R. Berlanga-Llavori, A language model approach for retrieving product features and opinions from customer reviews, IEEE Intell. Syst. 28 (3) (2013) 19–27.

[44] G. Di Fabbrizio, A. Aker, R. Gaizauskas, Summarizing on-line product and service reviews using aspect rating distributions and language modeling, IEEE Intell. Syst. 28 (3) (2013) 28–37.

[45] M. Vahdat, L. Oneto, D. Anguita, M. Funk, M. Rauterberg, Can machine learning explain human learning? Neurocomputing 192 (2016) 14–28.

[46] R. Socher, A. Perelygin, J.Y. Wu, J. Chuang, C.D. Manning, A.Y. Ng, C. Potts, Recursive deep models for semantic compositionality over a sentiment treebank, in: Proceedings of the Conference on Empirical Methods in Natural Language Processing, 2013.

[47] H. Yu, V. Hatzivassiloglou, Towards answering opinion questions: separating facts from opinions and identifying the polarity of opinion sentences, in: Proceedings of the 2003 Conference on Empirical Methods in Natural Language Processing, 2003.

[48] P. Melville, W. Gryc, R.D. Lawrence, Sentiment analysis of blogs by combining lexical knowledge with text classification, in: ACM SIGKDD International Conference on Knowledge Discovery and Data Mining, 2009.

[49] F. Bisio, P. Gastaldo, C. Peretti, R. Zunino, E. Cambria, Data intensive review mining for sentiment classification across heterogeneous domains, in: Advances in Social Networks Analysis and Mining (ASONAM), IEEE, 2013, pp. 1061–1067.

[50] B. Pang, L. Lee, Opinion mining and sentiment analysis, Found. Trends Inform. Retriev. 2 (1–2) (2008) 1–135.

[51] V. Hatzivassiloglou, K.R. McKeown, Predicting the semantic orientation of adjectives, in: Annual Meeting of the Association for Computational Linguistics and Eighth Conference of the European Chapter of the Association for Computational Linguistics, 1997.

[52] A.-M. Popescu, O. Etzioni, Extracting product features and opinions from reviews, in: Natural Language Processing and Text Mining, 2007.

[53] B. Snyder, R. Barzilay, Multiple aspect ranking using the good grief algorithm, in: Conference of the North American Chapter of the Association for Computational Linguistics—Human Language Technologies, 2007.

[54] A. Tsai, R. Tsai, J. Hsu, Building a concept-level sentiment dictionary based on commonsense knowledge, IEEE Intell. Syst. 28 (2) (2013) 22–30.

[55] S. Poria, A. Gelbukh, A. Hussain, N. Howard, D. Das, S. Bandyopadhyay, Enhanced SenticNet with affective labels for concept-based opinion mining, IEEE Intell. Syst. 28 (2) (2013) 31–38.

[56] C. Hung, H.-K. Lin, Using objective words in SentiWordNet to improve sentiment classification for word of mouth, IEEE Intell. Syst. 28 (2) (2013) 47–54.

[57] C. Bosco, V. Patti, A. Bolioli, Developing corpora for sentiment analysis and opinion mining: a survey and the Senti-TUT case study, IEEE Intell. Syst. 28 (2) (2013) 55–63.

[58] E. Kouloumpis, T. Wilson, J. Moore, Twitter sentiment analysis: the good the bad and the omg!, in: International AAAI Conference on Weblogs and Social Media, 2011.

[59] D. Davidov, O. Tsur, A. Rappoport, Enhanced sentiment learning using twitter hashtags and smileys, in: Proceedings of the 23rd International Conference on Computational Linguistics: Posters, 2010.

[60] S.M. Mohammad, S. Kiritchenko, X. Zhu, NRC-Canada: building the state-of-the-art in sentiment analysis of tweets, in: Joint Conference on Lexical and Computational Semantics, 2013.

[61] P. Chikersal, S. Poria, E. Cambria, SeNTU: sentiment analysis of tweets by combining a rule-based classifier with supervised learning, in: International Workshop on Semantic Evaluation (SemEval 2015), 2015.

[62] D. Tang, F. Wei, B. Qin, T. Liu, M. Zhou, Coooolll: a deep learning system for twitter sentiment classification, in: International Workshop on Semantic Evaluation, 2014.

[63] C.N. dos Santos, M. Gatti, Deep convolutional neural networks for sentiment analysis of short texts, in: International Conference on Computational Linguistics, 2014.

[64] D. Tang, F. Wei, N. Yang, M. Zhou, T. Liu, B. Qin, Learning sentiment-specific word embedding for twitter sentiment classification, in: Annual Meeting of the Association for Computational Linguistics, 2014.

[65] E. Cambria, A. Livingstone, A. Hussain, The hourglass of emotions, in: A. Esposito, A. Vinciarelli, R. Hoffmann, V. Muller (Eds.), Cognitive Behavioral Systems, Lecture Notes in Computer Science, vol. 7403, Springer, Berlin, Heidelberg, 2012, pp. 144–157.

[66] M. Rowe, J. Butters, Assessing trust: contextual accountability, in: European Semantic Web Conference, 2009.

[67] E. Cambria, P. Chandra, A. Sharma, A. Hussain, Do not feel the trolls, in: International Semantic Web Conference, 2010.

[68] R. Speer, C. Havasi, H. Lieberman, AnalogySpace: reducing the dimensionality of common sense knowledge, in: AAAI, 2008.

[69] E. Cambria, Y. Song, H. Wang, N. Howard, Semantic multi-dimensional scaling for open-domain sentiment analysis, IEEE Intell. Syst. 29 (2) (2014) 44–51.

[70] E. Cambria, P. Gastaldo, F. Bisio, R. Zunino, An ELM-based model for affective analogical reasoning, Neurocomputing 149 (2015) 443–455.

[71] E. Cambria, M. Grassi, A. Hussain, C. Havasi, Sentic computing for social media marketing, Multimedia Tools Appl. 59 (2) (2012) 557–577.

[72] M. Grassi, Developing HEO human emotions ontology, in: J. Fierrez, J. Ortega-Garcia, A. Esposito, A. Drygajlo, M. Faundez-Zanuy (Eds.), Biometric ID Management and Multimodal Communication, Lecture Notes in Computer Science, vol. 5707, Springer, Berlin, Heidelberg, 2009 pp. 244–251.

[73] A. Esuli, F. Sebastiani, SentiWordNet: a publicly available lexical resource for opinion mining, in: International Conference on Language Resources and Evaluation, 2006.

[74] B. Liu, M. Hu, J. Cheng, Opinion observer: analyzing and comparing opinions on the web, in: WWW, 2005.

[75] L. Oneto, S. Ridella, D. Anguita, Tikhonov, Ivanov and Morozov regularization for support vector machine learning, Mach. Learn. 103 (1) (2016) 103–136.

[76] A. Go, R. Bhayani, L. Huang, Twitter sentiment classification using distant supervision, in: CS224N Project Report, Stanford 1 (2009) 12.

[77] D. Anguita, A. Ghio, L. Oneto, S. Ridella, In-sample and out-of-sample model selection and error estimation for support vector machines, IEEE Trans. Neural Netw. Learn. Syst. 23 (9) (2012) 1390–1406.

[78] L. Oneto, A. Ghio, S. Ridella, D. Anguita, Fully empirical and data-dependent stability-based bounds, IEEE Trans. Cybernet. 45 (9) (2015) 1913–1926.

[79] P. Nakov, Z. Kozareva, A. Ritter, S. Rosenthal, V. Stoyanov, T. Wilson, Semeval-2013 task 2: sentiment analysis in twitter, in: Annual Conference of the North American Chapter of the Association for Computational Linguistics, 2013.

[80] S. Rosenthal, P. Nakov, A. Ritter, V. Stoyanov, Semeval-2014 task 9: sentiment analysis in twitter, in: Semantic Evaluation Exercises, (2014).

SENTIMENT ANALYSIS IN SOCIAL NETWORKS: A MACHINE LEARNING PERSPECTIVE

6

E. Fersini

University of Milano-Bicocca, Milan, Italy

1 INTRODUCTION

The continuous adoption of online social networks has generated several opportunities for capturing interest in multiple aspects both from an individual user point of view and from a collective perspective. The interconnections that the users create among themselves contribute to the establishment of a virtual discussion environment that allows people to express themselves and to influence others on the net, and provides the possibility of belonging to multiple virtual communities. Online social networks are therefore creating a digital revolution that is investing in the lives of every single individual on the net. People are free to express their thoughts and to have their virtual space in which to be themselves, with very few constraints and limits. The changes from social networks to *online* social networks are enabling people to talk about their emotions and opinions, and more importantly to share and spread their thoughts, with other people with no geographical barrier. This revolution has therefore contributed to the rise in a novel sentiment analysis tasks from a machine learning and natural language processing point of view. From a methodological perspective, the sentiment analysis models need to consider the actual virtual environment (where users interact) to capture and analyze *what people think*. The definition of complex supervised, unsupervised, and semisupervised models able to take into account the novel nature of expressions (language used on the network) and the novel way of communication (relationships established in the virtual space) becomes a mandatory step.

Considering the new scenario, we present in this chapter the most recent advancements regarding sentiment analysis in online social networks. The chapter is structured as follows. In Section 2 the key elements that characterize the online social networks for sentiment analysis purposes are described. In Section 3 a literature review of sentiment analysis from a machine learning perspective is presented, focusing on the nature of the social networks, which are actually rich in informal languages and relationships among users. According to these main characteristics, we analyze the state of the art by distinguishing between supervised, semisupervised, and unsupervised models. In Section 4, some possible applications of polarity classification are outlined. In Section 5 an overview of some possible future directions for the next generation of sentiment analysis models is presented. Finally, conclusions are drawn in Section 6.

Sentiment Analysis in Social Networks. http://dx.doi.org/10.1016/B978-0-12-804412-4.00006-1

2 POLARITY CLASSIFICATION IN ONLINE SOCIAL NETWORKS: THE KEY ELEMENTS

User-generated content has been proved to be of paramount importance both for users and organizations/institutions: on one hand, people can share their opinions in an unconstrained and unbiased environment, and on the other hand, corporations can extract useful insights for their decision making processes. To quantify *what people think* from qualitative raw textual data, a polarity classification task—aimed at detecting positive, negative, or neutral text—is necessary. Although there is a extensive state of the art regarding the analysis of well-formed documents such as newspaper articles, reviews, and official news, there are still several open issues to address to properly tackle the real nature of the message in the available online social networks. According to this novel communication scenario, the sentiment analysis solutions that need to be defined not only inherit a multitude of issues from traditional sentiment analysis and natural language processing but they also have to deal with new and complex challenges. Social network messages are one of the most challenging types of text to deal with. This complexity is mainly due to the following characteristics:

- **Short messages**: Social networks messages are usually very short, but rich in embedded semantics. To make explicit the hidden information, several methods have been proposed to bridge the semantic gap between the few words written by the user and the corresponding more complex meaning. Among the most recent investigations able to exploit extra information included in the text messages, we can broadly distinguish between approaches working on additional textual cues, such as hashtags in Twitter [1,2], and methods based on multimodal analysis, such as text and images [3,4].
- **Noisy content**: An additional aspect that should be explicitly modeled when one is dealing with sentiment analysis in social network relates to badly formed texts, where vocabulary, spelling, and syntax represent a linguistic challenge. Social network messages are characterized by colloquial expressions, abbreviations, emoticons, word lengthening, irregular capitalization, and emphatic expressions, and they usually do not conform to canonical grammatical rules. To deal with this novel type of language, two main paradigms can be followed: adapting and enhancing computational approaches of natural language processing to fit the text (ie, domain adaptation) [5–7] or adapting text to fit the language technologies (ie, normalization) [8,9].
- **Dynamics**: Social network content is characterized by a strong temporal dynamic because of the continuous evolution of trending topics and because of their potential to open a debate with content provided by other users. Addressing a polarity classification task, taking into account the temporal dimension on which opinions are provided, is a key challenge to capture the change in user interests and therefore to model the volatility of attitudes toward topics over time [10–13].
- **Explicit and implicit information**: The users of online social networks not only produce content but they are usually characterized by their own distinctive features (eg, gender, location, age), which can be used to improve a polarity detection task. Understanding the correlation between real-time expressions of individuals and additional exogenous/endogenous variables could help to derive more effective sentiment models [14–16].
- **Multilingualism**: Thanks to the worldwide diffusion of social networks, the computational models for sentiment analysis should be able to deal with the multitude of languages available: less than

50% of tweets are written in English, but Japanese, Spanish, Portuguese, and German ones are featuring prominently [17]. Although most of the technologies have been mostly focused on English, the adaptation to new languages is still an open issue. Very few investigations work on non-English text [18–21] but some recent studies are trying to move the attention of the sentiment analysis community to adaptation techniques for cross-lingual analysis [22–25].

- **Relationships**: The key aspect of online social networks is that they are rich in both content and relationships, pointing out new challenges and opportunities from the sentiment analysis perspective. Content can contribute to inferring the user sentiment even if the network structure is not informative. Conversely, the relationships established by the users can contribute to reasoning about a user when limited and ambiguous content information is available. Here the concept of homophily [26] plays a fundamental role: a contact among similar people is expected to occur at a higher rate than among dissimilar people, implying that differences in terms of social characteristics can be converted into network distances.

Among the above-mentioned characteristics, the two key elements on which the sentiment analysis community is working are the rich nature of the natural language and the rich nature of the network. Regarding the language used in social networks, the main effort of the sentiment analysis community has been devoted to capturing and modeling the typical expression on the network through text, part-of-speech tags (eg, adverbs and adjectives), and paralinguistic content (eg, emojis, slang, hashtags) to derive more effective prediction models. In this context, most of the literature is related to the traditional statistical learning paradigm, where the content obeys a specific language typical of the social network and is independent of the content of other users (independent and identically distributed assumption).

Concerning the nature of the network, different types of relationships based on different types of homophily have been investigated to derive computational models able to disregard the independent and identically distributed assumption. In [27], two types of homophily are distinguished: *status homophily*, in which similarity is based on informal, formal, or ascribed status, and *value homophily*, which is based on values, attitudes, and beliefs. Status homophily includes the major sociodemographic dimensions such as race, ethnicity, gender, or age, and acquired characteristics such as religion, education, occupation, or behavior patterns. Value homophily includes the wide array of internal states presumed to shape our orientation toward future behavior: attitude, belief, and value similarity lead to attraction and interaction. According to these distinctions, two kinds of approaches have been developed in the literature: methods grounded on status homophily relationships (such as friendships in Facebook and following/follower in Twitter) and approaches that exploit relationships based on value homophily (such as retweets in Twitter, +1 in Google+, and "like" in Facebook).

In the following sections the main advances in the machine learning literature will be discussed, focusing on the above-mentioned two main characteristics: *natural language* and *relationships*. A graphical representation that summarizes the key elements of machine leaning approaches for sentiment analysis purposes in given in Fig. 6.1.

The discussion of the state of the art regarding sentiment analysis techniques will be focused on the machine learning perspective, distinguishing between (1) *supervised learning*, where labeled observations are used to train a classifier, (2) *unsupervised learning*, where observations given to the learner are unlabeled, and (3) *semisupervised learning*, where both labeled and unlabeled data are used to derive the final sentiment model.

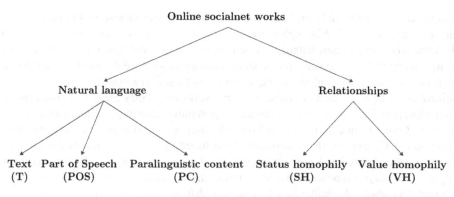

FIG. 6.1

Key elements of social networks.

3 POLARITY CLASSIFICATION: NATURAL LANGUAGE AND RELATIONSHIPS
3.1 LEVERAGING NATURAL LANGUAGE

Sentiment classification is usually treated as a traditional text classification problem where, instead of classifying documents of different topics (eg, politics, sciences, and sports), one estimates *positive*, *negative*, and *neutral* classes (or [−5,5], [0,100] intervals). According to this perspective, any existing supervised learning method, such as naïve Bayes and support vector machine classifiers, can be easily applied. However, in contrast to well-formed text, the natural language in online social networks has several distinctive features that can be exploited to approach the polarity classification problem:

- **Parts of speech**. Words belonging to different parts of speech should be treated according to their linguistic role (nouns, verbs, pronouns, etc.). When one is dealing with user-generated content, part-of-speech tags can be inferred if one adopts specific language models that are able to capture the structure of the expressive forms used in online social networks [5,6]. Among the available parts of speech, it has been shown that some specific elements (eg, adjectives, adverbs, interjection) are important indicators of subjectivity [28], polarity [29], and irony [30].
  An additional challenge relates to *sentiment shifters*; that is, those expressions used to alter the sentiment orientations (ie, from positive to negative or vice versa). Negation words (eg, *not, never, cannot*) [31], modal auxiliary verbs (eg, *would, should, could*) [32], and presuppositional words (eg, *strongly, smartly*) [33] are examples of sentiment shifters that have been shown to be relevant for sentiment analysis purposes.
- **Paralinguistic content**. Paralinguistic content is those pragmatic particles typically used in social networks to elicit a given message:
  - *Emoticons* are introduced as expressive, nonverbal components into the written language, mirroring the role played by facial expressions in speech [34]. To take advantage of these sentiment signals, several investigations have been conducted in different social networks [35–38]. Examples of lexicons containing positive emoticons (such as ☻, ☺, and ☻) and negative ones (such as ☹, ☹, and ☹) can be found in [39,40].

- *Initialisms for emphatic expressions* are an additional paralinguistic element used in nonverbal communication in online social networks. Although they act as a constituent, these emphatic abbreviations have been shown to play a role similar to that of emoticons [41]: expressions such as "ROFL" (meaning "rolling on floor laughing") can represent positive expressions, while abbreviations such as "BM" (meaning "bad manners") can denote negative statements.
- *Onomatopoeic expressions* in online social networks can help to convey emotions [42]: some expressions such as "bleh" and "wow" are clear indicators of negative and positive emotional states and therefore can help to distinguish the polarity of a text message.
- Word lengthening: Word styling (as bold, italic, and underlining) is not always available in online social network platforms and it is often replaced by some linguistic conventions. Word lengthening[1] (usually known as expressive lengthening or word stretching) is an example of such novel linguistic conventions that nowadays are extremely popular in online social networks. In [43,44] it was shown that such a commonly observed phenomenon is an indication of emphasis that is strongly associated with subjectivity and sentiment.
- *Capital letters.* Positive and negative expressions are commonly reported by capitalization of some specific words (eg, "*#StarWars was AMAZING!*") to express the intensity of the user sentiments. To take advantage of this indicator, it is possible either to give it more weight than other commonly occurring words when one is creating the text representation of the content [45] or to consider this indication as an additional feature (eg, count of capitalized words) to be exploited by any learning algorithm.
- *Hashtags.* A large number of posts in online social networks are characterized by a wide range of user-defined hashtags. Some of these tags are defined and used to express one or more specific sentiment associated with the corresponding text. However, the distinction between sentiment hashtags and topic hashtags is a challenge that needs to be properly addressed for polarity classification purposes [46–48].

In the following the state of the art will be distinguished according to three paradigms (ie, supervised, semisupervised, and unsupervised learning).

A graphical representation that summarizes the most recent literature leveraging the natural language used on social networks is presented in Fig. 6.2.

3.1.1 Supervised learning

There is extensive literature that leverages the combinations of the characteristics described earlier to train a supervised sentiment classification model [49]. In this research area we can roughly distinguish between the state of the art in two main fields (ie, baseline and ensemble models). Concerning the baseline models, several contributions have been provided in the last decade. Among the most recent approaches are those in [50–55].

Dhande and Patnaik [50] proposed a supervised machine learning approach that is able to combine naïve Bayes and neural network classifiers for sentiment categorization. In their investigation, they tried to overcome the attribute independence assumption underlying the naïve Bayes classifier by using a neural network to explicitly represent the dependencies among attributes (ie, words). The resulting

---

[1] An example of word lengthening is "*I loooooove you.*"

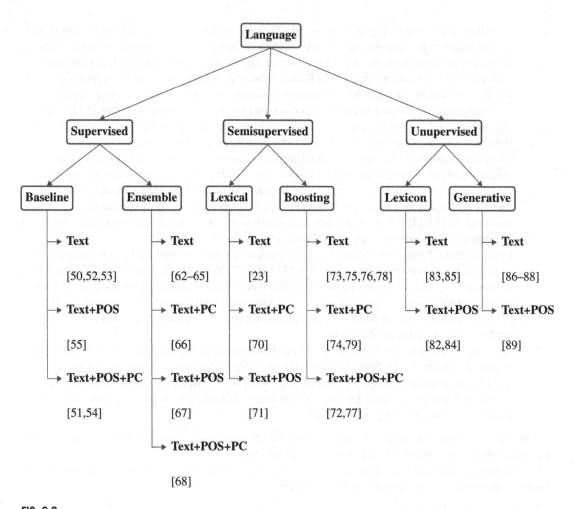

FIG. 6.2

State of the art of approaches based on natural language. *PC*, paralinguistic content; *POS*, parts of speech.

naïve Bayes neural classifiers have been shown to be able to achieve promising accuracy with use of a simple unigram representation of user messages.

Chikersal et al. [51] combine two main baseline approaches. The first one is a rule-based classifier that takes a decision about positive, negative, or unknown sentiment, using rules that are dependent on the occurrences of emoticons and opinion words in tweets (ie, lexicons). The second one, based on support vector machines, is trained on semantic, dependency, and sentiment lexicons to identify positive, negative, and neutral messages. The predictions provided by the two baseline approaches are subsequently combined to refine the support vector machine predictions. A further supervised approach based on sentiment lexicon construction was presented in [55]. The main goal is to deal with the problem of unavailability of labeled data by use of SentiWordNet [56]. The proposed framework, SWIMS (for "semisupervised subjective feature weighting and intelligent model selection"), starts by acquiring SentiWordNet as a labeled corpus to extract adjectives, verbs, adverbs, and nouns that are subjective. Then a new feature-weighting mechanism—based on the pointwise mutual information [57]—is used to finally train a supervised support vector machine for sentiment classification.

Even though the traditional supervised learning approaches have addressed several sentiment analysis tasks, most of the recent literature is moving toward a different perspective of the problem. In particular, the current research direction is related to the definition of novel representation spaces, by means of word embeddings [58], for subsequent training of traditional learning models [52–54]. Severyn and Moschitti [52] proposed a new model for initializing the parameter weights of a convolutional neural network [59] based on word embedding to finally train an accurate soft-max sentiment model. The solution they proposed successfully combines two important constituents for sentiment analysis: word embeddings for a rich language model and supervised learning on available data. A similar architecture was presented in [53]. A further investigation that exploits distributed word representations was proposed in [54], where two types of word embeddings were adopted (ie, the skip-gram model [60] and the sentiment-word model [61]) to subsequently train a support vector machine.

Although the above-mentioned approaches represent an important step toward the definition of robust systems, within the sentiment classification research field, none of the classification algorithms consistently performs better than the others and there is no consensus regarding which method should be adopted for a given problem in a given domain.

To overcome this limitation, the *ensemble learning* paradigm has been investigated recently [62–67]. The idea behind ensemble mechanisms is to take advantage of several independent classifiers by combining them to achieve better performance than the baseline ones.

A first approach to ensemble composition was presented in [62,63]. The main idea is for one to exploit all the possible baseline models in the hypothesis space by taking into account their marginal prediction capabilities and their reliabilities. One finally derives the optimal ensemble composition by taking advantage of a greedy model selection strategy able to find a good bias-variance trade-off among all the baseline models considered. Lin et al. [64] presented as a novel contribution a criterion for sentiment-based ensemble composition. In their work an approximate algorithm, which is able to exploit accuracy and diversity of baseline classifiers, is designed to tackle the combinatorial problem of classifier selection.

A different approach to ensemble learning is related to the feature space instead of the model space. Wang et al. [65] reported an extensive study of the traditional vector representations for inducing state-of-the-art ensemble methods. In particular, they investigated traditional bagging and boosting approaches [68] over different bag-of-word representations (unigram and bigram) and different weighting schema (Boolean, term frequency, and term frequency–inverse document frequency).

In [66] the hypothesis is that an appropriate feature engineering—known as feature hashing [69]—can lead to more accurate ensemble models. The original bag-of-word space is reduced by the hashing of the features into a lower-dimensional space, allowing multiple features to be mapped to the same hash key. An approach that tries to exploit the potentiality of baseline methods through ensemble learning and enriched word representation was presented by Zhang and He [67], who took advantage of two different feature sets: the first one describes the latent topics of the messages, while the second one is related to word embeddings. These feature sets are then used to tune the contribution of different learners in the ensemble model.

As a general consideration we can highlight that although the approaches based on supervised learning can lead to very high sentiment recognition performance, a drawback is concerned with the necessary human effort to label the data. To overcome this limitation, alternative solutions (grounded on semisupervised and unsupervised learning) have been developed.

3.1.2 Semisupervised learning

Several semisupervised approaches have recently been presented to address the well-known problem related to the acquisition of manually labeled data for sentiment classification. Generally, the semisupervised classification methods can be categorized into two types: approaches based on prior lexical knowledge combined with labeled (and unlabeled) data [23,70,71], and bootstrap techniques [72–78].

Concerning the *lexical-based approaches*, Ju et al. [71] addressed the seed-word selection for semisupervised sentiment classification through a joint lexicon-corpus learning approach. They investigated the (human) costs for annotating words to then measure their informativeness. Both the annotation cost and the informativeness measurement are taken into account to guide the selection strategy for good words for the final sentiment analysis task. Although the pure lexical-based approaches have shown promising results for tackling semisupervised sentiment classification, the most recent literature is focused on sentiment transfer learning. He et al. [23] proposed a transfer learning approach that is able to take advantage of the sentiment knowledge available in a resource-rich (source) language to restore the information lost during the transfer process in the new resource-poor (target) domain. Zhu et al. [70] presented an approach that combines lexicons and labeled and unlabeled data for sentiment transfer across different domains. First, several emotion keywords are used to automatically extract labeled samples and then both the automatically labeled samples from the target domain and the real labeled samples from the source domain are combined to create a new labeled data set. Finally, all the labeled and unlabeled data in the target domain are used to perform cross-domain sentiment classification with a standard label-propagation algorithm.

Regarding the *bootstrap techniques*, we can further distinguish between self-training [79] and co-training [80]. The main characteristic of *self-training* approaches is to adapt a predefined polarity lexicon with use of an unlabeled set of social network messages. Among the different self-training solutions for sentiment analysis, the most recent approaches are focused on the enrichment of existing vocabularies with (unsupervised) sentiment lexical items for a subsequent learning phase [72–74,78].

An additional strategy for semisupervised boosting is represented by the *co-training* approaches. The key characteristic of such methods is their ability to derive and take advantage of different "views" for the same opinionated text. Liu et al. [77] exploit both textual features (ie, opinionated words weighted according to WordNet-Affect [81]) and nontextual indications (ie, emoticons, temporal indications, and punctuation) to train two supervised classifiers. A further approach was presented in [76], where a semisupervised deep neural network framework was developed to co-train on the feature representation and pattern classification spaces. Yang et al. [75] recently investigated a combination of lexicon-based learning and corpus-based learning in a unified co-training framework.

After analyzing the current state of the art, we can affirm that although semisupervised methods for sentiment classification are still in their infancy, they are becoming ever more popular thanks to their ability to use both (small sets of) a labeled corpus and (huge sets of) unlabeled data.

3.1.3 Unsupervised models

Unsupervised approaches to sentiment classification can solve the problem of domain dependency and reduce the need for annotated training data. Most of the approaches available for unsupervised sentiment classification can be broadly distinguished into lexicon-based methods [82–85] and generative models [86–89].

Concerning the *lexicon-based approaches*, the first work was presented by Turney [82], who used two arbitrary seed words to compute the semantic orientation of a sentence (measured by pointwise mutual information [57]). An improvement on the above-mentioned approach was by Zagibalov and Carroll [83], who presented a method for the automatic seed word selection. The method requires information only about commonly occurring negations and adverbials to iteratively find sentiment-bearing items.

More recent methods are based on the automatic construction of lexicons. Lu et al. [85] addressed the problem of deriving a sentiment lexicon that is not only domain specific but also aspect dependent. To accomplish this task, an optimization framework was proposed to combine different sources of information for learning context-dependent sentiment lexicons.

Sheng et al. [84] proposed an automatic construction strategy for a domain-specific sentiment lexicon based on constrained label propagation. In particular, a set of candidate sentiment terms is extracted by use of the chunk dependency information and an a priori generic lexicon. Then a set of pairwise contextual and morphological constraints are extracted from a domain corpus and are exploited as prior knowledge to improve the sentiment lexicon construction.

The *generative models* represent an alternative and more flexible solution to the lexicon-based approaches. The main characteristic of this class of models is that they are able to simultaneously extract aspects and classify sentiments from textual messages. A sentence such as "*#iOS7: battery life is a plus, but the security is a big issue!*" is an example of different aspects, each having its own polarity, reported on the main target "iOS7." Several studies that deal with sentiment classification and topic modeling have been proposed in the literature.

A first generative model known as the *topic sentiment mixture model* to separate topics and sentiment words with use of an extended probabilistic latent semantic analysis model [90] was presented in [87]. Further investigations based on the latent Dirichlet allocation principle [91] can be found in [86,88], where an *aspect and sentiment unification model (ASUM)* and a *joint sentiment-topic (JST)* model were proposed respectively. The JST model is a fully unsupervised model that can capture the topic and sentiment at the same time. The ASUM is a model based on the JST model, characterized by a small adaption of the former one, that introduces the assumption that a sentence in a message can be related to only a specific aspect and sentiment. The main advantage of the JST model with respect to the ASUM comes from its ability to reciprocally reduce the noise of both topic and sentiment generation tasks.

A more recent generative model available in the literature was presented by He et al. [89]. They proposed a dynamic JST model that allows the detection and tracking of topics and sentiment over time: topic and sentiment dynamics are captured by the current time-dependent sentiment-topic word distributions and the word distributions at previous time stamps.

3.2 LEVERAGING NATURAL LANGUAGE AND RELATIONSHIPS

A key aspect of social networks is that they are rich both in content and in relationships, providing unprecedented challenges and opportunities from a sentiment analysis point of view. For instance, combining content and relationships could be useful when one is dealing with implicit (or implied) opinions, where textual features do not always provide explicit information about the sentiment orientation. However, as shown in the previous section, most of the state-of-the-art approaches are consistent with the classical statistical inference problem formulation, in which instances (posts/users) are represented as homogeneous, independent, and identically distributed. In other words, they consider textual information only, not taking into account that social networks are actually relational environments. Although relationships in online social networks have been extensively investigated from a sociological and psychological point of view, investigation of their role from a machine learning perspective is still in its infancy: most of the investigations are based on exploiting relationships from a propositional point of view (ie, flattening the social network connections by an aggregation function or including an additional attribute in the text representation to represent sentiment influence), while very few approaches tackle the networked environments in their native forms.

Analogously to the distinction provided in the previous section, in the following a description of approaches that combine content and relationships is provided, distinguishing between supervised, unsupervised, and semisupervised models. Focusing on these three main paradigms, we consider two types of relationships available in social networks; that is, *relationships based on status homophily* and *relationships based on value homophily*.

A graphical representation that summarizes the most recent literature based on relationships (and natural language) is reported in Fig. 6.3.

3.2.1 Supervised learning

The first and more popular investigations in the state of the art aimed at combining content and relationships are grounded on the status homophily sociological theory. Assuming *status homophily* as an underlying principle of online relationships between users implies the assumption that users form ties thanks to demographic factors (ie, race/ethnicity, sex/gender, age, religion, education, occupation, and social class). According to this principle the relationships between users have been modeled in online social networks both as directed and as undirected binary connections: friendships in Facebook,[2] Google+,[3] and Weibo,[4] and following/follower in Twitter.[5]

Concerning the state-of-the-art approaches that assume *relationships based on status homophily* jointly with text, we highlight the most recent supervised learning methods [92–94]. The first tentative approach exploiting the statistical relational learning paradigm for polarity classification purposes was presented Rabelo et al. [92], who investigated a relational neighbor classifier to estimate a polarity

---

[2]http://www.facebook.com
[3]https://plus.google.com/
[4]http://www.weibo.com/
[5]https://www.twitter.com

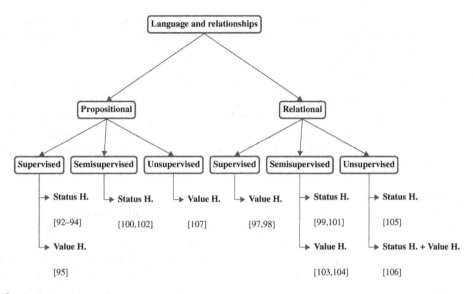

FIG. 6.3

State of the art of approaches based on relationships (and natural language). *H*, homophily.

probability model (based on text ad adjoining friends) and a relaxed collective inference approach to determine the sentiment of the users in the network. Hu et al. [93] presented a mathematical programming formulation that is able to capture the sentiment consistency (by means of user-content connections) and the emotional contagion (by taking advantage of user-user social relations) for networks of reduced size. Recently, an investigation into the emotional contagion in large social networks was presented by Coviello et al. [94], who modeled the emotions of the users as dependent not only on the endogenous and exogenous factors (eg, always being happy and rainfall effect) but also on contagion of groups of friends.

Although the above-mentioned investigations are characterized by consistent performance gains with respect to those approaches based purely on textual content, they strongly assume that the explicitly available relationships (friendships and following/follower connections) unconditionally represent the sentiment agreement between connected users. However, this assumption does not reflect what happens in the real world, where two structurally connected users can have divergent opinions on a given topic. To better capture the sentiment agreement among users, some recent approaches have been grounded on the *value homophily* theory. Considering this principle as underlying the online relationships between users implies the assumption that users create bonds thanks to attractions and interactions that contribute to their sharing of attitudes, abilities, beliefs, and aspirations. According to this principle the relationships between users have been modeled in online social networks as weighted directed connections: appreciations in Facebook (ie, "like") and Google+ ("+1") and retweets in Twitter ("RT").

Regarding those approaches in the literature that assume *relationships based on value homophily* together with text, we describe a few recent investigations. Jiang et al. [95] derived a probabilistic

Bayesian model that considers the text content posted by a user smoothed by the sentiment labels of neighbors directly connected through a structural connection (ie, a retweet in Twitter). Once the probabilistic model has been trained, a graph-based classification algorithm based on relaxation labeling [96] is used to infer the polarity of unobserved users.

Anjaria and Guddeti [97] proposed a supervised system that exploits the salient features of supervised machine learning algorithms for text-based sentiment classification to subsequently incorporate social network structural features (again a retweet in Twitter) as an approach to sentiment analysis at the user level. Finally, in [98] any kind of social interaction (eg, "like," comments, and sharing activities) is captured by a sentiment opinion graph. To derive the sentiment orientation of each user of the network, a relaxation labeling process is followed.

3.2.2 Semisupervised learning

Dealing with sentiment classification in networked environments usually requires a fully supervised learning paradigm, where the sentiment orientation must be known a priori to derive suitable predictive models. However, this does not always reflect the real setting of social networks, where some partial information can be grasped to derive a relational semisupervised model and therefore reduce the human effort related to the annotation process. Among the semisupervised techniques able to deal with content and relationships, we can again distinguish between models that include status homophily relationships and approaches that take advantage of value homophily relationships.

Among the models based on *status homophily relationships*, we highlight the most recent approaches presented in the literature [99–102]. Tan et al. [99] proposed a semisupervised approach to predict the user sentiment by introducing explicitly available undirected user-user relationships ("friendships") into a text-based factor-graph model. Speriosu et al. [100] proposed enriching the content representation by including directed user-user relationships as features additional to the text ones. The same kind of directed user-user social relationships (eg, "following" and "follower" in Twitter) was exploited in [101] to predict the sentiment orientation of users by a collective inference approach based on a partially labeled network. Tang et al. [102] recently presented a semisupervised version of the supervised model presented in [93]. The main rationale behind this recent approach is (1) content from the same author is likely to be more consistent in terms of polarity than two randomly selected messages and (2) content provided by connected friends is likelier than two randomly selected texts to have the same sentiment.

Concerning the *value homophily relationships*, only two semisupervised approaches have been found in the literature. Pozzi et al. [103] proposed a semisupervised sentiment learning approach that extends the model presented in [99] by introducing a social network representation based on the concept of an "approval network." Given a small proportion of users already labeled in terms of polarity, the model predicts the sentiments of the remaining unlabeled users by combining directly in the probabilistic model both the textual information and the retweet-based graph representation.

A subsequent contribution built on the work reported in [103] was presented by Nozza et al. [104]. In their investigation a social network is represented as a heterogeneous graph, where a latent representation of the nodes (both users and posts) is learned to infer the corresponding polarity labels.

3.2.3 Unsupervised learning

Similarly to the semisupervised paradigm, the unsupervised approaches in the literature able to leverage both content and relationships are very preliminary. The work in [105,106] represents the first tentative approaches to address the polarity detection task assuming *relationships based on status homophily*. The first explorative analysis in [105] proposed an unsupervised label propagation algorithm for dealing with both explicit and implicit opinion targets. The authors consider posts as nodes in the graph with a corresponding polarity label vector initialized by the hashtags reported in the text. Then at each iteration of the label propagation algorithm, the label vector of one node is propagated to the adjoining ones.

Ou et al. [106] proposed a content and link unsupervised sentiment model as a richer framework able to take advantage of four main components: content, same-user link (ie, two posts are provided by the same user), friend link (ie, the users of two messages are connected by a friendship relationship), and behavior link (two users are connected if any repost, reply, or comment activity is performed). These four ingredients were introduced in a unified probabilistic model, for which parameter estimation and inference can be approached by a maximum likelihood method and Gibbs sampling respectively.

Concerning the *value homophily relationships*, only one unsupervised approach has been found in the literature. Zhu et al. [107] proposed an unsupervised triclustering framework that is able to analyze both user-level and message-level sentiments through co-clustering of a tripartite graph. The most important contribution is concerned with the finding that making use of mutual dependency among aspects, messages, and user relationship can lead to effective unsupervised sentiment classification models.

4 APPLICATIONS

Polarity classification is well suited to various types of intelligence applications. Indeed, business intelligence seems to be one of the main factors behind corporate interest in the field. One of the most important needs of businesses and organizations in the real world is to find and analyze consumer or public opinions about their products and services (eg, *Why are consumers not buying our laptop?*). Polarity classification paves the way to several interesting applications, in almost every possible domain. For example, summarizing user reviews is a relevant task of analytics. Moreover, opinions matter a great deal in politics. Some work has focused on understanding what voters are thinking [108]. For instance, the US president Barack Obama used the polarity classification task of sentiment analysis to gauge feelings of core voters during the 2008 presidential election. A further task is the augmentation of recommendation systems, where the system might not recommend items that receive negative feedback several times [49].

However, polarity classification has also been applied to more ethical principles. For example, on the basis of observations of Twitter's role in the civilian response during the 2009 Jakarta and Mumbai terrorist attacks, Cheong and Lee [109] proposed a structured framework to harvest civilian sentiment and response on Twitter during terrorism scenarios. Arunachalam and Sarkar [110] monitored and analyzed several social networks to assess the citizens' perception of government agencies for several purposes: fine-tuning of policies, identification of best practices positively perceived, negative aspects of the actions and decisions. Polarity classification has also been applied to the medical field. Cobb et al. [111] examined how exposure to messages about a smoking-cessation drug affects smokers' decision making regarding its use. In recent years, social networks have emerged as a potential source of information for sentiment analysis in the financial domain. Financial tweets have been investigated to predict short- and long-term stock market evolutions [112–114].

Since sentiment analysis is nowadays accessible to a large audience (researchers, governments, institutions, companies, and corporations), we can expect even more upcoming applications: violence prevention, e-health intervention, monitoring of cyber bullying and cyber pedophilia, transportation optimization, and emergency management.

5 FUTURE DIRECTIONS

In the previous sections the most recent contributions to the state of the art of sentiment analysis were presented from a machine learning point of view. Concerning the future directions, some conclusions can be drawn. For the sentiment analysis methods focused on *natural language*, we can highlight the following:

- The *supervised models* that are able to leverage natural language are strictly focused on explicit opinions. A challenge that remains to be addressed relates to the more difficult task of identifying and properly dealing with implicit opinions (ie, objective statements that express a desirable or undesirable fact through regular or comparative statements). In this direction, not only syntactic cues could contribute to identifying text constituents that characterize implicit opinions, but also the semantics of co-occurrent patters in the language could provide a distinctive advantage.
- Regarding the future work on *semisupervised models*, a major challenge that remains to be addressed is related to incremental learning. While most of the available techniques are based on statistical learning and therefore assume a given stochastic distribution of the data they observe, an incremental learning model could be applied whenever new observations emerge and could adapt to what has been learned accordingly.
- According to the analysis of the literature on *unsupervised models*, we can affirm that although they represent a relevant alternative to the supervised and semisupervised ones, they can introduce bias when dealing with short and noisy text. The fact that social network text is composed of a few words poses considerable problems when one is applying traditional topic/sentiment models. These models typically suffer from data sparsity to estimate robust word co-occurrence statistics when they are dealing with short and ill-formed text. We can therefore expect as upcoming contributions several approaches able to adapt the generative process behind topic/sentiment modeling to the social network language.

For the sentiment analysis methods focused on both natural language and *relationships*, we highlight the following:

- As a future direction of *supervised models* that are able to leverage both information sources, we can expect several additional extensions of probabilistic learning/inference techniques to deal with complex relational structures (ie, connections based both on status homophily and on value homophily). From a machine learning point of view, we expect an increasing number of investigations that attempt to create a successful marriage between probability theory and several relational representations. In particular, the solutions to learn and infer over the relational environment of social networks are presumed to retain the relational data structure in its totality (ie, not focusing on directly connected users, but considering the whole network) and by adapting/enriching learning and/or inference algorithms to consider the real nature of the social networks.

- After analyzing the state of the art of this type of *semisupervised models*, we believe a possible future research direction relates to the uncertainty of relationships available in the social networks. The totality of the models (based on both status homophily and value homophily) assume certain relationships that do not evolve over time. In a more concrete scenario, all of these connections are uncertain: they can be broken, they can vary over time and with topic, and they can be latent (not directly observable). We can therefore expect ever richer models able to tackle the uncertainty over the relational structure to perform more accurate sentiment classification and propagation tasks.
- As a future direction of *unsupervised models*, we expect an extension of propositional generative models (presented in Section 3.1.3) for dealing with connections among users and relationships among messages. From a machine learning perspective, we expect an increasing number of investigations into the statistical relational learning domain able to explicitly model the relational component into the generative topic-sentiment models.

6 CONCLUSION

The growth of sentiment analysis as one of the most active research areas of the last 10 years is due to different reasons. First, sentiment analysis has a wide array of applications, in almost every domain. Second, it offers many challenging research problems that have never been studied before. Third, with the advent of the big data technologies, we now have a huge volume of opinionated data recorded and easily accessible in digital forms on the web. These reasons have motivated the recent advances in the state of the art presented in this chapter. Most of the work regarding polarity classification usually considers text as unique information to infer sentiment, disregarding that social networks are actually networked environments. To take advantage of both natural language and social networks relationships, a novel research branch is developing.

REFERENCES

[1] G. Petrovic, H. Fujita, Semi-automatic detection of sentiment hashtags in social networks, in: Intelligent Software Methodologies, Tools and Techniques, Springer, New York, NY, 2015, pp. 216–224.
[2] C. Simeon, R. Hilderman, Using combined lexical resources to identify hashtag types, in: Proceedings of the Sixth Workshop on Computational Approaches to Subjectivity, Sentiment and Social Media Analysis, 2015, pp. 169–174.
[3] C. Baecchi, T. Uricchio, M. Bertini, A. Del Bimbo, A multimodal feature learning approach for sentiment analysis of social network multimedia, Multimed. Tools Appl. (2015) 1–19.
[4] Y. Zhang, L. Shang, X. Jia, Sentiment analysis on microblogging by integrating text and image features, in: Advances in Knowledge Discovery and Data Mining, Springer, New York, NY, 2015, pp. 52–63.
[5] O. Owoputi, B. OConnor, C. Dyer, K. Gimpel, N. Schneider, N.A. Smith, Improved part-of-speech tagging for online conversational text with word clusters, in: Proceedings of the 2013 Conference of the North American Chapter of the Association for Computational Linguistics: Human Language Technologies, 2013, pp. 380–390.
[6] A. Ritter, S. Clark, Mausam, O. Etzioni, Named entity recognition in tweets: an experimental study, in: Proceedings of the Conference on Empirical Methods in Natural Language Processing, Association for Computational Linguistics, 2011, pp. 1524–1534.

[7] K. Bontcheva, L. Derczynski, A. Funk, M.A. Greenwood, D. Maynard, N. Aswani, TwitIE: an open-source information extraction pipeline for microblog text, in: Proceedings of the International Conference on Recent Advances in Natural Language Processing, Association for Computational Linguistics, 2013.

[8] M. Kaufmann, J. Kalita, Syntactic normalization of Twitter messages, in: Proceedings of the International Conference on Natural Language Processing, Kharagpur, India, 2010.

[9] B. Han, P. Cook, T. Baldwin, Automatically constructing a normalisation dictionary for microblogs, in: Proceedings of the 2012 Joint Conference on Empirical Methods in Natural Language Processing and Computational Natural Language Learning, 2012, pp. 421–432.

[10] D. Terrana, A. Augello, G. Pilato, Automatic unsupervised polarity detection on a Twitter data stream, in: Proceedings of the 2014 IEEE International Conference on Semantic Computing (ICSC), 2014, pp. 128–134.

[11] D. Quercia, J. Ellis, L. Capra, J. Crowcroft, Tracking gross community happiness from tweets, in: Proceedings of the ACM 2012 Conference on Computer Supported Cooperative Work, 2012, pp. 965–968.

[12] D. Das, A.K. Kolya, A. Ekbal, S. Bandyopadhyay, Temporal analysis of sentiment events-a visual realization and tracking, in: Computational Linguistics and Intelligent Text Processing, Springer, New York, NY, 2011, pp. 417–428.

[13] M. Dermouche, J. Velcin, L. Khouas, S. Loudcher, A joint model for topic-sentiment evolution over time, in: Proceedings of the 2014 IEEE International Conference on Data Mining (ICDM), 2014, pp. 773–778.

[14] L. Mitchell, M.R. Frank, K.D. Harris, P.S. Dodds, C.M. Danforth, The geography of happiness: connecting Twitter sentiment and expression, demographics, and objective characteristics of place, PLoS ONE 8 (5) (2013) e64417.

[15] J. Li, X. Wang, E. Hovy, What a nasty day: exploring mood-weather relationship from Twitter, in: Proceedings of the 23rd ACM International Conference on Conference on Information and Knowledge Management, 2014, pp. 1309–1318.

[16] S. Volkova, T. Wilson, D. Yarowsky, Exploring demographic language variations to improve multilingual sentiment analysis in social media, in: Proceedings of the 2013 Conference on Empirical Methods in Natural Language Processing, 2013, pp. 1815–1827.

[17] S. Carter, W. Weerkamp, M. Tsagkias, Microblog language identification: overcoming the limitations of short, unedited and idiomatic text, Lang. Resour. Eval. 47 (1) (2013) 195–215.

[18] I. Habernal, T. Ptáček, J. Steinberger, Sentiment analysis in czech social media using supervised machine learning, in: Proceedings of the Fourth Workshop on Computational Approaches to Subjectivity, Sentiment and Social Media Analysis, 2013, pp. 65–74.

[19] H.K. Aldayel, A.M. Azmi, Arabic tweets sentiment analysis—a hybrid scheme, J. Inform. Sci., doi: 10.1177/0165551515610513 (2015).

[20] Z. Huang, Z. Zhao, Q. Liu, Z. Wang, An unsupervised method for short-text sentiment analysis based on analysis of massive data, in: Intelligent Computation in Big Data Era, Springer, New York, NY, 2015, pp. 169–176.

[21] V. Perez-Rosas, C. Banea, R. Mihalcea, Learning sentiment lexicons in Spanish, in: LREC, vol. 12, 2012, pp. 73.

[22] A. Balahur, J.M. Perea-Ortega, Sentiment analysis system adaptation for multilingual processing: the case of tweets, Inform. Process. Manage. 51 (4) (2015) 547–556.

[23] X. He, H. Zhang, W. Chao, D. Wang, Semi-supervised learning on cross-lingual sentiment analysis with space transfer, in: Proceedings of the IEEE First International Conference on Big Data Computing Service and Applications, 2015, pp. 371–377.

[24] J. Brooke, M. Tofiloski, M. Taboada, Cross-linguistic sentiment analysis: from English to Spanish, in: RANLP, 2009, pp. 50–54.

[25] H. Ma, Y. Zhang, Z. Du, Cross-language sentiment classification based on support vector machine, in: Proceedings of the 2015 11th International Conference on Natural Computation, 2015, pp. 507–513.

[26] M. McPherson, L. Smith-Lovin, J.M. Cook, Birds of a feather: homophily in social networks, Ann. Rev. Sociol. 27 (1) (2001) 415–444.

[27] P.F. Lazarsfeld, R.K. Merton, Friendship as a social process: a substantive and methodological analysis, in: Freedom and Control in Modern Society Van Nostrand, New York, 1954, pp. 18–66.

[28] A. Pak, P. Paroubek, Twitter as a corpus for sentiment analysis and opinion mining, in: Proceedings of the International Conference on Language Resources and Evaluation, 2010, pp. 1320–1326.

[29] E. Fersini, E. Messina, F. Pozzi, Expressive signals in social media languages to improve polarity detection, Inform. Process. Manage. 52 (1) (2016) 20–35.

[30] E. Fersini, F.A. Pozzi, E. Messina, Detecting irony and sarcasm in microblogs: the role of expressive signals and ensemble classifiers, in: Proceedings of the IEEE International Conference on Data Science and Advanced Analytics, 2015, pp. 1–8.

[31] M. Wiegand, A. Balahur, B. Roth, D. Klakow, A. Montoyo, A survey on the role of negation in sentiment analysis, in: Proceedings of the Workshop on Negation and Speculation in Natural Language Processing, 2010, pp. 60–68.

[32] N. Hollenstein, M. Amsler, M. Bachmann, M. Klenner, SA-UZH: verb-based sentiment analysis, in: Proceedings of the Eighth International Workshop on Semantic Evaluation (SemEval 2014), Association for Computational Linguistics and Dublin City University, Dublin, Ireland, 2014, pp. 503–507.

[33] E.C. Dragut, C. Fellbaum, The role of adverbs in sentiment analysis, in: ACL 2014, vol. 1929, 2014, pp. 38–41.

[34] J.B. Walther, K.P. D'addario, The impacts of emoticons on message interpretation in computer-mediated communication, Soc. Sci. Comput. Rev. 19 (2001) 324–347.

[35] J. Zhao, L. Dong, J. Wu, K. Xu, MoodLens: an emoticon-based sentiment analysis system for Chinese tweets, in: Proceedings of the 18th ACM SIGKDD International Conference on Knowledge Discovery and Data Mining, ACM, New York, NY, 2012, pp. 1528–1531.

[36] K.-L. Liu, W.-J. Li, M. Guo, Emoticon smoothed language models for Twitter sentiment analysis, in: AAAI, 2012.

[37] F. Jiang, Y.-Q. Liu, H.-B. Luan, J.-S. Sun, X. Zhu, M. Zhang, S.-P. Ma, Microblog sentiment analysis with emoticon space model, J. Comput. Sci. Technol. 30 (5) (2015) 1120–1129.

[38] M. Steinbauer, M. Indrawan-Santiago, G. Anderst-Kotsis, Y. Yamamoto, T. Kumamoto, A. Nadamoto, Multidimensional sentiment calculation method for Twitter based on emoticons, Int. J. Pervas. Comput. Commun. 11 (2) (2015) 212–232.

[39] F. Bravo-Marquez, E. Frank, B. Pfahringer, Positive, negative, or neutral: learning an expanded opinion lexicon from emoticon-annotated tweets, in: Proceedings of the 24th International Conference on Artificial Intelligence, 2015, pp. 1229–1235.

[40] M. Boia, B. Faltings, C.-C. Musat, P. Pu, A:) is worth a thousand words: how people attach sentiment to emoticons and words in tweets, in: Proceedings of the 2013 International Conference on Social Computing (SocialCom), 2013, pp. 345–350.

[41] A. Agarwal, B. Xie, I. Vovsha, O. Rambow, R. Passonneau, Sentiment analysis of Twitter data, in: Proceedings of the Workshop on Languages in Social Media, 2011, pp. 30–38.

[42] T. Igarashi, R. Sasano, H. Takamura, M. Okumura, The use of sound symbolism in sentiment classification, in: PRICAI 2012: Trends in Artificial Intelligence, Springer, New York, NY, 2012, pp. 746–752.

[43] F.A. Pozzi, E. Fersini, E. Messina, D. Blanc, Enhance polarity classification on social media through sentiment-based feature expansion, in: WOA@ AI* IA, 2013, pp. 78–84.

[44] B. Brody, N. Diakopoulos, Cooooooooooooooooolllllllllllllll!!!!!!!!!!!!!!! using word lengthening to detect sentiment in microblogs, in: Proceedings of the Conference on Empirical Methods in Natural Language Processing, 2011, pp. 561–570.

[45] S. Mukherjee, A. Malu, A.R. Balamurali, P. Bhattacharyya, TwiSent: a multistage system for analyzing sentiment in Twitter, in: Proceedings of the 21st ACM International Conference on Information and Knowledge Management, ACM, 2012, pp. 2531–2534.

[46] D. Davidov, O. Tsur, A. Rappoport, Enhanced sentiment learning using Twitter hashtags and smileys, in: Proceedings of the 23rd International Conference on Computational Linguistics: Posters, 2010, pp. 241–249.

[47] X. Wang, F. Wei, X. Liu, M. Zhou, M. Zhang, Topic sentiment analysis in Twitter: a graph-based hashtag sentiment classification approach, in: Proceedings of the 20th ACM International Conference on Information and Knowledge Management, ACM, New York, NY, 2011, pp. 1031–1040.

[48] C. Simeon, R. Hilderman, Evaluating the effectiveness of hashtags as predictors of the sentiment of tweets, in: Proceedings of Discovery Science: 18th International Conference, DS 2015, Banff, AB, Canada, October 4–6, 2015, Springer International Publishing, New York, NY, 2015, pp. 251–265.

[49] B. Pang, L. Lee, Opinion mining and sentiment analysis, Found. Trends Inf. Retr. 2 (1–2) (2008) 1–135.

[50] L. Dhande, G. Patnaik, Analyzing sentiment of movie review data using Naive Bayes neural classifier, Int. J. Emerg. Trends Technol. Comput. Sci. 3 (2014) 313–320.

[51] P. Chikersal, S. Poria, E. Cambria, SeNTU: sentiment analysis of tweets by combining a rule-based classifier with supervised learning, in: Proceedings of the International Workshop on Semantic Evaluation, SemEval, 2015, pp. 647–651.

[52] A. Severyn, A. Moschitti, Twitter sentiment analysis with deep convolutional neural networks, in: Proceedings of the 38th International ACM SIGIR Conference on Research and Development in Information Retrieval, 2015, pp. 959–962.

[53] D. Stojanovski, G. Strezoski, G. Madjarov, I. Dimitrovski, Twitter sentiment analysis using deep convolutional neural network, in: Hybrid Artificial Intelligent Systems, Springer, New York, NY, 2015, pp. 726–737.

[54] D.-T. Vo, Y. Zhang, Target-dependent Twitter sentiment classification with rich automatic features, in: Proceedings of the Twenty-Fourth International Joint Conference on Artificial Intelligence (IJCAI 2015), 2015, pp. 1347–1353.

[55] F.H. Khan, U. Qamar, S. Bashir, SWIMS: Semi-supervised subjective feature weighting and intelligent model selection for sentiment analysis, Knowledge-Based Systems 100, 2016, pp. 97–111.

[56] A. Esuli, F. Sebastiani, Sentiwordnet: a publicly available lexical resource for opinion mining, in: Proceedings of LREC, vol. 6, 2006, pp. 417–422.

[57] K.W. Church, P. Hanks, Word association norms, mutual information, and lexicography, Comput. Linguist. 16 (1) (1990) 22–29.

[58] R. Collobert, J. Weston, A unified architecture for natural language processing: deep neural networks with multitask learning, in: Proceedings of the 25th International Conference on Machine learning, 2008, pp. 160–167.

[59] N. Kalchbrenner, E. Grefenstette, P. Blunsom, A convolutional neural network for modelling sentences, in: Proceedings of the 52nd Annual Meeting of the Association for Computational Linguistics, 2014, pp. 655–665.

[60] T. Mikolov, I. Sutskever, K. Chen, G.S. Corrado, J. Dean, Distributed representations of words and phrases and their compositionality, in: Advances in Neural Information Processing Systems, 2013, pp. 3111–3119.

[61] D. Tang, F. Wei, N. Yang, M. Zhou, T. Liu, B. Qin, Learning Sentiment-specific word embedding for Twitter sentiment classification, in: ACL (1), 2014, pp. 1555–1565.

[62] F.A. Pozzi, E. Fersini, E. Messina, Bayesian model averaging and model selection for polarity classification, in: Proceedings of the 18th International Conference on Application of Natural Language to Information Systems, 2013, pp. 189–200.

[63] E. Fersini, E. Messina, F.A. Pozzi, Sentiment analysis: Bayesian ensemble learning, Decis. Support Syst. 68 (2014) 26–38.

[64] Y. Lin, X. Wang, Y. Li, A. Zhou, Integrating the optimal classifier set for sentiment analysis, Soc. Netw. Anal. Min. 5 (1) (2015) 1–13.

[65] G. Wang, J. Sun, J. Ma, K. Xu, J. Gu, Sentiment classification: the contribution of ensemble learning, Decis. Support Syst. 57 (2014) 77–93.

[66] N.F. da Silva, E.R. Hruschka, E.R. Hruschka, Tweet sentiment analysis with classifier ensembles, Decis. Support Syst. 66 (2014) 170–179.

[67] P. Zhang, Z. He, Using data-driven feature enrichment of text representation and ensemble technique for sentence-level polarity classification, J. Inform. Sci. 41 (4) (2015) 531–549.

[68] J.R. Quinlan, Bagging, boosting, and C4.5, in: Proceedings of the 13th National Conference on Artificial Intelligence, 1996, pp. 725–730.

[69] K. Weinberger, A. Dasgupta, J. Langford, A. Smola, J. Attenberg, Feature hashing for large scale multitask learning, in: Proceedings of the 26th Annual International Conference on Machine Learning, 2009, pp. 1113–1120.

[70] Z. Zhu, D. Dai, Y. Ding, J. Qian, S. Li, Employing emotion keywords to improve cross-domain sentiment classification, in: Chinese Lexical Semantics, Springer, New York, NY, 2012, pp. 64–71.

[71] S. Ju, S. Li, Y. Su, G. Zhou, Y. Hong, X. Li, Dual word and document seed selection for semi-supervised sentiment classification, in: Proceedings of the 21st ACM International Conference on Information and Knowledge Management, 2012, pp. 2295–2298.

[72] L. Becker, G. Erhart, D. Skiba, V. Matula, Avaya: sentiment analysis on Twitter with self-training and polarity lexicon expansion, in: Proceedings of the Second Joint Conference on Lexical and Computational Semantics (* SEM), vol. 2, 2013, pp. 333–340.

[73] W. Baugh, bwbaugh: hierarchical sentiment analysis with partial self-training, in: Proceedings of the Second Joint Conference on Lexical and Computational Semantics (* SEM), vol. 2, 2013, pp. 539.

[74] Z. Liu, X. Dong, Y. Guan, J. Yang, Reserved self-training: a semi-supervised sentiment classification method for Chinese microblogs, in: Proceedings of the Sixth International Joint Conference on Natural Language Processing, Asian Federation of Natural Language Processing, Nagoya, Japan, 2013, pp. 455–462.

[75] M. Yang, W. Tu, Z. Lu, W. Yin, K.-P. Chow, LCCT: a semi-supervised model for sentiment classification, in: Human Language Technologies: Proceedings of the 2015 Annual Conference of the North American Chapter of the ACL, 2015, pp. 546–555.

[76] H.-Y. Chen, J.-T. Chien, Deep semi-supervised learning for domain adaptation, in: Proceedings of the 2015 IEEE 25th International Workshop on Machine Learning for Signal Processing (MLSP), 2015, pp. 1–6.

[77] S. Liu, W. Zhu, N. Xu, F. Li, X.-q. Cheng, Y. Liu, Y. Wang, Co-training and visualizing sentiment evolvement for tweet events, in: Proceedings of the 22nd International Conference on World Wide Web Companion, 2013, pp. 105–106.

[78] J. Zhao, M. Lan, T. Zhu, ECNU: expression- and message-level sentiment orientation classification in Twitter using multiple effective features, in: Proceedings of the Eighth International Workshop on Semantic Evaluation (SemEval 2014), Association for Computational Linguistics and Dublin City University, Dublin, Ireland, 2014, pp. 259–264.

[79] D. Yarowsky, Unsupervised word sense disambiguation rivaling supervised methods, in: Proceedings of the 33rd Annual Meeting on Association for Computational Linguistics, 1995, pp. 189–196.

[80] A. Blum, T. Mitchell, Combining labeled and unlabeled data with co-training, in: Proceedings of the Eleventh Annual Conference on Computational Learning Theory, 1998, pp. 92–100.

[81] C. Strapparava, A. Valitutti, et al., WordNet affect: an affective extension of WordNet, in: LREC, vol. 4, 2004, pp. 1083–1086.

[82] P.D. Turney, Thumbs up or thumbs down?: Semantic orientation applied to unsupervised classification of reviews, in: Proceedings of the 40th Annual Meeting on Association for Computational Linguistics, Association for Computational Linguistics, 2002, pp. 417–424.

[83] T. Zagibalov, J. Carroll, Automatic seed word selection for unsupervised sentiment classification of Chinese text, in: Proceedings of the 22Nd International Conference on Computational Linguistics—Volume 1, Association for Computational Linguistics, 2008, pp. 1073–1080.

[84] S. Huang, Z. Niu, C. Shi, Automatic construction of domain-specific sentiment lexicon based on constrained label propagation, Knowl. Based Syst. 56 (2014) 191–200.

[85] Y. Lu, M. Castellanos, U. Dayal, C. Zhai, Automatic construction of a context-aware sentiment lexicon: an optimization approach, in: Proceedings of the 20th International Conference on World Wide Web, 2011, pp. 347–356.

[86] Y. Jo, A.H. Oh, Aspect and sentiment unification model for online review analysis, in: Proceedings of the Fourth ACM International Conference on Web Search and Data Mining, ACM, 2011, pp. 815–824.

[87] Q. Mei, X. Ling, M. Wondra, H. Su, C. Zhai, Topic sentiment mixture: modeling facets and opinions in weblogs, in: Proceedings of the 16th International Conference on World Wide Web, ACM, 2007, pp. 171–180.

[88] C. Lin, Y. He, Joint sentiment/topic model for sentiment analysis, in: Proceedings of the 18th ACM Conference on Information and Knowledge Management, ACM, 2009, pp. 375–384.

[89] Y. He, C. Lin, W. Gao, K.-F. Wong, Dynamic joint sentiment-topic model, ACM Trans. Intell. Syst. Technol. 5 (1) (2013) 6.

[90] T. Hofmann, Probabilistic latent semantic indexing, in: Proceedings of the 22nd Annual International ACM SIGIR Conference on Research and Development in Information Retrieval, 1999, pp. 50–57.

[91] D.M. Blei, A.Y. Ng, M.I. Jordan, Latent dirichlet allocation, J. Mach. Learn. Res. 3 (2003) 993–1022.

[92] J. Rabelo, R.B. Prudencio, F. Barros, Collective classification for sentiment analysis in social networks, in: Proceedings of the 2012 IEEE 24th International Conference on Tools with Artificial Intelligence (ICTAI), vol. 1, 2012, pp. 958–963.

[93] X. Hu, L. Tang, J. Tang, H. Liu, Exploiting social relations for sentiment analysis in microblogging, in: Proceedings of the Sixth ACM International Conference on Web Search and Data Mining, 2013, pp. 537–546.

[94] L. Coviello, Y. Sohn, A.D. Kramer, C. Marlow, M. Franceschetti, N.A. Christakis, J.H. Fowler, Detecting emotional contagion in massive social networks, PLoS ONE 9 (3) (2014) e90315.

[95] L. Jiang, M. Yu, M. Zhou, X. Liu, T. Zhao, Target-dependent Twitter sentiment classification, in: Proceedings of the 49th Annual Meeting of the Association for Computational Linguistics: Human Language Technologies—Volume 1, 2011, pp. 151–160.

[96] R. Angelova, G. Weikum, Graph-based text classification: learn from your neighbors, in: Proceedings of the 29th Annual International ACM SIGIR Conference on Research and Development in Information Retrieval, 2006, pp. 485–492.

[97] M. Anjaria, R.M.R. Guddeti, A novel sentiment analysis of social networks using supervised learning, Soc. Netw. Anal. Min. 4 (1) (2014) 1–15.

[98] Y.-H. Kuo, M.-H. Fu, W.-H. Tsai, K.-R. Lee, L.-Y. Chen, Integrated microblog sentiment analysis from users social interaction patterns and textual opinions, Appl. Intell. (2015) 1–15.

[99] C. Tan, L. Lee, J. Tang, L. Jiang, M. Zhou, P. Li, User-level sentiment analysis incorporating social networks, in: Proceedings of the 17th ACM SIGKDD International Conference on Knowledge Discovery and Data Mining, 2011, pp. 1397–1405.

[100] M. Speriosu, N. Sudan, S. Upadhyay, J. Baldridge, Twitter polarity classification with label propagation over lexical links and the follower graph, in: Proceedings of the First Workshop on Unsupervised Learning in NLP, 2011, pp. 53–63.

[101] J.C. Rabelo, R.B. Prudêncio, F.A. Barros, Using link structure to infer opinions in social networks, in: Proceedings of the 2012 IEEE International Conference on Systems, Man, and Cybernetics (SMC), 2012, pp. 681–685.

[102] J. Tang, C. Nobata, A. Dong, Y. Chang, H. Liu, Propagation-based sentiment analysis for microblogging data, in: Proceedings of the SIAM International Conference on Data Mining, SIAM, 2015.

[103] F.A. Pozzi, D. Maccagnola, E. Fersini, E. Messina, Enhance user-level sentiment analysis on microblogs with approval relations, in: AI*IA 2013: Advances in Artificial Intelligence, vol. 8249, Springer International Publishing, New York, NY, 2013, pp. 133–144.

[104] D. Nozza, D. Maccagnola, V. Guigue, E. Messina, P. Gallinari, A latent representation model for sentiment analysis in heterogeneous social networks, in: C. Canal, A. Idani (Eds.), Software Engineering and Formal Methods: SEFM 2014 Collocated Workshops: HOFM, SAFOME, OpenCert, MoKMaSD, WS-FMDS, Grenoble, France, September 1–2, 2014, Revised Selected Papers, Springer International Publishing, New York, NY, 2015, pp. 201–213.

[105] X. Zhou, X. Wan, J. Xiao, Collective opinion target extraction in Chinese microblogs, in: EMNLP, vol. 13, 2013, pp. 1840–1850.

[106] G. Ou, W. Chen, B. Li, T. Wang, D. Yang, K.-F. Wong, CLUSM: an unsupervised model for microblog sentiment analysis incorporating link information, in: Proceedings of the Database Systems for Advanced Applications, 2014, pp. 481–494.

[107] L. Zhu, A. Galstyan, J. Cheng, K. Lerman, Tripartite graph clustering for dynamic sentiment analysis on social media, in: Proceedings of the 2014 ACM SIGMOD International Conference on Management of data, 2014, pp. 1531–1542.

[108] A.B. Goldberg, X. Zhu, S.J. Wright, Dissimilarity in graph-based semi-supervised classification, in: AISTATS, vol. 2, 2007, pp. 155–162.

[109] M. Cheong, V.C.S. Lee, A microblogging-based approach to terrorism informatics: exploration and chronicling civilian sentiment and response to terrorism events via Twitter, Inform. Syst. Front. 13 (1) (2011) 45–59.

[110] R. Arunachalam, S. Sarkar, The new eye of government: citizen sentiment analysis in social media, in: Sixth International Joint Conference on Natural Language Processing, 2013, pp. 23.

[111] N.K. Cobb, D. Mays, A.L. Graham, Sentiment analysis to determine the impact of online messages on smokers' choices to use varenicline, J. Natl. Cancer Inst. Monogr. 47 (2013) 224–230.

[112] J. Si, A. Mukherjee, B. Liu, Q. Li, H. Li, X. Deng, Exploiting topic based Twitter sentiment for stock prediction, in: ACL, 2013, pp. 24–29.

[113] J. Bollen, H. Mao, X. Zeng, Twitter mood predicts the stock market, J. Comput. Sci. 2 (1) (2011) 1–8.

[114] G. Ranco, D. Aleksovski, G. Caldarelli, M. Grčar, I. Mozetič, The effects of Twitter sentiment on stock price returns, PLoS ONE 10 (9) (2015) e0138441.

IRONY, SARCASM, AND SENTIMENT ANALYSIS

7

D.I. Hernández Farias[a,b], P. Rosso[a]

Technical University of Valencia, Valencia, Spain[a] University of Turin, Turin, Italy[b]

1 INTRODUCTION

Everyday, people make judgments about their environment. This is an inherent behavior of humans. There are different ways to express our opinions, one of the most interesting is by figurative language devices such as irony and sarcasm. This allows us to express ourselves in a particular way using words not only in their most salient meaning but also in a creative and funny sense. The use of words or expressions with a meaning that is different from the literal interpretation is known as *figurative language*.

Irony and sarcasm are two interesting and strongly related concepts. Usually people do not have a clear idea of what they are. However, from early childhood we begin to use them in our daily life. They have been a topic studied by different disciplines, such as linguistics, philosophy, psychology, psycholinguistics, cognitive science, and recently computational linguistics. Each discipline has tried to define what they are, how they are produced, and why they are used.

These figurative devices give us the opportunity to explore the interaction between cognition and language. Broadly speaking, irony and sarcasm are figurative language devices that serve to achieve different communication purposes. The commonest definition of irony refers to an utterance by which the speaker expresses a meaning opposite that literally said. There are different theories that attempt to explain what irony is. Grice's theory [1] points out that the speaker intentionally violates the "maxim of quality" (the speaker does not say what he or she believes to be false) when he or she expresses an ironic utterance. Some theories such the one described in [2] propose define it beyond the literal sense of the words: for Wilson and Sperber [2] an ironic utterance is an "echoic mention" that alludes to some real or hypothetical proposition to demonstrate its absurdity. Attardo [3] considers an ironic utterance as a form of "relevant inappropriateness" in which the speaker relies on the ability of the listener to reject the literal meaning on the basis of the disparity between what is literally said and the context in which it is said. On the other hand, the "failed expectation" intention (ie, the speaker's approval or disapproval of the entity or situation at hand) behind an ironic expression has been studied by Utsumi [4] and Kumon-Nakamura and Glucksberg [5].

Usually, *irony* is considered as a broader term that covers also sarcasm [6,7]. Irony may be positive (ie, noncritical), while sarcasm usually is not [8,9]. Sarcasm is commonly more aggressive and offensive than irony. In this work irony and sarcasm are treated as two different concepts.

Social media offer a face-saving way for people to express themselves, and they sometimes choose to use ironic or sarcastic utterances to communicate their attitude or evaluative judgment toward a particular target (eg, a public person, a product, a movie, or an event). The presence of ironic or sarcastic content in human communication may cause misunderstandings. Identification of this intention is not a trivial task even for humans: different cognitive processes are involved and knowledge of the environment is needed. For natural language processing tasks such as sentiment analysis, this kind of subjective user-generated content is a big challenge. In some cases the presence of ironic content plays a particular role: "polarity reversal." This means, for instance, that an utterance seems to be positive but its real intention is negative (or vice versa).

We introduce the following example, extracted from an ironic set of Amazon reviews collected by Filatova [10]: "*I would recomend this book to friends who have insomnia or those who I absolutely despise.*"[1] For a sentiment analysis system that exploits the basic approach of considering the frequency of positive and negative terms to assign a polarity, this sentence could be considered as positive. The words *recomend (recommend)*, *book*, and *friends* are positive terms, while *insomnia* and *despise* denote a negative sense. Therefore in the sentence there are three positive terms and two negative terms, and the sentence could be identified as positive. However, this review conveys a meaning far from positive. The author expresses a negative judgment against the book in an imaginative way. On one hand, the author writes about recommending the book, which can be considered as a positive aspect about the target (the book), but at the same time there is a point about "friends who have insomnia" or "those who I absolutely despise." Thus the author's hidden intention could be to state that the "book" is so boring as to induce sleep (even in those who have insomnia). Research in irony could not only improve the performance of sentiment analysis systems but could also help us to understand the cognitive process involved and how humans process and produce utterances of this kind. After introducing the state of the art in irony and sarcasm detection, we investigate the impact that the use of these figurative language devices may have on sentiment analysis.

This chapter is organized as follows. In Section 2 we describe the state of the art in irony and sarcasm detection. In Section 3 we address the impact that figurative language has on sentiment analysis. We analyze three shared tasks that have been recently organized. Section 4 discusses future trends and directions. In Section 5 we draw some conclusions.

2 IRONY AND SARCASM DETECTION

Irony and sarcasm detection are considered as special cases of text classification, where the main goal is to distinguish ironic (or sarcastic) texts from nonironic (or nonsarcastic) ones. To analyze figurative devices of this kind, it is necessary to consider not only the syntactic and lexical textual level (to extract salient features such as word position and punctuation marks) but also semantics (literal vs. nonliteral

---

[1]In this ironic utterance two examples of misspelling in social media texts can be noted. The author writes "recomend" instead of "recommend" and "who" rather than "whom".

meaning of the words), pragmatics (words matching with the appropriate context), and discourse analysis (relation between the utterance at hand and the way in which it is expressed). However, the progress so far has been a result of the use of mainly syntactic, lexical, and shallow semantics.

Dealing with social media texts is a challenging task. They have specific characteristics: they are informal and use ill-formed language. People express themselves in a face-saving way by unstructured content. Usually, social media texts contain spelling mistakes, abbreviations, and slang. In Twitter, the text should be written in a maximum of 140 characters; therefore figurative language is expressed in a very concise manner, which causes an additional issue. When people express their opinions by ironic or sarcastic utterances, they can choose how to use the language to achieve their communicative goals. There is no particular structure to construct ironic or sarcastic utterances.

In a such way the main objective of irony and sarcasm detection is to discover features that allow us to discriminate ironic (or sarcastic) texts from nonironic (or nonsarcastic) texts. The interest in irony and sarcasm detection in social media requires we have user-generated data that allow us to capture the real use of figurative language devices of this kind. As in most natural language processing tasks, the lack of corpora is an issue. There are two main approaches for ironic/sarcastic corpus construction: self-tagging and crowdsourcing. The first one considers as positive instances those texts in which the author points out her intention using an explicit label (eg, the hashtags #irony and #sarcasm). Therefore in this case we rely on the author's definition of what irony or sarcasm is. Crowdsourcing involves human interaction by the labeling of the content as ironic (or sarcastic). Mainly, the labeling process is done without any strict definition or guideline. Therefore it is a subjective task, where the agreement between annotators is often very low. In this way it is possible to obtain potential ironic and sarcastic texts produced by people in social media.

For computational linguistic purposes, *irony* and *sarcasm* are often considered as synonyms. The following subsections describe some proposed approaches to address irony and sarcasm detection. The first one is focused on work where the ironic intention was considered as an overall term, while the second one is focused on research where sarcasm was considered as a different concept.

2.1 IRONY DETECTION

One of the first studies in irony detection was by Carvalho et al. [11]. They worked on the identification of a set of surface patterns to identify ironic sentences in a Portuguese online newspaper. The most relevant features were the use of punctuation marks and emoticons. Veale and Hao [12] conducted an experiment by harvesting the web, looking for a commonly used framing device for linguistic irony: the simile (two queries "as * as *" and "about as * as *" were used to retrieve snippets from the web). They analyzed a very large corpus to identify characteristics of ironic comparisons, and presented a set of rules to classify a simile as ironic or nonironic.

Reyes et al. [13] analyzed tweets tagged with the hashtags #irony and #humor to identify textual features for distinguishing between them. They proposed a model that includes structural, morphosyntactic, semantic and psychological features. Additionally, they considered the polarity expressed in a tweet using the Macquarie Semantic Orientation Lexicon.[2] They experimented with

---

[2]http://www.saifmohammad.com/Release/MSOL-June15-09.txt

different feature sets and a decision tree classifier, obtaining encouraging results (*F* measure of approximately 0.80).

Afterward, Reyes et al. [14] collected a corpus composed of 40,000 tweets, relying on the "self-tagged" approach. Four different hashtags were selected: #irony, #education, #politics, and #humor. Their model is organized according to four types of conceptual features—signatures (such as punctuation marks, emoticons, and discursive terms), unexpectedness (opposition, incongruency, and inconsistency in a text), style (recurring sequences of textual elements), and emotional scenarios (elements that symbolize sentiment, attitude, feeling, and mood)—by exploiting the Dictionary of Affect in Language (DAL).[3] They addressed the problem as a binary classification task, distinguishing ironic tweets from nonironic tweets by using naïve Bayes and decision tree classifiers. They achieved an average *F* measure of 0.70.

Barbieri and Saggion [15] proposed a model to detect irony using lexical features, such as the frequency of rare and common terms, punctuation marks, emoticons, synonyms, adjectives, and positive and negative terms. They compared their approach with that of Reyes et al. [14] on the same corpus using a decision tree, and obtained results slightly better than those previously obtained. They concluded that rare words, synonyms ,and punctuation marks seem to be the most discriminating features. Hernández-Farías et al. [16] described an approach for irony detection that uses a set of surface text properties enriched with sentiment analysis features. They exploited two widely applied sentiment analysis lexicons: Hu&Liu[4] and AFINN.[5] They experimented with the same dataset used in [14,15]. Their proposal was evaluated with use of a set of classifiers composed of Naïve bayes, decision tree, support vector machine (SVM), multilayer perceptron, and logistic regression classifiers. The proposed model improved on the previous results (*F* measure of approximately 0.79). The features related to sentiment analysis were the most relevant.

Buschmeier et al. [17] presented a classification approach using the Amazon review corpus collected by Filatova [10], which contains both ironic and nonironic reviews annotated by Mechanical Turk crowdsourcing. They proposed a model that takes into account features such as *n*-grams, punctuation marks, interjections, emoticons, and the star rating of each review (a particular feature from Amazon reviews, which, according to the authors, seems to help result in good performance in the task. They experimented with a set of classifiers (composed of naïve Bayes, logistic regression, decision tree, random forest, and SVM classifiers), achieving an *F*-measure rate of 0.74.

Wallace et al. [18] attempted to undertake the study of irony detection using contextual features, specifically by combining noun phrases and sentiment extracted from comments. They proposed exploiting information regarding the conversational threads to which comments belong. Their approach capitalizes on the intuition that members of different user communities are likely to be sarcastic about different things. A dataset of comments posted on Reddit[6] was used.[7]

Karoui et al. [19] recently presented an approach to separate ironic from nonironic tweets written in French. They proposed a two-stage model. In the first part they addressed the irony detection as a

---

[3]http://www.cs.columbia.edu/~julia/papers/dict_of_affect/
[4]The resource is freely available: https://www.cs.uic.edu/~liub/FBS/sentiment-analysis.html#lexicon.
[5]The resource is freely available: http://github.com/abromberg/sentiment_analysis/blob/master/AFINN/AFINN-111.txt.
[6]http://www.reddit.com
[7]Particularly comments posted on two pairs of polarized user communities (or subreddits) were selected: progressive and conservative subreddits (related to the US political spectrum) and atheism and Christianity subreddits.

binary classification problem. Then the misclassified instances are processed by an algorithm that tries to correct them by querying Google to check the veracity of tweets with negation. They represented each tweet with a vector composed of six groups of features: surface (such as punctuation marks, emoticons, and uppercase letters), sentiment (positive and negative words), sentiment shifter (positive and negative words in the scope of an intensifier), shifter (presence of an intensifier, a negation word, or reporting speech verbs), opposition (sentiment opposition or contrast between a subjective and an objective proposition), and internal contextual (the presence/absence of personal pronouns, topic keywords, and named entities). The authors experimented with an SVM as a classifier, achieving an F measure of 0.87.

To sum up, several approaches have been proposed to detect irony as a classification task. Many of the features employed have already been used in various tasks related to sentiment analysis such as polarity classification. The ironic intention is captured by the exploitation of mainly surface features such as punctuation marks and emoticons. These kinds of lexical cues have been shown to be useful to distinguish ironic content, especially in tweets. It may confirm in some way the necessity of users to add textual markers to deal with the absence of paralinguistic cues. Besides, many authors point out the importance of capturing the inherent incongruity in ironic utterances. To achieve this goal, the presence of opposite polarities (positive and negative words) and the use of semantically unrelated terms (synonyms and antonyms) have been considered in many approaches. Both kinds of features seem to be relevant to distinguish ironic from nonironic utterances. Decision trees are among the classifiers that produced the best results.

2.2 SARCASM DETECTION

To determine whether specific lexical factors (eg, the use of some part of speech or punctuation marks) play a role in sarcasm detection, Kreuz and Caucci [20] asked some college students to read excerpts from paragraphs that originally contained the "said sarcastically" sentence (removed before the task). The participants were able to distinguish sarcastic from nonsarcastic utterances. This work represents a key to consider the influence that lexical factors can have in the analysis of social media content.

One of the first approaches that considered the #sarcasm hashtag as an indicator of sarcastic content was developed by Davidov et al. [21]. They introduced a semisupervised algorithm for sarcasm detection that considers as features frequent words, punctuation marks, and syntactic patterns so as to identify sarcastic utterances. They collected a dataset from both Amazon and Twitter; their results seem to be promising, with F measures close to 0.80.

Gonzalez et al. [22] performed an experiment on two datasets: a set of self-tagged tweets and a manually annotated set. They considered as sarcastic instances a set of self-tagged tweets containing the #sarcasm or #sarcastic hashtag, and as nonsarcastic instances some positive and negative tweets (retrieved with use of different hashtags, such as #happy, #joy, and #lucky and #sadness, #angry, and #frustrated respectively). As features they considered interjections and emoticons as well as some resources such as LIWC[8] and WordNet-Affect.[9] They attempted to distinguish between sarcastic, positive, and negative tweets. They applied an SVM and logistic regression as classifiers. Their reported

---

[8]http://www.liwc.net
[9]http://wndomains.fbk.eu/wnaffect.html

results are related to both datasets; the overall accuracy rate was around 0.57. They suggested that their results demonstrate the difficulty of sarcasm detection for both humans and machine learning methods.

According to Riloff et al. [23], a common form of sarcasm in Twitter consists of a positive sentiment contrasting with a negative situation (eg, *absolutely adore it when my bus is late #sarcasm*). The goal of their research was to recognize sarcasm instances containing this pattern.[10] They presented a boot-strapping algorithm that automatically learns phrases corresponding to negative situations. As sarcastic instances for the learning process, tweets that contained a sarcasm hashtag were retrieved. From the bootstrapping process they collected some positive sentiment verb phrases, predicative expressions, and negative situation phrases. They also performed some binary classification experiments using an SVM classifier. They used a set of features that contain not only their list of phrases but also n-grams and three sentiment and subjectivity lexicons (Hu&Liu, AFINN, and MPQA[11]). The best result (F measure 0.51) was achieved by a hybrid approach where a tweet is considered as sarcastic if either it contains a contrast (according to their list of phrases) or it is identified as such by the SVM (with unigram and bigram features).

Wang [24] presented a study to identify similarities and distinctions between irony and sarcasm. The study consisted of a quantitative sentiment analysis and a qualitative content analysis. A set of sarcastic and ironic tweets collected by the self-tagging approach was used. She found that sarcastic tweets were more positive that ironic ones.

Barbieri et al. [25] attempted to study the differences between ironic and sarcastic tweets. They addressed the problem as a binary classification task between tweets tagged with the #irony and #sarcasm hashtags. Their system is similar to the one presented in [15] for irony detection; they included two new features in their model: if a tweet contains a URL and named entities. The model was evaluated with use of a decision tree as a classifier. They obtained an F measure of 0.62; this result emphasizes the difficulty to distinguish between irony and sarcasm. Barbieri et al. mentioned the two most relevant features to distinguish between ironic and sarcastic tweets: the use of adverbs (more intense ones in sarcastic samples) and the sentiment value (sarcastic tweets are denoted by more positive words than ironic tweets).

Fersini et al. [26] addressed sarcasm detection by introducing an ensemble approach (the Bayesian model average). As features they used emoticons, punctuation marks, onomatopoeic expressions, part-of-speech labels, and a bag of words. They collected a set of tweets using the #sarcasm and #sarcastic hashtags, then three annotators were asked to determine the presence of sarcastic content in tweets. They also evaluated the ensemble method over the corpus presented in [14]. Their results, around 0.8 in F-measure terms in both corpora, seem to indicate that this strategy outperforms those that use traditional classifiers.

Rajadesingan et al. [27] developed a framework for sarcasm detection that uses a behavioral modeling approach. It defines some criteria so as to determine whether a tweet is sarcastic or not, by leveraging behavioral traits (using some of the user's past tweets) and textual-content features (such as punctuation marks, uppercase words, and parts of speech). Rajadesingan et al. collected tweets that contain the #sarcasm and #not hashtags as sarcastic instances; as negative instances the last 80 tweets from each sarcastic sample's author were retrieved. A binary classification task was performed between the sarcastic and nonsarcastic instances with use of decision tree, logistic regression, and SVM classifiers. Their results seem to be good, reaching rates above 0.70 in terms or accuracy.

---

[10]To identify "stereotypically" perceived negative situations is per se a big challenge.
[11]http://mpqa.cs.pitt.edu/lexicons/subj_lexicon/

A similar approach is that of Bamman and Smith [28], who stated that modeling the relationship between a sarcastic tweet and the author's past tweets can improve accuracy. They presented some experiments to discern the effect of sarcasm by using features derived not only from the local context of the message itself (words in the tweet and parts of speech, among others). They also used information about the author, the relationship with his or her audience, and the immediate communicative context they both share (such as salient historical terms and topics and profile information). For evaluation purposes, all tweets with #sarcasm or #sarcastic in the GardenHose sample of tweets in the period from August 2013 to July 2014 were used as sarcastic instances, while for the nonsarcastic ones the 3200 most recent tweets from each "sarcastic author" (ie, the user who posted a tweet labeled with #sarcasm or #sarcastic in the subset) were retrieved. As a classifier a binary logistic regression was employed, achieving an accuracy of 0.851.

To sum up, there is a consistent body of work focused on sarcasm detection. It is a controversial issue whether irony and sarcasm are considered to be similar linguistic phenomena. Almost the same features used for irony detection have been employed for sarcasm detection. Among the most widely applied features we mention punctuation marks and part-of-speech labels. As classifiers, logistic regression and SVMs have been the most used ones for sarcasm detection. Recent approaches on sarcasm detection consider information beyond the text itself, exploiting contextual information and information about the user.

3 FIGURATIVE LANGUAGE AND SENTIMENT ANALYSIS

In recent years the interest in understanding the role of irony and sarcasm in sentiment analysis has derived from different evaluation campaigns. Their main objective is not to identify ironic or sarcastic content but to develop systems that will be able to correctly classify the polarity of figurative language social media texts. The presence of figurative language devices such irony and sarcasm usually causes a polarity reversal. Irony and sarcasm detection is a necessary and important part for a sentiment analysis system because the performance of the latter is affected by the performance of the former. Maynard and Greenwood [29] performed an experiment to measure the effect of sarcasm on the polarity of tweets. They proposed a set of rules to improve the accuracy of sentiment analysis when sarcasm is present.

In the following, three different evaluation campaigns are introduced. In Section 3.1 we describe a pilot subtask to identify ironic content. A sentiment classification task in Twitter for both sarcastic and nonsarcastic social media text is presented in Section 3.2. Finally, a recent sentiment analysis task wholly dedicated to figurative language in Twitter is described in Section 3.3.

3.1 SENTIMENT POLARITY CLASSIFICATION AT EVALITA 2014

In the context of Evalita[12] 2014, the sentiment polarity classification task [30] was organized. Its main focus was the sentiment classification at the message level of Italian tweets. The task was divided into three independent subtasks: (1) subjectivity classification; (2) polarity classification, and (3) irony

[12]Evalita is an initiative devoted to the evaluation of natural language processing and speech tools for Italian: http://www.evalita.it/.

detection. Participants were provided with a dataset composed of a collection of 6448 tweets in Italian (70% for training and 30% for the test) derived from two existing corpora: SENTI-TUT [31] and TWITA [32]. Each tweet in the dataset was labeled according to subjectivity (subjective or objective), polarity (positive, negative, neutral, or mixed) and the presence of ironic content. The systems were evaluated by means of the F measure for each subtask. Eleven teams participated in the sentiment polarity classification task (further information about each system can be found in [33]). Table 7.1 summarizes the results obtained[13] by the teams that participated in the irony detection task.

All the participants outperformed the established baseline. The performance rates as the F measure for both subjectivity and polarity classification were near 0.70, while on subtask 3 the values were below 0.60. This confirms the difficulty of the ironic content–related subtask. The best ranked team for the first two subtasks (UNIBA2930 [34]) did not participate in the irony detection task (see Table 7.1). No system was developed to address particularly the irony detection subtask.

Most systems used supervised learning, and the SVM algorithm was the most popular. One further challenge for this task was the lack of Italian resources as well as natural language processing tools (such as tokenizers and part-of-speech taggers); however, some systems (eg, UNIBA2930 and IRADABE) translated some of the resources available in English into Italian. For classification purposes a variety of features were used such as a bag of words, punctuation marks, emoticons, and Twitter language markers (such as hashtags and mentions). UNITOR [35], the best ranked system in irony detection, proposed an "ironic vector" that captures the presence of some features such as punctuation marks, emoticons, a bag of words, and a sentiment analyis resource in Italian called Sentix[14] to train an SVM classifier. IRADABE [36] exploited two different sets of features: textual

Table 7.1 Sentiment Polarity Classification Task Results in *F*-Measure Terms			
Team	**Task 1**	**Task 2**	**Task 3**
UNIBA2930	0.71	0.67	–
UNITOR	0.68	0.62	0.57
IRADABE	0.67	0.63	0.54
SVMSLU	0.58	0.60	0.53
ITGETARUNS	0.52	0.51	0.49
Mind	0.59	0.53	0.47
fbkshelldkm	0.55	0.56	0.47
UPFtaln	0.64	0.60	0.46
Baseline	0.40	0.37	0.44

---

[13]For each task, two runs could be submitted: constrained (with use of only the training data provided) and unconstrained (with use of additional data for training). Table 7.1 presents the results for the constrained run; only three teams (UNIBA2930, UNITOR, and IRADABE) participated in both the constrained run and the unconstrained run on the three subtasks.
[14]http://wikis.fu-berlin.de/pages/viewpage.action?pageId=671548598

(eg, *n*-grams, emoticons, parts of speech, and uppercase words), and information extracted from the in-house Italian version of English resources such as AFINN, SentiWordNet,[15] Hu&Liu, DAL, and temporal compression and counterfactuality terms[16] together with an SVM classifier. The SVMSLU [37] system addressed the problem using an SVM for classification of binary vectors of tokens together with punctuation marks, hashtags, and retweet marks. In ITGETARUNS [38] a set of linguistic rules was defined to classify the tweets; the author considered some markers such as intensifiers and diminishers and modal verbs. The Mind system [39] is based on a multilayer Bayesian ensemble learning; the authors addressed the task under a hierarchical framework. If a given sentence is detected as ironic, then its positive or negative polarity is reversed. On the other hand, if the sentence is ironic but its polarity has been classified as mixed, then it is switched to negative. The system takes into account only a vector composed of terms for which a Boolean weight was computed; no additional information was added. The description of the fbkshelldkm system is not available on the proceedings of the task.

Finally, the UPFtaln [40] system addressed the task by a decision tree classifier. This approach is similar to the one presented in [15] for irony detection. The main difference is the use of Italian resources: Italian WordNet 1.6,[17] Sentix, and the CoLFIS corpus.[18]

3.2 SENTIMENT ANALYSIS IN TWITTER AT SEMEVAL 2014 AND 2015

In recent years, as part of SemEval,[19] a task on sentiment analysis in Twitter has been organized [41–43]. The participating systems were required to assign one of the following labels: positive, negative, or objective (neutral). The organizers provided two datasets[20] for training and the test, composed of social media texts, mainly from Twitter.

In both 2014 and 2015 the participating systems were evaluated also on a subset of sarcastic tweets. In 2014 a small set of tweets that contained #sarcasm was added to the test set, whereas in 2015 a set of tweets were manually labeled as "sarcastic" by human annotators. In Table 7.2 we show the seven best performing systems among the 44 participating systems.

The results obtained for the best ranked teams in the 2015 edition are shown in Table 7.3. The overall drop in the *F* measure between regular and sarcastic tweets is slightly less than in 2014. From the tables it can be seen there is an important drop in the performance when the systems were evaluated on the sarcastic tweets. Generally, sentiment analysis systems produce good results for regular content, but when the same systems are evaluated with sarcastic content the overall performance is affected. None of the proposed approaches directly tried to capture the sarcastic intention. All systems addressed the task as a supervised approach, taking into account features widely applied in sentiment analysis tasks such as a bag of words, part-of-speech tags, and punctuation marks.

Some of the systems used well-known resources such as, AFINN, Hu&Liu, and SentiWordNet. A more detailed description of the shared task and the participating systems can be found in [41,42].

---

[15]http://sentiwordnet.isti.cnr.it/

[16]The last three resources were previously used for irony detection in English by Reyes et al. [14].

[17]http://multiwordnet.fbk.eu/english/home.php

[18]http://linguistica.sns.it/CoLFIS/Home.htm

[19]SemEval is an ongoing series of evaluations of computational semantic analysis systems.

[20]More details about it can be found in [41,42].

Table 7.2 Sentiment Analysis Task in F-Measure Terms for Both Regular and Sarcastic Tweets in the 2014 Edition of SemEval

System	Twitter 2014	Sarcasm 2014
TeamX	70.96	56.50
coooolll	70.14	46.66
RTRGO	69.95	47.09
NRC-Canada	69.85	58.16
TUGAS	69.00	52.87
CISUC_KIS	67.95	55.49
SAIL	67.77	57.26

Table 7.3 Best Results in the Sentiment Analysis Task in F-Measure Terms for Both Regular and Sarcastic Tweets in the 2015 Edition of SemEval

System	Twitter 2015	Sarcasm 2015
Webis	64.84	53.59
unitn	64.59	55.01
lsislif	64.27	46.00
INESC-ID	64.17	64.91
Splusplus	63.73	60.99
wxiaoac	0.63	52.22
IOA	62.62	65.77

3.3 SENTIMENT ANALYSIS OF FIGURATIVE LANGUAGE IN TWITTER AT SEMEVAL 2015

Task 11 at SemEval 2015[21] was the first sentiment analysis task addressing figurative language devices such as irony, sarcasm, and metaphors. The goal of the task was not to directly detect any of the previously mentioned devices but to perform sentiment analysis in a fine-grained scale ranging from −5 (very negative) to +5 (very positive). Since irony and sarcasm are typically used to criticize or to mock, and thus skew the perception of sentiment toward the negative, it is not enough for a system to simply determine whether the sentiment of a given tweet is positive or negative [44]. The participants were asked to determine the degree to which a sentiment was communicated rather than to assign a more general score (such as in the previously described tasks).

---

[21] http://alt.qcri.org/semeval2015/

Table 7.4 Best Results in the Task on Sentiment Analysis of Figurative Language in Twitter (Cosine Similarity Measure)

Team	All	Irony	Sarcasm
ClaC	0.758	0.904	0.892
UPF-taln	0.711	0.873	0.903
LLT_PolyU	0.687	0.918	0.896
EliRF	0.658	0.905	0.904
LT3	0.658	0.897	0.891
ValenTo	0.634	0.901	0.895
HLT	0.630	0.907	0.887

A corpus composed of three subsets of tweets was supplied to the participants: trial (1025), training (8000), and test (4000). The corpus construction involved crowdsourcing and some tweets explicitly tagged with hashtags such as #irony, #sarcasm, #not, and #yeahright or that contained words commonly associated with the use of a metaphor (eg, "literally" and "virtually"). Further information can be found in [44].

Fifteen teams participated in the task on sentiment analysis of figurative language.[22] Table 7.4 shows the results of the seven best ranked systems according to the overall cosine similarity measure.

The best ranked system, ClaC [45], showed robustness across different sentiment analysis related tasks [46].[23] ClaC is based on a pipeline framework that groups different phases, from preprocessing to polarity induction. It exploits some resources such as NRC-lexicon,[24] Hu&Liu, and MPQA. In addition, the authors developed a new resource called Gezi (for more details, see [45,46]). The main difference between their proposal for both tasks was the machine learning algorithm used for polarity assignment, an SVM for the regular one and M5P (a decision tree regressor) for figurative language tweets. Nevertheless, it did not achieve the best performance either for ironic or for sarcastic tweets in the figurative language task. The UPF-taln [47] system presented an extended approach that considered frequent, rare, positive, and negative words and also exploited a bag of words as features. To assign the polarity degree, the authors used a regression algorithm (random subspace with M5P). Their system achieved second place in the overall ranking.

Two similar and efficient approaches were the ones proposed by LLT_PolyU [48] and EliRF [49]. They scored the best results in irony and sarcasm detection respectively. LLT_PolyU and EliRF considered as features *n*-grams, negation scope windows, and sentiment resources (LLT_PolyU exploited Hu&Liu, MPQA, AFINN, and SentiWordNet and EliRF used Pattern,[25] AFINN, Hu&Liu,

---

[22]Some systems such as Clac, UPF-taln, and EliRF participated also in the related task on sentiment analysis in Twitter at SemEval 2015.

[23]ClaC had the ninth best performance for both regular and sarcastic tweets in the task on sentiment analysis in Twitter [42].

[24]http://www.saifmohammad.com/WebPages/ResearchInterests.html

[25]http://www.clips.ua.ac.be/pattern

NRC-lexicon, and SentiWordNet). In both systems, regression models (RepTree in LLT_PolyU and a regression SVM in EliRF) were used to calculate the polarity value.

The LT3 [50] and ValenTo [51] systems included in their set of features the presence of punctuation marks, emoticons, and hasthags. To capture potential clues of figurative content in tweets, LT3 took advantage of features to detect changes in the narrative as well as contrasting, contradictory, and polysemic words. In the LT3 system an SVM classifier was used to determine the polarity value of tweets. Furthermore, the ValenTo system exploits sentiment analysis resources (such as AFINN, Hu&Liu, General Inquirer,[26] and SentiWordNet) as well as some containing emotional and psycholinguistic information (ANEW,[27] DAL, SenticNet,[28] and LIWC. Besides, a feature to reverse the polarity valence of a tweet when it contains a sarcastic intention was considered. In ValenTo a linear regression model was used to assign the polarity value. Finally, the HLT system [44] used an SVM approach together with lexical features such as negation and intensifiers and some markers of amusement and irony.

4 FUTURE TRENDS AND DIRECTIONS

Irony detection and sarcasm detection have been addressed as a text classification task. Salient features such as lexical marks are mainly used to characterize ironic and sarcastic utterances. As figurative language devices, irony and sarcasm need to be studied beyond the scope of the textual content of the utterance. In this regard both the context in which utterances are expressed and common knowledge should be considered to identify the real intention behind an ironic or sarcastic expression. There are some attempts to take advantage of this kind of information. Wallace et al. [18] exploited contextual information of the forum where a comment was posted. Information about users who wrote sarcastic tweets (such as their past tweets) was considered by Rajadesingan et al. [27] and Bamman and Smith [28] so as to distinguish between sarcastic and nonsarcastic tweets.

Besides, it is necessary to consider how affective and emotional content is implicitly embedded in irony and sarcasm. Some work in the literature has already started to exploit affective information by using sentiment and affective lexica such as DAL [14,16], AFINN and Hu&Liu [16], and SentiWordNet [15,25].

With regard to the impact of sentiment analysis on irony and sarcasm detection, before the polarity of an utterance is determined it would be helpful to identify if the utterance expresses either ironic or sarcastic intention. Further investigations are needed to develop approaches that could efficiently identify ironic and sarcastic content to avoid misclassification of the polarity score of a subjective text.

5 CONCLUSIONS

People communicate their ideas in complex ways. Figurative language devices such as irony and sarcasm are often used to express evaluative judgments in an unconventional way. Irony and sarcasm

---

[26]http://www.wjh.harvard.edu/~inquirer/
[27]http://csea.phhp.ufl.edu/media/anewmessage.html
[28]http://sentic.net/

are concepts that are difficult to define; however, they are often used in social media. In this sense user-generated content represents a big challenge. The progress achieved so far in irony and sarcasm detection has been a result of the exploitation of mainly the syntactic, lexical, and semantic levels of natural language processing. Similar approaches have been proposed to address the task as a binary classification. Currently, the biggest effort concerns identification of the most salient features that allow one to determine when the intended content of an utterance is ironic or sarcastic.

From the sentiment analysis perspective, the presence of irony and sarcasm affects the performance of the task. As we pointed out, state-of-the-art systems generally have good results when they are dealing with regular content, but when they are evaluated with ironic or sarcastic content, there overall performance is affected. Therefore robust sentiment analysis systems will need to understand when human communications in social media make use of figurative language devices such as irony and sarcasm.

ACKNOWLEDGMENTS

This work was done in the framework of the SomEMBED MINECO TIN2015-71147-C2-1-P research project. The National Council for Science and Technology (CONACyT Mexico) funded the research of Delia Irazú Hernández Farias (grant no. 218109/313683 CVU-369616).

REFERENCES

[1] H.P. Grice, Logic and conversation, in: P. Cole, J.L. Morgan (Eds.), Syntax and Semantics: Vol. 3: Speech Acts, Academic Press, San Diego, CA, 1975, pp. 41–58.
[2] D. Wilson, D. Sperber, On verbal irony, Lingua 87 (1–2) (1992) 53–76.
[3] S. Attardo, Irony as relevant inappropriateness, J. Pragmat. 32 (6) (2000) 793–826.
[4] A. Utsumi, Verbal irony as implicit display of ironic environment: distinguishing ironic utterances from nonirony, J. Pragmat. 32 (12) 1777–1806.
[5] S. Kumon-Nakamura, S. Glucksberg, How about another piece of pie: the allusional pretense theory of discourse irony, J. Exp. Psychol. Gen. 124 (1) (1995) 3.
[6] R.W. Gibbs, Irony in talk among friends, Metaphor Symbol 15 (1–2) (2000) 5–27.
[7] J.M. Whalen, P.M. Pexman, A.J. Gill, S. Nowson, Verbal irony use in personal blogs, Behav. Inform. Technol. 32 (6) (2013) 560–569.
[8] L. Alba-Juez, S. Attardo, The evaluative palette of verbal irony, Eval. Context Pragmat. Beyond New Ser. 242 (2014) 93–116.
[9] R. Giora, S. Attardo, Irony, in: Encyclopedia of Humor Studies, Sage, Thousand Oaks, CA, 2014, pp. 397–401.
[10] E. Filatova, Irony and sarcasm: corpus generation and analysis using crowdsourcing, in: Proceedings of the Eighth International Conference on Language Resources and Evaluation, 2012, pp. 392–398.
[11] P. Carvalho, L. Sarmento, M.J. Silva, E. de Oliveira, Clues for detecting irony in user-generated contents: Oh..!! it's "so easy" ;-), in: Proceedings of the First International Conference on Information Knowledge Management Workshop on Topic-Sentiment Analysis for Mass Opinion, 2009, pp. 53–56.
[12] T. Veale, Y. Hao, Detecting ironic intent in creative comparisons, in: Proceedings of the 19th European Conference on Artificial Intelligence, IOS Press, 2010, pp. 765–770.

[13] A. Reyes, P. Rosso, D. Buscaldi, From humor recognition to irony detection: the figurative language of social media, Data Knowl. Eng. 74 (2012) 1–12, Applications of Natural Language to Information Systems.

[14] A. Reyes, P. Rosso, T. Veale, A multidimensional approach for detecting irony in Twitter, Lang. Resour. Eval. 47 (1) (2013) 239–268.

[15] F. Barbieri, H. Saggion, Modelling irony in Twitter, in: Proceedings of the Student Research Workshop at the 14th Conference of the European Chapter of the Association for Computational Linguistics, 2014, pp. 56–64.

[16] I. Hernández Farías, J.-M. Benedí, P. Rosso, Applying basic features from sentiment analysis for automatic irony detection, in: R. Paredes, J.S. Cardoso, X.M. Pardo (Eds.), Pattern Recognition and Image Analysis, LNCS, vol. 9117, Springer International Publishing, 2015, pp. 337–344.

[17] K. Buschmeier, P. Cimiano, R. Klinger, An impact analysis of features in a classification approach to irony detection in product reviews, in: Proceedings of the Fifth Workshop on Computational Approaches to Subjectivity, Sentiment and Social Media Analysis, 2014, pp. 42–49.

[18] B.C. Wallace, D.K. Choe, E. Charniak, Sparse, contextually informed models for irony detection: exploiting user communities, entities and sentiment, in: Proceedings of the 53rd Annual Meeting of the Association for Computational Linguistics and the 7th International Joint Conference on Natural Language Processing (Vol. 1: Long Papers), Beijing, China, 2015, pp. 1035–1044.

[19] J. Karoui, F. Benamara, V. Moriceau, N. Aussenac-Gilles, L. Hadrich-Belguith, Towards a contextual pragmatic model to detect irony in tweets, in: Proceedings of the 53rd Annual Meeting of the Association for Computational Linguistics and the 7th International Joint Conference on Natural Language Processing (Volume 2: Short Papers), 2015, pp. 644–650.

[20] R.J. Kreuz, G.M. Caucci, Lexical influences on the perception of sarcasm, in: Proceedings of the Workshop on Computational Approaches to Figurative Language, 2007, pp. 1–4.

[21] D. Davidov, O. Tsur, A. Rappoport, Semi-supervised recognition of sarcastic sentences in Twitter and Amazon, in: Proceedings of the Fourteenth Conference on Computational Natural Language Learning, 2010, pp. 107–116.

[22] R. González-Ibá nez, S. Muresan, N. Wacholder, Identifying sarcasm in Twitter: a closer look, in: Proceedings of the 49th Annual Meeting of the Association for Computational Linguistics: Human Language Technologies, 2011, pp. 581–586.

[23] E. Riloff, A. Qadir, P. Surve, L.D. Silva, N. Gilbert, R. Huang, Sarcasm as contrast between a positive sentiment and negative situation, in: Proceedings of the 2013 Conference on Empirical Methods in Natural Language Processing, 2013, pp. 704–714.

[24] A.P. Wang, #irony or #sarcasm—a quantitative and qualitative study based on twitter, in: Proceedings of the 27th Pacific Asia Conference on Language, Information, and Computation, National Chengchi University, 2013, pp. 349–356.

[25] F. Barbieri, H. Saggion, F. Ronzano, Modelling sarcasm in Twitter, a novel approach, in: Proceedings of the Fifth Workshop on Computational Approaches to Subjectivity, Sentiment and Social Media Analysis, 2014, pp. 50–58.

[26] E. Fersini, F.A. Pozzi, E. Messina, Detecting irony and sarcasm in microblogs: the role of expressive signals and ensemble classifiers, in: Proceedings of the IEEE International Conference on Data Science and Advanced Analytics, 2015.

[27] A. Rajadesingan, R. Zafarani, H. Liu, Sarcasm detection on Twitter: a behavioral modeling approach, in: Proceedings of the Eighth ACM International Conference on Web Search and Data Mining, 2015, pp. 97–106.

[28] D. Bamman, N.A. Smith, Contextualized sarcasm detection on Twitter, in: Proceedings of the Ninth International Conference on Web and Social Media, 2015, pp. 574–577.

[29] D. Maynard, M. Greenwood, Who cares about sarcastic tweets? Investigating the impact of sarcasm on sentiment analysis, in: Proceedings of the Ninth International Conference on Language Resources and Evaluation, 2014, pp. 4238–4243.

[30] V. Basile, A. Bolioli, M. Nissim, V. Patti, P. Rosso, Overview of the Evalita 2014 SENTIment POLarity classification task, in: Proceedings of the First Italian Conference on Computational Linguistics and the Fourth International Workshop EVALITA 2014, pp. 50–57.

[31] C. Bosco, V. Patti, A. Bolioli, Developing corpora for sentiment analysis: the case of irony and Senti-TUT, IEEE Intell. Syst. 28 (2) (2013) 55–63.

[32] V. Basile, M. Nissim, Sentiment analysis on Italian tweets, in: Proceedings of the Fourth Workshop on Computational Approaches to Subjectivity, Sentiment and Social Media Analysis, 2013, pp. 100–107.

[33] R. Basili, A. Lenci, B. Magnini (Eds.), Proceedings of the First Italian Conference on Computational Linguistics and the Fourth International Workshop EVALITA 2014, Pisa University Press, Pisa, Italy, 2014.

[34] P. Basile, N. Novielli, UNIBA at EVALITA2014-SENTIPOLC Task: predicting tweet sentiment polarity combining micro-blogging, lexicon and semantic features, in: Proceedings of the First Italian Conference on Computational Linguistics and the Fourth International Workshop EVALITA 2014, pp. 58–63.

[35] G. Castellucci, D. Croce, D. De Cao, R. Basili, A multiple kernel approach for Twitter sentiment analysis in Italian, in: Proceedings of the First Italian Conference on Computational Linguistics and the Fourth International Workshop EVALITA 2014, pp. 98–103.

[36] I. Hernandez-Farias, D. Buscaldi, B. Priego-Sánchez, IRADABE: adapting English lexicons to the Italian sentiment polarity classification task, in: Proceedings of the First Italian Conference on Computational Linguistics and the Fourth International Workshop EVALITA 2014, pp. 75–81.

[37] A. Anisimovich, Self-evaluating workflow for language-independent sentiment analysis, in: Proceedings of the First Italian Conference on Computational Linguistics and the Fourth International Workshop EVALITA 2014, pp. 108–111.

[38] R. Delmonte, ITGETARUNS a linguistic rule-based system for pragmatic text processing, in: Proceedings of the First Italian Conference on Computational Linguistics and the Fourth International Workshop EVALITA 2014, pp. 64–69.

[39] E. Fersini, E. Messina, F.A. Pozzi, Subjectivity, polarity and irony detection: a multi-layer approach, in: Proceedings of the First Italian Conference on Computational Linguistics and the Fourth International Workshop EVALITA 2014, pp. 70–74.

[40] F. Barbieri, R. Francesco, S. Horacio, Relying on intrinsic word features to characterize subjectivity, polarity and irony of tweets, in: Proceedings of the First Italian Conference on Computational Linguistics and the Fourth International Workshop EVALITA 2014, pp. 104–107.

[41] S. Rosenthal, A. Ritter, P. Nakov, V. Stoyanov, SemEval-2014 Task 9: sentiment analysis in Twitter, in: Proceedings of the Eighth International Workshop on Semantic Evaluation (SemEval 2014), ACL and Dublin City University, Dublin, Ireland, 2014, pp. 73–80.

[42] S. Rosenthal, P. Nakov, S. Kiritchenko, S. Mohammad, A. Ritter, V. Stoyanov, SemEval-2015 Task 10: sentiment analysis in Twitter, in: Proceedings of the Ninth International Workshop on Semantic Evaluation, 2015, pp. 451–463.

[43] P. Nakov, T. Zesch, D. Cer, D. Jurgens (Eds.), Proceedings of the 9th International Workshop on Semantic Evaluation, Association for Computational Linguistics, Denver, CO, 2015.

[44] A. Ghosh, G. Li, T. Veale, P. Rosso, E. Shutova, J. Barnden, A. Reyes, SemEval-2015 Task 11: sentiment analysis of figurative language in Twitter, in: Proceedings of the Ninth International Workshop on Semantic Evaluation, 2015, pp. 470–478.

[45] C. Özdemir, S. Bergler, CLaC-SentiPipe: SemEval2015 Subtasks 10 B,E, and Task 11, in: Proceedings of the Ninth International Workshop on Semantic Evaluation, 2015, pp. 479–485.

[46] C. Özdemir, S. Bergler, A comparative study of different sentiment lexica for sentiment analysis of tweets, in: Proceedings of the International Conference Recent Advances in Natural Language Processing, INCOMA Ltd. Shoumen, 2015.

[47] F. Barbieri, F. Ronzano, H. Saggion, UPF-taln: SemEval 2015 tasks 10 and 11. Sentiment analysis of literal and figurative language in Twitter, in: Proceedings of the Ninth International Workshop on Semantic Evaluation, 2015, pp. 704–708.

[48] H. Xu, E. Santus, A. Laszlo, C.-R. Huang, LLT-PolyU: identifying sentiment intensity in ironic tweets, in: Proceedings of the Ninth International Workshop on Semantic Evaluation, 2015, pp. 673–678.

[49] M. Giménez, F. Pla, L.-F. Hurtado, ELiRF: A SVM approach for SA tasks in Twitter at SemEval-2015, in: Proceedings of the Ninth International Workshop on Semantic Evaluation, 2015, pp. 574–581.

[50] C. Van Hee, E. Lefever, V. Hoste, LT3: sentiment analysis of figurative tweets: piece of cake #notreally, in: Proceedings of the Ninth International Workshop on Semantic Evaluation, 2015, pp. 684–688.

[51] D.I. Hernández Farías, E. Sulis, V. Patti, G. Ruffo, C. Bosco, ValenTo: sentiment analysis of figurative language tweets with irony and sarcasm, in: Proceedings of the Ninth International Workshop on Semantic Evaluation, 2015, pp. 694–698.

SUGGESTION MINING FROM OPINIONATED TEXT

8

S. Negi, P. Buitelaar
National University of Ireland, Galway, Ireland

1 INTRODUCTION

Conventionally, opinion mining aims to summarize the amount of appreciation and criticism in a given text, which is performed with use of sentiment analysis methods. Opinionated text from reviews, blogs, discussion forums, and social networking sites is considered as a source for identifying appreciation or dissatisfaction of people toward certain aspects of a product, service, or topic under discussion. This chapter highlights a different kind of information in the opinionated text on social media, which could be exploited in numerous ways, and has been attracting the attention of the research community lately. People often tend to include information such as advice, tips, and wishes among the online expression of their opinions toward products and services. We collaboratively refer to this kind of information as *suggestions*.

Such suggestions are either useful to brand owners, since they can be about improvement in the product/service, or useful for the customers since these provide relevant tips, and advice in the context of a commercial entity. Mining such suggestion-bearing textual units from a large amount of opinionated text can be referred to as *suggestion mining*. Suggestion mining and retrieval can be a potential new research area emerging from this kind of research. The detection of suggestions in text goes beyond the scope of sentiment polarity detection, and opens up new challenges in the areas of subjectivity analysis, social media analysis, and extrapropositional semantics.

Some of the related work refers to customer suggestions for improvements and new features as *wishes*, while other work refers to them as *suggestions*. The problem was first introduced in the context of opinion mining by Goldberg et al. [1], and was termed the *wish detection problem*. It was emphasized by another line of work [2] that not all the wishes are relevant for opinion mining, and only the detection of *wishes for improvements and new features* was performed. Later, such information was termed *suggestions for improvements* by Brun and Hagege [3].

Advice mining on discussion forums was performed by Wicaksono and Myaeng [4], which is primarily the extraction of suggestions and advice for the readers about the entity under discussion. In our work [5] we introduced the term *customer-to-customer (CTC) suggestions*, pertaining to the suggestions in reviews that are meant to help the fellow customers, excluding the suggestions for improvements in the product or service.

Sentiment Analysis in Social Networks. http://dx.doi.org/10.1016/B978-0-12-804412-4.00008-5

Therefore a suggestion can be referred to as a wish, advice, or a suggestion, depending on the specific use case and the task definition. However, *suggestion mining* seems to be an appropriate term for broadly referring to this area of research. The presence of suggestions across various social media platforms has been verified in some of the related work. Below are the different domains of opinionated texts from which suggestions have been automatically extracted:

1. **Product reviews:** In [1–3] wishes and suggestions for improvements were detected in the products reviews. Suggestions of this kind are targeted to the product manufacturers.
2. **Discussion forums on travel:** Extraction of advice-revealing sentences from travel-related discussion forums was performed by Wicaksono and Myaeng [4,6]. *Advice* was defined by them as the sentences which contain advice or information relevant to the original question in the post.
3. **Discussion forums on sociopolitics:** Wish detection in political discussion forums was performed by Goldberg et al. [1]. But these wishes were about social and political issues rather than suggestions for improvement in products and services.
4. **Twitter:** People often write about their opinions on products and services on social networking websites such as Facebook, and Twitter. Tweets about Microsoft Windows phones were collected by Dong et al. [7], and the tweets that suggested improvements in the Windows phone were extracted from them.

2 SENTIMENTS AND SUGGESTIONS

Although most of the opinion mining work so far revolves around the identification of sentiments [8], the presence of suggestions in opinionated texts was noticed as early as 2006, but mostly in the context of sentiment analysis. Chesley et al. [9] indicated that suggestions appear among the sentiment-bearing texts, which are marked by the *suggesting* category of verbs. They identified different verb categories as features for sentiment-based text classification, and showed that the removal of suggesting verbs from the feature set increases the accuracy of sentiment classification.

Sentiment analysis is always performed toward a target, mainly a person, product, service, etc. However, the retrieved opinionated text corresponding to the target is often a mixture of positive and negative statements about the target and *another* category of statements such as wishes, conditionals, neutral statements, and objective statements. Therefore some studies focused on the features that can distinguish other statements from the positive and negative ones, so as to increase the sentiment prediction accuracy [10]. In previous work [11] we pointed out that such nonpolar sentences should also be the focus of attention, rather than the positive and negative sentences, for nonsentiment analysis tasks such as suggestion mining.

Sentiments can minimally appear at the word level, while suggestions can only appear at or above clause level in the texts. If one compares the sentiments and suggestions at sentence level, a suggestion-bearing sentence can simultaneously exhibit positive, negative, or neutral sentiments. In previous work [5] we labeled sentiment-tagged sentences as *suggestions* and *nonsuggestions*, and showed that CTC suggestions do not always contain one particular sentiment. For a sentence classification task in suggestion mining, unlike sentiment analysis, only the positive class holds importance for the extraction of suggestions from a given text, while in sentiment analysis both positive and negative classes are important for the generation of sentiment summaries.

Table 8.1 Examples of Suggestions Appearing in Sentiment Analysis Datasets and the Labels Assigned to Them

Sentence	Domain	Sentiment	Aspect
One more thing- if you want to visit the Bundestag it is a good idea to book a tour (in English) in advance	Hotel	Neutral	Null
For those of you who already bought this camera, I suggest you buy a hi-ti dye-sub photo printer	Camera	Neutral	Null
If only it played stand alone avi files	DVD player	Neutral	Null
The dial on the original zen was perfect and i wish it was on this model	Jukebox	Neutral	Null
Would be really good if they have given an option to stop this autofocussing	Camera	Null	Null

Another significant variation is in the topic, entity, or context of sentiment- and suggestion-bearing texts. Sentiment analysis is always performed in the context of mining consumer sentiments from the relevant data, which are targeted toward a particular entity and its aspects. State-of-the-art sentence-level sentiment analysis datasets tag the sentences that do not bear sentiment toward the target entity as objective or neutral (see Table 8.1). For example, a hotel review sentence such as "Make sure you bring plenty of suntan lotion—very expensive in the gift shop," would be labeled as neutral since it does not express any sentiment for the hotel. Suggestions in hotel reviews can range from tips and advice about the reviewed entity to suggestions and recommendations about the neighborhood, transportation, and things to do. Similarly, in product reviews, suggestions can be about how to make better use of the product, accessories that go with it, availability of better deals, etc., which may not necessarily contribute to the sentiment toward the reviewed entity [5].

3 TASK DEFINITION AND TYPOLOGY OF SUGGESTIONS

Suggestion mining is a recently introduced research problem, and therefore the task definition is still evolving. The task can be framed as a statement classification task, as indicated by most of the related work. A statement can be considered as a unit of text that has a complete meaning of its own. Therefore the smallest suggestion can be a main clause. A high-level task definition can be framed as follows: Given a set S of statements $\{s_1, s_2, s_3, \ldots, s_n\}$, predict a label l_i for each statement in S, where $l_i \in \{\text{suggestion, nonsuggestion}\}$.

In [5] we proposed that the terms *statement* and *suggestion* in this high-level definition are required to be explicitly defined for each suggestion mining task. Therefore we proposed three parameters to formulate a fine-grained definition of suggestion mining tasks:

1. **The textual unit of a suggestion:** All the studies that performed suggestion extraction considered sentences as the units of suggestions; however, it was observed that sentences might miss the context or might refer to something mentioned in the previous sentence. Furthermore, punctuation marks are often erroneously used in social media text, so automatic sentence splitting does not work well with such text. Some of the studies also performed a manual split of training set sentences. A possible solution was provided in 2014 by [16] who built a dataset of hotel reviews, where reviews are segmented into statements, so that each statement has only one sentiment. They defined a statement to be at least a clause and at most a sentence from the reviews that is meaningful on its own. To ensure replicability, they provided the algorithm that automatically splits a given opinionated text into such statements.

2. **Beneficiary of a suggestion:** As explained in Section 1, product- and service-related suggestions on social media are aimed at two kinds of stakeholders: either the manufacturer/provider or the fellow consumers. All the related work in suggestion mining focused on one beneficiary at a time. As mentioned previously, we refer to the suggestions meant for fellow customers as *CTC suggestions*. The linguistic nature of suggestions seems to differ from one kind of beneficiary to another. More details on the linguistic observations will follow in Section 5.

3. **Definition of a suggestion:** The term *suggestion* is defined in the *Oxford English Dictionary* as "an idea or plan put forward for consideration." Synonyms of *suggestion* are *proposal*, *proposition*, *recommendation*, *advice*, *hint*, *tip*, and *clue*. In a general scenario, this definition of *suggestion* easily distinguishes suggestions from other kinds of texts. However, when suggestions are required to be identified in the space of opinionated sentences, humans seem to perceive most of the sentences as suggestions. In previous work [5] we performed a survey on what kind of sentences laymen perceive as suggestions. Asher et al. [12] defined 20 types of opinion expressions, including suggestions and recommendations, which appear in opinionated text. A representative sample of 20 sentences from hotel and electronics reviews was chosen, corresponding to the predefined 20 types of opinion expressions. Ten annotators (laymen) were asked to determine if the given sentences are suggestions to other customers (CTC suggestions) or not. Table 8.2 shows sentences for which 50% or more people agreed they were CTC suggestions. Except for the suggest and recommend categories, suggestions in rest of the categories are in an implicit form (ie, the intention of giving a suggestion is not explicitly expressed). Since humans can inherently infer suggestions from a given statement or information, the layman annotators did not distinguish between implicit and explicit forms of suggestions. However, in the case of automatic detection, it would be challenging to automatically infer suggestions from their implicit forms. Therefore we proposed [5] two forms of suggestions so as to define the scope of suggestion mining tasks:
   (a) *Explicit*: Directly suggests or recommends an entity or action.
   (b) *Implicit*: Does not explicitly suggest an entity or action but only provides the information from which a suggestion can be inferred.

4 DATASETS

There is a clear lack of annotated datasets for the problem of suggestion mining, because the problem has only recently been identified and some of the datasets are not publicly available. Additionally, the available datasets do not use a well-formulated guideline and definition of suggestions. In our most

Table 8.2 Sentences Labeled as Customer-to-Customer Suggestions by 50% or More of Annotators

Sentence	Category	Annotators (%)	Suggestion Type
Concierge is not available 24 hours	Inform	70	Implicit
We did not have breakfast at the hotel but opted to grab breads/pastries/coffee from the many food-outlets in the main stations	Tell	80	Implicit
Room was very quiet despite being close to the elevator	Remark	50	Implicit
The staff was nice and friendly	Praise	60	Implicit
Double bed quite narrow and not as comfortable as expected	Disappoint	60	Implicit
The view from the 7th floor was amazing	Fascinate	50	Implicit
If you do end up here, be sure to specify a room at the back of the hotel	Suggest	100	Explicit
I recommend going for a Trabi Safari	Recommend	90	Explicit

Courtesy: S. Negi, P. Buitelaar, Towards the extraction of customer-to-customer suggestions from reviews, in: Proceedings of the 2015 Conference on Empirical Methods in Natural Language Processing, Association for Computational Linguistics, Lisbon, Portugal, 2015, pp. 2159–2167.

recent work [5], we provided more detailed guidelines and task definition, leading the path for well-defined datasets in the future. Unlike others, our dataset makes a distinction between implicit and explicit forms of suggestions. To the best of our knowledge, all of the related work with datasets that are publicly available is listed below:

- **Reviews:** We provide a dataset of sentences from hotel (8000 sentences) and electronics (3700 sentences) reviews, which are labeled as CTC suggestions or non-CTC suggestions. We labeled both explicitly and implicitly expressed suggestions in this dataset as different categories. Less than 10% of sentences were labeled as explicit suggestions, and about 35% were labeled as implicit suggestions. The original data were obtained from an existing sentiment analysis dataset, which was pretagged with the type of sentiment toward the reviewed entity.
  A corpus of 1200 sentences from product reviews is provided by Goldberg et al. [1], labeled as wish or nonwish. All wish-expressing sentences are labeled, and sum up to 12% of the total sentences. However, not all the wishes express suggestions for improvements. We [11] relabeled this dataset with suggestion and nonsuggestion labels, where the suggestions are explicit in nature and are suggestions for improvements in the products.
- **Twitter:** A dataset of 3000 tweets about Microsoft Windows phone, labeled as suggestion or nonsuggestion, is provided by Dong et al. [7]. These are suggestions for improvements in the product.
- **Discussion forums:** A dataset of 6300 sentences from political discussions is provided by Goldberg et al. [1], of which 34% are labeled as wishes, where not all the wishes are suggestions. Another dataset of 5000 sentences from a travel discussion forum is provided by Wicaksono and Myaeng [4], and contains advice and nonadvice labels for the sentences.

A study of various domains of opinionated texts such as newspaper articles, blogs, and reviews was performed by Asher et al. [12]. The distribution of various opinion expressions was observed across these domains, and it was reported that suggestions and recommendations constitute about 10% of the opinion expressions in reviews, while judgments (blame, praise) and sentiments (love, fascinate, hate, disappoint, sad) constitute about 80%. This linguistic study referred to the explicit forms of suggestions when they refer to the recommendation and suggestion category of expressions. Our review dataset also shows a similar distribution of explicit suggestions.

5 APPROACHES FOR SUGGESTION DETECTION

Two main types of approaches are used for suggestion mining: statistical classifiers and rule-based classifiers. All the existing work performed either the detection of suggestions for improvements in products or the detection of suggestions to fellow customers, but as not an integrated system. The features and rules used in these approaches are derived from the linguistic properties that characterize expression of suggestions.

5.1 LINGUISTIC OBSERVATIONS IN SUGGESTIONS

The presence of a variety of linguistic strategies in the suggestion-expressing sentences makes this problem interesting from a computational linguistics perspective. One such characteristic is modality. It is a grammatical category that allows the expression of aspects related to the attitude of a speaker toward his or her statement in terms of the degree of certainty, reliability, subjectivity, sources of information, and perspective [13].

In [11] we presented evidence of the subjunctive mood in suggestions for improvements. This is mainly because suggestions for improvements are often expressed in the form of wishes (see Table 8.3). The subjunctive mood is a commonly occurring language phenomenon in Indo-European languages, and is a verb mood typically used in subordinate clauses to express action that has not yet occurred, in the form of a wish, possibility, necessity, etc. [14].

Table 8.3 Examples of Wishes, and the Subjunctive Mood

Sentence Type	Examples
Wishes in product reviews	I wanted a DVD player that had basic features and would be able to play DVD or format discs that I had made myself
Wishes in political discussions	I wish Canon works out some way for that issue
	I wish someone said that to Teddy at the meeting yesterday
	Perhaps I should have stopped at 8 or 9 years old
	I would like to know if you are a purist or a hypocrite
Subjunctive mood	I wish it were summer
	I suggest that Dawn drive the car

Two of the related studies [4,5] observed the presence of the imperative mood in advice and suggestions in reviews and discussion forums respectively that were addressed to fellow customers or bloggers. Both studies used features that represent the imperative mood (see Section 5.2 and 5.3).

Although these features proved to be effective, they work well only as complementary features with other lexical and syntactic features. It was observed in the data that suggestions tend to contain the imperative mood and the subjunctive mood but this might not always be the case. Also, the features used might not have precisely represented the imperative mood and the subjunctive mood.

5.2 DETECTION OF SUGGESTIONS FOR IMPROVEMENTS

Experiments using support vector machine classifiers with features such as words, manually identified wish templates, and automatically extracted wish templates from a corpus containing new year wishes were performed by Goldberg et al. [1] to identify the wishes in product reviews. The evaluations were performed on two manually labeled datasets comprising product reviews and political discussions, where each sentence was classified as a wish or nonwish sentence. Later we [11] also used a support vector machine classifier and improved on the results achieved by Goldberg et al. by employing features based on the subjunctive mood. It was observed by Ramanand et al. [2] that wish is a broader category, and some wishes might not be suggestions. They performed experiments on suggestion detection, where they focused only on suggestion-bearing wishes, and used manually formulated syntactic patterns for their detection.

Another system for the detection of suggestions for improvements was proposed by Brun and Hagege [3]. One of the components was a structured terminology of products, and their features. The terminology comprised concepts such as "part of" (eg, a paper tray is a part of printer) and technical characteristics such as speed, price, and noise. Another component was a thesaurus for suggestion expressions, which comprised expressions used in sentences denoting wishes, regrets, and misses. The central component of their system was a syntactic-semantic pattern-based classifier for identifying suggestions and nonsuggestions. These patterns comprised arguments belonging to a structured terminology and domain thesaurus, and linguistic information such as dependency relations and tense. They performed an evaluation on a set of manually labeled reviews but this evaluation dataset is not publicly available.

The features used in all of these studies were lexical and syntactic in nature, such as n-grams of words and part-of-speech tags, frequent part-of-speech sequences, frequent part-of-speech sequences in the subjunctive mood, and frequent dependency relations.

5.3 DETECTION OF SUGGESTIONS TO FELLOW CUSTOMERS

In [5] we emphasized the existence of suggestions to fellow customers in the reviews, defined the task of CTC suggestion detection, and prepared datasets for the same. We performed experiments using a support vector machine classifier, and features other than the n-gram features were identified so as to improve the classification accuracy. The additional features were part-of-speech patterns for the imperative mood, sentiment-based features, and arguments of the *nsubj* dependency present in the sentence.

Three types of sentiment-based features were compared. An important observation from the experiments was that the sentiment score summation of words in a given sentence produced better results than the manually labeled sentiments that were expressed toward the reviewed entity. The sentiment scores of words were obtained from SentiWordNet [15]. This showed that the suggestions to fellow customers can appear in the sentences regardless of the sentence being positive, negative, or neutral toward the reviewed entity. For example, *"Room was big, bath was lovely, but watch out for the tile floor after you shower"* is marked as positive, while *"Smokers beware: the hotel only has a few smoking rooms, all located on the second floor"* is marked as negative. The training dataset used in this work is publicly available (see Section 4). One challenge associated with the task was that the dataset was highly imbalanced, with less than 10% of sentences labeled as CTC suggestions.

6 APPLICATIONS

The importance of the extraction of suggestions for customers can be validated from sections such as "Room Tips" (see Fig. 8.1) on websites of companies such as TripAdvisor.[1] Likewise, tips on restaurants, shops, sightseeing, etc., that are relevant to a person's stay in a particular hotel can also be extracted from the reviews. The suggestions that are recommendations for third-party entities such as shops, cafes, restaurants, etc., in the vicinity of a hotel or business are of great importance in the case when there are no dedicated reviews available for these entities.

The website of Yelp[2] is another very popular review website that features "tips" provided by customers for other customers, in addition to detailed reviews. Such tips are often suggestions, or some important information that a user wants to convey to others. It was also observed that product reviews on websites of companies such as Amazon[3] contain recommendations for accessories that go with the product being reviewed, troubleshooting and usage tips, information about better deals, etc., which are

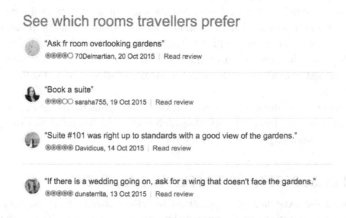

FIG. 8.1

Room tips on the website of TripAdvisor.

[1]https://www.tripadvisor.ie/
[2]http://www.yelp-support.com/article/What-are-tips
[3]http://www.amazon.com

all different forms of suggestions. With the use of suggestion mining, such information can be automatically acquired from a large amount of already existing text rather than it having to be explicitly sought. Suggestions are often explicitly sought in feedback forms, discussion forums, and question answering sections on websites of companies such Amazon and TripAdvisor. The suggestion-seeking questions require manual answering, while the answers might already exist at a different location in the form of reviews and entries in discussion forums. Suggestions extracted from a large number of reviews can also be seen as a type of opinion summarization, in addition to sentiment summarization over the reviews.

It can be argued that suggestions for improvements can be explicitly sought from platforms that are dedicated to collecting suggestions from consumers. There are two problems associated with such platforms. Usually, fewer people tend to write on these platforms because of time constraints and lack of ideas at that particular moment; on the other hand, they tend to convey the suggestion in a flow when they provide overall opinions in reviews and their discussion forum and social media status. Another problem is although the platform is dedicated for suggestions, the text often contains different elements of discourse around the core suggestion-expressing sentences, therefore creating a need for summarization of suggestions. Some examples of these discourse elements are the context sentences that do not convey any new information since the context is already known, humor, and sarcasm. Extraction of explicitly expressed suggestions can help identify the concrete suggestions, leading to an extractive approach for summarization of suggestion forums. Below is an example of a suggestion post from a dedicated suggestion forum for Visual Studio 2015:

> Yesterday was announced that Xbox One will allow indie developer to easily publish games on Xbox One. Lots of indie developers and small game company are using .NET to develop games. Today, we are able to easily target several Windows platforms (Windows Desktop, Windows RT and Windows Phone 8) as well as other platforms thanks to Mono from Xamarin. As we don't know yet the details about this indie developer program for Xbox One, we would love to use. NET on this platform - with everything accessible, from latest 4.5 with async, to unsafe code and native code access through DLLImport (and not only through WinRT components). Please make .NET a compelling game development alternative on Xbox One!

In the example given, the last two sentences convey the actual suggestion, while the rest of the text contains the context. It is highly likely that the context is not new information for the suggestion seekers when the entity about which a suggestion is targeted is predetermined. Therefore performing suggestion mining from such forums can help in an extractive summarization of the posts.

7 FUTURE TRENDS AND DIRECTIONS

Because there has been a limited amount of research into the problem of suggestion mining, there are many aspects of the problem that remain unexplored. Semantics-based features have not yet been employed for the classification task in suggestion mining. However, the available datasets are still inadequate i to train statistical classifiers, and dataset expansion is specially needed. Once bigger datasets are available, it will be possible to effectively employ deep learning methods for this task.

Another direction can be to perform a clustering over the detected suggestions, based on common topics and themes, which is similar to aspect-based sentiment analysis. Because of the lack of labeled data, experiments with semisupervised and unsupervised methods can be other possible avenues.

From a computational linguistics perspective, the study of suggestions deals with a variety of linguistic phenomena, especially moods and modality [11]. There has been a considerable amount of linguistic research on modality; however there has been much less computational work, and there are fewer tools available for the detection of linguistic moods in text. The focus on suggestion mining would also revive interest in the computational approaches toward mood and modality analysis.

8 SUMMARY

Most existing work has approached suggestion mining as a sentence classification problem, and trained statistical classifiers experimenting with a variety of features. The classification accuracies obtained so far show that there is a lot of scope for improvement in the existing suggestion mining algorithms, and the training datasets. Because of the novel nature of this text classification problem, there is also scope for dedicated algorithms, and feature engineering with existing classification algorithms. Part-of-speech tagging and sentence splitting of the text obtained from social media tends to be inaccurate, which also increases the classification error, since suggestions are mostly present at the sentence level. The manual annotation guidelines for this task also demand attention, since decisions on whether a statement is a suggestion or not tend to be subjective for humans.

The study of suggestions across different sources of text, and the variation of linguistic strategies employed in them, is an interesting study from a computational linguistics perspective. Similarly to the sentiment summaries, automatically extracted suggestions are useful to both future customers and sellers and service providers. Our study of the use cases for suggestion mining indicates a strong commercial potential for this research.

ACKNOWLEDGMENTS

This work was funded by the European Union Horizon 2020 program under grant agreement no. 644632 (MixedEmotions) and by Science Foundation Ireland under Grant No. SFI/12/RC/2289 (Insight Centre for Data Analytics).

REFERENCES

[1] A.B. Goldberg, N. Fillmore, D. Andrzejewski, Z. Xu, B. Gibson, X. Zhu, May all your wishes come true: a study of wishes and how to recognize them, in: Proceedings of the 2009 Annual Conference of the North American Chapter of the Association for Computational Linguistics, NAACL '09, Association for Computational Linguistics, 2009, pp. 263–271.

[2] J. Ramanand, K. Bhavsar, N. Pedanekar, Wishful thinking—finding suggestions and 'buy' wishes from product reviews, in: Proceedings of the NAACL HLT 2010 Workshop on Computational Approaches to Analysis and Generation of Emotion in Text, Association for Computational Linguistics, Los Angeles, CA, 2010, pp. 54–61.

[3] C. Brun, C. Hagege, Suggestion mining: detecting suggestions for improvement in users comments, Res. Comput. Sci. 70 (2013) 199–209.

[4] A.F. Wicaksono, S.-H. Myaeng, Automatic extraction of advice-revealing sentences for advice mining from online forums, in: Proceedings of the Seventh International Conference on Knowledge Capture, ACM, 2013, pp. 97–104.

[5] S. Negi, P. Buitelaar, Towards the extraction of customer-to-customer suggestions from reviews, in: Proceedings of the 2015 Conference on Empirical Methods in Natural Language Processing, Association for Computational Linguistics, Lisbon, Portugal, 2015, pp. 2159–2167.

[6] A.F. Wicaksono, S.-H. Myaeng, Mining advices from weblogs, in: Proceedings of the 21st ACM International Conference on Information and Knowledge Management, CIKM '12, ACM, New York, NY, 2012, pp. 2347–2350, doi:10.1145/2396761.2398637.

[7] L. Dong, F. Wei, Y. Duan, X. Liu, M. Zhou, K. Xu, The automated acquisition of suggestions from tweets, in: Proceedings of the Twenty-Seventh AAAI Conference on Artificial Intelligence, AAAI Press, 2013.

[8] B. Liu, Sentiment analysis and opinion mining, Synth. Lect. Hum. Lang. Technol. 5 (1) (2012) 1–167.

[9] P. Chesley, Using verbs and adjectives to automatically classify blog sentiment, in: Proceedings of AAAI-CAAW-06, the Spring Symposia on Computational Approaches, 2006, pp. 27–29.

[10] K. Bloom, Sentiment analysis based on appraisal theory and functional local grammars, PhD thesis, Illinois Institute of Technology, 2011.

[11] S. Negi, P. Buitelaar, Curse or boon? presence of subjunctive mood in opinionated text, in: Proceedings of the 11th International Conference on Computational Semantics, Association for Computational Linguistics, London, UK, 2015, pp. 101–106.

[12] N. Asher, F. Benamara, Y. Mathieu, Appraisal of opinion expressions in discourse, Lingvist. Investig. 31.2 (2009) 279–292.

[13] R. Morante, C. Sporleder, Modality and Negation: an introduction to the special issue, Comput. Linguist. 38 (2) (2012) 223–260.

[14] F.R. Palmer, Mood and Modality, Cambridge University Press, Cambridge, UK, 1986.

[15] A. Esuli, F. Sebastiani, SENTIWORDNET: a publicly available lexical resource for opinion mining, in: Proceedings of the Fifth Conference on Language Resources and Evaluation, 2006, pp. 417–422.

[16] H. Wachsmuth, M. Trenkmann, B. Stein, G. Engels, T. Palakarska, A review corpus for argumentation analysis, in: Computational Linguistics and Intelligent Text Processing, Springer Berlin Heidelberg, 2014, pp. 115–127.

OPINION SPAM DETECTION IN SOCIAL NETWORKS

G. Fei, H. Li, B. Liu

University of Illinois at Chicago, Chicago, IL, United States

1 INTRODUCTION

The increasing popularity of social media such as Facebook and Twitter has provided a great platform for campaign promoters to conduct targeted campaign and for spammers to spread misleading information. Opinions in reviews or social feeds are increasingly used by individuals and organizations to make purchase decisions, for marketing, and for product design. Positive opinions often mean profit and fame for businesses and individuals, which, unfortunately, provides strong incentives for imposters to post fake reviews to promote or to discredit some target products or services. Such individuals are called *opinion spammers* and their activities are called *opinion spamming* [1]. Researchers focusing on analyzing one review or one reviewer at a time neglected the potential relationships among multiple reviews or reviewers [1–7]. In the past few years, more researchers have started taking a different approach by modeling the relationship among different entities in the reviewing system such as reviewers and products so as to gain deeper insight into the problem itself and achieve better results [8–11]. In this chapter we introduce the most recent approaches for detecting opinion spam that incorporate user-user collaborations and in the framework of collective positive-unlabeled (CPU) learning.

2 RELATED WORK

This chapter focuses on review spam, but social relations between other forms of spammers and nonspammers have been studied by many researchers [12,13]. Their work showed that acquiring followers for a user not only increases the size of the audience but also boosts the ranking of the user's tweets. Although some promoters behave in a way similar to spammers, there are also a large number of promoters who are participating in a campaign legitimately, especially in nonprofit campaigns. SPOT [14] can catch suspicious Twitter profiles by learning content-based features from text and malicious URLs in tweets and scoring their suspiciousness. Aggarwal and Kumaraguru [15] noticed that purchased Twitter follower accounts have a difference in their interaction and content-sharing patterns in comparison with random Twitter users. Other recent studies on detecting social spammers include [16–18]. Aggarwal [17] deploys social honeypots to obtain deceptive spam profiles from social networking communities. These spam profiles can be used for future statistical analysis of their properties to create better spam classifiers. SYBILRANK [19] relies on social graph properties to rank users according to their perceived likelihood of being sybils. SSDM [20] is a sociological framework that models social network information and content information for spammer detection. Those methods paved the way for the models we are going to introduce in the following sections.

3 REVIEW SPAMMER DETECTION LEVERAGING REVIEWING BURSTINESS

In this section we discuss one approach to fight against spamming reviews on review websites by exploiting the burstiness nature of online reviews [8]. In normal situations, reviews for a product should arrive randomly. However, there are areas (time periods) where the reviews for a product are bursty, meaning that there are sudden concentrations of reviews in these areas or periods. These areas are called *review bursts*. This method makes some important assumptions about the formation of review bursts and uses them to build connections among seemingly unrelated reviewers so as to detect spamming reviewers/reviews. It is different from other methods in that it tries to directly model the reviewer-reviewer relationship without using any social network information such as "friend" or "follow" information.

This approach assumes that bursts in reviews can be due to either the sudden popularity of products/services or spam attacks. For example, a TV may suddenly become popular because of a successful TV commercial, followed by a large number of customers purchasing the TV and writing reviews for it in a short period. In this case, most reviewers appearing within this burst of reviews tend to be honest reviewers. On the other hand, if a product is undergoing spam attacks, a number of spamming or fake reviews may be posted in a short period. Spam attacks usually involve multiple reviews. Compared with multiple fake reviews, a single one can hardly make enough impact to change the overall sentiment toward the product. And multiple reviews may be posted in a short period because of group spam [6], meaning a group of spammers working together to promote or demote a product. These two possibilities lead to an important hypothesis about bursts in reviews; that is, reviewers co-occurring in the same bursts tend to have a similar nature, meaning that they are either mostly spammers or mostly genuine reviewers.

This approach involves two independent steps. The first step is review burst detection, which looks for dense areas in the arrival pattern of reviews. The second step is review spammer detection. Given the review bursts detected in the first step and the reviewers appearing in the bursts, it models the reviewer-reviewer relationship using Markov random fields (MRFs) [21] and employs loopy belief propagation (LBP) [22] to infer the real identities of reviewers.

3.1 BURST DETECTION

We first introduce review burst detection. As mentioned already, this step detects bursts in reviews, allowing the second step to model the reviewers appearing within these bursts. As the modeling is based on several important assumptions regarding the properties of bursts, detecting real bursts is crucial to the performance of the spammer detection algorithm. However, since it is a step independent of the real spammer detection and is thus beyond the scope of this chapter, we will only briefly introduce one method, which is based on kernel density estimation [23]. Kernel density estimation is a nonparametric way to estimate the probability density of a random variable on the basis of a finite data sample. Given a sample $S = \{x_i\}_{i=1...N}$ from an unknown distribution, its density function $f(x)$ can be estimated with Eq. (9.1):

$$\hat{f}(x) = \frac{1}{N}\sum_{i=1}^{N}K_h(x - x_i), \qquad (9.1)$$

where K_h is called the *scaled kernel* with a bandwidth (scale) h such that $K_h(t) = hK(t/h)$. K is called the *kernel*, which should satisfy $K(u) \geq 0$ and $\int K(u)du = 1$. One can think of Eq. (9.1) as estimating the probability distribution function by averaging the effect of a set of kernel functions centered at each data point. In kernel density estimation a range of kernel functions are commonly used. In this method, a Gaussian kernel is used.

Assume we have a product p that has a set of m reviews $\{p_1, \ldots, p_m\}$, and each review is associated with a review date $\{t_1, \ldots, t_m\}$. The method first chooses a bin size that is equal to a time period (eg, 2 weeks). Then the reviews are separated into subintervals on the basis of their time stamps to generate a histogram of review counts. The last step is to fit the histograms via kernel density estimation and select bursts by the setting of proper burst thresholds.

3.2 SPAMMER DETECTION UNDER REVIEW BURSTS

Now we introduce the algorithm for detecting spammers within bursts. The algorithm uses several important assumptions about review bursts and models the co-occurrence of reviewers using a probabilistic graphical model called MRFs. We start by introducing MRFs.

3.2.1 Reviewer modeling using Markov random fields

MRFs (also called *Markov networks*) are undirected graphical models that deal with inference problems with uncertainty in observed data. MRFs work on an undirected graph $G = (V, E)$, where each vertex or node $v_i \in V$ represents a random variable and each edge (v_i, v_j) represents a statistical dependency between the pair of variables indexed by i and j. A set of potential functions is defined on the cliques of the graph to measure compatibility among the nodes involved. MRFs thus define a joint distribution over all the nodes in the graph/network. Each random variable can be in any of a finite number of states S and is independent of other random variables given its immediate neighbors. The inference task is to compute the maximum likelihood assignment of states; that is, classes for classification. In this approach, the network of reviewers are represented by pairwise MRFs [24]. Instead of imposing potential functions on large cliques, the potential functions in pairwise MRFs are over single variables and pairs of variables (or edges). The state of a node is assumed to be dependent only on its neighbors and to be independent of all other nodes in the graph. We use $\phi_i(\sigma_i)$ to denote the potential function on a single variable (indexed by node i), indicating the prior belief that the random variable v_i is in state σ_i. We also call it the *prior of the node*. We use $\psi_{i,j}(\sigma_i, \sigma_j)$ to denote the potential that node i is in state σ_i and node j is in state σ_j for the edge of the pair of random variables (v_i, v_j), which is also called the *compatibility potential*. To reduce the number of model parameters, the compatibility potentials are often shared.

Now we show how this approach models the reviewers in bursts and their co-occurrences as pairwise MRFs. Reviewers co-occur if they wrote reviews in the same bursts. Each reviewer is represented by a node in the graph, and has a state to indicate his/her real but as yet unknown identity, which can take any of three values; spammer, mixed identity, and nonspammer. The reason for our using mixed identity as a state is because some reviewers sometimes write fake reviews for profit and at other times are legitimate buyers and write genuine reviews. The co-occurrence between two reviewers within the same burst is represented by an edge between their corresponding nodes. So all reviewers that appear in the same burst form a clique. To simplify the problem the approach does not distinguish how many times two reviewers appear in the same bursts. To completely define MRFs, the prior potentials and compatibility potentials need to be defined.

Node prior potentials

Node prior potentials, which represent initial class probabilities for each node, are often initialized on the basis of prior knowledge. If no external information or domain knowledge is available, one can set all the priors as unbiased/uninformative (ie, equal probability for each class). In this approach, several spammer behavior features serve as the prior knowledge;

- **Rating deviation**: A reasonable reviewer is expected to give ratings similar to other reviewers of the same product. Ratings given by spammers can be quite different from those give by other reviewers. We define the rating deviation of a reviewer as

$$RD(a) = \underset{p \in P_a}{\text{avg}} \frac{|r_{ap} - \bar{r}_{ap}|}{4}, \tag{9.2}$$

where r_{ap} is the rating given by reviewer a toward product $p \in P_a$, and $\bar{r}_{ap}$ refers to the average rating of the product given by other reviewers. We normalized the value by 4, which is the maximal possible rating deviation on a 5-star rating scale.

- **Burst review ratio**: This feature computes the ratio of a reviewer's reviews in bursts to the total number of reviews that he/she wrote. Since we expect the arrival of normal reviews to be random, if a reviewer has a high proportion of reviews in bursts, he/she is likelier to be a spammer. The burst review ratio of reviewer a is computed as

$$BRR(a) = \frac{|B_{a*}|}{|V_{a*}|}, \tag{9.3}$$

where B_{a*} represents the set of reviews that reviewer a wrote that have appeared in review bursts.

- **Review content similarity**: We define v_a as the set of reviews that reviewer a wrote, and $v_{a,i}$ is his/her ith review. Review content similarity measures the average pairwise similarity of all reviews that a reviewer wrote. Since spammers normally do not spend as much time as genuine reviewers in writing a completely new review, the words they choose every time are expected to be similar. A bag-of-words model and cosine similarity can be used to represent each review text and measure the similarity as shown in Eq. (9.4) for the review content similarity for reviewer a:

$$RCS(a) = \underset{v_{a,i}, v_{a,j} \in V_a : i < j}{\text{avg}} \cos(v_{a,i}, v_{a,j}) \tag{9.4}$$

- **Reviewer burstiness**: If the reviews appearing in some product review bursts happen to be the reviews in a reviewer's own review burst, he/she is likelier to be a spammer. Reviewer burstiness is computed as

$$RB(a) = \begin{cases} 0, & L(B_{a^*}) - F(B_{a^*}) > \lambda, \\ 1 - \frac{L(B_{a^*}) - F(B_{a^*})}{\lambda}, & \text{otherwise}, \end{cases} \tag{9.5}$$

where $L(B_{a^*})$ and $F(B_{a^*})$ are the latest time and the earliest time respectively for the reviews that reviewer a wrote that appear in the burst, and λ is the time window parameter representing a burst in a customer's own review pattern. λ is set equal to 2 months on the basis of the observation in [25].

Given a set of values for the features of node i as prior knowledge, the next step is compute the prior potential ϕ_i, which is a real-valued vector of size 3, representing the prior probability of node i being a spammer, a reviewer with mixed identity, and a nonspammer. The expected value of the above features is first computed to represent the overall spamming indicator. One way this can be done for a node with three states is as follows.

Given a normalized value ω, we use a Gaussian distribution $N(\omega, \sigma^2)$ to compute a reviewer's probability of being a spammer, a reviewer with mixed identity, and a nonspammer as in Eq. (9.6).

$$p(x_i|\omega) = k \int_{\frac{1}{3}*i}^{\frac{1}{3}*(i+1)} f(t)dt, (i = 0, 1, 2), \tag{9.6}$$

where $f(t)$ is the density function of $N(\omega, \sigma^2)$, and x_i is the random variable representing the possible state of each reviewer, with x_0 representing nonspammer, x_1 representing mixed identity, and x_2 representing spammer. k is the normalization factor such that the sum of the three probabilities equals 1. In this method, $\sigma = 0.25$.

Edge compatibility potentials

On the other hand, the compatibility potentials are ideally estimated from labeled data. In a problem setting such as opinion spam detection, however, obtaining a reasonable amount of labeled data is extremely difficult because of the challenges that human annotators face. Therefore these parameters are set on the basis of intuition reflecting the hypothesized properties of different types of reviewers within the same bursts. Under these assumptions a sample instantiation of the compatibility potentials is shown in Table 9.1.

This instantiation is based on the following intuition. In a review burst a spammer is most likely to co-occur with other spammers so as to have a major impact on the sentiment toward the product being

Table 9.1 An Example Propagation Matrix

	Spammer	Nonspammer	Mixed Identity
Spammer	0.4	0.25	0.35
Nonspammer	0.25	0.4	0.35
Mixed identity	1/3	1/3	1/3

reviewed. Because reviewers with mixed identity could also act as spammers, a spammer is likelier to appear with them than with genuine reviewers. Similarly, genuine reviewers are likelier to appear with other genuine reviewers because of the possibility that the product becomes popular suddenly; and they are likelier to appear with reviewers with mixed identity than with heavy spammers. However, a reviewer with mixed behavior is equally likely to appear with spammers, reviewers with mixed identity, or nonspammers.

3.2.2 Reviewer identity inference using loopy belief propagation
Given the reviewer network represented as pairwise MRFs and on which the potential functions are defined, the next step is to compute the posterior probability over the states/labels of each node. For specific graph topologies such as chains, trees, and other low tree width graphs, there are efficient algorithms for exact inference. However, for a general graph, the exact inference is computationally intractable. Therefore approximate inference is typically used. One of the most popular algorithms is the LBP algorithm, which is extended from the belief propagation algorithm.

The belief propagation algorithm was first proposed Pearl [26] to find exact marginals on trees. The same algorithm can be applied to general graphs that contain loops [27]. The algorithm is thus called LBP. However, LBP is not guaranteed to converge to the correct marginal probabilities. But Murphy et al. [22] indicate that it often converges and the marginals are a good approximation to the correct posteriors.

The key idea of LBP is iterative message passing between the connected nodes. The message represents the belief of i about j (ie, what i "thinks" j's label distribution is). More formally, $m_{i,j}$ captures the probability distribution over the class labels of j, and is computed on the basis of the class priors of i, the compatibility potentials of the edge that connects i and j, and the messages that i receives from its neighbors excluding j. Eq. (9.7) gives the formula for message passing:

$$m_{i,j}(\sigma_j) = Z_1 \sum_{\sigma_i \in S} \psi_{i,j}(\sigma_i, \sigma_j)\phi_i(\sigma_i) \prod_{k \in N(i)\backslash j} m_{k,i}(\sigma_i), \tag{9.7}$$

where Z_1 is the normalization constant and σ_j is one component of the message $m_{i \to j}(\sigma_j)$, which is proportional to the likelihood of node j being in state σ_j given the evidence from i in all possible states σ_i. $N(i)$ represents all the neighbors of node i. Eq. (9.7) is called the *sum-product algorithm* because the inner product is over the messages from other nodes to node i and the outer summation sums over all states that node i can take. At the beginning of LBP, all messages are initialized to 1. Then the messages of each node from its neighbors are alternately updated until the messages stabilize or the threshold of a maximum number of iterations is reached. The final belief $b_i(\sigma_i)$ of a node i is a vector of the same dimension as the message that measures the probability of node i being in state σ_i. The belief of node i is the normalized messages from all its neighbors shown in Eq. (9.8):

$$b_i(\sigma_i) = Z_2 \, \phi_i(\sigma_i) \prod_{k \in N(i)} m_{k,i}(\sigma_i), \tag{9.8}$$

where Z_2 is the normalization factor that ensures $\sum_{\sigma_i} b_i(\sigma_i) = 1$.

In the end, for each node the state with the highest belief score is chosen as the final state.

4 DETECTING CAMPAIGN PROMOTERS ON TWITTER

As social media platforms have become more and more important for marketing and advertising, detecting malicious promoters in social media campaigns is also an important task in detecting social media spam. Since tweets can be posted and accessed from a wide range of web-enabled services, real-time propagation of information to a large audience has become the focus of merchants, governments, and even malicious spammers. Unlike campaigns on traditional mass media platforms, social media campaigns often influence people in a hidden or implicit manner without disclosing their true intention. The readers are thus often unaware that the messages they see are strategic campaign posts aimed at persuading them to buy some target products/services or to accept some target ideas or ideologies. It is thus important to discover such campaigns, their promoter accounts, and how the campaigns are organized and executed. The goal is to classify two types of user accounts, those involved in promotion and those not involved.

Similarly to the approach introduced in the last section, this algorithm [28] also formulates the promoter detection problem with MRFs. Because Twitter allows only 140-character-long messages (called tweets), they are often too short for effective promotion of targeted products/services. Promotional tweets typically have to include URLs pointing to the full messages, which may include pictures, audio, and videos. Three different types of entities are considered jointly to detect campaign promoters; namely, users, URLs, and bursts. And different types of entities have different states. For example, a user can be either a promoter or a nonpromoter; a URL can be either a promoted or an organic URL; and a burst can be either a planned or a normal burst.

To jointly model different types of entities (different types of nodes) and their relationship, this algorithm generalizes the classic MRF to the typed MRF (T-MRF), which allows nodes of different types connecting to each other in the network. The relationship between different entities is based on the following intuition. If one user has a higher probability of being a promoter, then the URLs in his/her tweets are likely to be promoted URLs. Likewise, the burst that he/she is in is likely to be a planned burst. Such relationships can be modeled in the T-MRF, and the above intuition is the key for defining the potential functions in a T-MRF.

4.1 CAMPAIGN PROMOTER MODELING USING TYPED MARKOV RANDOM FIELDS

In contrast to a classic MRF, a T-MRF defines a graph with typed nodes $T = \{t_1, t_2 \ldots, t_n\}$. Each t_i is an element of a finite set of types H; that is, $t_i \in H$. For example, we use three node types in this work; that is, $H = \{$user, URL, burst$\}$. Each type of node represents a type of entity of interest (eg, user, URL, or burst in our case), and the edges between nodes represent their dependency relationships. For example, there will be a user-URL edge if a user's tweet contains a certain URL. Again, two kinds of potential functions are defined on the T-MRF: the prior potential $\phi_i(\sigma_i|t_i)$ and the compatibility potential $\psi_{i,j}(\sigma_i, \sigma_j|t_i, t_j)$. The compatibility potential gives the probability of a node v_j of type t_j being in the state σ_j given its neighboring node v_i of type t_i being in state σ_i. Now we introduce how prior potentials and compatibility potentials are set.

4.1.1 Node prior potentials

In this method, there are three types of nodes and each type of node needs a different way of estimating priors given the available prior knowledge:

Table 9.2 Propagation Matrix $\psi_{i,j}(\sigma_i, \sigma_j | t_i, t_j)$ for Each Type of Edge Potential

t_i = User	t_j = URL	
	Promoted	Organic
Promoter	$1 - 2\epsilon$	2ϵ
Nonpromoter	2ϵ	$1 - 2\epsilon$

(a)

t_i = User	t_j = Burst	
	Planned	Normal
Promoter	$0.5 + \epsilon$	$0.5 - \epsilon$
Nonpromoter	$0.5 - \epsilon$	$0.5 + \epsilon$

(b)

t_i = URL	t_j = Burst	
	Planned	Normal
Promoted	$0.5 + \epsilon$	$0.5 - \epsilon$
Organic	$0.5 - \epsilon$	$0.5 + \epsilon$

(c)

t_i = User	t_j = User	
	Promoter	Nonpromoter
Promoter	$0.5 + \epsilon$	$0.5 - \epsilon$
Nonpromoter	0.5	0.5

(d)

- **User prior**: Here supervised classification is used to compute the state priors for each user node. Since promoters and nonpromoters have different goals, they differ greatly in how they behave. We can train a classifier from a set of labeled users and to estimate the state probability distribution for the unlabeled users. Both content features and behavioral features are considered. Content features may include the number of URLs per tweet, the number of hashtags per tweet, the number of user mentions per tweet, the percentage of retweets for each user, and the number of URLs per tweet. The abuse of user mentions is also an important feature for the learner. Behavior features may include the maximum, minimum, and average number of tweets per day, the maximum, minimum, and average time between two consecutive tweets, the total number of tweets, and the number of unique URLs tweeted. For classification, we use logistic regression because it can give the estimated posterior probability for each class, which can be directly used as the node prior in the T-MRF.
- **URL and burst prior**: Using the same strategy, one can classify a URL into the promoted or organic class. However, labeling URLs is difficult because there are usually a large number of tweets containing a URL, which increases the cost of labeling tremendously. Instead, one can obtain directly estimates of class/state probabilities for URL nodes using the labels of users. The idea is if a URL is tweeted more by promoters than by nonpromoters, it is believed to be promoted. URLs that are tweeted neither by labeled promoters nor by labeled nonpromoters have equal probabilities of being in the two states. Even if there are many more unique URLs than labeled users, the number of popular URLs in the campaign could be estimated approximately. Similarly, the prior belief of a burst can be estimated. Planned bursts are dominated by promoters, while natural bursts are dominated by normal users.

4.1.2 Compatibility potentials

Since we have three types of nodes, the interactions or dependencies among different nodes (or random valuables) are also different. There are thus six kinds of edges in this model, user-URL, user-burst, user-user, burst-burst, URL-burst, and URL-URL. However, only four are found to be useful: user-URL, user-burst, URL-burst, and user-user (see Table 9.2). Compatibility potentials for these four types of edges are defined on the basis of the following intuition:

- **User-URL potentials**: A user and a URL form an edge if the user has tweeted the URL at least once. If a URL is heavily promoted, the users who tweet the URLs are likely to be promoters. In contrast, URLs that are relatively less promoted are usually mentioned by nonpromoters. URLs in the tweets of promoters are called *promoted URLs*.
- **User-burst potentials**: A user and a burst form an edge if the user posted at least one tweet in the burst. The arrival of a large number of tweets forming a burst is either a natural reaction to a successful campaign or a deliberate promoting activity from real promoters and/or their Twitter bots. We assume planned bursts contain primarily promoters and normal bursts are mostly formed by normal users who are attracted by the campaign.
- **URL-burst potentials**: A URL and a burst form an edge if the URL has been tweeted at least once in the burst. To maximize the influence of a campaign, campaign promoters have to continuously post tweets to maintain the advertising balance for URLs of interest. Similarly to user-burst potentials, URLs mentioned within a planned burst are likely to be promoted and URLs in a normal burst are likely to be organic.
- **User-user potentials**: Rather than working alone, campaign promoters can be well organized. A group of campaign accounts that work collaboratively can attract a greater audience and increase their credibility. If the group of accounts is not consider collectively, it is often difficult to detect some individual promoters because of insufficient features. Thus links between users are created if two users are considered similar in their behaviors. Similarity can be measured on the basis of the content similarity of their tweets, URL similarity, and "following" similarity. The last two similarity measures can be computed on the basis of the Jaccard coefficient.

4.2 INFERENCE

Similarly to the inference algorithm in the first algorithm, LBP is used to approximate the posterior probability over the states/labels of each node. In the T-MRF the message passing assignment of LBP is as shown in Eq. (9.9):

$$m_{i,j}(\sigma_j|t_j) = Z_1 \sum_{\sigma_i \in S} \psi_{i,j}(\sigma_i, \sigma_j|t_i, t_j)\phi_i(\sigma_i|t_i) \prod_{k \in N(i)\backslash j} m_{k,i}(\sigma_i|t_i). \qquad (9.9)$$

Eq. (9.10) shows the final belief $b_i(\sigma_i|t_i)$ of a node i of type t_i, which is a vector of the same dimension as the message that measures the probability of node i of type t_i being in state σ_i:

$$b_i(\sigma_i|t_i) = Z_2 \, \phi_i(\sigma_i|t_i) \prod_{k \in N(i)} m_{k,i}(\sigma_i|t_i). \qquad (9.10)$$

4.3 OPINION SPAM EVALUATION

One of the major obstacles toward review spammer detection is the evaluation because ground truth data are hard to obtain for comparison with the model output. Here we introduce two approaches to opinion spam/spammer evaluation:

- **Human evaluation**: Researchers have used human evaluation to judge if a system produces correct results for opinion spam detection [3,6,9,25]. It is commonly accepted that just by reading a single review without any context, it is very hard to determine whether a review is fake (spam) or not [1,4]. However, it has been shown [6] that when a context is provided (eg, reviewing patterns, ratings, posting activity trails), human expert evaluation becomes easier. Normally, several domain expert judges are hired to evaluate the results produced by the system. Given a reviewer and his/her reviews, the judges are asked to independently examine his/her entire profile (along with relevant metadata) to provide a label as a spammer or a nonspammer. In the end, the label with the maximum number of votes from different judges is taken as the real label and an agreement score is computed. Although commonly adopted, human evaluation is not perfect because human evaluation is subjective and different evaluators often have different tolerance toward even the same set of behavioral indicators.
- **Supervised text classification**: Supervised text classification can be considered as complementary to human evaluation. In spam review detection, we can treat the spam reviews as belonging to the positive class and nonspam reviews as belonging to the negative class. A classifier can then be built to separate the two classes of reviews. This evaluation can be applied only when an underlying assumption holds. It assumes that a set of features different from the text features are used in the spam detection step. In the review classification, we use purely linguistic features. If the classification shows good accuracy, we know that the reviews written by reviewers labeled as spammers and nonspammers on the basis of their behaviors are also separable on the basis of their review text. The mixed class is not used in this evaluation because it contains a mixture of spam and nonspam reviews, which are harder to separate.

5 SPOTTING SPAMMERS USING COLLECTIVE POSITIVE-UNLABELED LEARNING

Almost all the social media platforms and review-hosting websites have built their own spam detection systems based on either hand-crafted rules or machine learning algorithms. But all of them are facing the critical problem that they tend to only spot spammers or spam that is extremely abnormal. The high precision and unknown recall of filtered reviews leads to a positive-unlabeled (PU) learning problem. Li et al. [29] applied PU learning algorithms to a real-life fake review dataset shared by Dianping.com, which is the equivalent of Yelp in China. By taking the application of PU learning to Dianping as an example, we discuss why PU learning is more suitable than traditional supervised learning in datasets where label precision is high and recall is unknown. Li et al. [30] proposed the CPU learning method to perform the task; it outperforms existing PU learning models as it leverages the intricate dependencies among different entities. In this section, our discussion will be mainly about CPU learning.

5.1 PROBLEM DEFINITION

Dianping's filtering system has a very high precision, but unknown recall. This means almost all fake reviews detected are certainly fake but the remaining ones may not all be genuine. As reviews passed by its system may still contain many fake reviews, it is more appropriate to treat negative examples as

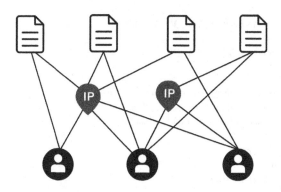

FIG. 9.1

Sample network of the users, reviews, and IP addresses.

an unlabeled set. In this section we will first introduce some notation and concepts and then define the CPU learning problem in a heterogeneous network.

A heterogeneous network is defined as $\mathcal{G} = (V, T, E)$, where $V = \{v_1, v_2, \ldots, v_{|V|}\}$ is a set of nodes representing the entities of different types and E is the set of edges incident on V. $e_{i,j} \in E$ if v_i has a link to v_j. In Dianping's problem, the heterogeneous network is defined as an undirected graph; that is, if $e_{i,j} \in E$, then $e_{j,i} \in E$. $T = \{t_1, t_2, \ldots, t_{|V|}\}$ is the set of corresponding entity types of nodes. Each t_i is an element of a finite set of types Γ (ie, $t_i \in \Gamma$). For example, in the defined heterogeneous network, there are three types of nodes; users, reviews, and IP addresses. That is, $\Gamma = \{$user, review, IP address$\}$. The edges between nodes represent their dependency relationships. Fig. 9.1 schematically shows three types of nodes and some edges between them.

Each node v_i is associated with a class label y_i, which is an element of a set of states S_{t_i} that the node belongs to with respect to its entity type t_i. Thus we have $y_i \in S_{t_i}$. In the PU learning setting, a review has three states; *fake* (positive class), *truthful* (negative class), and a special state called *unlabeled*. A user has two states: *spammer* and *nonspammer*. An IP address can be either *suspicious* or *organic*.

ALGORITHM 9.1 COLLECTIVE POSITIVE-UNLABELED LEARNING ALGORITHM

Input: Heterogeneous network $\mathcal{G} = \{V, T, E\}$
        Training dataset indices A Testing dataset indices D
        Feature matrix $\mathcal{X}^R$, $\mathcal{X}^U$, $\mathcal{X}^I$
        Labels $\mathcal{Y}_A^R = \{y_i \mid i \in A, y_i \in \{+, u\}\}$, $\mathcal{Y}^U$, $\mathcal{Y}^I$
Output: $\mathcal{Y}_D^R = \{y_i \mid i \in D, y_i \in \{+, -\}\}$
Note: superscripts R, U, I stand for reviews, users, and IPs respectively

---

1: $\mathcal{N}, \hat{y} = \text{INITIALIZE}(\mathcal{G}, A, D, \mathcal{X}^R, \mathcal{X}^U, \mathcal{X}^I, \mathcal{Y}_A^R, \mathcal{Y}^U, \mathcal{Y}^I)$

2: **while** $\hat{y}$ not stabilized and maximal iterations have not elapsed **do**

3:     $\mathcal{M} = \varnothing$ //*adjacent matrix of relational features*

4:     $\hat{y} = \text{PREDICT}(\mathcal{N}, \mathcal{M}, A, D, \mathcal{X}^R, \mathcal{X}^U, \mathcal{X}^I, \mathcal{Y}_A^R, \mathcal{Y}^U, \mathcal{Y}^I)$

5: **end while**

6: Output $\mathcal{Y}_D = \{\hat{y}_i \mid i \in \mathcal{D}, \hat{y}_i \in \hat{y}\}$

7:

8: **procedure** $\text{PREDICT}(\mathcal{N}, \mathcal{M}, A, D, \mathcal{X}^R, \mathcal{X}^U, \mathcal{X}^I, \mathcal{Y}_A^R, \mathcal{Y}^U, \mathcal{Y}^I)$

9: 　**for** $i \in \{1, 2, ..., |V|\}$ **do**

10: 　　$\mathcal{M}_i = \{\hat{y}_j \mid j \in \mathcal{N}_i, \hat{y}_j \in \hat{\mathcal{Y}}^R \cup \hat{\mathcal{Y}}^U \cup \hat{\mathcal{Y}}^I\}$

11: 　　Append $\mathcal{M}_i$ to $\mathcal{M}$

12: 　**end for**

13: 　Train a logistic regression classifier f^R from $\mathcal{X}_A^R$, $\mathcal{Y}_A^R$ and $\mathcal{M}$

14: 　Train a logistic regression classifier f^U from $\mathcal{X}^U$, $\mathcal{Y}^U$ and $\mathcal{M}$

15: 　Train a logistic regression classifier f^I from $\mathcal{X}^I$, $\mathcal{Y}^I$ and $\mathcal{M}$

16: 　//update $\hat{\mathcal{Y}}^R, \hat{\mathcal{Y}}^U, \hat{\mathcal{Y}}^I$

17: 　$\hat{\mathcal{Y}}^R = \varnothing, \hat{\mathcal{Y}}^U = \varnothing, \hat{\mathcal{Y}}^I = \varnothing$

18: 　**for** $i \in \{1, 2, ..., |V|\}$ **do**

19: 　　$k = t_i$　//$t_i \in \{R, U, I\}$ t_i is the entity type

20: 　　$\hat{y}_i = f^k(x_i, \mathcal{M}_i)$

21: 　　Append $\hat{y}_i$ to $\hat{\mathcal{Y}}^k$

22: 　**end for**

23: 　Compute the mean μ_k and σ_k of $\hat{\mathcal{Y}}^k$ of all three types

24: 　**for** $i \in \{1, 2, ..., |V|\}$ **do**

25: 　　$k = t_i$　// $t_i \in \{R, U, I\}$ t_i is the entity type

26: 　　**if** $\hat{y}_i >= \mu_k + \sigma_k$ **then** // reliable positive data

27: 　　　update $\mathcal{Y}^k$ with label y_i set to $+$

28: 　　　**if** $i \in D$ **then**

29: 　　　　//reliable positive in testing reviews for training

30: 　　　　move i from D to A

31: 　　　**end if**

32: 　　**else if** $\hat{y}_i < \mu_k - \sigma_k$ **then** // reliable negative data

33: 　　　**if** $i \in D$ or y_i is not $+$ **then**

34: 　　　　update $\mathcal{Y}^k$ with label y_i set to $-$

35: 　　　**end if**

36: 　　　**if** $i \in D$ **then**

37: 　　　　//reliable negative in testing reviews for training

38: 　　　　move i from D to A

39: 　　　**end if**

40: 　　**end if**

41: 　**end for**

42: 　**return** $\hat{\mathcal{Y}}$

43: **end procedure**

5.2 COLLECTIVE CLASSIFICATION

CPU learning uses an iterative classification algorithm (ICA) [31] as its underlying relational classifier. While a conventional classifier is a function f that maps the observed feature matrix $\mathcal{X}$ onto the class label space $\mathcal{Y}$, the ICA breaks the independence assumption. Consider a node v_i whose class label $y_i \in \mathcal{Y}$ needs to be determined and suppose a neighborhood function $\mathcal{N}_i = \{j \mid e_{i,j} \in E\}$ returns the indices of its neighbors. $\mathcal{M}_i = \{\hat{y}_j \mid j \in \mathcal{N}_i, \hat{y}_j \in \hat{\mathcal{Y}}\}$ is the class label vector of the neighbors of node i that is derived from $\mathcal{N}_i$ and the estimated class labels matrix $\hat{\mathcal{Y}}$. The ICA trains a local classifier f, whose input is the observed features x_i of v_i as well as the estimated labels from its neighbors $\mathcal{M}_i$. Because many labels of nodes are unknown, this process has to be executed iteratively, and in each iteration the label y_i of each node is assigned the current best estimates from the local classifier $y_i = f(x_i, \mathcal{M}_i)$. The base learner used by the ICA can be any conventional classifier that gives probabilistic outputs such as logistic regression or support vector machines.

As the network is heterogeneous, Li et al. [30] divide the network into multiple networks, each of which is homogeneous. Nodes in the resulting networks are connected if they share common neighbors in the original network. Unlike the ICA, CPU learning allows initial labels to be violated if the current probability estimate strongly indicates the opposite prediction. This is especially useful for the mining of fake reviews that are identified by the collective classifier but not identified by Dianping's filter [32]. During each iteration, the model produces new estimates of nodes for all three types. For each type of node, the probability is assumed to be a normal distribution such that a set of reliable positive and reliable negative data instances can be extracted. Once a reliable positive data instance is identified, its label is changed from unlabeled to positive. However, relying on the fact that Dianping's filter has a very high precision, the label of a reliable negative is updated only if its label was previously unlabeled. Algorithm 9.1 outlines the CPU learning model.

5.3 MODEL EVALUATION

The effectiveness of the CPU learning model was evaluated on gold standard data from Dianping's system.[1] Tenfold cross validation was performed for each model. F_1, precision, recall, and accuracy are reported in Table 9.3. Compared with the other collective classification models ICA and MHCC [33], the CPU learning model achieves much better classification results (F_1 scores, precision, and accuracy) than nonrelational classifiers, which classify each instance independently. Nonrelational PU learning models (PU-LEA [34], Spy-EM [35], Spy-SVM [35]) have higher recall than the traditional supervised classifier logistic regression (LR) despite some loss in precision. This is because Dianping's unlabeled reviews contain hidden positives that provide purer positive and negative instances for training.

Table 9.3 Results of 10-Fold Cross-Validation				
	Accuracy	**Precision**	**Recall**	F_1
LR	0.679	0.557	0.536	0.546
PU-LEA	0.664	0.53	0.611	0.567
Spy-EM	0.595	0.468	0.891	0.613
Spy-SVM	0.626	0.488	0.733	0.585
ICA	0.788	0.761	0.601	0.671
MHCC	0.804	0.777	0.643	0.702
CPU	0.840	0.829	0.700	0.759

CPU, collective positive-unlabeled; ICA, iterative classification algorithm; LR, logistic regression.

[1] http://liu.cs.uic.edu/download/dianping/

5.4 TRENDS AND DIRECTIONS

Although many algorithms have been proposed to detect fake reviews, there is still a long way to go before we can weed out opinion spamming activities. There are also many interesting research directions that have not been or have barely been explored. Here we describe several such directions based on [36]:

- **Multiple site comparisons**: Spammers who promote or demote some target products may write fake reviews on multiple sites to achieve the maximum effect as many websites may sell the products or host reviews about the products. It is interesting to compare reviews of the same product across these sites to discover abnormalities; for example, similar reviews (contents or ratings) that are written at about the same time, similar user ids, and the same or a similar IP address. It is quite unlikely for a genuine reviewer to be bothered to post a positive review for a product on multiple sites.

- **Language inconsistency**: To suit different products and to stress personal experiences, fake reviewers may write something that is inconsistent or against social norms in different reviews. For example, to promote a woman's watch, a spam reviewer may write "*I bought this watch for my wife and she simply loved it.*" Later, to promote a man's shirt, the same reviewer may write "*I bought this shirt for my husband yesterday.*" The two sentences indicate gender inconsistency. There are many other possible inconsistencies that can be detected (eg, age, with/without children, ethnicity).

- **Nature of business**: In many cases the nature of the product or business can help to detect fake reviewing activities. For example, if all positive reviews of a hotel come from people living in the area near the hotel (on the basis of their IP addresses), these positive reviews are clearly suspicious because few people would stay in a hotel if they have homes nearby. However, there are so many types of businesses, and manually compiling such normal and abnormal behavior patterns is very difficult. The challenge is how we can design an algorithm to automatically discover such abnormal behavioral patterns for each domain.

- **Web use abnormality**: Web servers record almost everything that a person does on a website, which is valuable for detecting fake reviews. For example, using the IP address information and click behaviors, we may find that all positive reviews for a product are from the same or a similar IP address, or many reviewers who have never visited the website suddenly came to a product page directly and wrote positive reviews. In the first case, all the reviews might have come from the same person, and in the second case, the seller of the product might have paid people to write reviews for the product and also provided a link to the product page. The fake reviewers simply clicked on the link and posted fake reviews. Again, there are a large number of abnormal web use behavior patterns, and the challenge is how to automatically mine such patterns.

- **Early detection**: Most existing algorithms rely on patterns detected from review contents and reviewers' behaviors. It takes some time for most types of patterns to form. However, when the patterns finally show themselves, some major damage might already have been done. Thus it is important to design algorithms that can detect fake reviews as soon as possible, ideally immediately after they have been posted.

6 CONCLUSION

In this chapter we have discussed the use of network information from various social media entities in opinion spam detection. In particular, two techniques were introduced. MRFs combined with belief propagation are applied to model and infer the user-user, user-URL, and user-burst relationships, and CPU learning is employed to make use of existing commercial spam detection systems whose filtered reviews have high precision but unknown recall. The increasing dynamics and number of ways users may interact on social media websites brings both challenges and opportunities for researchers and engineers who fight against opinion spam. With an increasing number of ways users may interact on social media, opinion spammers may have more ways to subtly manipulate the systems and influence genuine users. At the same time, this gives us more room to design more accurate filtering systems by combining spammers' footprints from different aspects of their social media interactions.

ACKNOWLEDGMENTS

This work was supported in part by a grant from the National Science Foundation under grant no. IIS-1407927, a NCI grant under grant no. R01CA192240, and a gift from Bosch. The content of this chapter is solely the responsibility of the authors and does not necessarily represent the official views of the National Science Foundation, NCI, or Bosch.

REFERENCES

[1] N. Jindal, B. Liu, Opinion spam and analysis, in: WSDM, 2008, pp. 219–230.

[2] N. Jindal, B. Liu, E.-P. Lim, Finding unusual review patterns using unexpected rules, in: CIKM, 2010, pp. 1549–1552.

[3] E.-P. Lim, V.-A. Nguyen, N. Jindal, B. Liu, H.W. Lauw, Detecting product review spammers using rating behaviors, in: CIKM, 2010, pp. 939–948.

[4] M. Ott, Y. Choi, C. Cardie, J.T. Hancock, Finding deceptive opinion spam by any stretch of the imagination, in: ACL, 2011, pp. 309–319.

[5] F. Li, M. Huang, Y. Yang, X. Zhu, Learning to identify review spam, in: IJCAI, 2011, pp. 2488–2493.

[6] A. Mukherjee, B. Liu, N.S. Glance, Spotting fake reviewer groups in consumer reviews, in: WWW, 2012, pp. 191–200.

[7] J. Li, M. Ott, C. Cardie, E. Hovy, Towards a general rule for identifying deceptive opinion spam, in: ACL, 2014, pp. 1566–1576.

[8] G. Fei, A. Mukherjee, B. Liu, M. Hsu, M. Castellanos, R. Ghosh, Exploiting burstiness in reviews for review spammer detection, in: ICWSM, 2013, pp. 175–184.

[9] G. Wang, S. Xie, B. Liu, P.S. Yu, Review graph based online store review spammer detection, in: ICDM, 2011, pp. 1242–1247.

[10] L. Akoglu, R. Chandy, C. Faloutsos, Opinion fraud detection in online reviews by network effects, in: ICWSM, 2013, pp. 2–11.

[11] S. Rayana, L. Akoglu, Collective opinion spam detection: bridging review networks and metadata, in: KDD, 2015, pp. 985–994.

[12] S. Ghosh, B. Viswanath, F. Kooti, N.K. Sharma, G. Korlam, F. Benevenuto, N. Ganguly, P.K. Gummadi, Understanding and combating link farming in the twitter social network, in: WWW, 2012, pp. 61–70.

[13] C. Yang, R.C. Harkreader, J. Zhang, S. Shin, G. Gu, Analyzing spammers' social networks for fun and profit: a case study of cyber criminal ecosystem on Twitter, in: WWW, 2012, pp. 71–80.

[14] C. Perez, M. Lemercier, B. Birregah, A. Corpel, SPOT 1.0: scoring suspicious profiles on Twitter, in: ASONAM, 2011, pp. 377–381.

[15] A. Aggarwal, P. Kumaraguru, Followers or phantoms? An anatomy of purchased Twitter followers, CoRR abs/1408.1534 (2014).

[16] G. Stringhini, C. Kruegel, G. Vigna, Detecting spammers on social networks, in: ACSAC, 2010, pp. 1–9.

[17] C.C. Aggarwal, An introduction to social network data analytics, in: Social Network Data Analytics, Springer, New York, 2011, pp. 1–15.

[18] E. De Cristofaro, A. Friedman, G. Jourjon, M.A. Kaafar, M.Z. Shafiq, Paying for Likes?: Understanding Facebook like fraud using Honeypots, in: IMC, 2014, pp. 129–136.

[19] Q. Cao, M. Sirivianos, X. Yang, T. Pregueiro, Aiding the detection of fake accounts in large scale social online services, in: NSDI, 2012, pp. 197–210.

[20] X. Hu, J. Tang, Y. Zhang, H. Liu, Social spammer detection in microblogging, in: IJCAI, 2013, pp. 2633–2639.

[21] Y. Boykov, O. Veksler, R. Zabih, Markov random fields with efficient approximations, tech. rep., Ithaca, NY, 1997.

[22] K.P. Murphy, Y. Weiss, M.I. Jordan, Loopy belief propagation for approximate inference: an empirical study, in: UAI, 1999, pp. 467–475.

[23] G.R. Terrell, D.W. Scott, Variable kernel density estimation, Ann. Statist. 20 (3) (1992) 1236–1265.

[24] W. Pieczynski, A.-N. Tebbache, Pairwise Markov random fields and its application in textured images segmentation, in: SSIAI, 2000, pp. 106–110.

[25] S. Xie, G. Wang, S. Lin, P.S. Yu, Review spam detection via temporal pattern discovery, in: KDD, 2012, pp. 823–831.

[26] J. Pearl, Reverend Bayes on inference engines: a distributed hierarchical approach, in: AAAI, 1982, pp. 133–136.

[27] J.S. Yedidia, W.T. Freeman, Y. Weiss, Understanding belief propagation and its generalizations, Exploring Artificial Intelligence in the New Millennium, vol. 8, Morgan Kaufmann, Burlington, MA, 2003, pp. 236–239.

[28] H. Li, A. Mukherjee, B. Liu, R. Kornfield, S. Emery, Detecting campaign promoters on Twitter using Markov random fields, in: ICDM, 2014, pp. 290–299.

[29] H. Li, B. Liu, A. Mukherjee, J. Shao, Spotting fake reviews using positive-unlabeled learning, Comput. Sist. 18 (3) (2014) 467–475.

[30] H. Li, Z. Chen, B. Liu, X. Wei, J. Shao, Spotting fake reviews via collective positive-unlabeled learning, in: ICDM, 2014, pp. 899–904.

[31] P. Sen, G. Namata, M. Bilgic, L. Getoor, B. Gallagher, T. Eliassi-Rad, Collective classification in network data, AI Mag. 29 (3) (2008) 93–106.

[32] H. Li, Z. Chen, A. Mukherjee, B. Liu, J. Shao, Analyzing and detecting opinion spam on a large-scale dataset via temporal and spatial patterns, in: ICWSM, 2015, pp. 634–637.

[33] X. Kong, P.S. Yu, Y. Ding, D.J. Wild, Meta path-based collective classification in heterogeneous information networks, in: CIKM, 2012, pp. 1567–1571.

[34] D. Hernández, R. Guzmán, M. Móntes y Gomez, P. Rosso, Using PU-learning to detect deceptive opinion spam, in: Proceedings of the Fourth Workshop on Computational Approaches to Subjectivity, Sentiment and Social Media Analysis, 2013, pp. 38–45.

[35] B. Liu, Y. Dai, X. Li, W.S. Lee, P.S. Yu, Building text classifiers using positive and unlabeled examples, in: ICDM, 2003, pp. 179–188.

[36] B. Liu, Sentiment Analysis—Mining Opinions, Sentiments, and Emotions, Cambridge University Press, Cambridge, UK, 2015.

OPINION LEADER DETECTION

10

P. Parau, C. Lemnaru, M. Dinsoreanu, R. Potolea
Technical University of Cluj-Napoca, Cluj-Napoca, Romania

1 INTRODUCTION

Analyzing social networks allows one to gain valuable insights into the structure, dynamics, and flow of information within a group of people. This claim is especially true considering the number of interactions the Internet facilitates as a social communication framework. A task in the field of social network analysis is identifying relevant or out of the ordinary individuals. Among these, opinion leaders are individuals who can influence and shape the opinions of others. Identifying opinion leaders is useful in domains such as health care, for raising awareness on important issues, in advertising and marketing, or in the political domain. Therefore it is important to have methods and measures to objectively and accurately detect opinion leaders. This chapter presents approaches that can be used for detecting opinion leaders and discusses the advantages and drawbacks of different types of methods in different contexts. We also present general methods for identifying leaders or influencers, on the basis of the idea that an influential or important individual in a social network, or more generally a communication network, is likely to be an opinion leader as well.

The chapter is structured as follows: Section 2 contains the problem definition and application examples. Section 3 contains a description of various approaches for identifying opinion leaders, classified in categories based on the type of data analyzed. Section 4 contains a high-level critical discussion of the approaches presented. The chapter ends with concluding remarks in Section 5.

2 PROBLEM DEFINITION

Opinion leaders are individuals who exert a significant amount of influence within their network and who can affect the opinions of connected individuals. Opinion leaders play an important role within the two-step flow of communication model, where information is transferred from the mass media to the public in two steps: first, from the media to opinion leaders and then from opinion leaders to the larger audience [1]. The two-step flow is therefore relevant to the process of influencing and changing people's opinions [2]. According to Katz [1], the following three factors impact the status of opinion leadership: (1) personification of certain values, (2) personal competence, and (3) strategic social location. The status of opinion leadership might change with time and different individuals may be opinion leaders in different domains.

There are many domains in which information can be disseminated more effectively when opinion leaders are targeted. For instance, in the medical field, detecting opinion leaders has been used to raise awareness and promote new and effective treatments [3], as in HIV prevention or child health promotion [4]. Climate change awareness campaigns have also relied on opinion leaders to effectively disseminate information [5]. Two such examples are campaigns led by Al Gore in the mid-to-late years of the first decade of this century that involved selecting opinion leaders to give presentations and inform the larger public on climate change issues. Opinion leader identification is also of interest in advertising, marketing, and product adoption [3], where companies are interested in attracting potential clients to their products as effectively as possible. Political campaigns can also benefit from identifying and targeting opinion leaders, as evidenced by the 2004 US presidential election campaign of George W. Bush, where opinion leaders were selected to promote the campaign [5]. Knowing who the opinion leaders are can yield benefits in a variety of domains, which makes their correct and efficient identification a very important task.

Traditionally, sociological approaches rely on manual or explicit collection of leader information via questionnaires or interviews [1]. A survey covering 191 articles in the field of sociology found that the main strategies for leader identification are distributed as follows: 19% use sociometric methods, 13% use self-selection, 12% use positional approaches, 11.5% use judges' ratings methods, and the rest do not reveal the identification mechanism [6]. Such approaches possess several drawbacks: On one hand, self-reported information is subjective by nature and self-claimed influence is likely to be a reflection of self-confidence [3]. Having an objective assessment of opinion leadership would lead to more reliable methods of finding leaders. On the other hand, sociological studies are limited in scope by the resources needed to undertake them; having scalable algorithms that can accurately identify opinion leaders allows us to take advantage of the ever-growing quantities of social data generated on the Internet. Thus methods that rely on network science and data mining techniques to identify opinion leaders have been developed, and such approaches are the focus of this chapter.

3 APPROACHES

This section presents the most important approaches for opinion leader identification, grouped, according to the characteristics of the available data, into four categories: methods that rely on static measures extracted from the network topology, either at global level or at community level; methods that additionally employ interaction information, which are suitable in contexts in which such information can be observed or approximated; a third category encompasses approaches that extract— totally or partially—network data from the content generated by users; finally several approaches employ both interaction and content information to determine influential users within the network. For each category we present relevant approaches, highlighting the methods and metrics employed and some evaluation results. We also present several approaches for related challenges, whose solutions can be applied to the leader detection problem.

3.1 MEASURES BASED ON NETWORK STRUCTURE

This section presents measures for assessing leadership on the basis of the structure of the network, considering topological factors as indicators for influential nodes. Heuristics based on vertex degree, network paths, or the community structure are used to identify potential leaders by their position within the network, considering that social location is an important factor in opinion leadership [1].

3.1.1 Centrality measures

A straightforward method of assessing the relevance of a vertex is to compute its centrality. The centrality of a vertex is a measure of its importance in the network in a given perspective [7] and can be expressed in various ways; thus there are multiple types of centrality measures. Which measure is suitable in a given context depends on which aspect of the network topology the centrality measure captures.

The simplest centrality measure is the degree of the vertex, also called *degree centrality* [7]. This measure suggests that the better connected a vertex is, the more important it is in the network. From the perspective of opinion leaders, it seems intuitive that the potential for communication and influence is greater for individuals with more connections. *Eigenvector centrality* attempts to capture the qualitative aspect of the connections of a vertex. On the basis of the premise that connections to more influential vertices are more important than connections to less influential vertices, the measure also takes the centrality of the neighbors into account [7]. Similarly to eigenvector centrality is *PageRank*, which assesses the importance of webpages in a search engine [8]. PageRank models the probability that a "random" web surfer, who starts at a random webpage and continues following links, will visit a webpage (or vertex in the webpage network). The measure also introduces a damping factor that expresses the probability at each step that the surfer will not continue with a link but will jump to a random webpage. Other centrality measures explicitly consider the indirect connectivity to other vertices in the network. *Closeness centrality* is such a measure, and it represents the average distance, or average shortest path, to all other vertices in the network [7]. The basic idea here is that a central vertex will be closer on average than other, less central vertices. This also makes sense from an influence perspective: a person who can easily reach other people will be more effective in spreading influence. *Betweenness centrality*, on the other hand, attempts to capture the ability of a vertex to control the flow of communication: it indicates how many times a vertex is located on the shortest path between two other vertices [9]. A vertex situated on a large number of such paths has an increased power to control communication since any information passing through those paths will pass through the vertex.

As stated earlier, different centrality measures are suitable for identifying the most important vertices in different contexts, contexts that match the assumptions implied by the specific formulation of the measure. Whether a centrality measure truly reflects importance in a network depends on how information flows in that particular network [10]. Next we look at several findings on centrality measures as indicators of leadership. The findings of a study on opinion leadership in smartphone adoption suggest that degree centrality does indeed indicate opinion leadership [11]. In the same study it was found that, as expected, social influence is greater over stronger connections or ties, but no significant interaction between the connection strength and degree centrality was found. The findings in [12] suggest that degree centrality is an indicator of local opinion leadership, since a high degree centrality means many connections in the direct environment of a vertex. To assess global opinion leadership, the closeness and betweenness centrality measures are better suited. The reason for this, Bodendorf and Kaiser [12] argue, is that individuals who are easily reachable by others have a higher chance of being noticed (closeness centrality), while individuals who lie on communication paths can exert a greater influence on that communication (betweenness centrality). Shafiq et al. [13], in experiments on data collected from Facebook, found that leaders tend to have significantly higher degree centrality on average than other types of individuals, which supports the idea that being well connected and having a high degree centrality is beneficial to the opinion leader status. However, they also noted that a large number of leaders do not have a high degree centrality, which suggests that degree centrality does not capture all aspects of leadership. The best closeness centrality is found among leaders, especially among introvert leaders. In their experiments, eigenvector centrality could not differentiate between leaders and followers but was significantly lower for neutral nodes (neither leaders nor followers). PageRank, on the other hand, was higher for leaders than for followers. Despite these differences in PageRank and degree centrality between leaders and nonleaders, Shafiq et al. do not recommend these measures for detecting leaders in interaction data.

Lu et al. [14] found the PageRank measure to be less effective in networks of people than in webpage networks, so they propose LeaderRank as a more effective way for ranking people in a network. LeaderRank is similar to PageRank but is parameter free: it introduces a ground node, which is connected to all other nodes in the network, and it has a role similar to that of the damping factor in PageRank. This factor is thus absent, which eliminates the need for calibration. Their experiments on data from Delicious, a social bookmarking service, suggest that LeaderRank outperforms PageRank in the task of identifying influential users. They also found that this algorithm has better performance than just taking into account the number of followers a user has (i.e., degree centrality).

Chen et al. [15] proposed a new semilocal centrality measure that relies on the nearest and the next nearest neighbors to identify the most influential nodes in an undirected network. The proposed approach seems to identify influential nodes better than degree centrality–based and betweenness centrality–based methods. However, other existing random-walk approaches such as PageRank and LeaderRank seem to be better indicators of influential nodes but less computationally efficient. The method was tested on four different real-life networks: bloggers on the MSN Spaces (Windows Live Spaces) website, coauthors in network science a router-level topology, and e-mails of the members of a university. The method performed differently depending on the network structure and is recommended for heterogeneous networks and less for tree-shaped networks. Chen et al. also analyzed the relation between the centrality measures considered, showing that, in general, the proposed local centrality has a strong positive correlation with closeness centrality, and a weak correlation with betweenness centrality and degree centrality.

Cho et al. [16] conducted a systematic study using a stochastic cellular automata model associated with the small-world assumption to analyze the effect of different centrality metrics and network properties on the diffusion speed and maximum cumulative number of adopters in the context of the diffusion of innovation. The experimental results reveal that distance centrality and rank-nomination centrality are the best for maximizing the cumulative number of adopters, whereas sociality provides the best speed of diffusion.

3.1.2 Community-driven measures

There are a variety of measures for assessing the importance of an individual in a network, but many of them—for instance, the classic centrality measures mentioned in the previous section—do not take the community structure of the network into account. A common definition for a community is an area of the graph that has a higher connection density [17], and is usually formed by vertices that share common properties [18]: individuals who are friends, who frequently communicate with each other, or groups of like-minded individuals. From the perspective of social location as a factor for opinion leadership, both the connections to people inside the group and also external connections are important [1]. The community structure is an important characteristic of networks, and it seems natural to take the position of individuals within it into account when one is assessing their importance.

One of the simplest measures that can be used to discover relevant vertices in the community structure of a network is *embeddedness* [19–21]. It is defined as the ratio between the internal degree (the number of connections to other vertices within the community) and the total degree (all connections, including ones with vertices outside the community). This measure quantifies how strongly a vertex belongs to its community, however, in real-world networks many vertices have no connections to other communities and they have high embeddedness values [19,20,22]. In such cases the ability of embeddedness to distinguish between important and unimportant vertices is diminished. Parau et al. [22] proposed the *relative commitment* measure, which is simple to compute yet captures more information than embeddedness. On one hand, relative commitment takes the magnitude of the internal degree of a vertex into account and, on the other hand, it represents a weighted measure: connections to highly committed vertices will have a greater impact on the score than connections to less committed vertices. This can be viewed as a force acting on the vertex, pulling it towards the community of the connected vertex with a force that depends on the commitment of the latter. Rosvall and Bergstrom [23] presented a method for quantifying the *statistical significance* of vertices in a community structure and identifying the significance clusters of vertices within communities. Their method consists in generating a number of bootstrap networks in which the connections are modified to a certain extent compared with the original network. The community structure of all of these networks is compared and the largest subset of vertices in a community that appear together in the same community in at least 95% of the bootstrap networks is the significance cluster of that community. The significance of a vertex, defined as the percentage of bootstrap networks in which the vertex maintained its original community membership, can thus be viewed as a measure of the membership strength of that vertex, and the findings in [22] suggest that it is a superior measure compared with embeddedness and relative commitment. A disadvantage of significance is that it is computationally intensive. Guimera and Amaral [24] proposed two measures that are jointly used to classify vertices in a community structure in seven roles. The *z score* measures how well connected a vertex is within its own community, and the *participation coefficient* quantifies the degree to which the connections of a vertex are distributed among the communities of the network. On the basis of the *z* score, vertices are classified as hubs and nonhubs, which are then further classified on the basis of the participation coefficient.

The previously mentioned community-driven measures are classified in [22] as measures of commitment to a community. Parau et al. argue that there is also another dimension of the community-driven relevance of a vertex—community importance—and propose a categorization of vertices based on these two dimensions. Commitment is an indicator of the membership strength of a vertex toward its community, while community importance shows how prominent a role the vertex plays for the structure of the community. Parau et al. proposed a community importance measure called *community disruption*, which assesses the importance of a vertex by examining the effects on the community of removing the vertex from the network. The measure is based on the idea that the removal of an important vertex will cause greater changes in the community (e.g., the community splitting into subcommunities, vertices migrating to other communities) than unimportant vertices. A disadvantage of this measure is that it is computationally intensive.

A category among the community-driven approaches to detect relevant vertices is represented by methods that aim to identify community kernels: the core members of a community. In [25] the kernel of a community consists of influential vertices inside that community: each community is composed of such a kernel and an auxiliary community of nonkernel members. Wang et al. [25] argue that kernel members can be detected with use of a centrality measure such as degree centrality or PageRank followed by a community detection method on these kernels only, but that doing so ignores the connections to auxiliary members. Thus they propose two algorithms to find the kernels and conduct experiments on coauthorship networks and on a Twitter dataset. An extension of these algorithms is presented in [26], where the attributes of vertices (eg, gender, age) are also considered while the community kernels are found. Du et al. [27] found community kernels by using overlapping maximal cliques. They also performed a step of community naming in which they identify the central entities of each community through a central entity resolution algorithm and build a community profile based on them.

3.1.3 Summary
The findings presented in this section suggest that while measures based solely on the topological properties of a network capture important aspects of leadership, there are other factors that can influence the status of a vertex that are not captured by these measures. In the following sections, we examine approaches that consider additional factors to identify opinion leaders.

3.2 METHODS BASED ON INTERACTION
Network topology information captures the relationships between individuals at a certain moment in time. By contrast, interaction information captures dynamic exchanges between individuals, usually also considering the temporal dimension of these exchanges. Analyzing user interactions can help establish the flow of influence in a network, which can provide significant insights into the leading individuals within the network. The flow of influence in a network is closely related to information diffusion processes, in the sense that the global (or local) influence of a node can be generally inferred if the diffusion process is known, or modeled correctly. All approaches in this section rely on interaction information and most consider structural network information also; in terms of the algorithms employed, the approaches range from greedy search strategies to frequent pattern mining, or clustering.

A general framework for modeling the diffusion process in a dynamic network is presented in [28]. The diffusion is modeled as a discrete network of continuous, conditionally independent, temporal processes that may occur at different rates. Rodriguez et al. [28] start by considering three well-known functions to model the conditional transmission likelihood between two nodes (exponential, power-law and Rayleigh). On the basis of these, survival and hazard functions are defined, which leads to the definition of the likelihood of a cascade. The proposed solution managed to track near perfect performance in the evaluations performed, for both continuous and discontinuous transmission rates. Although it does not explicitly identify leaders, the approach is relevant because it models the information flow in the network, and can be used to infer the influential nodes.

In the domain of advertising in marketing, analyzing the purchasing habits of users can be used not only to predict purchases but also to identify how user influence acts on the decision to buy a product. Richardson and Domingos [29,30] proposed probabilistic models for networks extracted from knowledge-sharing sites to estimate customer network value, so as to devise the best viral marketing plan. The motivation for their approach is the fact that many markets possess strong network effects (i.e., an individual's decision to purchase is influenced both by an intrinsic motivation and by the influence exerted by people whose opinion he/she values). Therefore each potential customer possesses an intrinsic value and a network value, which captures the strength of the influence the particular customer has on the probability of a purchase by other customers.

Kempe et al. [31] proposed a greedy hill climbing approach for the problem of detecting the k most influential individuals, and then proved that it provides a solution within 63% of the optimal solution, for several diffusion models. They explicitly consider two classes of diffusion models—the independent cascade model and the linear thresholds model—and use the theory of submodular functions to prove the quality of the greedy approach. Comparisons performed with centrality-based heuristics show that the greedy approach achieves a greater number of adopters than the other heuristics, which confirms that approaches that consider network dynamics perform better than ones that rely on the structural properties of the graph alone.

Another approach that considers user interactions is presented in [32]. It relies on frequent pattern mining and integrates an undirected social network with a log of actions performed by the nodes to build a directed acyclic propagation graph. Leadership is defined in terms of the number of nodes that perform the same action as an initial user, after the initial user but within a time frame, and are reachable from that initial user via social links. On the basis of the propagation graph, user influence subgraphs are generated, from which leaders and tribe leaders are identified. Additional measures are considered, such as confidence and genuineness. The approach is also related to the community detection problem if a correlation between tribes and communities is considered. The evaluation data were obtained by the integration two real data subsets: one from Yahoo! Movies ratings and one from Yahoo! Messenger.

The *longitudinal user centered influence* model [13] relies on directed user interactions and computes two coefficients by means of linear regression: the ego coefficient and the network coefficient, correlating the user past interaction and the past inward interaction, respectively, with the future outward one. The approach relies on a generalization of the Friedkin-Johnsen influence model. A kernel k-means algorithm is employed to cluster individuals into introvert leaders, extrovert leaders, followers, and neutrals. Shafiq et al. [13] also examined the characteristics of the identified classes on a dataset extracted from Facebook, considering properties such as centrality measures, the number of triangles, and the clustering coefficient. The fact that different classes of users have different average values and distributions for these properties suggests that the selected classes are relevant, but also that some of these measures can be used to discriminate between members of different classes.

Diffusion processes can also be represented within the community structure of the network. Amor et al. [33] presented a method for community detection and role identification that relies on the analysis of a Markov process in the graph and defines the quality of the partition in terms of trapping the flow of the diffusion process. The users have different roles in the propagation of information, defined by similar in and out flow patterns. The solution employs the role-based similarity (cosine) measure to generate a role-based similarity graph by using the relaxed minimum spanning tree algorithm. The Markov stability function was used on the similarity graph to identify communities of users having similar in and out flow patterns (roles). Although this method does not explicitly identify leaders, nodes exhibiting leader behavior can be easily identified. The solution was evaluated on topic-specific Twitter data (the care.data debate). The community detection solution was applied on two networks—the follower and the retweet networks—yielding the interest communities and the conversation communities respectively. Roles were identified in the interest communities.

The approaches reviewed in this section consider the flow of information so as to identify the most influential nodes. The solutions generally combine centrality-based metrics with various models of information propagation such as random walk, Markov processes, and probabilistic models. They include methods for analyzing the models obtained via classification, clustering, or simple threshold-based functions to determine the most influential nodes. The most prominent application field for this category of methods is marketing.

3.3 METHODS BASED ON CONTENT MINING

This category of strategies relies on network structure and information extracted from the content various nodes in the network are exposing and sharing. The content is used to extract topic information (since opinion leadership is topic dependent), explicit user features (eg, expertise, geographical location, post time), or sentiment. Although not all strategies are specifically designed for leader identification, the approaches are applicable to such a context as well.

Song et al. [34] proposed the *InfluenceRank* algorithm to identify opinion leaders among blogs. The algorithm considers not only how central a blog is compared with others but also how novel the information posted on that blog is, and Song et al. argue that both properties are important. They claim that information posted on a blog may originate from other linked blogs or from a source not present in the blog network, or that it may be original. The latter sources of information can be viewed as a hidden node connected to that blog from which information novelty originates. They used latent Dirichlet allocation as a topic model and the cosine similarity measure to assess the novelty of a blog's entries and subsequently the information novelty of the blog. The InfluenceRank measure contains a parameter that controls the extent to which novelty affects the score, and if that parameter is 0, the measure reduces to PageRank.

An original strategy (*BARR—blog content, author, reader properties, relationship*) for opinion leader identification in social blogs was presented in [35]. The method relies on the observation that the influence of a blogger can be estimated as the weighted sum of the quality and the quantity of blogs created. The method combines several data sources (keywords, blog portals, and web sources) and applies an ontology-based extraction method to collect values for 11 parameters, such as the number of visits per blog, the author's expertise, author blog preference, reader expertise, homophily, and tie strength. The method uses the technique for order preference by similarity to the ideal solution (TOPSIS) to compute the related similarity of each blog to the ideal solution, and compute the hot blog of an author. Ultimately, it expresses the influence of an author as the weighted sum of the quality (the normalized, largest related similarity) and the quantity of his/her blogs.

Huang et al. [36] presented the *positive opinion leader detection* method, which starts from a graph-based three-level structure representing the topic, comments, and users. The approach performs sentiment analysis on the comments, classifying them as positive, negative, or neutral. The weights of the edges are computed on the basis of the sentiment similarities of the comments. The impact of time (i.e., the older a comment, the weaker its influence) is also considered as a function used to reduce the probability of the selection of a comment. On the basis of the time-weighted, normalized weights, an improved finite Markov chain is defined.

Opinion leadership can be reflected in the way the content individuals produce is distributed and shared across social media or even more traditional forms of media. For instance, Niculae et al. [37] presented an unsupervised prediction setting to quantify media bias, by means of identifying the quotes an outlet will broadcast. *QUOTUS* was developed on the basis of data represented by 6 years of speeches by Barack Obama and the way they were reflected in the media. The solution requires the identification of patterns in the outlet-to-quote bipartite graph. While the authors do not explicitly refer to detection of opinion leaders, the principles presented may be applied to identify leaders of a community: if, instead of speeches we consider content produced by individuals and instead of quotes by the media we consider sharing and distributing the said content or parts thereof in different forms of media, we obtain a picture of what content is shared the most and which individuals produce the most shared content.

As mentioned previously, there is value in taking into account the community structure of a network when one is attempting to identify opinion leaders. Considering the observations in [1]—that different individuals can be opinion leaders in different domains—communities in a network can be viewed as an environment in which local opinion leaders act (depending on how they are constructed). Taking into account the characteristics of people when one is building the communities may help one in finding groups of similar people and subsequently finding leaders within them. In this sense, McAuley and Leskovec [38] presented a strategy to identify circles (i.e., communities) in ego networks on the basis of both profile similarity and network structure, which also allows for overlapping circles (relying on different, but not necessary disjoint dimensions of the profile). The evaluations were performed on data harvested from Facebook, Google+, and Twitter. Parau et al. [39] built networks based on the opinions of individuals, both based on the opinion target and aggregated across multiple opinion targets. These networks and their community structure could also be useful for detecting opinion leaders.

3.4 METHODS BASED ON CONTENT AND INTERACTION

The approaches falling into this category rely on both interaction information and content in addition to the network topology to identify opinion leaders. Temporal cues such as novelty, feedback flow, and explicit temporal data are exploited by the methods, together with specific content extracted, such as topic identification and user-related features (expertise, opinions, etc.). Some approaches in this category consider network topology information, while others rely solely on content and temporal information.

Li et al. [40] presented *ENIA*—a framework for ranking opinion leaders in online learning communities on the basis of four indicators: expertise, novelty, influence, and activity. They are extracted from three sources of information—textual content, observed user behavior, and temporal information—to compute a score for each of the four indicators. These scores are then multiplied to obtain the user score. The solution quality is evaluated with use of metrics to estimate longevity and centrality. ENIA was compared with PageRank and HITS on two datasets for online learning communities, showing superior correlation between the estimated ratings and the human-produced ratings compared with the other two approaches.

An opinion leader can also be viewed as an active member of a community whose produced content and feedback is important to other individuals. The findings in [41] suggest that received feedback impacts future user behavior asymmetrically on the basis of the feedback polarity. The approach employs binomial regression, considering only textual features from post content to predict the quality of the post. The outcomes of the evaluations are relevant in the context of the opinion leader by estimating the quality of the posts and measuring the feedback they receive, which would allow the detection of users who are likeliest to polarize interest.

The experiments reported in [42] provide understanding of how information spreads online and are relevant for predicting cascade growth. Moreover, the study identifies that the breadth of the initial growth in a cascade is an indicator of larger cascades and the depth is not. The features engineered for learning are grouped into four types: content-related features, original poster/resharer features, structural features, and temporal features. The experiments were conducted on Facebook photos uploaded within 1 month and reshares within 28 days of the initial upload. The findings of the study show that temporal and structural features are the most predictive, while the set of temporal features in isolation outperforms all other individual feature sets. Relevant for opinion leader detection are the observations that the star configuration tends to grow into the largest yet slowest cascades, that a median resharer has 35 fewer friends than someone who is active on the site nearly every day, and that cascades with initial fast reshares are likelier to grow significantly. Moreover, the finding that temporal and structural features are key predictors of cascade size allows efficient identification of relevant features for the community growth.

A good strategy to identify an opinion leader would be by predicting the number of reshares of a given post. On the basis of the theory of a self-exciting point, Zhao et al. [43] presented a theoretical framework to explain the temporal patterns of information cascades. The main advantage of the strategy is that it requires only the time history of reshares together, the degrees of the resharing nodes, and minimal knowledge about the information cascade and the underlying network structure. The method needs no feature engineering, hence it is not context dependent, and scales linearly (on the number of reshares of a given post). The mechanism was compared against four methods, and it is better and faster than each of them. *SEISMIC* can make an initial prediction of leading tweets in the first 5 minutes after the original post (with the time to learn parameter and time for prediction of just 0.02 seconds), with 25% error rate after 10 minutes and 15% error rate after 1 hour of tweet surveillance; moreover, just knowing the delay (of a retweet) allows one to accurately model the speed of a cascade spreading. The leader identification can be seen as identifying breakout tweets, applicable in contexts such as trend forecasting and rumor detection.

4 DISCUSSION

The first challenge for identifying opinion leaders is to determine how a leader is defined in different contexts. If we consider opinion leaders as individuals who have the ability to significantly influence other individuals, there are multiple perspectives from which leadership can be viewed. Firstly, a leader must have the ability to transmit influence, and this can be intuitively seen as being reflected in the structural properties of the social network. The leader concept is also commonly defined as the starting point of an action that propagates farther and faster than other actions. Therefore the leader detection problem is closely related to the dynamic propagation problem in networks, process modeling and process mining in networks, and influence modeling. A holistic solution can be achieved by integration of the structural properties, influence flow, and diffusion processes in networks. An important factor for identifying opinion leaders is who they are, their intrinsic properties, which, together with other factors, leads to their status. On can indirectly study these intrinsic properties by looking at personal characteristics, and also by examining the content produced by leaders, whether we talk about posts on social media, blogposts, comments on news articles, or even endorsements of other's content through sharing. In reality, all these elements factor into the opinion leader status, and ideally methods for detecting them would consider all these aspects. However, designing generally applicable methods that consider all these factors is a difficult task. As such, which method is best applicable to a specific problem depends naturally on the context. In some contexts a certain factor may outweigh the others significantly, such that a method specifically tailored to measure it (eg, degree centrality as a structural measure) can yield good results. In others the leader status is determined significantly by multiple factors, so the best results would be gained by the use of multiple methods, or hybrid methods.

Precisely defining what a leader is in a certain context is the first step in choosing the most appropriate methods or metrics to detect leadership. A further challenge is to identify the leader features in the available data. Even if the characteristics to be measured have been defined, they may not be clearly expressed in the available data, or they may not even be present. So the decision as to what approach to use in identifying opinion leaders is dependent on two factors: defining the concept of opinion leader in a particular context and identifying the defined features in the available data.

In the remaining paragraphs of this section we critically analyze the approach categories presented in Section 3. The advantage of using centrality measures to identify important individuals is that they rely only on the topology of a graph to assess the importance of its vertices. All such approaches are based on examination of the connectivity between vertices, which makes them relatively easy to use as long as the available data can be represented as a graph. This does not mean that they are universally suitable as leadership metrics, but it does represent an advantage over more specific measures: centrality measures generally capture fundamental network properties, which lends them intrinsic value. Whether they are used as is to assess importance or as input for a more complex measure, they can be useful in a variety of contexts.

The community structure of a network is an important property, especially in social contexts, where it can reflect the social structure present in such networks. The community topology shapes the flow of communication in a network and implicitly the flow of influence. Communities may form around important individuals who play an important role in their structure. Individuals may be leaders just in their own community, or they may influence multiple communities, and they can have varying degrees of commitment to different groups. Community-driven measures rely on the topology of the community structure, and as such the advantages and drawbacks mentioned in the previous paragraph apply here as well. On the basis of the idea that leaders are the most important or central individuals in a network, algorithms that search for the group of individuals who form the kernel of a community can also be useful to identify leaders or to select a set of candidates and thus limit the search space of the problem.

The generality of centrality or community-driven measures is simultaneously an advantage and a drawback: the information captured by them may be limited. Their usefulness is tightly coupled with how the network is built and what relationships between individuals it models. In cases where leadership is a combination of more factors than can be easily and effectively represented as network properties, more advanced centrality measures or other methods or algorithms may be needed to fully capture the concept of leadership.

Structural approaches consider only static properties of the network. To take advantage of the dynamic processes occurring in a network, one must consider the flow of influence, the communication processes, and the information diffusion model. Influential individuals can be viewed as hubs, playing important roles in the flow of influence in a network. Interactions in the network can offer important information on how influence flows between different categories of individuals: influence may flow from opinion leaders toward followers, followers may further contribute to the diffusion of influence by sharing or passing on information from the leaders they follow, etc.

To assess not only how individuals are communicating but also what they are communicating, one must examine the content they produce. Analyzing the topics, determining the sentiment, and assessing the novelty and originality of what someone posts are all factors that allow us to understand the characteristics of individuals. In social media especially, the type and quality of the content an individual produces is as important as his or her ability to distribute it effectively. Analyzing the content is perhaps a more difficult task since it addresses the question of why a certain type of content or certain opinions appeal to a larger audience and other types do not. We believe that while analyzing content can add great value to the task of identifying opinion leaders, content analysis techniques must be accompanied by methods that also assess an individual's ability to communicate: an individual can post the most interesting and original ideas, but he or she will never be an opinion leader if no one reads them.

Trends and directions in this domain can be observed from three main perspectives: approaches, evaluation, and applicability. The first important thing to note is that there is no universal approach. Even if solutions based on network structure and those that consider diffusion models possess a higher degree of generality, many recent methods have shifted toward trying to estimate the intrinsic features of individuals, by considering the content produced by them in conjunction with their observable relations (modeled as a social network) and (possibly) behavior. A potentially promising development would be to correlate the models with external events that might influence the behavior of the individuals, or to use several sources of data to extract information on the same individual (eg, intersocial networks). Analyzing multimedia content in addition to text could also provide a better assessment of an individual's characteristics.

Given the heterogeneity of existing solutions, it is natural that there are no established metrics and evaluation scenarios. This makes it difficult to compare methods. However, several measures that might be used to compare the methods have emerged recently, and it is important to note the evolution from human evaluation toward quantitative metrics.

While initially triggered by a pure economic necessity, with important marketing applications even nowadays, opinion leader detection has gained interest in other fields, such as online learning, disease awareness campaigns, and politics. There is an increasing interest in analyzing/predicting viral content, thus producing a focus shift from the individual toward the information an individual produces. This is strongly related to the emergence of solutions that exploit content.

5 CONCLUSIONS

The aim of this chapter was to present an overview of opinion leader detection approaches. To that end we described the problem of identifying opinion leaders and then reviewed various solutions categorized on the basis of the type of features they measure. We examined structural methods, including centrality and community-driven measures, approaches that focus on interaction data and influence diffusion processes within a network, and approaches that also consider the content of information posted by individuals.

The approaches, models, and processing flows, however, are highly dependent on the problem domain and the specific data available; therefore general-purpose solutions are extremely difficult to devise. However, practically speaking, the objective is to identify leaders on specific topics and in specific contexts (available data, domain); therefore the best specifically tuned methods have to be employed. The approaches presented in this chapter reflect these observations and allow the reader, we believe, to appropriately choose a method or an approach suited to a particular context.

REFERENCES

[1] E. Katz, The two-step flow of communication: an up-to-date report on an hypothesis, Public Opin. Quart. 21 (1) (1957) 61–78.

[2] V.C. Troldahl, A field test of a modified "two-step flow of communication" model, Public Opin. Quart. 30 (4) (1966) 609–623.

[3] R. Iyengar, C. Van den Bulte, J. Eichert, B. West, T.W. Valente, How social networks and opinion leaders affect the adoption of new products, GfK Market. Intell. Rev. 3 (1) (2011) 16–25.

[4] K. Guldbrandsson, M.K. Nordvik, S. Bremberg, Identification of potential opinion leaders in child health promotion in Sweden using network analysis, BMC Res. Notes 5 (1) (2012) 1–4.

[5] M.C. Nisbet, J.E. Kotcher, A two-step flow of influence? Opinion-leader campaigns on climate change, Sci. Commun. 30 (3) (2009) 328–354.

[6] T.W. Valente, P. Pumpuang, Identifying opinion leaders to promote behavior change, Health Educ. Behav. 34 (6) (2007) 881–896.

[7] M.E.J. Newman, The mathematics of networks, in: L.E. Blume, S.N. Durlauf (Eds.), The New Palgrave Encyclopedia of Economics, Palgrave Macmillan, Basingstoke, second ed., 2008, pp. 1–12.

[8] S. Brin, L. Page, The anatomy of a large-scale hypertextual web search engine, Comput. Netw. ISDN Syst. 30 (1–7) (1998) 107–117.

[9] L.C. Freeman, A set of measures of centrality based on betweenness, Sociometry 40 (1) (1977) 35–41.

[10] S.P. Borgatti, Centrality and network flow, Soc. Netw. 27 (1) (2005) 55–71.

[11] H. Risselada, P.C. Verhoef, T.H.A. Bijmolt, Indicators of opinion leadership in customer networks: self-reports and degree centrality, Market. Lett. (2015) 1–12, http://link.springer.com/article/10.1007/s11002-015-9369-7.

[12] F. Bodendorf, C. Kaiser, Detecting opinion leaders and trends in online communities, in: ICDS, 2010, pp. 124–129.

[13] M.Z. Shafiq, M.U. Ilyas, A.X. Liu, H. Radha, Identifying leaders and followers in online social networks, IEEE J. Sel. Areas Commun. 31 (9) (2013) 618–628.

[14] L. Lu, Y.-C. Zhang, C.H. Yeung, T. Zhou, Leaders in social networks, the delicious case, PLoS ONE 6 (6) (2011) e21202.

[15] D. Chen, L. Lu, M.-S. Shang, Y.-C. Zhang, T. Zhou, Identifying influential nodes in complex networks, Physica A 391 (4) (2012) 1777–1787.

[16] Y. Cho, J. Hwang, D. Lee, Identification of effective opinion leaders in the diffusion of technological innovation: a social network approach, Technol. Forecast. Soc. Change 79 (1) (2012) 97–106.

[17] M.E.J. Newman, The structure and function of complex networks, SIAM Rev. 45 (2) (2003) 167–256.

[18] S. Fortunato, Community detection in graphs, Phys. Rep. 486 (3-5) (2010) 75–174.

[19] A. Lancichinetti, M. Kivela, J. Saramaki, S. Fortunato, Characterizing the community structure of complex networks, PLoS ONE 5 (8) (2010) e11976.

[20] G.K. Orman, V. Labatut, H. Cherifi, Comparative evaluation of community detection algorithms: a topological approach, J. Stat. Mech. vol. 2012 (08) (2012) P08001.

[21] G. Palla, A.L. Barabasi, T. Vicsek, Quantifying social group evolution, Nature 446 (7136) (2007) 664–667.

[22] P. Parau, C. Lemnaru, R. Potolea, Assessing vertex relevance based on community detection, in: IC3K, 2015, pp. 46–56.

[23] M. Rosvall, C.T. Bergstrom, Mapping change in large networks, PLoS ONE 5 (1) (2010) e8694.

[24] R. Guimera, L.A.N. Amaral, Cartography of complex networks: modules and universal roles, J. Stat. Mech. 2005 (2) (2005) P02001.

[25] L. Wang, T. Lou, J. Tang, J.E. Hopcroft, Detecting community kernels in large social networks, in: ICDM, 2011, pp. 784–793.

[26] D. Maccagnola, E. Fersini, R. Djennadi, E. Messina, Overlapping kernel-based community detection with node attributes, in: IC3K, 2015, pp. 517–524.

[27] N. Du, B. Wu, X. Pei, B. Wang, L. Xu, Community detection in large-scale social networks, in: WebKDD/SNA-KDD, 2007, pp. 16–25.

[28] M.G. Rodriguez, J. Leskovec, D. Balduzzi, B. Scholkopf, Uncovering the structure and temporal dynamics of information propagation, Netw. Sci. 2 (1) (2014) 26–65.

[29] M. Richardson, P. Domingos, Mining knowledge-sharing sites for viral marketing, in: KDD, 2002, pp. 61–70.

[30] P. Domingos, M. Richardson, Mining the network value of customers, in: KDD, 2001, pp. 57–66.

[31] D. Kempe, J. Kleinberg, E. Tardos, Maximizing the spread of influence through a social network, in: KDD, 2003, pp. 137–146.

[32] A. Goyal, F. Bonchi, L.V. Lakshmanan, Discovering leaders from community actions, in: CIKM, 2008, pp. 499–508.

[33] B. Amor, S. Vuik, R. Callahan, A. Darzi, S.N. Yaliraki, M. Barahona, Community detection and role identification in directed networks: understanding the Twitter network of the care.data debate (2015), arXiv:1508.03165.

[34] X. Song, Y. Chi, K. Hino, B. Tseng, Identifying opinion leaders in the blogosphere, in: CIKM, 2007, pp. 971–974.

[35] F. Li, T.C. Du, Who is talking? An ontology-based opinion leader identification framework for word-of-mouth marketing in online social blogs, Decis. Supp. Syst. 51 (1) (2011) 190–197.

[36] B. Huang, G. Yu, H.R. Karimi, The finding and dynamic detection of opinion leaders in social network, Math. Prob. Eng. vol. 2014 (2014), Article ID 32840.

[37] V. Niculae, C. Suen, J. Zhang, C. Danescu-Niculescu-Mizil, J. Leskovec, QUOTUS: the structure of political media coverage as revealed by quoting patterns, in: WWW, 2015, pp. 798–808.

[38] J. McAuley, J. Leskovec, Discovering social circles in ego networks, ACM Trans. Knowl. Discov. Data 8 (1) (2014) 4:1–4:28.

[39] P. Parau, A. Stef, C. Lemnaru, M. Dinsoreanu, R. Potolea, Using community detection for sentiment analysis, in: ICCP, 2013, pp. 51–54.

[40] Y. Li, S. Ma, Y. Zhang, R. Huang, Kinshuk, An improved mix framework for opinion leader identification in online learning communities, Knowl. Based Syst. 43 (2013) 43–51.

[41] J. Cheng, C. Danescu-Niculescu-Mizil, J. Leskovec, How community feedback shapes user behavior, in: ICWSM, 2014.

[42] J. Cheng, L. Adamic, P.A. Dow, J.M. Kleinberg, J. Leskovec, Can cascades be predicted? in: WWW, 2014, pp. 925–936.

[43] Q. Zhao, M.A. Erdogdu, H.Y. He, A. Rajaraman, J. Leskovec, SEISMIC: a self-exciting point process model for predicting tweet popularity, in: KDD, 2015, pp. 1513–1522.

OPINION SUMMARIZATION AND VISUALIZATION

11

G. Murray[a], E. Hoque[b], G. Carenini[b]

University of the Fraser Valley, Abbotsford, BC, Canada[a] University of British Columbia, Vancouver, BC, Canada[b]

1 INTRODUCTION

There are many cases where it would be useful to be able to analyze opinions contained in a large amount of social media text. For example, it could help inform the decision making of an organization regarding development and marketing of a product. However, the vastness of textual data in social networks makes this a challenging and time-consuming proposition. For that reason it would be highly desirable to generate natural language summaries of opinions in social media, and present these summaries to the user in an easily understood format.

This chapter presents an overview of a set of computational methods for summarizing opinions from textual data. In particular, it discusses how various approaches for performing opinion detection and sentiment analysis can be used in generating textual summaries. It gives an overview of several extractive and abstractive summarization systems along with their relative trade-offs.

Once summaries have been generated from a large set of opinions, a further challenge is how to effectively present these summaries to the user. Information visualization can play a critical role here by creating visual representations of summaries along with important attributes of the underlying opinions (eg, strength, polarity). Often, visualizations can be interactive (eg, the user may filter and zoom into the actual opinions and get detailed information on demand). In this way, interesting patterns, trends, and outliers among opinions can be easily perceived, thus enhancing the ability of the user to make informed decisions. In the second part of the chapter, an overview of various visualization tools will be provided.

2 OPINION SUMMARIZATION

The task of automatically summarizing documents has been researched for several decades [1–6]. Most of this work has been on summarizing highly structured documents such as news articles and scientific journals. As a result, summarization researchers have focused a great deal on well-formed, grammatical documents that are mostly devoid of sentiment and opinion. Most of this work has also been *extractive*, meaning that sentences in the source document(s) are classified as informative or noninformative, and those informative sentences are simply concatenated to form a summary.

Recently, those trends have shifted. Researchers have focused on new domains such as automatic summarization of meeting transcripts [7], written conversations [8], lectures [9,10], and increasingly social media text. In general, the natural language processing community has become more interested in "noisy" text, which may include ungrammatical sentences, misspellings, fragments, and slang [11]. Documents in these domains are also likelier to contain opinions, sentiment, and disagreements.

Simultaneously, the summarization research community has started moving increasingly toward *abstractive* summarization approaches. The loosest definition of *abstractive* is that the summary sentences do not occur in the original source documents. By this definition, sentence compression approaches would qualify as abstractive [12,13]. In a stricter sense, abstractive approaches should mimic human-authored summarization by following steps roughly corresponding to understanding, synthesis, and creation of summary text. Spärck Jones [3] termed those steps *interpretation*, *transformation*, and *generation*. This type of abstraction is clearly more difficult than extraction, not least because it requires a natural language generation component, but it also offers the hope of more fluent and informative summaries than extractive techniques can offer. Many current abstractive summarization systems in truth fall somewhere between extractive and abstractive [14].

In the following sections we describe the challenges associated with summarizing opinion-filled social media text, and the approaches that researchers have taken.

2.1 CHALLENGES

There are two main challenges associated with summarizing social media text: the documents tend to be noisy and ungrammatical, and they are filled with opinions that may be very diverse and conflicting. Those challenges are addressed in turn.

2.1.1 Challenges of summarizing noisy text

The noisy nature of social media text poses challenges for all summarization systems but the challenges are different for extractive versus abstractive systems.

For an extractive system the output sentences are a subset of the input sentences. This means that the summary will reflect any ungrammaticalities, disfluencies, and slang that are in the input unless care is taken to remove them. This type of postprocessing can include expansion of acronyms, correction of misspellings, appropriate capitalization, and sentence compression. Sentence fragments and ungrammatical sentences are more difficult to deal with; they can be filtered out altogether, at the cost of reducing coverage of the document, or they can be left in the summary as is, at the cost of reducing readability and coherence of the summary.

Abstractive systems do not suffer from the same problem. We can use natural language generation to create well-formed sentences that describe the input documents at a high level. The natural language generation component gives us some control over readability, coherence, conciseness, and vocabulary. However, abstractive systems may be more reliant than extractive systems on syntactic and semantic parsing to represent the meaning of the input sentences at a deeper level. In some domains it is very difficult to get good parsing performance because of the noisy nature of the text. It may be possible to improve parsing by preprocessing the sentences, similar to the extractive postprocessing steps described above. Alternatively, systems could try to incorporate parsers, partial parsers, chunkers, or ontology mappers that have been specifically trained on such noisy data.

In one evaluation and comparison of extractive and abstractive summarizers in the similarly noisy domain of meeting speech [15], user study participants were extremely dissatisfied with extractive summaries and many participants remarked that the extracts did not even constitute summaries. Abstraction seems to have a clear advantage in such domains.

2.1.2 Challenges of summarizing opinion-filled text

The main challenge in summarizing opinion-filled text is to generate a summary that accurately reflects the varied, and potentially conflicting, opinions. If the system input consists of social media posts in which the vast majority of social media users share similar opinions about a person, organization, or product, then simple extractive approaches may suffice: just find some exemplar posts and make those the summary sentences. However, if the social media users disagree about that entity, or have a similar opinion but for different reasons, extraction alone may not be enough. For instance, if the group exhibits binary polarization about an issue or entity, we may be able to identify a mix of positive and negative exemplar texts, but concatenating them has the potential to create a very incoherent summary.

So abstractive approaches seem well suited to the task of summarizing opinion-filled text. The system can generate high-level sentences that describe the differing opinions and any information or evidence that seems to be driving those opinions. Further, a hybrid system can have each abstractive sentence linked to extracts that exemplify the viewpoint being described.

2.2 EVALUATION

We briefly describe two types of summarization evaluation that have been used in the literature.

2.2.1 Intrinsic evaluation

Intrinsic evaluation measures are so-called because they attempt to measure intrinsic properties of the summary, such as informativeness, coverage, and readability. These qualities are sometimes rated by human judges (eg, using Likert-scale ratings).

For system development purposes, human ratings are often too expensive and so are used sparingly. As an alternative, automatic intrinsic evaluation can be done by comparison of machine-generated summaries with multiple human-authored reference summaries. Multiple reference summaries are used because even human-authored summaries will often exhibit little overlap with one another. A very popular automatic summarization evaluation suite is ROUGE [16], which measures n-gram overlap between machine summaries and reference summaries. However, in other noisy domains it has been observed that ROUGE scores do not always correlate well with human judgments [17].

Another intrinsic evaluation technique is the pyramid method [18], which is more informative than ROUGE because it assesses the content similarity between machine and reference summaries in a more fine-grained manner. However, the pyramid method is much more time-consuming and only recently has a partially automatic version been proposed [19].

2.2.2 Extrinsic evaluation

The ideal evaluation is an extrinsic one, where one tests whether the generated summaries are actually effective in assisting users in some realistic task. Like human ratings of intrinsic summary qualities, extrinsic evaluations can be very expensive and so are rarely used during the system development process. Rather, they are employed after a system has been developed and has already been tested with intrinsic measures.

To give the most general example of an extrinsic summary evaluation, one can test whether user study participants are able to find information in the source documents more quickly when they have a generated summary to assist them. The required information may be in the form of a set of questions that the user needs to answer in a limited amount of time. Depending on the types of questions and the relevant documents, in some cases it may be easier and quicker for the user to simply do a keyword search. If the information need is more complex (eg, requiring the user to understand some aspect of group interaction in the source documents), a summary may be very valuable in completing the task.

2.3 OPINION SUMMARIZATION APPROACHES

Some of the most widely cited work on opinion summarization is by Hu and Liu [20], who developed a system for automatic generation of summaries for product reviews. They do not take a purely extractive or abstractive approach, instead developing a hybrid system that analyzes product features and creates a structured summary with links to actual review sentences.

The Hu and Liu system has three major steps:

1. identify product features from the customer reviews;
2. identify opinion sentences from the reviews, and determine whether they are positive or negative;
3. generate a concise summary of the results.

For identification of frequent features, they use a type of association mining based on the *Apriori* algorithm. They also develop a simple procedure for identifying infrequent features that may be of interest to some customers.

For identification of opinion words, they use adjectives and exploit WordNet's synonym and antonym sets to predict "semantic orientation" of adjectives.[1] They begin with a seed list of positive adjectives (eg, *fantastic*, *nice*) and negative adjectives (eg, *boring*, *dull*) and consult WordNet to expand the adjective lists. Identification of opinion sentences is done by analysis of the constituent opinion words of each sentence.

The actual summary generation component of the Hu and Liu system works in two steps:

- For each feature, the relevant opinion sentences are put into positive and negative categories, and a count is displayed for each.
- Features are ranked according to how often they are mentioned in reviews.

For a particular feature such as the *picture* feature of a camera, the summary snippet might show that there are 12 positive comments, including the following example: *"Overall this is a good camera with a really good picture clarity."*

To continue that example, it might also show that there are two negative comments, including: *"The pictures come out hazy if your hands shake even for a moment during the entire process of taking a picture."*

---

[1] https://wordnet.princeton.edu/

Hu and Liu performed three types of intrinsic evaluation corresponding to the various system components described above, and found the coverage and performance to be very satisfactory.

Carenini et al. [21] explored extractive versus abstractive approaches for summarization of product reviews. They began by distinguishing between *crude features* that can be extracted from product reviews and user-defined features that represent a more abstract taxonomy of product characteristics. They derived a mapping between crude features and user-defined feature; for example, the crude features "unresponsiveness" and "lag time" are mapped to the user-defined feature "delay between shots." Each crude feature cf_i is associated with a set of polarity and strength evaluations $ps(cf_i)$ derived from the product reviews. With the mapping between crude features and user-defined features, they can also derive the polarity and strength evaluations associated with each user-defined feature.

Their extractive approach relies on the MEAD open-source summarization framework [22]. A summarization feature they found particularly useful is defined in Eq. (11.1).

$$CF_{\text{sum}}(s_k) = \sum_{ps_i \in \text{eval}(s_k)} |ps_i|, \tag{11.1}$$

where s_k is a sentence and $\text{eval}(s_k)$ is a set of evaluations of crude features associated with the sentence. Their extractive system also used reranking i to reduce redundancy.

Carenini et al. compared this MEAD-based extractive system with an abstractive system wherein they first calculate the direct importance of each feature in the user-defined feature according to Eq. (11.2):

$$\text{dir\_moi}(\text{udf}_i) = \sum_{ps_k \in PS_i} |ps_k|^2, \tag{11.2}$$

where ps_i is the set of polarity and strength evaluations directly associated with feature udf_i. They then use a dynamic greedy selection algorithm to determine the most important features for the product that will need to be described in the summary. They calculate a polarity for each user-defined feature, and also assess the distribution of opinions. If the distribution is bimodal, users are split on whether they like the feature, and both viewpoints will need to be included in the summary. They generated the actual summaries using the GEA natural language generation system [23].

A key finding of their evaluation is that the two approaches performed similarly well but that the extractive summaries sometimes fail to give a thorough overview of the opinions expressed, while abstractive summaries can be repetitive or "robotic." The complementary nature of the strengths and weaknesses suggests that hybrid approaches should be feasible.

Carenini and Cheung [24] further investigated such issues and found that abstractive approaches are superior precisely when the products are more controversial. Extraction may not suffice when there are many viewpoints to be represented.

Nishikawa et al. [25] developed an opinion summarization system with a focus on online product reviews and restaurant reviews. They framed the summarization task as an integer linear programming problem, a strategy that was explored previously in other domains as well [26,27]. In their approach, maximizing the objective function results in a summary that covers the core concepts *and* has maximum coherence. More specifically, the objective function is given by Eq. (11.3):

$$\max \lambda \sum_{e_i \in E} w_i e_i + (1 - \lambda) \sum_{a_{i,j} \in A} c_{i,j} a_{i,j}. \tag{11.3}$$

Here e_i represents an opinion, which is a tuple $< target, aspect, polarity >$, where *target* is an entity and *aspect* is a feature of the entity. The tuple has an associated weight w_i, for which they use the frequency of the opinion in the document. The term $a_{i,j}$ represents an arc between sentences i and j, and $c_{i,j}$ represents the coherence of that arc. This is a constrained optimization problem, with example constraints being the length of the summary and constraints that tie together opinions and sentences.

Nishikawa et al. used two types of intrinsic evaluation: ROUGE and human ratings. They outperformed two state-of-the-art systems according to the ROUGE evaluations, but there were no significant differences according to human readability scores.

Potthast and Becker [28] described an opinion summarization system for web comments, which combines elements of summarization and visualization. Related to our earlier point about the risk of extractive summarization on noisy documents, Potthast and Becker state that it is "pointless" to extract sentences from web comments, and they instead focus on extracting words. Given a positive sentiment lexicon V^+ and negative sentiment lexicon V^-, they calculate the semantic orientation of a word using Eq. (11.4);

$$SO(w) = \sum_{w^+ \in V^+} \text{assoc}(w, w^+) - \sum_{w^- \in V^-} \text{assoc}(w, w^-), \qquad (11.4)$$

where assoc() is calculated as pointwise mutual information. If the semantic orientation of some word w is greater than a threshold ϵ, it is added to V^+. If it is below $-\epsilon$, it is added to V^-1. This has the effect of adapting the sentiment lexicon to the particular domain. They can then detect the commonest positive and negative words in Flickr images and YouTube videos. Finally, they arrange these words as positive and negative tag clouds.

Recently, Gerani et al. [29] have also explored how to leverage the discourse structure of product reviews to generate better abstractive summaries of those reviews. The discourse trees of all the reviews are aggregated in a graph that provides both content and structure for the summary. Two intrinsic crowdsourced evaluations in which users expressed pairwise preferences between summaries show that the proposed approach significantly outperforms extractive and abstractive baselines.

In this section we have focused on opinion-based summarization of web text such as weblogs and product reviews. We conclude the section by noting that there is also research on summarization of web text that does not focus on opinions. For example, Sharifi et al. [30] generate short summaries explaining why Twitter users are tweeting about a particular subject, but they do not incorporate opinion modeling in their work. There has also been some work on opinion summarization on data from nonweb sources (eg, telephone speech [31]).

3 OPINION VISUALIZATION

So far in this chapter we have discussed different methods for summarizing opinions from textual data in social media. However, a further challenge is how to support the user in understanding and analyzing the results of such summarization methods.

It is well known that information visualization techniques can be very useful to support the user in exploring a large amount of data [32]. Information visualization techniques take advantage of our visual information processing ability by creating visual representations of the large dataset. As a result, various interesting patterns, trends, and outliers can be much more easily observed.

An information visualization system initially shows an overview of the dataset; however, the user can get more detailed information on demand through interactive techniques. Showing such detailed information on demand is critical because we may lose important information in the summarization process [32]. For instance, if an opinion visualization for customer reviews presents the keyphrase "terrible display," only after reading texts from original reviews may the user realize that the keyphrase is concerned with the low-resolution display of a smartphone. In such situations, interactive techniques can help the user to read the original text on demand to understand the context of the summary. Another reason for introducing interactivity is that when we deal with large datasets, given the display limitations, a static visualization cannot show all the data at once. In such situations, interactive techniques can deal with large datasets by changing the view from an overview to more detailed data through direct manipulation, filtering, and zooming [33].

3.1 CHALLENGES FOR OPINION VISUALIZATION

A fundamental challenge of designing any information visualization system arises from the human and display limitations. Our perceptual and cognitive abilities are limited, which must be taken into account to design an effective visualization. Moreover, the limited display size often means there are trade-offs regarding what data should be shown and how they should be shown to the user.

Even if we assume that the visualization addresses these limitations successfully, it could be still ineffective if it does not match the specific task that users care about. In other words, a visualization can be comprehensible by humans but not well suited for the intended task. Therefore it is important to understand the user tasks and carefully choose the best possible visualization design by consideration of multiple alternatives.

There are also some design challenges that are very specific to opinion visualization for social media text data. One particular challenge arises from the noisy nature of social media text, as pointed out earlier in this chapter. As a consequence of noisy text, the results of text mining and summarization methods can be inaccurate. If the visualization does not account for such inaccuracy or uncertainty, the user may reach wrong conclusions after analyzing the data, or may lose trust in the system after realizing that the results are unreliable [34].

In this era of big data, another challenge emerges from the fact that social media data are often generated at a volume and velocity that cannot be handled by most of the existing tools. When we need to deal with such a large amount of data, many basic visualization techniques such as bar charts or scatter plots may not be sufficient to display the information. In such cases, a more complicated visualization may be needed to link multiple types of visualizations through interactions.

In the reminder of the section, we discuss a set of opinion visualization techniques for different text genres and how they address specific design challenges that we have pointed out.

3.2 TEXT GENRES AND TASKS FOR OPINION VISUALIZATION

Most of the previous work on opinion visualization in social media can be broadly categorized on the basis of the text genres and subsequently by the task characteristics, as shown in Table 11.1. We now provide an overview of the key text genres and possible tasks for each of these genres.

Table 11.1 Summary of the Work on Opinion Visualization Discussed in This Chapter, Organized on the Basis of Text Genres (Row) and Tasks (Column)

Text Genre	Task
Customer feedback	Explore opinions of a single entity Static data: Gamon et al. [35], Carenini et al. [36], Yatani et al. [37], Wu et al. [38] Streaming data: Hao et al. [39]
	Compare opinions between multiple entities Static data: Liu et al. [40], Carenini and Rizoli [41]
User reactions to large-scale events via microblogs	Explore opinions for large-scale events Static data: Diakopoulos et al. [42] Streaming data: Marcus et al. [43]
	Discover opinion diffusion for large-scale events Static data: Wu et al. [34]
Asynchronous conversations	Explore opinions in asynchronous conversations Static data: Hoque and Carenini [44]

3.2.1 Customer feedback
Early work on opinion visualization was done for customer review datasets with a focus on feature-based (aka *aspect-based*) sentiment analysis. When one is performing feature-based sentiment analysis, it is assumed that given an entity of interest (eg, a smartphone model), opinions are expressed on its features (eg, cameras, battery, screen). The goal is to support a potential customer to either explore what opinions were expressed on different features of an entity [35–37] or compare multiple entities [40,41]. In contrast, a business analyst may be interested in performing more complex tasks; for example, finding correlation between opinions and various data dimensions, such as geographical, demographical, and temporal aspects [38,39].

3.2.2 User reactions to large-scale events
Many news stories or events trigger a huge amount of discussion in social media, especially via microblogs such as Twitter. Analyzing people's opinions about such events is of great interest to business analysts, market intelligence analysts, and social scientists. The visualizations for large-scale events have mainly focused on supporting the user in analyzing overall sentiment trends; namely, how the sentiment evolves over time [42,43] and how a particular opinion spreads among users [34].

3.2.3 Online conversations
Online conversations in social media such as Facebook discussions or blog conversations exhibit several unique characteristics: unlike microblogs or messaging [45], they do not have fixed-length comments; furthermore they have a finer conversational structure as participants often reply to a post and/or quote fragments of other comments [46]. These unique characteristics need to be taken into account when one is designing both mining and visualization techniques. For this text genre, users can be categorized into two groups on the basis of their activities: (1) *participants* who have already contributed to the conversations, and (2) *nonparticipants* who wish either to join the conversations or to analyze the

conversations. A few visualization tools [44] have been developed recently to support the exploration of online conversations.

3.3 OPINION VISUALIZATION OF CUSTOMER FEEDBACK

Opinion visualizations on customer review datasets mainly focused on two major tasks: (1) explore opinions on a single entity and (2) compare opinions across features for multiple entities.

3.3.1 Explore opinions on a single entity

Often it is useful to organize the features of an entity into a hierarchy to provide a more structured view of opinions. Treemapping is a hierarchical visualization technique that was applied to represent the sentiment associated with different features of a product [35,36]. Within a treemap, each node is represented as a rectangle with nested rectangles that indicates the descendants of the node. The Pulse system clusters the sentences of reviews into different topics and visualizes these topic clusters and their opinions using a treemap [35]. Carenini et al. [36] extracted a set of features from reviews and automatically mapped these features into a user-defined hierarchy. The resultant hierarchy is visualized with use of treemaps, where each feature is represented as a rectangle as shown in Fig. 11.1. The size of the rectangle is used to represent the importance of that feature in the hierarchy, while color is used to represent the polarity (positive in green vs. negative in red) of customer opinions about that feature. In addition, a textual summary based on an abstractive method is presented to provide an overview of all reviews. The user can zoom into any node in the hierarchy by clicking on it, and eventually drill down to individual feature nodes decomposed into squares, one for each evaluation the feature received. The user can then click on an evaluation and see the original review from which the evaluation was extracted. This interface was tested in a user study, where some participants liked the visualization, but most of the participants preferred the text-based interface.

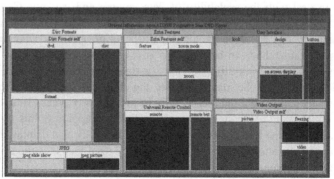

FIG. 11.1

A screenshot showing the opinions expressed about a DVD player [36]. The treemap represents sentiment information for each feature in the user-defined hierarchy of features. The interface additionally shows a textual summary of the reviews (left).

Review Spotlight presents an alternative visualization that is based on tag clouds [37]. The interface shows a list of adjective and noun word pairs that appeared most frequently. The font size of a noun word is proportional to its frequency in the reviews, whereas the font size of an adjective is determined by the number of occurrences of the word pair consisting of it and the associated noun. Also, the font color indicates the sentiment of each word, where the color hue represents sentiment polarity (green, red, and blue for positive, negative, and neutral respectively) and the saturation represents sentiment strength (darker tone indicates strong sentiment). A laboratory-based study revealed that the participants were able to perform the given decision making task faster with Review Spotlight than with the traditional customer review interface.

Both treemap-based visualization and tag cloud–based visualization have own advantages and limitations. The tag cloud–based visualization provides an arguably more compact representation than a treemap. However, if the features of an entity can be organized into a hierarchy, a treemap visualization technique would be arguably more suitable than a tag cloud one.

While earlier work mainly focused on just visualizing sentiment of different features of an entity, recent work has focused more on the tasks involving finding correlations between opinions and other important dimensions, such as temporal, spatial, and demographic information. OpinionSeer [38] supports the analysis of hotel customers' feedback data based on a combination of tag clouds, scatter plots, and radial visualizations. Here, opinions are represented as points on a scatter plot that is placed inside a triangle. The position of an opinion is determined according to its distance from the three triangle vertices representing the most positive, negative, and uncertain sentiment. For example, an opinion shown in the lower left center of the triangle indicates a highly negative opinion. The opinion rings surrounding the triangle are designed to explore the correlations between the customer opinions and other data dimensions, such as time, location, and demographic information, such as age range. While OpinionSeer may support the user to perform more complex analytical tasks than earlier approaches, a critical limitation is that presenting a large number of reviews within a scatter plot may lead to potential overlapping and visual clutter.

With the proliferation of web-based social media, new challenges have emerged because of the high volume and high velocity at which customer feedback data can be generated. Therefore the visualization needs to deal with the scalability of data volume and velocity. Considering these challenges, Hao et al. [39] presented a visual analysis system that facilitates exploration and analysis of customer feedback streams based on geotemporal aspects of opinions. Geotemporal aspects are important to analysts because they can be useful to answer some critical questions; for instance, how a product or service is received in different cities or states over time. Hao et al. present sentiment information as colored pixels on the map. However, the challenge then is how to represent the large number of opinions as points on a map, especially in high-density areas. To address this challenge, they apply a pixel placement algorithm that replaces the overlapping points by a circle of points, positioning them at the nearest free position within the circle. They also display the most significant term in each geographical location, where the color of a key term indicates the average sentiment value of all the sentences containing that term.

3.3.2 Compare opinions for multiple entities

A common task performed by consumers is making a preferential choice (ie, given a set of alternative products or services, find the best alternatives on the basis of the opinions expressed about those products or services. In such a case it is useful to compare the alternatives across different features of those products. Such comparisons of quantitative values can be made easier with small, multiple bar charts. For instance, Opinion Observer presents multiple bar graphs where each bar graph represents the sentiment value of a feature for different alternatives [40]. Carenini and Rizoli [41] focused on a similar task of comparing opinions using small, multiple bar graphs. However, their visualization addresses two key limitations of Opinion Observer. First, unlike the earlier system, they compare entities across features on the basis of three levels of strength of opinions for both positive polarity $(+3, +2, +1)$ and negative polarity $(-3, -2, -1)$, thus providing more accurate comparisons. Another difference is that they organize the features into a hierarchy, and then represent the opinions of features for each entity using stacked bars.

3.4 OPINION VISUALIZATION OF USER REACTIONS TO LARGE-SCALE EVENTS VIA MICROBLOGS

Recent work on visualizing opinions has focused on supporting the exploration of people's reactions to large-scale events [42,43]. Diakopoulos et al. [42] presented *Vox Civitas*, which supports journalists in their analysis and making sense of the large amount of tweets generated for a news event. The visual interface shows a sentiment timeline that aggregates sentiment responses into four different categories: positive, negative, controversial, or neutral (see Fig. 11.2). In addition, the system shows the volume of tweets over time, the keywords over time, and the detailed twitter messages.

A limitation of this visualization is that it is designed to deal with an archived collection of tweets. However, we often need to analyze a huge amount of tweets for an event in real time. To address this challenge, *TwitInfo* [43] supports the user in browsing a large collection of tweets in real time. The system applies a streaming algorithm that identifies the peaks (subevents) within the event timeline and labels these peaks with meaningful text from the related tweets. Users can then zoom into the timeline to discover more peaks and subevents. It also presents the total proportion of positive and negative tweets during the event or subevent by means of a pie chart.

Another key analytical task in exploring reactions to large-scale events is to investigate how opinions propagate among users. This task can be very important in several situations; for instance a business analyst may want to detect the diffusion of negative opinions early, so that her company can address the issue, before it goes viral. *OpinionFlow* [34] focuses on this task by visualizing the spreading of opinions among participants with a combination of a density map and a Sankey diagram. The Sankey diagram shows the flow of users across different topics in an event over time, where each horizontally arranged strip is associated with a topic and each line that connects two topic strips represents the transition of user attention between the two corresponding topics. Within the Sankey diagram, density maps are encoded by application of kernel density estimation with scaled and oriented Gaussian kernels to convey the density and orientation information of opinion diffusion among users. Finally, a hierarchical topic structure represented as a stacked tree allows analysts to select topics of interest at different levels of granularity and examine how opinions spread for those topics.

3.5 VISUALIZING OPINIONS IN ONLINE CONVERSATIONS

Today it is quite common for people to exchange hundreds of comments in online conversations (eg, blogs, Facebook conversations). However, it can often be very difficult to analyze and gain insights from such long conversations. To address this problem, a number of visualization approaches have been proposed (eg, [44,47–49]). Among them, ConVis has been the most recently proposed system, and it is designed by consideration of the unique characteristics of online conversations.

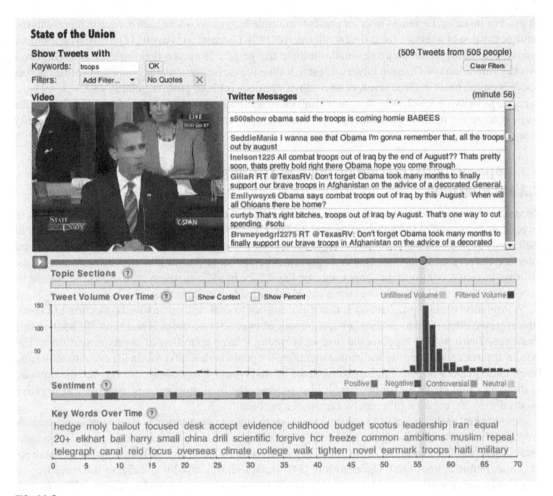

FIG. 11.2

The Vox Civitas user interface [42], showing the Twitter messages along with the volume of tweets, the trend of overall sentiment, and keywords over time.

As shown in Fig. 11.3, ConVis consists of an overview (Thread Overview) of the conversation along with two primary facets, topics and authors, which are presented circularly around this overview. The Thread Overview visually represents the sentiment distribution of each *comment* of the conversation as a stacked bar. A set of five diverging colors is used to visualize the distribution of sentiment orientation of a comment in a perceptually meaningful order, ranging from purple (highly negative) to orange (highly positive). In addition, three different metadata are encoded within the stacked bar: the comment length (height), the ordinal position of the comment in the conversation (vertical position), and the depth of the comment (horizontal position). To indicate the topic-comment-author relationship, the

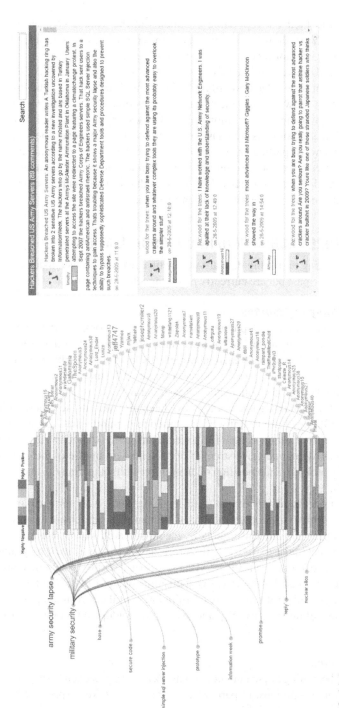

FIG. 11.3

A snapshot of ConVis for exploring blog conversation. The Thread Overview visually represents the whole conversation encoding the thread structure and how the sentiment is expressed for each comment, the Facet Overview presents topics and authors circularly around the Thread Overview, and the Conversation View presents the actual conversation in a scrollable list (right). Here topics and authors are connected to their related comments via curved links.

facet elements are connected to their corresponding comments in the Thread Overview via curved links. Finally, the Conversation View shows the actual text of the comments as a scrollable list.

The user can start exploring the conversation by causing the mouse to hover over topics, which highlights the connecting curved links and related comments in the Thread Overview. As such, one can quickly understand how topics may be related to different comments and authors. If the user clicks on a topic, a thick vertical outline is drawn next to the corresponding comments in the Thread Overview. Such outlines are also mirrored in the Conversation View. Besides exploring by the topics/authors, the reader can browse individual comments by causing the mouse to hover over them and clicking on them in the Thread Overview. In particular, when the mouse hovers over a comment, its topic is highlighted, while when the user clicks on a comment, the actual text for that comment is shown in the Conversation View (by scrolling). A user study [50] showed that ConVis outperformed traditional interfaces for several subjective metrics (eg, usefulness, enjoyable).

3.6 CURRENT AND FUTURE TRENDS IN OPINION VISUALIZATION

Visualizing uncertainty and scaling up for big data are two critical aspects of visualizing opinions that have been underresearched in the past but are currently receiving a lot of attention.

3.6.1 Visualizing uncertainty in opinions

Uncertainty may arise when one is making a prediction with noisy or incomplete data, which is quite common for opinion mining in social media. When the results are presented to the user without the uncertainty being taken into account, she may reach incorrect conclusions. To tackle this problem, it is important to convey the degree of uncertainty to the user as auxiliary information. In this way users can decide how confident they should be in the conclusions they are drawing from the data.

While several techniques for visualizing uncertainty have been proposed in the generic information visualization literature [51–53], they have recently been applied to opinion visualization. One notable exception is the Opinion Seer visualization system [38], where the degree of uncertainty of an opinion is encoded along with the positive and negative strength of its sentiment by use of the distance to the three vertices of a triangle. By looking at the position of an opinion within the triangle, one can perceive how uncertain that opinion is.

Recall that bar graph–based visualization was used in some early work on opinion visualization [40,41]. A common approach to encode uncertainty within such bar graphs is to introduce error bars to represent the confidence interval. Unfortunately, recent research shows that error bars have many drawbacks from the perceptual perspectives; therefore new techniques such as gradient plots (use transparency in bars to encode uncertainty) and violin plots (use width) should be considered as alternatives to bar charts with error bars [54]. For text visualization, other visual attributes such as color hue, or saturation of the background, or use of the border thickness of the surrounding box of the text have been used for the encoding of uncertainty [52], and this could be adopted for opinion visualization involving text data.

3.6.2 Scaling up for big data

As social media text data are becoming larger and more complex at an unprecedent rate, new challenges have emerged for visualization of opinions. In particular, we discuss two key aspects of big data that need to be addressed for opinion visualization:

1. **Volume**: Opinion visualization needs to deal with challenges that arise from the massive amount of data. Unfortunately, most of the visualizations discussed in this chapter would be inadequate to handle very large amounts of raw opinion data. To tackle such situations, data reduction methods such as filtering and sampling, and aggregation should be applied before visualization [55]. Then the reduced data could be presented along with various interactive techniques to progressively reveal the data from a high-level overview to low-level details, similarly to what was done in [21].
2. **Velocity**: The high velocity of big data poses enormous challenges for the opinion mining and visualization methods. For instance, immediately after a product is released, a business analyst may want to analyze text streams in social media to identify problems or issues, such as whether customers have started complaining about a feature of the product. In such cases, timely analysis of the streaming text can be critical for the company's reputation. For this purpose, a combination of efficient opinion mining and streaming text visualization is required. This subject is beyond the scope of this chapter, and interested readers are referred to [56] for various ways of visualizing streaming text in real time.

4 CONCLUSION

In this chapter we have discussed how a large set of opinions extracted from social media can be effectively summarized and visualized. The generation of textual summaries in this domain is particularly challenging because the source documents tend to be noisy and ungrammatical, and are often filled with diverse and conflicting opinions. In the first part of the chapter, we described how these challenges can be addressed by the application of both extractive and abstractive summarization methods. In the second part of the chapter, we discussed how large sets of opinions extracted from social media can be effectively visualized. We focused on three key text genres that are typically rich in opinions: customer feedback in the form of reviews, user reactions to large-scale events via microblogs, and online blog conversations.

REFERENCES

[1] H.P. Luhn, The automatic creation of literature abstracts, IBM J. Res. Dev. 2 (2) (1958) 159–165.
[2] H.P. Edmundson, New methods in automatic extracting, J. ACM 16 (2) (1969) 264–285.
[3] K.S. Jones, Automatic summarizing: factors and directions, in: I. Mani, M. Maybury (Eds.), Advances in Automatic Text Summarization, MITP, 1999, pp. 1–12.
[4] I. Mani, Automatic Summarization, John Benjamin, Amsterdam, The Netherlands, 2001.
[5] A. Nenkova, K. McKeown, Automatic summarization, Found. Trends Inform. Retr. 5 (2–3) (2011) 103–233.
[6] J.-M. Torres-Moreno, Automatic Text Summarization, Wiley, London, UK, 2015.
[7] T. Kleinbauer, G. Murray, Summarization, in: Multimodal Signal Processing: Human Interactions in Meetings, Cambridge University Press, Cambridge, UK, 2012, pp. 170–192.
[8] G. Carenini, G. Murray, R. Ng, Methods for Mining and Summarizing Text Conversations, Morgan Claypool, San Rafael, CA, 2011.
[9] Y. Fujii, N. Kitaoka, S. Nakagawa, Automatic extraction of cue phrases for important sentences in lecture speech and automatic lecture speech summarization, in: Proceedings of Interspeech, 2007, pp. 2801–2804.

[10] J. Zhang, H. Chan, P. Fung, L. Cao, Comparative study on speech summarization of broadcast news and lecture speech, in: Proceedings of Interspeech, 2007, pp. 2781–2784.

[11] A. Farzindar, D. Inkpen, Natural Language Processing for Social Media, Morgan & Claypool Publishers, San Rafael, CA, 2015.

[12] D. Zajic, B. Dorr, J. Lin, Single-document and multi-document summarization techniques for email threads using sentence compression, Inform. Process. Manage. 44 (2008) 1600–1610.

[13] F. Liu, Y. Liu, Towards abstractive speech summarization: exploring unsupervised and supervised approaches for spoken utterance compression, IEEE Trans. Audio Speech Lang. Process. 21 (7) (2013) 1469–1480.

[14] G. Murray, Abstractive summarization as a Markov decision process, in: Advances in Artificial Intelligence, Springer, New York, 2015, pp. 212–219.

[15] G. Murray, G. Carenini, R. Ng, Generating and validating abstracts of meeting conversations: a user study, in: Proceedings of INLG, 2010, pp. 105–113.

[16] C.-Y. Lin, Rouge: a package for automatic evaluation of summaries, in: Proceedings of ACL, 2004, pp. 74–81.

[17] F. Liu, Y. Liu, Correlation between rouge and human evaluation of extractive meeting summaries, in: Proceedings of ACL, 2008, pp. 201–204.

[18] A. Nenkova, R. Passonneau, K. McKeown, The pyramid method: incorporating human content selection variation in summarization evaluation, ACM Trans. Speech Lang. Process. 4 (2) (2007) 4.

[19] R. Passonneau, E. Chen, W. Guo, D. Perin, Automated pyramid scoring of summaries using distributional semantics, in: Proceedings of ACL, 2013, pp. 143–147.

[20] M. Hu, B. Liu, Mining and summarizing customer reviews, in: Proceedings of KDD, 2004, pp. 168–177.

[21] G. Carenini, R. Ng, A. Pauls, Multi-document summarization of evaluative text, in: Proceedings of EACL, 2006, pp. 3–7.

[22] D. Radev, s. Teufel, H. Saggion, W. Lam, J. Blitzer, H. Qi, A. Celebi, D. Liu, E. Drabek, Evaluation challenges in large-scale document summarization, in: Proceedings of ACL, 2003, pp. 375–382.

[23] G. Carenini, J. Moore, Generating and evaluating evaluative arguments, Artif. Intell. 170 (11) (2006) 925–952.

[24] G. Carenini, J.J. Cheung, Extractive vs. NLG-based abstractive summarization of evaluative text: the effect of corpus controversiality, in: Proceedings of INLG, 2008, pp. 33–41.

[25] H. Nishikawai, T. Hasegawa, Y. Matsuo, G. Kikui, Opinion summarization with integer linear programming formulation for sentence extraction and ordering, in: Proceedings of ACL, 2010, pp. 910–918.

[26] D. Gillick, K. Riedhammer, B. Favre, D. Hakkani-Tür, A global optimization framework for meeting summarization, in: Proc. ICASSP, 2009, pp. 4769–4772.

[27] S. Xie, B. Favre, D. Hakkani-Tür, Y. Liu, Leveraging sentence weights in a concept-based optimization framework for extractive meeting summarization, in: Proceedings of Interspeech, 2009, pp. 1503–1506.

[28] M. Potthast, S. Becker, Opinion summarization of web comments, in: Advances in Information Retrieval, Springer, New York, 2010, pp. 668–669.

[29] S. Gerani, Y. Mehdad, G. Carenini, R. Ng, B. Nejat, Abstractive summarization of product reviews using discourse structure, in: Proceedings of EMNLP, 2014, pp. 1602–1613.

[30] B. Sharifi, M.-A. Hutton, J. Kalita, Summarizing microblogs automatically, in: Proceedings of NAACL, 2010, pp. 685–688.

[31] D. Wang, Y. Liu, A pilot study of opinion summarization in conversations, in: Proceedings of ACL, 2011, pp. 331–339.

[32] T. Munzner, Visualization Analysis and Design, CRC Press, Boca Raton, FL, 2014.

[33] B. Shneiderman, The eyes have it: a task by data type taxonomy for information visualizations, in: Proceedings of IEEE Symposium on Visual Languages, 1996, pp. 336–343.

[34] Y. Wu, S. Liu, K. Yan, M. Liu, F. Wu, OpinionFlow: visual analysis of opinion diffusion on social media, Proc. IEEE Trans. Vis. Comput. Graphics 20 (12) (2014) 1763–1772.

[35] M. Gamon, A. Aue, S. Corston-Oliver, E. Ringger, Pulse: mining customer opinions from free text, in: Advances in Intelligent Data Analysis VI, Springer, New York, 2005, pp. 121–132.

[36] G. Carenini, R. Ng, A. Pauls, Interactive multimedia summaries of evaluative text, in: Proceedings of IUI, 2006, pp. 124–131.

[37] K. Yatani, M. Novati, A. Trusty, K. Truong, Review spotlight: a user interface for summarizing user-generated reviews using adjective-noun word pairs, in: Proceedings of SIGCHI Conference on Human Factors in Computing Systems, 2011, pp. 1541–1550.

[38] Y. Wu, F. Wei, S. Liu, N. Au, W. Cui, H. Zhou, H. Qu, OpinionSeer: interactive visualization of hotel customer feedback, IEEE Trans. Vis. Comput. Graphics 16 (6) (2010) 1109–1118.

[39] M.C. Hao, C. Rohrdantz, H. Janetzko, D.A. Keim, U. Dayal, L. erik Haug, M. Hsu, F. Stoffel, Visual sentiment analysis of customer feedback streams using geo-temporal term associations, Inform. Vis. 12 (3–4) (2013) 273–290.

[40] B. Liu, M. Hu, J. Cheng, Opinion Observer: analyzing and comparing opinions on the web, in: Proceedings of WWW, 2005, pp. 342–351.

[41] G. Carenini, L. Rizoli, A multimedia interface for facilitating comparisons of opinions, in: Proceedings of IUI, ACM, 2009, pp. 325–334.

[42] N. Diakopoulos, M. Naaman, F. Kivran-Swaine, Diamonds in the rough: social media visual analytics for journalistic inquiry, in: Proceedings of IEEE VAST, 2010, pp. 115–122.

[43] A. Marcus, M.S. Bernstein, O. Badar, D.R. Karger, S. Madden, R.C. Miller, Twitinfo: aggregating and visualizing microblogs for event exploration, in: Proceedings of CHI, 2011, pp. 227–236.

[44] E. Hoque, G. Carenini, ConVis: a visual text analytic system for exploring blog conversations, Comput. Graphics Forum (Proc. EuroVis) 33 (3) (2014) 221–230.

[45] A. Ritter, C. Cherry, B. Dolan, Unsupervised modeling of twitter conversations, in: Proceedings of ACL, 2010, pp. 172–180.

[46] S. Joty, G. Carenini, R.T. Ng, Topic segmentation and labeling in asynchronous conversations, J. Artif. Intell. Res. 47 (2013) 521–573.

[47] W. Sack, Conversation map: an interface for very-large-scale conversations, J. Manage. Inform. Syst. 17 (3) (2000) 73–92.

[48] K. Dave, M. Wattenberg, M. Muller, Flash forums and forumReader: navigating a new kind of large-scale online discussion, in: Proc. ACM Conf. CSCW, 2004, pp. 232–241.

[49] B. Kerr, Thread arcs: an email thread visualization, in: Proceedings of the IEEE Symposium on Information Visualization, 2003, pp. 211–218.

[50] E. Hoque, G. Carenini, ConVisIT: interactive topic modeling for exploring asynchronous online conversations, in: Proceedings of IUI, 2015, pp. 169–180.

[51] A.T. Pang, C.M. Wittenbrink, S.K. Lodha, Approaches to uncertainty visualization, Vis. Comput. 13 (8) (1997) 370–390.

[52] C. Collins, S. Carpendale, G. Penn, Visualization of uncertainty in lattices to support decision-making, in: Proceedings of EuroVis, 2007, pp. 51–58.

[53] J. Sanyal, S. Zhang, G. Bhattacharya, P. Amburn, R. Moorhead, A user study to compare four uncertainty visualization methods for 1D and 2D datasets, IEEE. Trans. Vis. Comput. Graphics 15 (6) (2009) 1209–1218.

[54] M. Correll, M. Gleicher, Error bars considered harmful: exploring alternate encodings for mean and error, IEEE Trans. Vis. Comput. Graphics 20 (12) (2014) 2142–2151.

[55] Z. Liu, B. Jiang, J. Heer, imMens: real-time visual querying of big data, in: Proceedings of EuroVis, 2013, pp. 421–430.

[56] D.A. Keim, M. Krstajic, C. Rohrdantz, T. Schreck, Real-time visual analytics for text streams, Computer 46 (7) (2013) 47–55.

SENTIMENT ANALYSIS WITH SPAGOBI

12

I. Iennaco[a], L. Pernigotti[b], S. Scamuzzo[c]

Engineering Ingegneria Informatica, Turin, Italy[a] Engineering Ingegneria Informatica, Bologna, Italy[b] Engineering Ingegneria Informatica, Assago (MI), Italy[c]

1 INTRODUCTION TO SPAGOBI

SpagoBI is an open source business intelligence suite, developed and governed by Engineering Group, covering all areas of business intelligence with a set of analytical capabilities and cross-domain functionalities.

The suite has been developed by the balancing of open source flexibility and industry-grade software quality. It is released under an Open Source Initiative–approved license, namely the Mozilla Public License version 2.0. Everyone can study, use, modify, and distribute modified copies of SpagoBI under the terms of its license. The software can be downloaded from the forge of the OW2 consortium,[1] a nonprofit and independent open source community.

Different kinds of documents can be built and different kinds of tasks can be performed with SpagoBI:

- reports
- charts
- dashboards and cockpits
- online analytical processing analysis on cubes
- Ad hoc querying and reporting
- location intelligence
- data mining
- network analysis
- what-if simulations

All SpagoBI documents can be linked to each other, if needed, and can be combined in the context of interactive cockpits. Data can come from different sources, including data warehouses, SQL and NoSQL databases, services, and files. In this way the final user has a coherent and secure environment

---

[1] https://www.ow2.org

Sentiment Analysis in Social Networks. http://dx.doi.org/10.1016/B978-0-12-804412-4.00012-7

in which to perform analysis on different sets of data by using the most appropriate tool for his specific requirements.

Different analytical scenarios can be implemented by use of SpagoBI; in this chapter will we focus in particular on how to leverage the SpagoBI tools to support scenarios of sentiment analysis on data collected from social networks. The approach that we describe is generic enough to be applied also to different usage scenarios. It relies on a data collection component, an engine to implement sentiment analysis algorithms by using statistical functions, and several visualization tools to present the results in effective ways.

2 SOCIAL NETWORK ANALYSIS WITH SPAGOBI

2.1 MAIN PURPOSE

SpagoBI provides a specific tool for social network listening to and monitoring social networks (eg, Twitter). The end user can perform analysis on real-time data, such as streams of tweet data, as well as on historical data defined by a specific time period.

The main purpose of the SpagoBI Social Network Analysis module is to monitor tweets corresponding to particular keywords or accounts and to analyze them to provide the end user with the most meaningful information. This ranges from basic information (ie, number and trend of tweets and retweets, top tweets and top influencers, etc.) to more advanced analysis, such as topic extraction and sentiment classification of tweets' texts derived from statistical algorithms written in R.

In the next sections we describe SpagoBI Social Network Analysis module's main features with a particular focus on the sentiment analysis tool implemented.

2.2 FEATURES

The SpagoBI Social Network Analysis module allows the end user to search for tweets without the need to use directly the Twitter Search application programming interface because they are managed directly in the module. The end user needs only to register its own app on Twitter to retrieve the consumerKey, consumerSecret, accessToken and accessTokenSecret to configure the SpagoBI Social Network Analysis module. In this way the end user can search tweets that contain hashtags or keywords specified simply by completing the Twitter Search Form.

In the form it is possible to choose between two search modalities:

- **streaming**: Tweets that contain the hashtags or keywords specified in the form are downloaded in real time starting at the moment at which the search is activated until the end user decides to stop it. Because of limitations imposed by Twitter, it is possible to maintain only one twitter search active.
- **historical**: Indexed tweets associated with the keywords specified by the end user are downloaded. The search retrieves tweets starting from the moment at which the search is begun up to 6–9 days before. Moreover, it is possible to specify the temporal range and schedule the search to repeat it.

In the form the end user can also specify resources and accounts to monitor:

- **twitter accounts**: Through the module it is possible to monitor up to three twitter accounts so that it is possible to see the trend of their number of followers over time.

- **bitly shortened links**: By specifying up to three bitly shortened links in the search form, the end user can monitor the number of clicks over time.
- **SpagoBI documents**: The end user can choose up to three SpagoBI documents, such as reports, charts, or online analytical processing cubes (see Section 1 for the full list of SpagoBI documents), to visualize and refresh the data updated up to the date of the last executed search.

The different searches created are shown in tables in the Twitter Search Form and the end user can execute different actions on them, as detailed below:

- **continuous scanning table**: This table shows the streaming search results:
  - *Start/stop.* According to the search status, the end user can start or stop it. Starting a search will stop other active searches.
  - *Delete.* Remove the search and the associated resources.
  - *Analyze.* If the streaming search is in stop status, the end user can access the tab to visualize the results of his search.
- **timely scanning table**: This table shows the historical search results:
  - *Delete*: Remove the search and the associated resources.
  - *Analyze*: Once the downloading of the results is terminated, the end user can visualize it by clicking on this button.
  - *Scheduler*: If the search is scheduled, the end user can stop it so that it will not be repeated.

Once the search has been stopped, the end user can visualize the results of his search in the Twitter Results tabs. In these tabs the results are divided into areas of interest and shown through different tools such as graphs, timelines, and maps.

The first tab is the *Summary* tab, where general information about the downloaded tweets is visualized. In particular, the total number of results, the total number of twitter users, and their diffusion in the social network are highlighted. In particular, the end user can visualize:

- **tweets timeline**: In this plot the end user can visualize a graphical representation of the trend of the tweets and retweets over time according to their publication date.
- **tweets origin**: Through pie charts it is possible to access information about the nature of the tweets (ie, if they are tweets, retweets, or replies) and the device used to publish the tweets.
- **top and recent tweets**: The end user can read the most relevant tweets and the most recent ones.

In the *Topic* tab, word clouds with hashtags and topics are shown. The topics are retrieved by means of a text mining algorithm.

The *Network* tab contains information based on the users who published the tweets downloaded by the search. The end user in this tab can visualize:

- **top influencers**: The users are ordered according to the number of their followers, and a description of their twitter profile is shown.
- **mentions**: With this word cloud, the mentions are shown and the dimension of the mention is correlated with the number of occurrences in the tweets downloaded.
- **users' interactions graph and map**: The interactions between two users such as retweets or replies are shown in a network and in a map.

The end user can also find information about the geographical distribution of the tweets in the *Distribution* tab. To have temporal information about the number of clicks on the bitly resources and the followers monitored, the end user can select the *Impact* tab. Finally, the *ROI* tab shows the SpagoBI document associated with the twitter search updated to the last monitoring.

Together with all the graphs, visualizations, and information given by the tabs described that are made available, the SpagoBI Social Network Analysis module performs a sentiment analysis on the tweets downloaded, retrieving the polarity of the tweets in terms of positive, negative, or neutral tweets. In the *Sentiment* tab the user can see the percentage and number of positive (green), neutral (yellow), and negative (red) tweets and the distribution of the sentiment across the different topics of the tweets. This distribution is displayed in a radar graph and bar charts.

2.3 USE CASE

Among all the possible applications, social network listening can be a powerful customer intelligence tool. It allows you to improve your market positioning and build stronger brand loyalty, but also to check what people are saying about your competitors or stem any negative social buzz.

A typical use case for the SpagoBI Social Network Analysis module is marketing campaign monitoring and analysis. As an example, we consider the launch of a new SpagoBI release. This event is usually associated with a marketing campaign, performed also on the main social networks.

Let us suppose that the launch of the new release is scheduled for November 1 and you want to monitor the impact of your marketing campaign on Twitter. You would like to define a continuous scanning search starting from October 28, a few days before the official launch, just to check the actual impact compared with the previous days.

Let us also suppose that you are using two accounts—@SpagoBI and @spagoworld—to promote your campaign, that you are always using the bitly URL http://bit.ly/1uCUO7X to redirect people to the website with all the event-related information, and that you have launched a new hashtag (#spagobi5) to refer to the new release.

You can then define a new online monitoring search in the SpagoBI Social Network Analysis module using:

- "spagobi" and "spagobi5" (your new hashtag) as keywords
- @SpagoBI and @spagoworld as accounts to monitor
- http://bit.ly/1uCUO7X as a resource to monitor

As explained in the previous section, this will allow you to check the number of followers of the monitored account and the numbers of clicks on the monitored resources. You can also schedule the accounts and resource monitoring to start 2 or 3 days after the monitoring of tweets. This can be useful since, very often, it is important to monitor tweets from the very beginning of the launch of the campaign, but, for instance, the impact on the number of followers of the corresponding accounts becomes visible starting from a few days later.

Once monitoring has been scheduled, the *Summary* results of your campaign monitoring will look like the ones shown in Fig. 12.1 plus additional information on the tweet sources and nature and two lists of the top and most recent tweets.

As shown in Fig. 12.1, in our case there is a high peak immediately after November 1: the number of tweets is almost four times the corresponding amount of the previous days. This could mean that the launch campaign has been very effective and has generated a good response in the social network.

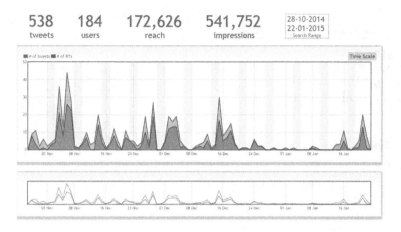

FIG. 12.1

Summary tab results—upper part.

Exploring the other sections, you can check the most discussed topics in the corresponding tab. For instance, you would like to know which of the new features of SpagoBI are the ones most discussed in the network. You can also compare the retrieved topics with the most used hashtags: sometimes hashtags correspond to the main topic of the tweet, other times they are just used to refer to other discussions or popular trends.

In the *Network* tab, shown in Fig. 12.2, you can investigate how the different accounts tweeting about your campaign interact with each other.

For instance, when one is performing a marketing campaign, it is very important to know who the top influencers are. On one hand, you can directly address them with the main information that you want to spread over the network; on the other hand, you need to keep a careful eye on them: if they are not happy with your campaign, they could generate a negative social buzz. The user interaction graph, shown on the lower right in Fig. 12.2, can provide insights into the level of clustering of the network. A network split into different subgraphs (clusters) could suggests a in-depth analysis aimed at unveiling differences between the subgraphs: this knowledge can then be used to plan different customized subcampaigns directed at the different subgroups.

Geolocalized information can be recovered from the user interaction map located in lower part of the *Network* tab (shown on right in Fig. 12.2) and from the *Distribution* tab. Here you can check if the area where your customers are located has been effectively reached by your campaign, and you can identify new potential marketing areas among the interested ones.

Finally, the *Sentiment* tab is where you can monitor the polarity of the tweets related to your campaign, as shown in Fig. 12.3. This is one of the most important pieces of information when one is monitoring a marketing campaign: it allows you to understand the general network's feeling about the new release and to quickly identify potential negative elements that require intervention. Indeed, in this tab the polarity information is also split according to the main topics: you can therefore discover immediately what people are happy or unhappy about and tune your campaign plan accordingly.

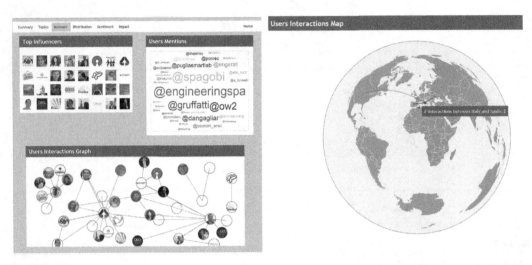

FIG. 12.2

Network tab results: top influencers, top accounts, and network interactions (left) and geographical distribution of interactions (right).

3 ALGORITHMS USED

The SpagoBI Social Network Analysis module supports sentiment analysis to detect in an automatic way the polarity of the tweet concerning a specific argument. To perform this task, a supervised algorithm to assign labels to the tweets that indicate if the tweet is positive, negative, or neutral has been adopted. The specific method used is the naïve Bayes classification algorithm.

In machine learning, naïve Bayes classification algorithms are a family of probabilistic classifiers based on the Bayes theorem. In the specific case of sentiment analysis the goal is to classify text or documents in the positive, negative, or neutral class. The implementation of the classifier is characterized by three phases:

- **training phase**: In this phase the system is trained with use of a training set constituted by previously classified texts to obtain the probability that a word is positive, negative, or neutral given the class assigned to the text.
- **testing phase**: The algorithm is tested to calculate the accuracy of the method.
- **classification phase**: In this phase the input of the algorithm is a set of not classified texts and it is determined if they are positive, negative, or neutral.

A preprocessing phase precedes the steps described. In this phase, spaces, URLs, tags, and numbers are deleted, all the words are set to lowercase, and the emoticons are replaced by placeholders so they can be used in the classification.

The algorithm used is implemented in the R language. R is a programming language and software environment for statistical computing that is integrated into SpagoBI. The SpagoBI Social Network

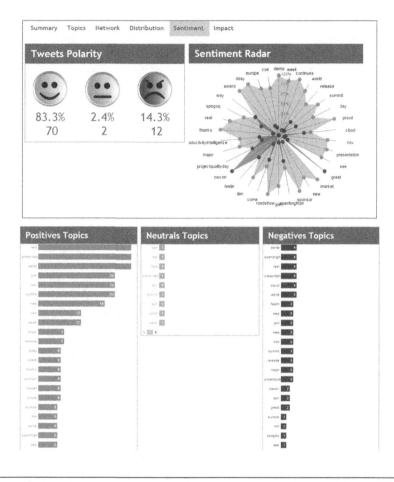

FIG. 12.3

Sentiment tab results—upper part.

Analysis module uses R to perform sentiment analysis and topic modeling. Advanced users can also use R inside SpagoBI to perform their own analysis and visualize the results in SpagoBI.

4 CONCLUSION

In this chapter we illustrated how the SpagoBI open source business intelligence suite supports social network analysis through data mining algorithms and data visualization techniques. The main value associated with the integration of social network analysis in a business intelligence suite relies on its mutual benefit: business intelligence brings to social network analysis several tools and techniques to make the results of the analysis easier to communicate with efficacy and attractiveness to final users, while social network analysis brings extended valuable data to make effective analysis and drive better decisions.

SOMA: THE SMART SOCIAL CUSTOMER RELATIONSHIP MANAGEMENT TOOL: HANDLING SEMANTIC VARIABILITY OF EMOTION ANALYSIS WITH HYBRID TECHNOLOGIES

13

L. Dini[a], A. Bittar*[,a], C. Robin[†,a], F. Segond[‡,b], M. Montaner[§,c]

Holmes Semantic Solutions, Gières, France[a] Viseo Technologies, Grenoble, France[b] Strategic Attention Management, Girona, Spain[c]

1 INTRODUCTION

Sentiment and emotion are key elements for companies to understand their customers so as to improve customer relationship management, to adapt both their services and their products and to optimize marketing strategies. In recent years social media have become a new channel of communication between companies and customers and, therefore, the most appropriate place to analyze and try to achieve their satisfaction.

SOMA (for "Smart Media Management for Social Customer Attention") is an innovative R&D project cofunded by Eurostars aiming to create a corporate tool that allows companies to understand and interact efficiently with their customers through social media (eg, Facebook, Twitter, LinkedIn). The main objectives of the SOMA project are threefold. First, to monitor and analyze from a strategic point of view what is happening in the different social media channels of the company (eg, evaluate if the different customers use social media as a channel to complain, ask questions, give opinions, etc., or analyze the impact of a marketing campaign on the sentiment of the customers). Second, the definition of a common corporative strategy of communication through social media channels by means of suggested/automatic actions (eg, create critical alerts when complaints of influencers arrive or suggest

*www.ho2s.com
[†]www.ho2s.com
[‡]www.viseo.com
[§]www.blueroominnovation.com/

cross-selling actions when congratulations or positive opinions arrive). Third, automatically incorporate all this valuable social information into the company's customer relationship management, which is usually totally disconnected from social media. In other words, SOMA is merging unstructured and structured information to improve customer satisfaction. The unstructured information is that contained in social networks that relates to customers' sentiments and emotions.

In this chapter we focus on emotion detection. Unlike opinion analysis, emotion analysis cannot be reduced to the categorization between positive, negative, and neutral, as expression of emotion is often much more nuanced and subtler than this. In what follows we first build a corpus. We then perform two tasks: classifying emotions into different types (eg, anger, disgust, fear, surprise) and distinguishing between emotional and nonemotional texts (not all the social media posts have emotions in them) using a hybrid approach. Finally, we provide the first evaluation results that we obtained.

2 DEFINITION OF SENTIMENT AND EMOTION MINING

In recent years, so-called emotional marketing has become a key factor of success for many business-to-consumer companies, especially global ones. Simply put, emotional marketing has the basic goal of convincing customers that a brand or a product is not just a brand or a product, but a kind of "friend." Any emotional marketing strategy starts with an in-depth understanding of customers' emotional or motivational drivers, and this is achieved either via open question surveys or by analysis of emotional reactions on social media. As mentioned already, sentiment and opinion analysis consists in "classifying a piece of text into positive versus negative classes," while emotion analysis consists in "multiclassifying" text into different types of categories (anger, disgust, fear, happiness, sadness, and surprise).

Opinions can map to a multidimensional space of emotions with different activation levels, and this certainly gives more insights compared with traditional sentiment analysis techniques.

This chapter has the goal of validating the feasibility of automatic emotion analysis on social media. It should be noted that standard sentiment analysis, intended as opinion detection (positive vs. negative), possibly ranked on an intensity scale, is inappropriate for our purposes, both practically and conceptually. Practically, the fact that a customer expresses, for instance, a positive opinion has no impact on an emotional evaluation: the sentences "*I love this cup*" and "*This cup is very good*" have an identical opinion value but definitely a different emotional tonality. Conceptually, whereas opinions are usually expressed in a quite explicit way, the language of emotions is much more difficult to interpret as it relies on indirect signals and implicit knowledge (eg, "*Harley isn't just a motorcycle, it's a lifestyle*").

3 PREVIOUS WORK

Much research has been performed on sentiment analysis in the past decade. Wiebe et al. [1] performed an ambitious annotation effort, producing a 10,000-sentence corpus of world news texts marked up for a range of sentiment-related phenomena, although the typology of emotions focused on polarity rather than actual emotion types.

Alm et al. [2] created a corpus of children's tales where each sentence (1580 in total) was annotated with one of the six emotions of Ekman [3] or a neutral value. They also describe a supervised machine learning system that detects emotional versus neutral sentences and detects emotion polarity within a sentence. Although this work captures actual emotion types, rather than just polarity, the type of texts is not compatible with the domain of corporate customer relationship management or social media.

Pak and Paroubek [4] created a corpus of tweets for sentiment analysis, but again focused only on emotion polarity rather than capturing the values of emotion types—the information that is crucial to our project.

Vo and Collier [5] created a corpus of Japanese tweets annotated according to an ontology of five emotions (similar to the Ekman typology [3]) and a system to automatically detect the prevalent emotion in a tweet, achieving a global F score of 64.7. This work is similar to our current project in that it deals with emotion types, although the language (Japanese) is not pertinent to our work.

Finally, the numerous SemEval campaigns that have included various tasks on emotion analysis have almost exclusively focused on the assignment of a polarity value to detected emotions. An exception is the 2007 campaign [6], Task 14: Affective Text, in which participants were required to detect and classify emotions and/or determine their polarity in a corpus of manually annotated news headlines extracted from news websites. In the annotated corpus, each headline is annotated with a numeric interval (0–100) that indicates, for each of the six emotions (anger, disgust, fear, joy, sadness, surprise), its strength in the headline. The six human annotators who prepared the corpus were instructed to "select the appropriate emotions for each headline on the basis of the presence of words or phrases with emotional content, as well as the overall feeling invoked by the headline." The nature of this task is highly subjective, relying heavily on each annotator's interpretation of a given headline and his or her emotional response. Furthermore, requesting annotation over such a fine-grained interval for each emotion allows even further room for disagreement. This high degree of subjectivity is reflected in the reported interannotator agreement (Pearson correlation coefficient) for the task, which "is not particularly high" (an average agreement of 53.67 across the six emotions). The resulting "gold standard" corpus for this task is, therefore, not a reliable yardstick against which to evaluate system performance. Indeed, evaluation results for the participating systems were relatively quite low (F scores ranging from 16.00 to 42.43).

To the best of our knowledge, no suitable corpus for the task exists: we created a new corpus of emotion-annotated tweets for the future evaluation of the SOMA system. This corpus of tweets represents the social media component of the global SOMA corpus that is to be created for use in the project.

4 A SILVER STANDARD CORPUS FOR EMOTION CLASSIFICATION IN TWEETS

The first corpus, which we will call the "Emotion Tweet Corpus for Classification" (ETCC), is a "silver standard" in which each tweet is classified with a single emotion. In creating this corpus, we relied on the basic premise that some Twitter users, when expressing emotions, also tag their message with emotional hashtags. On the basis of this assumption we tried to construct a corpus where tweets are classified according to the six emotional classes used in SemEval 2007 (anger, disgust, fear, joy, sadness, and surprise) [6]. The choice of hashtag to be associated with emotions (one hashtag per emotion) was very important, as the hashtags needed to be common enough to allow the retrieval of a significant number of tweets, and to be unambiguous: for instance, for the emotion surprise we could not use the hashtag #surprise as it is semantically highly ambiguous (as an interjection, *Surprise!* is a noun meaning something that surprises, an act of surprising, etc.). Instead, we opted for the unambiguous hashtag #astonished. The six emotion hashtags we used were #angry, #astonished, #disgusted, #happy, #sadness, and #scared. The corpus collection phase was made much easier by the fact that since November 2014 [7] Twitter has a search interface not emphasizing recentness and allowing the retrieval of tweets since 2006: emotional hashtags could then be used as search keywords, and the necessary number of tweets for each emotion was collected (20,000 per emotion) with use of the approach described in [8].

We then performed some filtering to remove inappropriate tweets (formal filtering). We eliminated non-English tweets by specifying the language in the search query. We also removed tweets that were not composed of text (eg, by filtering out tweets that had a higher proportion of hashtags than other tokens). Tweets containing links to multimedia content were also filtered out, as in general the emotional hashtag in such tweets relates to the indicated media rather than the textual content of the tweet. After manual inspection we noticed that the number of tweets containing an emotional tag but no emotional text was still high. We therefore applied a further filter (affect filter) based on WordNet-Affect [9], we indexed all content with Lucene, and then we ran a fuzzy search, selecting only tweets containing an emotional word from the WordNet-Affect lexicon. Figures for the resulting corpus are given in Table 13.1.

Finally, all hashtags appearing at the end of a tweet were removed and hashtags that occurred within (ie, before the end of the text) a tweet had their hash sign removed as in such cases they are often used in the place of regular words. For example, after this step, tweet 1 below becomes tweet 2:

1. #MoodSwings are a #symptom of being #Bipolar. If you're #scared, #sad, #paranoid, or #suicidal, There's help here: http://ow.ly/tByb6.
2. MoodSwings are a symptom of being Bipolar. If you're scared, sad, paranoid, or suicidal, there's help here: http://ow.ly/SBtb6.

Although the corpus was not created via a full manual annotation (whence its "silver" status), the criteria used for retrieval and selection of the texts were anchored in the actual textual forms of the tweets, as opposed to our relying on highly subjective annotator judgments, as was the case in SemEval 2007.

Table 13.1 Figures for the Corpus of Emotion-Classified Tweets

SemEval 2007 Emotion	Hashtag	After Formal Filtering	After Affect Filtering
Anger	#angry	8738	5105
Surprise	#astonished	16,970	8635
Disgust	#disgusted	14,508	9084
Joy	#happy	3574	2009
Sadness	#sadness	3364	1724
Fear	#scared	10,525	5750

5 GENERAL SYSTEM

In our work we have been pursuing and comparing two approaches: a symbolic approach to emotion analysis and one based on machine learning. It shows that while the task of classifying emotions in a closed-world assumption (each text has an emotional value) is relatively easy, the real challenge is to distinguish emotional from nonemotional text. We also show that a statistical approach outperforms a symbolic one in emotion classification, while the opposite is true when information filtering is considered.

Concretely, this work focused on two different tasks. The first is the categorization of tweets according to the emotion they express, a single emotion per tweet among a set of six basic emotions. As we explained in detail in the previous section, currently available corpora do not, to our knowledge, provide appropriate data for evaluation of the automation of this task, and a major objective of this work was to make up for this shortfall. The second task was to distinguish tweets that express an emotion from those that do not. We also created a corpus as evaluation data for this task.

5.1 HYBRID OPERABLE PLATFORM FOR LANGUAGE MANAGEMENT AND EXTENSIBLE SEMANTICS

The Hybrid Operable Platform for Language Management and Extensible Semantics (HOLMES) [10] is a natural language processing platform developed by Holmes Semantic Solutions. The main assumption behind the design of HOLMES is that the combination of different technologies (statistical and machine learning methods and symbolic or rule-based methods) is indispensable to achieve superior performance in generic text mining and information extraction tasks. HOLMES is based on a flexible processing model (similar to that of Stanford CoreNLP) where different annotators are arranged in a pipeline and each annotator has access to the annotations added in all previous stages of processing. The general strategy adopted in HOLMES is to introduce into the pipeline pairs of annotators with comparable functionalities, one based on (most often supervised) machine learning and the other based on symbolic methods. The role of the linguist then becomes to correct the output of the statistical model on the basis of appropriate rules. For example, HOLMES has both a conditional random field (CRF)–based named entity recognition module [11] and a correction module based on TokensRegex [12], a stochastic part-of-speech tagger and a linear pattern matching rule component, a MaltParser-based model for dependency parsing, and a graph transformation–based component for detecting and correcting parsing errors and for performing semantic analysis, which we describe below.

As outlined in [13], a prevailing trend in computational semantics is to suppose that a graph is an optimal representation of semantic structures. HOLMES's semantic layer (which includes the sentiment analysis module) is based on this assumption. Basically predicates (in a first-order logic sense) are represented by arcs connecting nodes, which correspond to entities (tokens) detected in the text and that are enriched with specific semantic information. For example, the sentence "*John ate an apple yesterday*" has the semantic graph representation shown in Fig. 13.1.

Given that HOLMES performs syntactic analysis using a dependency graph output, it was natural to conceive the process of semantic analysis as graph transformation. HOLMES makes use of the Stanford Semgrex engine [14] to transform the dependency structure into a semantic graph. An in-house formal grammar was developed to provide linguists with a user-friendly interface for encoding the syntax-to-semantics transformations.

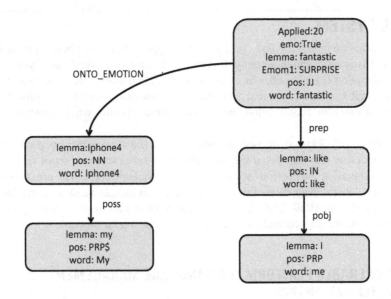

FIG. 13.1

Semantic graph for the sentence *"John ate an apple yesterday."*

5.2 THE MACHINE LEARNING APPROACH

The first test we ran, on the ETCC, was to use a classifier to discern the emotion expressed in each tweet. The corpus was split via random sampling into 80% training and 20% test. We used a multiclass linear classifier associated with a quasi Newton minimizer [15], under the Stanford natural processing language implementation.[5] We paid particular attention to the feature selection process, and after several tests the best results were obtained with the following set of features:

- **Word**: The sequence of characters composing the word as they appear in the text.
- **Lemma**: Lemma and part-of-speech tag, as resulting from part-of-speech disambiguation.
- **Noun phrase**: We use the output of the dependency grammar to produce all possible well-formed noun phases out of input text. Noun phrases are passed to the classifier both as sequences of word forms and as sequences of lemmas.
- **Dependencies**: A certain subset of grammatical dependencies is passed to the classifier as a set of triples. For instance (verb, SUBJ, noun), (verb, OBJ, noun), (noun, MOD, adj), etc., where parts of speech are obviously replaced by the relevant lemma (eg, (hate, SUBJ, i), (have, OBJ, money)). As the grammar we use produces Stanford-style dependencies [16], the dependency features are close to a semantic representation.

For each tweet the classifier assigns a probability for each emotion (the total probability mass being 1), and each tweet is assigned the emotion with the highest probability.

---

[5]http://nlp.stanford.edu/nlp/javadoc/javanlp/edu/stanford/nlp/optimization/QNMinimizer.html

5.3 **THE SYMBOLIC APPROACH**

Our symbolic approach to emotion annotation was done with our in-house system, Senti-Miner, developed within the company over several years [17,18]. Senti-Miner is based on the HOLMES platform. Processing consists of three main stages that integrate into the usual preprocessing pipeline (sentence detection, tokenization, part-of-speech tagging, morphological analysis and lemmatization, dependency parsing). These stages are lexical tagging, token-based regular expression annotation, and dependency graph transformation. Each of these is described below:

- **Lexical tagging with gazetteers**: The main lexical resource used in Senti-Miner is a gazetteer of emotions (1577 lemmas) automatically extracted from the WordNet-Affect database. A mapping between the WordNet-Affect emotions and the six basic emotions used for this experiment was established. Classes of emotions that did not have a coherent mapping were discarded.
  Classes that had multiple mappings were split. The resulting gazetteer used for this experiment contains 1302 lemmas. Furthermore, a separate gazetteer of Internet slang terms and their corresponding emotions (eg, LOL = JOY, WTF = SURPRISE), containing 416 entries, was also used.
  A third gazetteer is used to disambiguate lemmas that are only emotions when presented with specific parts of speech. For example, "like" is an emotion as a verb, but not as a preposition; "close" is an emotion as an adjective or adverb, but not as a verb, etc. This gazetteer contains 1547 emotion lemmas with their possible parts of speech.
  After part-of-speech tagging, all lexical items in the input text that have a lemma in one of the emotion gazetteers are tagged with their corresponding emotion and possible parts of speech. An example of output at this stage is shown in Fig. 13.2 (note that no disambiguation has occurred at this stage).
- **Token-based regular expression annotation (cf. Stanford TokensRegex [12])**: After lexical tagging, a set of token-based grammar rules are first applied to correct emotion annotations on the basis of possible parts of speech. For example, the preposition "like" in "*John eats like a pig*" is not an emotion, and this is taken into account. A further set of rules is used to process certain

Id	Word	Lemma	Char begin	Char end	POS	EmoPOS	Emo	EmoL-1
1	My	my	0	2	PRPS			
2	iPhone4	iphone4	3	10	NN			
3	is	be	11	13	VBZ			
4	fantastic	fantastic	14	23	JJ			SURPRISE
5	.	.	23	24	.			
6	like	like	25	29	IN			JOY
7	me	I	30	32	PRP			
8	!	!	32	33	.			

FIG. 13.2

Example output after lexical tagging.

Id	Word	Lemma	Char begin	Char end	POS	EmoPOS	Emo	EmoL-1
1	My	my	0	2	PRPS			
2	iPhone4	iphone4	3	10	NN			
3	is	be	11	13	VBZ			
4	fantastic	fantastic	14	23	JJ		TRUE	SURPRISE
5	.	.	23	24	.			
6	like	like	25	29	IN			
7	me	I	30	32	PRP			
8	!	!	32	33	.			

FIG. 13.3

Example output after token-based regular expression annotation.

multiword expressions that are able to be dealt with by a regular grammar without a deep syntactic analysis. These rules remove emotions from certain contexts; for example, *"close minded"* (sic), *"with respect to,"* etc. An example of output after this stage is shown in Fig. 13.3.

- **Dependency graph transformation grammar (using the Stanford Semgrex engine [14]):** After dependency parsing, the final step is the sequential application of a set of graph transformation grammars that mark relations between emotion words and their arguments. These grammars have access to all annotations added during previous processing. Certain rules are used to remove emotions from certain contexts; for example, in the scope of a modal operator (eg, *"You would be astonished,"* *"You should be happy,"* etc.), to remove emotions from common interjections (eg, *"Good night!,"* *"Happy Birthday/New Year/Anniversary,"* *"Merry Christmas!"*), and in certain expressions (eg, *"You have got to be kidding me"*). Other rules add an EMOTION relation between an emotion word and its syntactic argument. For example:
  - *"John is angry"*—EMOTION(*"angry,"* *"John"*).
  - *"This is a frightening book"*—EMOTION(*"frightening,"* *"book"*).
  - *"John has sympathy for Mary"*—EMOTION(*"sympathy,"* *"John"*).
  - *"John's sympathy for Mary"*—EMOTION(*"sympathy,"* *"John"*).

Furthermore, our grammar assigns one of two relations to indicate the status of the experiencer with respect to the emotion (causative or stative):

1. *"John is a **shy** person."*
2. *"This film **impresses** me."*

For example, in sentence 1, the grammar marks EXPERIENCER_STAT(*"shy,"* *"John"*), indicating that *"shy"* is a state of its subject, while in sentence 2 the grammar assigns EXPERIENCER_CAUSE(*"film,"* *"impresses"*), indicating that the subject of the emotion word *"impresses"* is the cause of the emotion. Although these two relations are output by our system, they were not used for the purposes of the current experiments. Example output of graph transformation is shown in Fig. 13.4.

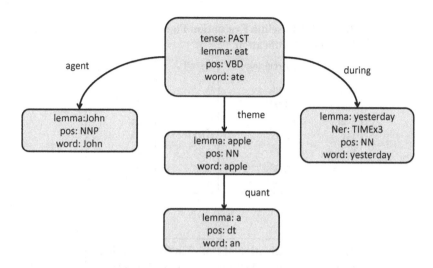

FIG. 13.4

Example output after dependency graph transformation.

The annotated relations, aside from the two just mentioned, mark the presence of an emotion in the final output. The final emotion is assigned to a given tweet, firstly, according to the number of occurrences found. If all detected emotions occur in equal numbers, the first one (from left to right) is assigned.

6 RESULTS AND EVALUATION

6.1 TWEET EMOTION DETECTION

For this task we determined a baseline against which to gauge the performance of our classifiers by calculating precision, recall, and F score for each emotion in the ETCC (see Section 4) according to the simple presence or absence of the appropriate emotion hashtag in the tweet text (eg, "anger" in the ANGER tweets were considered true positives, "anger" absent from an ANGER tweet was a false negative, and so on). Baseline figures are presented in Table 13.2.

Evaluation results for the machine learning classification of tweets (see Table 13.3) on the ETCC show differing performance across emotion types, reflecting the amount of data available for training for each emotion (see Table 13.1). The classifier achieved an average improvement in the F score of 9 percentage points over the baseline.

Evaluation results for the classification of tweets using the symbolic classifier are presented in Table 13.4. The figures are significantly lower than those obtained via machine learning (F score lower by 17 percentage points) and are also lower than the proposed baseline (F score lower by 8 percentage points). The relatively low performance of the symbolic classifier can be explained by the fact that the system was not developed for this particular type of corpus (it was initially developed to extract emotional responses—to products or brands, etc.—provided in user-generated feedback). Indeed, the

Table 13.2 Baseline Evaluation Figures for Emotion Classification

	Precision	Recall	F Score
Anger	0.96	0.37	0.53
Disgust	1.00	0.33	0.49
Fear	0.98	0.17	0.28
Joy	0.78	0.62	0.69
Sadness	0.99	0.32	0.48
Surprise	0.98	0.28	0.43
Average	0.95	0.35	0.49

Table 13.3 Evaluation of Emotion Classification of Tweets via the Machine Learning Classifier

	Precision	Recall	F Score
Anger	0.53	0.46	0.49
Disgust	0.66	0.72	0.69
Fear	0.61	0.65	0.63
Joy	0.63	0.6	0.62
Sadness	0.54	0.37	0.44
Surprise	0.62	0.61	0.62
Average	0.6	0.57	0.58

Table 13.4 Evaluation of Emotion Classification of Tweets via the Symbolic Classifier

	Precision	Recall	F Score
Anger	0.75	0.33	0.46
Disgust	0.76	0.24	0.37
Fear	0.72	0.35	0.47
Joy	0.26	0.68	0.37
Sadness	0.24	0.37	0.29
Surprise	0.84	0.37	0.52
Average	0.60	0.39	0.41

symbolic classifier proves less robust when faced with texts from a domain different from that for which it was developed.

6.2 TWEET RELEVANCE

To evaluate the performance of the classifier in detecting emotional tweets in the ETCC, we ran the classifier with different score thresholds for emotion detection. For example, with a threshold set at 0.4, at least one emotion must have a score above 0.4 for the tweet to be classified as emotional. The reasoning behind this is that for a tweet with no emotional content, one would expect the classifier to attribute equal scores to all emotions and in the case of emotional ones different scores for each emotion. By varying the threshold score for emotion classification, we hoped to determine the optimal score for detecting the emotional relevance of a tweet. We did not include tweets with no emotions, as, in order to achieve balance in this domain-nonspecific corpus, such tweets would have to encompass an enormous range of varied data from all possible domains, which is obviously infeasible.

The graph in Fig. 13.5 shows the F-score results of the evaluation for each of the thresholds tested. As expected, lower score thresholds favored recall, with relatively low precision, while precision, although still mediocre, was better at higher thresholds. Best performance for the classifier was an F score of 0.26.

As for the symbolic approach, always assigning the nonemotional category to tweets in the corpus provides the baseline figures shown in Table 13.5.

Evaluation figures for the symbolic methods for detecting emotional versus nonemotional tweets (Table 13.6) show a major improvement over the baseline (average F score of 0.72 vs. 0.48). The figures also show a major improvement over those obtained by the classifier (F score of 0.48 vs. 0.26 for detection of emotional tweets).

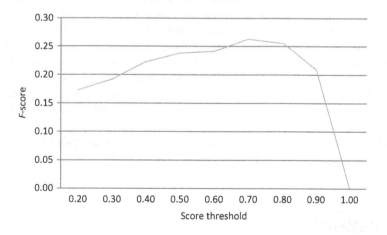

FIG. 13.5

F score for the detection of emotional versus nonemotional tweets with respect to the minimum score threshold.

Table 13.5 Baseline Figures for Detecting Emotional Versus Nonemotional Tweets via Symbolic Methods

	Precision	Recall	F Score
Emotional	0	0	0
Nonemotional	0.91	1.00	0.95
Average	0.45	0.50	0.48

Table 13.6 Figures for Detecting Emotional Versus Nonemotional Tweets With Symbolic Methods

	Precision	Recall	F Score
Emotional	0.54	0.43	0.48
Nonemotional	0.94	0.96	0.95
Average	0.74	0.69	0.72

7 CONCLUSION

Companies know that customer satisfaction means business. Monitoring and analyzing customers in social media, making decisions on the basis of this strategic information, and analyzing the results of the marketing actions performed are nowadays essential, especially for business-to-consumer companies. SOMA will provide companies with an advanced tool to help them achieve these results by analyzing customers' sentiments and emotions in social media with advanced techniques that allow deeper and more exhaustive analysis. Because of the nature of the corpus, our evaluation results for the task of emotion detection do not allow us to conclude that one type of method (symbolic or machine learning) is generally more successful than the other, although, in our particular case, the machine learning approach did perform better. In the task of detecting emotional versus nonemotional texts, which we evaluated on a gold standard corpus, the results are more reliable, and we may conclude that for this type of task, symbolic methods perform better.

In the SOMA project we also plan to use this work on emotion analysis to detect influencers in social networks (see Chapter 10 for more information on this topic).

ACKNOWLEDGMENTS

This work was partially funded by the Eurostars program, project SOMA number E!9202 (2015–17).

REFERENCES

[1] J. Wiebe, T. Wilson, C. Cardie, Annotating expressions of opinions and emotions in language, Lang. Resour. Eval. 39 (2) (2005) 165–210.

[2] C. Alm, D. Roth, R. Sproat, Emotions from text: machine learning for text-based emotion prediction, in: Proceedings of HLT/EMNLP, 2005.

[3] P. Ekman, Facial expression and emotion, Am. Psychol. 48 (4) (1993) 384–392.

[4] A. Pak, P. Paroubek, Twitter as a corpus for sentiment analysis and opinion mining, in: Proceedings of the Seventh International Conference on Language Resources and Evaluation (LREC 2010), 2010, pp. 1320–1326.

[5] H. Vo, N. Collier, Twitter emotion analysis in earthquake situations, Int. J. Comput. Linguist. Appl. 4 (1) (2013) 159–173.

[6] C. Strapparava, R. Mihalcea, SemEval-2007 task 14: affective text, in: Proceedings of the Fourth International Workshop on the Semantic Evaluations (SemEval 2007), 2007, pp. 70–74.

[7] Y. Zhuang, Building a Complete Tweet Index, 2013. https://blog.twitter.com/2014/building-a-complete-tweet-index.

[8] T. Dickinson, Scraping Tweets Directly from Twitter, 2015. http://tomkdickinson.co.uk/2015/01/scraping-tweets-directly-from-twitters-search-page-part-1/.

[9] R. Valitutti, WordNet-Affect: an affective extension of WordNet, in: Proceedings of the Fourth International Conference on Language Resources and Evaluation (LREC 2004), 2004, pp. 1083–1086.

[10] L. Dini, A. Bittar, M. Ruhlmann, Approches hybrides pour l'analyse de recettes de cuisine DEFT, TALN-RECITAL 2013, in: Proceedings of Défi Fouille de Textes, 2013, pp. 53–65.

[11] J. Lafferty, A. McCallum, F. Perreira, Conditional random fields: probabilistic models for segmenting and labeling sequence data, in: Proceedings of the International Conference on Machine Learning—ICML, 2001, pp. 282–289.

[12] A. Chang, C. Manning, TokensRegex: defining cascaded regular expressions over tokens, tech. rep., Stanford University, 2014.

[13] J. Sowa, Conceptual graphs, in: Handbook of Knowledge Representation, Elsevier, Amsterdam, The Netherlands, 2008.

[14] N. Chambers, D. Cer, T. Grenager, D. Hall, C. Kiddon, B. MacCartney, M.-C. de Marneffe, D. Ramage, E. Yeh, C. Manning, Learning alignments and leveraging natural logic, in: Proceedings of the Workshop on Textual Entailment and Paraphrasing, 2007.

[15] J. Nocedal, S. Wright, Quasi-newton methods, in: Numerical Optimization, Springer, New York, 2006, pp. 135–163.

[16] M.-C. de Marneffe, C. Manning, The stanford typed dependencies representation, in: Coling 2008: Proceedings of the Workshop on Cross-Framework and Cross-Domain Parser Evaluation, 2008.

[17] S. Maurel, P. Curtoni, L. Dini, Classification d'opinions par méthodes symbolique, statistique et hybride, in: Proceedings of Défi Fouille de Textes, 2007, pp. 121–127.

[18] A. Bittar, L. Dini, S. Maurel, M. Ruhlmann, The Dangerous myth of the star system, in: Proceedings of the Ninth International Conference on Language Resources and Evaluation (LREC 2014), 2014, pp. 2237–2241.

THE HUMAN ADVANTAGE: LEVERAGING THE POWER OF PREDICTIVE ANALYTICS TO STRATEGICALLY OPTIMIZE SOCIAL CAMPAIGNS*

14

B.H.B. Honan, D. Richer
KRC Research, New York, NY, United States

1 INTRODUCTION

In today's increasingly digitally connected world, content publishing is an imperative, and it is increasingly becoming essential to brands for their social media marketing purposes. Social media content can be vital fuel, a force field that creates a certain amount of gravitational pull, drawing in customers and stakeholders to join and engage with a brand, product, or service in new and interesting ways.

Historically, marketing was a means for brands and companies to broadcast messages to their customers but it was a one-way street; essentially, people sitting at home watching commercials on television, receiving direct mail, or seeing a point-of-sale display. For consumers it was possible to experience a brand when they bought it or if they knew someone who used the product but otherwise there was very little interaction between the consumer and the brand, leading to a gap between the brand and the consumer's experience as a prospect.

Now companies and brands are using social media as a key mechanism to stay involved in the ongoing conversation in their particular space, whether that space is health insurance or consumer technology. To that end, brands today are creating social media content and driving forward thought leadership conversations. They are trying to relate to consumers and connect with them in a way that is no longer a monologue but a two-way street, largely through social media platforms such as Twitter, Facebook, Vine, Instagram, and Pinterest, which people use to converse and visually communicate with their family and friends. In this way brands are now reaching people—and their friends, families, and

*Throughout this chapter, we have presented case studies to illustrate our social and digital media content analytics method. While we cannot give the names of the organizations with which we have worked, we think these case studies are instructive lessons that apply broadly beyond their respective categories. Thus you will notice that information has been redacted in some of the figures.

Sentiment Analysis in Social Networks. http://dx.doi.org/10.1016/B978-0-12-804412-4.00014-0

peers—where they live and breathe, and are becoming much more a part of consumers' daily lives and daily conversations.

However, as more resources are dedicated to this space, marketers are growing frustrated with traditional automated analytical tools, software, and techniques that aim to measure impact. Marketers see many of these automated tools as too often simply "data dumps" where a lot of information is provided yet there are no actionable or prescriptive insights into the target audience. Today, the number of scorecards, dashboards, and other technologies has exploded. But what do they really tell us about customers? What insights do they actually provide besides providing a snapshot?

On the basis of our work we are hearing the same questions. Automated tools on their own are not providing very much and are not providing what is needed; namely, strategy to drive social campaigns. We live in the era of big data but marketers do not have the right data.

We have therefore concluded that sentiment analysis is at an important inflection point: chief marketing officers and chief communications officers need the tools to understand the whole picture about their customers and audience. They increasingly want to know the reasons behind consumer behavior online, not simply what their customers do, but why they do it.

The automation of sentiment and content analysis is in its infancy but as more marketing dollars are dedicated to social and digital programs, marketers need far better analytics to provide a clear strategy for where to go and how to get there. What is missing in many social media campaigns is a deep strategic approach and road map for how to develop content that drives the most effective engagement.

Content and data-driven marketing have become mission critical because marketers are actively searching for insights and information in all different formats. Data-driven marketing offers companies a way to analyze the way the customer interacts with the brand and use that to design strategic communications that have a much higher likelihood of engaging consumers. Ultimately, data-driven marketing is a means to satisfy customers' desires—often through direct communication with the customers.

While understanding sentiment is key, there remains a significant amount of social media content that does not perform well. A surprising number of social media campaigns are simply not breaking through the clutter and are not being heard, so they end up simply cluttering the digital space. Businesses are thus missing an opportunity to share their message and get the word out about their brand—and thus clients are missing an opportunity to grow their brand and improve their reputation.

Even more concerning, marketers are in many cases being misled by false sentiment data and are creating the wrong content and the wrong campaigns. It is important for marketers to know not only whether content is performing but also what they can do or change to improve performance. Often, social media analytics fails to improve performance because the algorithms generate misleading counts, and because counting alone does not offer any explanation as to the why. To provide an explanation, methods that draw statistical connections and test hypotheses are required.

If we acknowledge that simply creating content for the sake of creating content does not make sense, we then must ask what does effective social media content look like? What is the right strategy for creating it? The growing consensus is that it is crucial to move beyond simply counting the number of likes, shares, and retweets to understand the true sentiment behind these numbers. KRC Research has developed a way to marry social media measurement with human intervention that can transform data to answers, and tell us not just what is working but why and what might work better.

2 THE CURRENT PHILOSOPHY AROUND SENTIMENT ANALYSIS

Part of the answer for marketers is smart, actionable analytics, which connects content and engagement to a business or communications goal or objective. Smart analytics matters because it helps in devising and developing strategies that will engage people. Optimizing social media marketing strategy is very important to brands so that they can best connect with consumers and achieve their organization's mission and goals. More should be done to help marketers make decisions so that they are not wasting time and resources developing suboptimal content.

At the same time, companies do not need to conduct a "census"; meaning they do not need to analyze every single piece of content individually, which is neither cost-efficient nor time-efficient. Yet far, far too often the philosophy in social media analytics is that only a census is sufficient—every single piece of social media content must be studied and analyzed—and that means deferring to the computer software and taking humans largely out of the equation.

Automated listening tools and dashboards are powerful and impressive tools that have the capacity to code and analyze hundreds of millions of pieces of content, and do it in a matter of minutes. However, with technology in the driver's seat, this type of analysis does not always equal strategic campaign planning or actionable insights. While automated dashboards are necessary, they are not sufficient in and of themselves because they cannot tell marketers everything they need to know. In fact, this philosophy carries many pitfalls for companies, many of which are being overlooked.

Coding errors are chief among these pitfalls. Computers are fallible, and bad data ensures bad analysis. As an example, computers do not understand language nuances. For example, with sentiment coding, there is no way to determine if *"this pizza is hot"* means that it is at a high temperature and thus might burn your mouth, or that it is spicy, or that it is popular/desirable. Yes, algorithms can learn over time; for example, while *"this pizza is hot"* can have several meanings, if qualified with explanation and context in the form of *"this pizza is hot, so I need to get a glass of water,"* a computer can be trained to understand the statement. Yet despite the fact that computers can learn, social monitoring platforms consistently make coding errors. For this reason, we believe that automated monitoring alone is an insufficient measurement if the goal is to improve engagement because it does not result in a strategy for engagement.

Monitoring and listening can tell you that, for example, in the last hour, 1000 people retweeted a specific keyword, and in the hour before that, only 900 people retweeted that keyword. If a brand is trying to run a successful campaign, what does this information really tell it and how do you interpret it? And what are you supposed to really do? In addition, all too often, monitoring is an afterthought and is not integrated into a campaign's strategic direction. Monitoring is not leading strategy the way it should.

The ever-popular and often-used dashboard is not by itself a strategy creation tool either. Dashboards belong in the category of monitoring and listening. A dashboard is essentially a data dump. It allows readers to get an at-a-glance snapshot of important data but it cannot tell clients how and what they need to do to optimize their social media marketing strategy. See Fig. 14.1 for an example.

3 KRC RESEARCH'S DIGITAL CONTENT AND SENTIMENT PHILOSOPHY

While unactionable data and information abounds, new techniques—that combine human intelligence with the right kind of advanced analytical techniques—offer considerable promise and offer the next

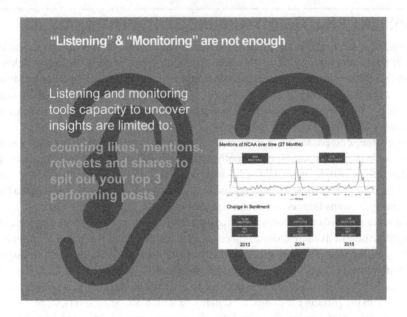

FIG. 14.1

Real-world example of a dashboard that shows spikes in mentions over time but does not provide any context for this information.

place that the industry must go. KRC Research's vision is about evolving the traditional approaches away from research programs that involve creating endless static scorecards and dashboards to a dynamic technique designed to iteratively improve our understanding of the underlying sentiment behind social media posts online—a process that reveals actionable insights and helps develop strategic marketing strategy.

How do we do this? In a word, people. Marketers need smart, analytical people working side by side with them to build a strategy and a real game plan for effectively engaging with their target audience and ensuring it is being executed efficiently. Existing automated social listening tools and software monitor sentiment and count likes and tweets, but, with technology in the driver's seat, automated analyses do not always equal powerful or even more than basic insights. To accurately analyze the conversation around sustainability on social channels, we need humans. Humans can interpret social media context and dual word meanings where and in ways that machines often cannot. And humans can code and categorize content that can then be studied and analyzed in ways that computers cannot.

KRC Research's four-pillar social media and sentiment philosophy centers on the basic premise that we can and must treat social data in the same way we would likely treat traditional quantitative research and analysis. Social media posts demonstrate opinions and behavior just as survey responses do, and with the right curating, a collection of tweets can be analyzed to provide meaningful and nuanced findings.

The four pillars of KRC Research's philosophy are:

1. Robust pretesting is crucial—not optional—to eliminate work and ideas that are of little or no use.
2. We must continuously and iteratively learn how to get better.
3. We must use scientific sampling rather than reviewing every piece of content.
4. We must build predictive models to improve/increase the likelihood of driving desired actions, outcomes in social media.

The resulting output for our clients is a clear and precise strategy, not guesswork, that helps us identify what content is most sharable, most engaging, and helps move the brand or company forward. Let us look at each of these pillars in more detail.

3.1 PRETESTING IS CRUCIAL

We often see programs that are creative and have an interesting tag line, along with flashy apps, great tools, and compelling marketing collateral. Yet simply developing a campaign, rolling it out, and hoping it works is not a wise expenditure of money and resources. It is not enough to design a campaign, no matter how brilliant it is.

KRC Research believes in creating smaller bits of social media content that can be pushed out in advance of a campaign to see if they have resonance and then learn iteratively from them. One tweet or Facebook post may not have all the creative assets behind it, nor does it represent the fully developed campaign, but it is still sufficient to test the waters. This is a very simple, easy step that does not require a lot of time or cost, yet a lot of companies are skipping it. They are not doing the initial groundwork to figure out if an idea really works and if they are on the right track.

One way in which KRC Research tests the waters for clients is with a proprietary tool we developed called the *Social Sandbox*. This is a Facebook-like, customizable secure platform that lets us "road test" potential ideas in a safe environment. By recruiting frequent social media users as we would a focus group, and asking them to browse and comment on the conversation, we can determine which communication platforms elicit a strong response from the target audience and which individual messages are particularly successful in driving engagement.

Respondents are able to "like," share, and comment on as many posts as they wish. Results are then tallied, detailing which messages seem to be most strongly resonating. This is a very simple thing to do, yet is also very effective in ultimately determining if a campaign or communication is going to be sharable or highly unpopular.

Clients can use the Social Sandbox to test ideas, campaigns, and programs in advance before they create content. For instance, if Major League Baseball wanted to develop a campaign to promote the World Series, it could talk about sharing memories with your children and your experiences growing up watching baseball, or it could talk about bragging rights; for example, "*I was at the game and I saw history in the making.*" But which approach will work best? Which strategy is the right one? What tactics will most effectively drive the greatest degree of engagement? The Social Sandbox will tell you.

We have also used the Social Sandbox to stop campaigns in the testing stage because they simply were not working, and in turn we have seen campaigns that tested well go on to be highly successful for our clients. This success is due to our discovery, through our testing, that people wanted to be involved in the call to action. The Social Sandbox lets us continuously learn how to improve so we can advise our clients of when they need to course correct a campaign.

3.2 CONTINUOUSLY LEARN HOW TO IMPROVE

One thing that digital analytics and sentiment analysis requires is that companies not rest on their laurels. In traditional advertising campaigns, they use time-tested tools such as surveys and focus groups to gauge how their target audience responds to the ad, and how and where campaigns need to be adjusted and course corrected. We believe that companies should use this same thought process applied to the digital space to refine what they are doing and optimize the social media content they are putting out.

Our work for a life insurance organization is a good example of this practice (see the case study at the end of this chapter for more information). For this client, our approach was to examine the social media content that was being created and analyze the sentiment around that content in a robust way. We were then able to help this client optimize its content creation so it could develop something that is even more effective.

Specifically, we found that its messaging on Twitter was not well matched with its Twitter audience. Its tweets focused on fear, such as *"what happens to your children if you are killed in an accident?"* Unfortunately that kind of message does not work well on Twitter. Our insights helped the company to change its content so that it was much more uplifting, focusing on success stories (such as *"John was able to go to college and start his own business because his father had life insurance when he passed away"*) rather than worst-case scenarios (see Fig. 14.2).

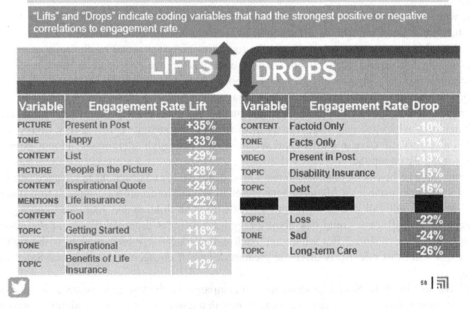

Summary: Twitter Elements & Engagement Rates

"Lifts" and "Drops" indicate coding variables that had the strongest positive or negative correlations to engagement rate.

LIFTS / DROPS

Variable	Engagement Rate Lift		Variable	Engagement Rate Drop	
PICTURE	Present in Post	+35%	CONTENT	Factoid Only	-10%
TONE	Happy	+33%	TONE	Facts Only	-11%
CONTENT	List	+29%	VIDEO	Present in Post	-13%
PICTURE	People in the Picture	+28%	TOPIC	Disability Insurance	-15%
CONTENT	Inspirational Quote	+24%	TOPIC	Debt	-16%
MENTIONS	Life Insurance	+22%			
CONTENT	Tool	+18%	TOPIC	Loss	-22%
TOPIC	Getting Started	+16%	TONE	Sad	-24%
TONE	Inspirational	+13%	TOPIC	Long-term Care	-26%
TOPIC	Benefits of Life Insurance	+12%			

FIG. 14.2

KRC Research's analytics show topics and types of Twitter posts that lift and drop the engagement rate.

At KRC Research we often say the only bad mistake is one that you keep repeating. Our work with this life insurance organization is a strong example of how important it is for marketers to learn from their mistakes and to optimize content so that it works better for the company and its audience. We should never take anything for granted. It is crucial for companies to experiment, admit when they are wrong, and change strategy and execution accordingly.

3.3 USE SCIENTIFIC SAMPLING RATHER THAN REVIEWING EVERY PIECE OF CONTENT

We believe that the current "census philosophy" that advises companies to analyze every piece of content is just plain wrong. This census mentality posits that everything every person tweets or posts is important and must be analyzed; however, this is not the wisest path forward—actually far from it.

Consider that the US Constitution stipulates that the country is required to count the number of people living in the United States every 10 years. Yet there are tens of millions of people that the US Census is unable to reach. To compensate, the US Census conducts numerous studies and sampling between the decennial census to gain a better understanding of trends and patterns. The point is that the US Census does not—and cannot—analyze every household. Unfortunately this philosophy is not shared by many clients. At a recent Super Bowl half-time show, a celebrity performer tweeted about something that contained a brand message for a popular beverage. Some 2 million people commented on her tweet. A lot of the conversation among people who were working on the campaign for this beverage focused on how it was crucial to examine all 2 million tweets.

The problem is that to analyze that much content you have to use computers, and this can lead to coding errors and nonactionable analysis. Why? Computers simply cannot think. Even the best software has significant limitations for developing marketing strategy. Increasingly with social media campaigns it is not sufficient to conduct analysis that lacks actionability. That is not what clients, account teams at agencies, or campaigns need. Rather, what they need is a clear strategy for how to drive engagement forward. And no computer, no dashboard, and no software package can outline that.

This is not to say that computers have no use—far from it. For sure, computers do a great job at looking at millions of pieces of data and producing, within a few minutes, how many tweets are related to certain mentions. We use computers all the time to look at all the tweets or posts related to a hashtag, and the computer is able to provide us with a random sampling of 1000 pieces of social media content in a matter of minutes. This is valuable because it would take an enormous amount of time for us to collect all the content and determine the random sampling.

Computers are also valuable in creating statistical models. Once each piece of content has been coded by hand by a person, the data are fed into a computer program that produces the statistically generated model. It is a human, however, that interprets the data that are fed into the computer. When the computer produces the statistical model, a person interprets the model and makes sense of it. That is an approach different from having someone hit computer keys to produce a graph in less than 15 seconds purporting to show "analysis."

In no uncertain terms, the only way to help clients drive engagement is with people who understand the business and communications needs and objectives; who can determine if brand content is meeting those needs, and whether one tactic or strategy is more engaging than another. When people, rather than computers, look at a sampling of the content, those people can deduce errors that a computer may likely overlook, and their analytical edge far surpasses that of any software program.

Similarly, humans need to play an active role in model development, specifically in the exploratory data analysis/identification of data structures and phases and more importantly the model generation and validation process. Just as humans code content by hand, they are responsible for establishing the parameters, modeling inputs, and optimization for model fit based on their analysis of fit statistics, prediction errors, and other factors. Humans are also needed to determine the appropriate modeling technique for the data available and the desired outcome.

Additionally, computers can only pull out a basic aggregation of data—basic sentiment such as negative, neutral, or positive and how many likes a topic receives. If you ask a computer to analyze comments that appear on Twitter about, for example, a news item, the computer will tell you what percentage of comments are negative, neutral, or positive. Yet knowing the percentages of positive, negative, and neutral comments is not very helpful to a company that is trying to develop or improve on a campaign, nor does it help us determine how to change the conversation.

We have found that in the vast majority of cases, regardless of what topic or product the comments or tweets are about, the computer analysis reaches the same conclusion: approximately the same percentages are ascribed to positive, neutral, and negative. It is rare to have deviations, even though we know that the conversation about a serious news topic cannot be the same as, say, the conversation about a food product. This indicates that there are serious flaws with the computer analysis.

Thus a census, when all is said and done, is a superficial analysis. We know that automated coding of sentiment, as well as automating counting of themes, can be inaccurate. Yet to understand what types of social media content are delivering engagement, it is critical to be accurate about both sentiment and themes. The only way to be sure of accuracy is through human coding. At the same time, it is impossible and impractical for humans to code the vast quantity of social media content generated about and by most brands. This is where probability theory comes in. Probability theory tells us that random samples have an enormously high probability of mirroring the population they are drawn from; in other words, if you have a statistically valid sample that is balanced across gender, race, age, and geography (eg, urban and rural), you can purport to know the viewpoint of all Americans on the basis of your sample.

We believe this same approach should apply to social media analysis—a census is not needed; real sampling is. By applying probability theory to social media analysis, we can make it possible to conduct the kind of analysis required to understand how to continually improve the performance of social media content.

One final note about sampling is that it is important to consider whether you are analyzing audience posts (high volume) or owned social posts (low volume). Sampling makes sense with social listening—campaign mentions that are driven by the marketing messages—given the vast volume of content; however, sampling of owned social media comments is not relevant or needed because the volume of content is low and, therefore, sampling could cause you to miss important nuances.

3.4 BUILD PREDICTIVE MODELS

Using sophisticated analytical and statistical tools, we build predictive models for clients. A predictive model is a tool that allows us to look at a lot of data about past behavior and then, to a great extent, make some predictions about future behavior.

For example, if a food manufacturer continues to produce content about recipes on its Facebook page and this content has received a modest level of engagement from consumers, we can presume this level of engagement will continue in the future unless there is a dramatic change. In the case of the food manufacturer, we were able to predict how many people would continue to share information related to a specific hashtag, whereas communications about the health benefits of a specific food would yield a smaller number of shares.

Our point of view is that you have to be clear with clients at the beginning of campaigns, and predictive models allow us to do that, providing we have the relevant historical data to support the model. For new campaigns/digital properties, there is a lag time for model development because we must allow the campaign to mature over time to produce the 12–18 months' worth of data needed for the modeling. Once we have the data, predictive models help clients understand what does and does not work so that they and their agency partners can build or revise their campaigns on the basis of the results of the predictive model. We can also use predictive models to analyze campaigns that are not achieving a good return on investment and redirect them to a more efficient direction.

4 KRC RESEARCH'S SENTIMENT AND ANALYTICS APPROACH

Our sentiment analysis approach begins with a random sampling of comments on social media. We conduct a strategic examination of a client's existing social media content so we can identify trends and patterns. We then create a custom social media codebook or coding framework, based on the core objectives of the client's campaign, to capture variables that we identify as most essential on which to evaluate content.

A team of KRC Research researchers then codes, or categorizes, by hand the thousands of hashtags, tweets, posts, and comments randomly selected. Each piece of content is placed into categories on the basis of the theme, sentiment, and other components (eg, photos, links) within the content. For a life insurance client we looked at each tweet and determined if the tone was uplifting or sad, whether life insurance was mentioned, what the topic was (eg, bereavement), and whether video or photo links were present (eg, this tweet went out on Thursday in the morning; it was about getting one's financial house in order and included an infographic with a rhetorical question; it had a serious tone). By coding individual pieces of content across dozens of categories, one can create a robust dataset that can then be analyzed quantitatively.

We utilize the information obtained from our hand coding to determine the most effective content and sentiment among target audiences. Once we have manually coded the relevant content, we develop a statistical predictive model for each channel to understand the relationship between each variable and outcome measure(s). A statistical model focuses not on the highest number of tweets or posts but on patterns, themes, and trends. We can tell a client, for example, that putting out a tweet on a Tuesday afternoon results in more retweets than putting that same tweet out on a Saturday, or we can say that a video is retweeted more than a photo.

The statistical model is essentially a tool that lets us look at trends across the entire exercise. It allows us to understand the relationships between various factors and to what extent one factor versus another has more impact on the audience. We can then accurately predict what types of content will be most impactful. See Fig. 14.3 for an outline of our approach.

As a result of our approach, clients are able to produce strategic, mediable content including potential headlines, social media content, and engagements; visual storytelling elements including infographics that they can integrate into their current campaigns; meaningful subgroup analysis that gives key insights into the behavior of their target audiences; and strategic recommendations for communications that build on existing consumer sentiment.

Social Content Evaluation Modeling

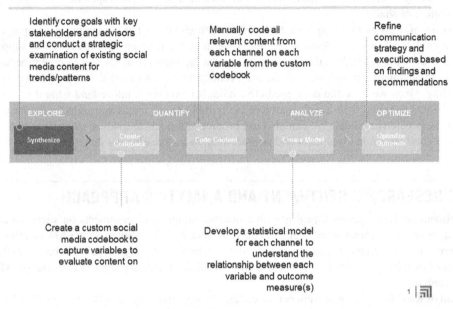

FIG. 14.3

KRC Research's step-by-step proprietary process to enable clients to engage better with target audiences.

5 CASE STUDY

The following example shows how KRC Research has helped one of its clients optimize its communications through actionable insights and guidance on the basis of our sentiment analysis method. This real-life example illustrates how this work can be applied to drive thought leadership, campaign evaluation and planning, and, ultimately, engagement.

5.1 LIFE INSURANCE ORGANIZATION

A life insurance organization commissioned KRC Research to conduct an in-depth review and statistical analysis of the content on its traditional channels such as email and webinars, and its Twitter and LinkedIn channels. The organization wanted to gain a deeper understanding of its overall communications channels, as well as to clarify any questions about each of them. KRC Research also analyzed its Twitter followers by demographics, including age, gender, location, occupation, relationship status, and social interests, to gain a better understanding of the profile of the organization's Twitter followers.

    KRC Research began with a high-level overview of the current content. Each piece of content posted on the organization's Twitter page, LinkedIn page, and LinkedIn group in a 1-year period

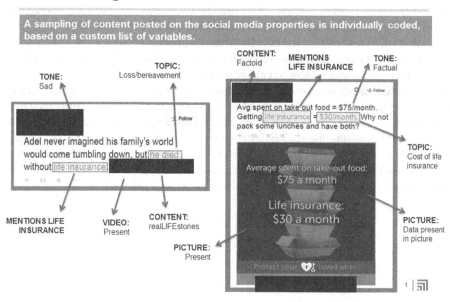

Social Decoded
Content Coding

A sampling of content posted on the social media properties is individually coded, based on a custom list of variables.

FIG. 14.4

KRC Research's coding method in which custom variables in social media posts (such as the presence of a photo or video) are categorized.

was individually coded on the basis of 20 different custom variables, including the intended audience, keywords, type of content, and tone. See Fig. 14.4 for an example.

Having manually coded more than 1500 pieces of content, KRC Research created a predictive model that identified key themes, tones, and words within and across channels that were driving engagement with that brand.

The key output of this effort was a strategic game plan for how the organization could most effectively use and target resources toward industry and consumer communications in the next 12 months. Ultimately, this analysis provided this client with actionable insights on which elements, such as topic, tone, and content type, most effectively drive engagement so as to optimize the organization's outreach strategy on its social channels. Examples of our key findings include:

- Content designed to educate its followers, both consumers and industry, resonated strongly.
- There are some clear differences in the types of topics and formats that best resonate on each channel.
- Compared with text-only submissions, images greatly increase engagement across Twitter and LinkedIn platforms.

6 CONCLUSION

It is now commonplace for companies to leverage data to help them make business decisions. When we talk about data, it is not simply a matter of generating more data; rather; we are leveraging the right kinds of tools to help address the needs of brands and companies. At KRC Research, we believe there is value in tools such as automated dashboards. When companies need to know if they are a part of the social media conversation, dashboards have enormous value, but at the same time, dashboards and similar tools cannot tell companies how to engage people.

The pendulum has swung to a pivotal point where marketers are realizing that software alone is not sufficient to explain the "why" behind social media sentiment or to provide insights into the target audience. Brands need human intelligence, along with the more traditional analytical tools, to develop a solid strategy for influencing the social/digital conversation. Machine learning and algorithms are simply too fallible for us to rely on them exclusively. KRC Research's dynamic approach generates meaningful, nuanced findings that inform strategic marketing strategy, and allow brands and companies to be heard by breaking through the glut of social content.

PRICE-SENSITIVE RIPPLES AND CHAIN REACTIONS: TRACKING THE IMPACT OF CORPORATE ANNOUNCEMENTS WITH REAL-TIME MULTIDIMENSIONAL OPINION STREAMING

K. Moilanen[a,b], S. Pulman*[,a,b]

TheySay Ltd., London, United Kingdom[a] University of Oxford, Oxford, United Kingdom[b]

1 INTRODUCTION

Publicly quoted companies have rigorous regulatory requirements and fiduciary responsibilities to make official announcements and to release potentially price-sensitive information at regular intervals (eg, at the end of financial accounting periods) or when some material events or changes in a corporation's circumstances and operational environments have occurred. Such announcements have to be released in an orderly manner so as not to leak any insider knowledge that may give a person or an organization an advantage in the market.

Formal financial announcements typically contain a full report including quarterly profit and loss figures and balance sheet performance, and often compare current performance with prior performance (eg, year-to-date performance). Corporate announcements are traditionally followed by a public conference for both analysts and the press in which senior management can be questioned further about the latest announcement. In essence, the audience in a public forum are scrutinizing whether the company is performing well or poorly, particularly against prior expectations. The expectations of the audience (and the market) are a function of what was promised by the company in previous financial announcements and any previously announced material contracts (sales or mergers and acquisitions) that have been secured and executed by the company. In particular, analysts, brokers, fund managers, and shareholders will be listening for any signals that can indicate (1) better-than-expected performance (indicating that the company is undervalued), (2) worse-than-expected performance (indicating that the company is overvalued), or (3) obfuscation (indicating potential threats or problems). On the basis of

---

*https://www.cs.ox.ac.uk/people/stephen.pulman

Sentiment Analysis in Social Networks. http://dx.doi.org/10.1016/B978-0-12-804412-4.00015-2

such assessment, investment decisions (to buy, sell, or hold) will be made and reports will be issued to downstream clients concerning their assessment and interpretation of the company. Depending on the level of optimism versus pessimism, a company may start to be seen in positive or negative light. In addition, regular announcements by larger, higher-profile companies may attract further negative or positive press in the financial columns.

Many other emergent material announcements can also have a similar positive versus negative effect, such as major product releases, changes in organization structure (eg, CEOs resigning or being fired unexpectedly, unexpected senior management changes, new board announcements), mergers and acquisitions events and activities, sales (eg, winning or losing major contracts), legal events (eg, litigation threats, regulatory changes), and unforeseen crises and disasters (eg, the Volkswagen emissions scandal, car recalls, deepwater oil spills, civil war).

Regular announcements are still reported primarily through traditional[1] news channels, which can be described as typically regulated, non-real-time, structural, formal, and factual, and their primary audience is mostly made up of professionals and organizations in and around the financial services industry (eg, analysts, traders, investors, companies).

Regular announcements are of critical intrinsic importance to the market because announcements often contain a great many price-sensitive financial performance cues—explicit as well as implicit references to the fitness, activities, circumstances, and prospects of a given company. Although such intrinsic upstream performance cues alone constitute a clear market-moving force, an even greater variety of performance cues are present in the extrinsic downstream public reaction to and conversation around corporate announcements that can create potentially very strong ripple effects in the market. In particular, rich streams of less formal and regulated, instantaneous, more rampant, less structural, less factual, more subjective, and more emotional reactions can be mined and gauged across a multitude of social media channels that can reach a much wider audience faster than any traditional public forums and conferences.

This chapter describes our approach to monitoring and quantifying in real time the impact of corporate announcements and other related events using deep, multidimensional opinion streaming that is powered by a large-scale natural language processing (NLP) pipeline and seeded with financial feeds, social media firehoses, blogs, forums, and news. Our main focus is on affective "soft" metrics derived from sentiment, emotion, speculation, intent, risk, and other related signals that augment traditional, more factual "hard" metrics such as raw volume or share price. The main goal of our streaming system is to provide feedback and rich price-sensitive insights for the end users who want to shed light on the following key questions:

1. Who is talking about the announcement and the company (when, where, how, and in what contexts)?
2. How do people feel about the announcement (company)?
3. How does the conversation around the announcement (company) evolve?
4. What drives sudden peaks (or troughs) in public opinion around the announcement (company)?

---

[1]Note that Twitter is gaining prominence as a primary channel for corporate announcements as well (see Justin Baer (2015). Goldman Sachs earnings are moving to Twitter. *The Wall Street Journal*. Accessed October 7, 2015. http://www.wsj.com/articles/goldman-sachs-earnings-are-moving-to-twitter-1444261919).

2 ARCHITECTURE

2.1 DATA SOURCES AND FILTERS

The real-time opinion streams are derived from two main sources; namely, (1) a full, unthrottled Twitter[2] firehose and (2) a pool of mixed streams from general news, blog, post, and forum sites that are polled approximately 3000 times a day. All raw data sources are filtered with multiple keyword and other content filters to make them maximally relevant to a specific corporate announcement for a specific end user. We employ simple Boolean keyword filters that rely on positive and suppressive negative matching as well as the ability to specify additional context anchors.

The keyword-filtered streams vary dramatically in terms of their average keyword hit levels, reflecting corporations, events, and circumstances in the financial world. While announcements about large multinational corporations (eg, IBM, Berkshire Hathaway) are understandably voluminous and often bursty, smaller corporations (eg, Thundermin Resources) tend to be mentioned considerably less frequently, as can be seen in the raw keyword hit estimates in Table 15.1, for example. Such variance poses a challenge for real-time opinion streaming in that no single data filtering precision versus recall trade-off point will be able to cover all corporate announcements across all individual end users. In particular, low-volume corporate announcements are especially troublesome because their recall levels may be too low and because they may also reveal deficiencies in the underlying NLP analyses, both of which can have a devastating impact on the usability of the system.

Typical content aggregation platforms attempt to remove or normalize duplicate documents and messages reposted and syndicated by upstream sources or social media users. Corporate announcements behave differently in this regard because repeated (and therefore amplified) content

Table 15.1 Sample Frequency Estimates of Raw Keyword Hit Rates on Google (https://www.google.com), Bing (http://www.bing.com/), and Topsy (Accessed November 29, 2015. The service is no longer available.)

Raw Keyword Query	Hits	Search Engine
Berkshire Hathaway		
"Berkshire Hathaway"	14,600,000	Google (all time)
	5,320,000	Bing (all time)
	6188	Topsy (last 30 days)
with +earnings +results +2015	331,000	Google (all time)
	325,000	Bing (all time)
Thundermin Resources		
"Thundermin Resources"	24,700	Google (all time)
	4140	Bing (all time)
	11	Topsy (last 30 days)
with +earnings +results +2015	15,300	Google (all time)
	959	Bing (all time)

[2]http://support.gnip.com/sources/twitter

can constitute a highly relevant price-sensitive signal in itself. For this reason, we do not apply any deduplication filters.

Although Boolean keyword filters can generate sufficiently clean and focused topical data streams for most corporate announcements, they cannot eradicate all forms of irrelevant content—ostensibly accurate keyword matches in contexts which do not contain any useful information for the end user. To make the opinion streams even more relevant and focused, and to aid downstream opinion signal creation, we run as secondary filters three additional soft classifiers, the sensitivity of which the end user can control. These secondary filters, which all use standard supervised classifier architectures with trigram features, target (1) sarcasm and irony, (2) advertisements (cf. spam), and (3) humor.

Sarcasm is of particular importance in that it can skew sentiment classifiers' predictions. While the noise caused by sarcasm is typically marginal or tolerable in high-volume opinion streams from formal news sources, it can have a detrimental impact on the sentiment predictions in low-volume opinion streams from social media sources. Although current sarcasm and irony detection performance levels are far from perfect [1–3], standard supervised classifiers can be useful as additional relevance filters, especially at high confidence levels. Advertisements that refer to a company directly or indirectly via references to product or services can in turn skew sentiment predictions toward positive sentiment. Positive spam is a particular problem with high-volume opinion streams tracking extremely popular companies (eg, Apple, Tesla, Visa). Humor generates yet another kind of noise in that references to a given company in humorous contexts may well contain relevant sentiment signals but they are axiomatically less important than those from factual contexts. Considering the limited capabilities of current humor approaches [4,5], we similarly apply humor filtering only at high confidence levels.

2.2 CORE NATURAL LANGUAGE PROCESSING AND OPINION METRICS

We process each keyword-filtered text with an NLP pipeline with the aim of capturing and profiling as many direct and indirect references to a specific corporation and its announcement as possible. We first tokenize text with a custom tokenizer that supports (1) finite-state patterns for domain-specific multiword expressions to capture complex company names and symbol sequences (eg, *"SPDR S&P MidCap 400"*) that may not align fully with downstream syntactic parses (which typically reflect formal grammars), (2) generic complex emoji and emoticon sequences, and (3) hashtag-internal tokenization with character-level CKY chart parsing (eg, *"#beatsstreet"*). Deeper and richer tokenization, an often overlooked task, can boost downstream processing; for example, part-of-speech tagging, dependency parsing, sentiment analysis, and emotion tagging [6,7].

We use a similar finite state approach for sentence breaking. Our custom sentence breaker exploits rich resources optimized for the financial genre and accounts for peripheral hashtag, social media user ID, and other symbolic fields around core sentence content (eg, *"$WSM $AXP $VOYA $NTAP $RRGB $WDC $KMX - all new 52-week lows - yep, it's all about the oil! $SPY $QQQ $IWM $DIA"*[3]), again to reduce noise in downstream processing.

After tokenization and sentence breaking, each sentence is processed by a Hidden Markov model part-of-speech tagger and a (nonrecursive) noun phrase/verb group chunker. These preparsing components have been trained on (among other) text from the British National Corpus,[4] with the tagset

---

[3]http://stocktwits.com/coolkevs/message/47079864
[4]http://www.natcorp.ox.ac.uk

then being mapped so as to be compatible with that used in the Penn Tree Bank.[5] The preparsing components have been further engineered over a number of years so as to perform accurately on the various kinds of phenomena found in naturally occurring text out in the wild beyond limited gold standards used in academic experiments, including structural intricacies of language use in social media and complex constructs in the financial genre.

Part-of-speech-tagged and shallow-chunked sentences are then processed by a deterministic, incremental, dependency parser [8,9]. Again, intensive feature engineering and generalization means that this parser performs quite accurately even when faced with text that is not very well behaved linguistically. The set of dependency relations used is compatible with those produced by the Stanford Parser [10] (and this is one possible output format) but internally they are further mapped to a richer set of dependencies based on the *Cambridge Grammar of the English Language* formalism and approach to the description of English [11].

2.3 OPINION METRICS

Using the output of the core NLP components described earlier, we generate, for each document, multidimensional opinion metrics for corporate announcements at multiple structural and syntactic levels that encompass (1) individual and aggregated noun phrases (cf. "entities," terms, keywords, key phrases), (2) syntactic relations between noun phrases, (3) sentences, and (4) documents.

2.4 INDEXING

Having generated the opinion metrics (see Section 3), we then index and time-stamp them for (1) each sentence, (2) each individual entity mention, and (3) the top n most salient sentiment relations between entities. Unlike partial aspect-level sentiment analysis approaches that are grounded on the interdependencies between opinion expressions and opinion targets and holders [12], we index all noun phrases detected in text. Exhaustive coverage is critical in our target domain because corporate announcements and unrestrained conversation around them involve not only explicit, subjective opinions (eg, *"Many regard the company's plan as overly optimistic"*) (often with explicit opinion holders or targets) but also implicit sentiment in the form of references to states of affairs and events in the world that have positive or negative connotations (eg, *"The company has appointed a new CEO"*) that can axiomatically cover an extremely diverse range of topics, among which implicit opinion holders and targets are not uncommon. The ranking function that is used to determine which sentiment relations are indexed takes into account raw frequencies, syntactic salience estimates that favor specific grammatical roles, extreme positive/negative sentiment distributions, and other factors.

2.5 REAL-TIME OPINION STREAMING

The resultant time-stamped data points are then aggregated into various temporal buckets at various resolution levels ranging from seconds to months that eventually render real-time opinion streams, each with multidimensional opinion metrics with which the end user can monitor specific corporate announcements and conversation around them. Typical practical use cases involve (1) querying the

---

[5]http://www.cis.upenn.edu/~treebank/home.html

streams with a specific time window and resolution; (2) searching the streams with full-text search; (3) filtering the streams to focus on specific opinion metrics (and ranges and combinations thereof); (4) sorting and manipulating query results to detect and visualize extreme values, peaks, troughs, outliers, and interesting (salient or frequent) noun phrases; (5) comparing opinion streams; and (6) piping the streams into external trading or other predictive models. The end user can also set up alerts for specific keyword occurrences and thresholded triggers for the opinion metrics.

3 MULTIDIMENSIONAL OPINION METRICS

In the context of corporate announcements, "sentiment" is an imprecise umbrella term for a very large number of both subjective and objective, and factual and nonfactual dimensions and topics that go beyond the typical distinction between *positive* versus *negative* evaluative polarity (cf. *good* vs. *bad*; *favorable* vs. *unfavorable*; *desirable* vs. *undesirable*; *thumbs up* vs. *thumbs down*; *one star* vs. *five stars*) that characterize what generic subjectivity classification, sentiment analysis, and opinion mining approaches [13–16] assume and focus on. In practical use cases in and around the finance industry, "sentiment" is taken to refer to any circumstances, states of affairs, dependencies, and events in the world that ultimate lead to *positive* financial performance (ie making money) versus *negative* financial performance (ie losing money) in some form [17]. In other words, financial sentiment expressions do not need to express an opinion but can describe or refer to some fact and still have an implied evaluative orientation (unlike, say, pure opinion statements in movie reviews). Financial sentiment therefore covers a vast range of extralinguistic factors such as the general market mood (*bullish* vs. *bearish*); recommendations for stocks (*buy* vs. *sell*); general stock *demand* versus *supply* levels; product *releases* vs. product *recalls*; *beating* versus *missing* expectations in earnings results or general performance; mergers, acquisitions, and takeovers (which can be *advantageous* or *disadvantageous* to a company); *securing* versus *losing* contracts; senior management changes and employee layoffs (*hiring* vs. *firing*); litigation (*guilty* vs. *not guilty*); overall state of the economy (*boom* vs. *recession*); governmental regulations and policies (*relaxed* vs. *tightened*); environmental issues; catastrophes; overall corporate reputation and trust image; and scandals.

It is evident that generic sentiment analysis is not in itself enough to fully capture distinctions of the above kind. We therefore argue that sentiment analysis of corporate announcements is best viewed and approached as a multidimensional task that goes beyond vanilla opinion-oriented sentiment analysis. Our system accordingly profiles corporate announcements and conversation around them with multidimensional opinion metrics that emerge from (1) fine-grained multilevel sentiment analysis, (2) affect analysis, (3) irrealis analysis, (4) comparative analysis, and (5) topic tagging, which we describe next.

3.1 FINE-GRAINED MULTILEVEL SENTIMENT

3.1.1 Compositional sentiment parsing

To capture and profile all topics, issues, and events related to a corporate announcement, exhaustive coverage is highly desirable. To achieve that, we parse each document with an exhaustive compositional multilevel sentiment parser [18] that assigns fine-grained sentiment distributions to all syntactic constituents in a sentence. The sentiment parser consults a sentiment grammar to compose sentiment recursively from word-level leaf nodes all the way to the sentence root, and hence generates, for each sentence, a stack of sentiment (sub)contexts with fine-grained distributions of all positive/

neutral/negative sentiment detected in them. Each composition step has access to information about lexical prior polarities, lexical sentiment reversal potential (eg, *none, decreasing*), lexical sentiment ambiguity potential (eg, two-way or three-way ambiguous sentiment carriers such as *crude, aggressive*, or *old*), morphosyntactic features, and compositional tendencies pertaining to the commonest syntactic constructions in English (reflecting the *Cambridge Grammar of the English Language* grammar [11]).

Although compositional sentiment parsing is relatively robust toward lexical sentiment ambiguity, domain dependency effects, and incomplete or fragmentary syntactic parses, we disambiguate specific frequent sentiment-ambiguous words and constructions with syntactic dependency predicates before sentiment composition. For example, in the genre of corporate announcements, the three-way ambiguous adjective *legal* can be disambiguated and asserted as negative when it acts as a prehead modifier to a noun such as *cost* or *challenge*, while the three-way ambiguous verb *beat* can be asserted as positive when it hosts as its direct object complement a noun phrase headed by a noun such as *analysts* or *street*.

3.1.2 Entity scoring

Once exhaustive compositional sentiment parses have been generated, we score each noun phrase using its weighted (sub)sentential sentiment distribution stack [19], and, for some specific predicators, lexical shallow-semantic entity frames [20,21].

Example 15.1 illustrates how entities in various contexts are scored by the entity scorer:

(15.1) a. *Apple stock* 86.4% negative | *results* 56.6% negative | *quarter* 87.9% negative |
   "*Apple stock is pretty flat in the wake of the results, hovering around the $100 mark in after-hours trading - with so many cuts by analysts after supply chain warnings earlier in the quarter, was the bad news already priced in?*"[6]

   b. *fulfillment costs* 100% negative | *company* 54.7% negative 45.3% positive | *logistics* 66% positive
   "*To Jeremy's point about fulfillment costs, that's a big problem for the company as it has worked to improve its fulfillment and logistics in recent years.*"[7]

   c. *fourth-quarter 2015 adjusted earnings* 63% negative 37% positive | *economic growth* 73.1% negative 26.9% positive | *mining and oil and gas industries* 75.5% negative
   "*Caterpillar's fourth-quarter 2015 adjusted earnings declined 45% to 74 cents per share, reflecting weakening economic growth primarily in developing countries, and ongoing weakness in mining and oil and gas industries.*"

3.1.3 Sentiment confidence estimation

Some end users and use cases require extremely high precision levels in the sentiment predictions even if that leads to reduced volume levels in the opinion streams. Increased precision can be achieved by suppression of sentiment predictions that the system regarded as more difficult in some way. To enable the end user to threshold the system's confidence in this regard, the sentiment parser provides a sentiment confidence estimate for each sentiment prediction it makes. In our case, confidence is not

[6]http://blogs.ft.com/tech-blog/liveblogs/2016-01-26
[7]http://blogs.marketwatch.com/thetell/2016/01/28/amazon-earnings-expected-to-show-record-holiday-quarter-live-blog

a typical probability measure against some underlying training data but rather is a direct estimation of the structural complexity, sentiment ambiguity, and error potential of a piece of text.

The ambiguity indicators used by the parser detect (1) three-way-ambiguous and two-way-ambiguous sentiment carriers (eg, *old*, *upturn*), (2) reversal operators (eg, *never*, *decreasing*), (3) unknown out-of-vocabulary words, and (4) complexity and saturation measures targeting various grammatical, morphosyntactic, and lexical dimensions. Example 15.2 illustrates how sentiment confidence estimates can be used to rank sentiment predictions for the end user:

(15.2) a. *conf*: 0.84 | *"Burge In Talks Over New Deal"*

b. *conf*: 0.64 | *"Reforms for state-owned companies including CITIC Group and Sinopec may fuel a rerating of state-owned entities, HSBC adds but cautions "we think a rally might be underway due to the cheap valuations but this is more likely to be a short-term rebound than a new cyclical bull market.""*

c. *conf*: 0.56 | *"Mr. Chu confirmed that he has no disagreement with the Board and there are no matters relating to his resignation that need to be brought to the attention of The Stock Exchange of Hong Kong Limited and the shareholders of the Company."*

3.1.4 Relational sentiment analysis

Exhaustive sentiment parses—fine-grained sentiment distributions assigned to all syntactic constituents and all entity noun phases in a sentence—have an added benefit in that they can be used as useful proxies for intrasentential relational entity sentiment analysis. Because they consider entity noun phrase pairs that are bridged syntactically, relational sentiment distributions are subtly different from those assigned to individual entity noun phrases. Sentiment relations allow the end user to keep track of specific aspects and features of a given corporation. Consider the sample sentence in Example 15.3 (nonpronominal entities in head noun and genitive subject-determiner positions underlined):

(15.3) *"The stable <u>outlook</u> reflects our <u>expectation</u> that @COMPANY@'s operating <u>performance</u> will be stable over the next 12–24 <u>months</u> and its financial <u>position</u> will not significantly weaken despite <u>difficulties</u> in the <u>Middle East</u>."*

Exhaustive, pairwise relational sentiment analysis across the entities in the sentence can be used to determine that most aspects of the company that the sentence is about are strongly or mostly positive but also that some negativity is implied. The relation *(outlook, expectation)* is strongly positive, *(outlook, position)* is slightly less positive, and *(performance, months)* is strongly positive; at the same time, a moderate amount of negativity exists in the relation *(outlook, Middle East)*, while *(difficulties, Middle East)* is strongly negative.

Instead of being presented with only one flat sentential sentiment score or scores for only some entities in the sentence, the end user can exploit deep sentiment relations of the above kind to formulate highly focused queries about a much greater number of aspects, facets, or features.

3.2 MULTIDIMENSIONAL AFFECT

Sentiment analysis can provide the end user with a holistic assessment of positive versus negative aspects of a corporate announcement. It does not, however, provide any signals pertaining to basic (primary) versus complex (secondary) emotions that go beyond positive versus negative evaluative polarity. Of the most commonly agreed on basic emotion categories and dimensions [22,23], two are particularly important in corporate announcements; namely, calmness versus agitation (cf. activity, potency, arousal) and fear. To enable the end user to detect emotion signals in the data streams, we enrich document-level and sentence-level sentiment predictions with multidimensional emotion scores that are provided by a shallow-compositional emotion tagger. The model provides fine-grained emotion scores along (1) bipolar (happy⟷sad; calm⟷uncalm; like⟷dislike) and (ii) unipolar (anger→; fear→; shame→; surprise→) emotion dimensions [22,23].

These seven dimensions are scored jointly and individually by a transition graph that is seeded with prior emotion weights assigned to each word. The weights are obtained from an emotion lexicon that specifies probabilistic weights for all likely emotion dimensions (or emotion senses) that a given word can have. The graph traverses through the text and considers all possible scopes and transitions across all emotion dimensions activated by the seeds detected in the text. The transitions are scored and disambiguated with weighted transducers that target specific emotion compositions that are specified in a calculus that has access to syntactic and linear temporal information. All emotion scores are provided as raw, unbounded values and as five normalized bands that mimic Kappa correlation levels—*weak* (0.0, 0.2), *fair* (0.2, 0.4), *moderate* (0.4, 0.6), *strong* (0.6, 0.8), and *extreme* (0.8, 1.0)—so that the end user can align the affect scores with other bounded opinion metrics, and Threshold the signals at a less granular level.

Example 15.4 illustrates the kinds of multidimensional affect signals that the end user can detect:

(15.4) a. calm: 0.428 | happy: 0.673 | like: 0.54
"*As the company's founder, Dorsey is likely to be afforded a respect and even reverence which an external appointment would need to work for.*"[8]

b. calm: −0.283 | fear: 0.98 | happy: −0.588 | like: −1.062 | sure: −0.444
"*However, @COMPANY@'s management believe that it is not a sign of the company making any mistakes or losing out to competitors, but rather that of general global slowdown in the industry and natural changes in their business model.*"

c. calm: 0.452 | fear: 0.512 | happy: −1.037 | like: −0.39 | sure: −0.451 | surprise: 0.166
"*Given the unexpected fall in @COMPANY@'s EBITDA and revenue in 2014 as compared to 2013, as well as the continuing bleak outlook for steel prices and seaborne iron ore price, there is worse to come in 2015...*"

3.3 IRREALIS MODALITY

The distinction between *realis* and *irrealis* mood plays a central role in the analysis of corporate announcements. Irrealis mood covers various forms of (1) speculation (cf. "*forward-looking language*" hedges, conditionals, wishes, predictions, forecasts, warnings), (2) intent (cf. plans), and (3) imperatives (commands), et cetera [24]. Irrealis signals allow the end user to explore, partition, and interpret sentiment and affect metrics in an even more flexible manner.

[8]http://europe.newsweek.com/twitters-new-ceo-five-challenges-facing-jack-dorsey-333956

We capture multiple irrealis types at the sentence level using finite-state taggers with rich hand-crafted shallow-semantic patterns over words and part-of-speech sequences [25]. The taggers detect three higher-level irrealis types (speculation, intent, and risk), as well as more specific subtypes such as speculation.prediction, speculation.conditional, intent.buy, intent.expand (a business), risk.estimate (failing estimates), and risk.legal.

Examples of prototypical irrealis signals present in many corporate announcements are shown in Example 15.5, together with the tags assigned by the taggers:

(15.5) a. *"The <u>stable outlook</u>"* speculation.prediction *reflects our <u>expectation</u>* speculation.prediction *that the* @COMPANY@*'s operating performance <u>will be stable</u>* speculation.prediction *over the <u>next 12–24 months</u>* speculation.future *and its financial position <u>will not significantly weaken</u>* speculation.prediction *despite high capital expenditure.*

b. *"<u>Liability claims</u>"* risk.legal *related to our products or our handling of hazardous materials <u>could damage</u>* speculation *our reputation and have a <u>material adverse effect</u>* risk *on our financial results.*

c. *"The <u>plan to merge</u>"* intent.merge *@COMPANY@ and @COMPANY@ <u>should lead to</u>* speculation.prediction *cost savings and <u>will result in</u>* speculation *a more balanced exposure in emerging markets.*

Although all irrealis expressions are highly informative and useful for the end user, the system needs to be particularly sensitive toward any and all negative signals and cues pertaining to uncertainties and risks as they are symptomatic of negative financial performance—one of the key signals analysts and the wider public look for in corporate announcements. To account for such interpretative sensitivity bias, we weight irrealis sentences that exhibit negative sentiment polarity by a very large amount in sentiment aggregation and suppress positive irrealis sentences by a moderate amount.

3.4 COMPARISONS

Corporate announcements typically contain price-sensitive comparative information about a company, its past, its competitors, and the market. Unlike approaches that approach sentiment and comparative constructions jointly [26] and hence pay less attention to noncomparative sentiment signals, we analyze the two dimensions separately so as to ensure exhaustive sentiment coverage and to offer more flexible queries for the end user.

We tag comparative sentences with finite-state taggers with rich hand-crafted shallow-semantic patterns over words and part-of-speech sequences. The taggers, which are functionally akin to the irrealis taggers described earlier, capture generic comparison expressions [27,28], as well as more detailed comparison subtypes such as comparison.money, comparison.time, and comparison.evaluation. Example 15.6 illustrates sample comparative expressions detected by the taggers:

(15.6) a. *"EBITDA amounted to € 60.3 million over the first nine months of 2014, up 3.2% <u>compared with a year earlier</u>"* comparison.time.

b. *"Landing Jack Dorsey as the permanent CEO is the <u>by far the best</u>"* comparison.evaluation *choice Twitter can make right now.*

c. *"Meanwhile, <u>higher revenues</u>"* comparison.money *and <u>lower net credit losses</u>* comparison.money *were offset by <u>higher operating expenses</u>* comparison.money *and a <u>higher effective tax rate</u>* comparison.money.

3.5 TOPIC TAGGING

The system lastly tags entity mentions, sentences, and documents with topic tags that reflect some desired classification and aggregation criteria; for example, tax, m&a, board_of_directors, or legal_issues. The topic tags serve two main purposes; namely, (1) to make it easier for the end user to query and filter the opinion streams at a higher conceptual or topical level and (2) to profile and summarize corporate announcements through aggregated sentiment and emotion predictions. Multiclass topic tagging is achieved with a classifier society with simple finite-state taggers alongside standard supervised learning architectures with trigram features. Because of the inherent variation in the actual topic tag sets used by different end users, the system exposes user-definable resources for both classifier types.

4 DISCUSSION

Whenever a publicly quoted company makes an official announcement, a series of events is triggered in its audience of analysts, traders, investors, other companies, the press, and the wider public. Seen from the point of view of the market, upstream financial performance cues in announcements—explicit and implicit evidence about the fitness, activities, circumstances, and prospects of a given company— are obviously of critical intrinsic importance. Seen from the point of view of a company that makes an announcement, it is equally essential to be able to capture the even greater variety of performance cues that abound in the (typically more subjective) extrinsic downstream public reaction around the announcement in the form of formal and informal discussions, analyses, recommendations, predictions, and speculation. Accordingly, the main goal of our real-time opinion streaming system is to enable companies to track, understand, quantify, and react to the ripple effects and chain reactions that official announcements trigger.

The core analytical tasks required for such a system pose many computational and practical challenges. Considering the range of topics, issues, and events that will ultimately surface in the ensuing downstream public commentary, and the way they are interpreted, it is evident that standard sentiment analysis is not enough to fully support the task and that it has to be augmented with other opinion metrics that touch on affect, irrealis modality, comparisons, general topics, and other related dimensions in language. Even though the affective "soft" metrics that are derived from such analyses can be rich and highly informative, many end users use them as a powerful complement to typical factual "hard" metrics (eg, raw volume of mentions, share price, volatility, number of followers, and number of retweets) to yield even richer signals. Accordingly, real-time opinion streaming is best viewed and approached as a holistic, multifaceted problem to which sentiment analysis provides an essential but partial solution.

Unlike in academic experiments and laboratory conditions, only some challenges pertain to the actual intrinsic classification and scoring accuracy of the underlying sentiment, affect, and other related core NLP analyses. On the one hand, rather broad relative[9] temporal changes tend to matter more than individual low-level data points to users who monitor high-volume and high-velocity opinion streams.

---

[9]Especially with bursty high-volume opinion streams, many end users merely monitor the relative ups (peaks) and downs (troughs) in the streams at a relatively superficial level until sudden relative changes (or alerts) catch their attention (colloquially referred to as *ocular regression*).

Such streams can in this sense exploit the boost and protection ("statistical whitewash") provided by large data distributions to mask many errors, anomalies, or biases in the underlying analyses (or in the raw streams themselves). On the other hand, low-volume opinion streams can expose individual data points, in which case intrinsic accuracy does matter greatly as even a handful of incorrect or anomalous analyses can skew the opinion streams and decrease the end user's confidence in the system.

This dichotomy means that an opinion streaming system needs to be able to support multiple users' unique precision-versus-recall criteria, preferences, requirements, and resources, all of which can change frequently in demanding real-world conditions. Such flexibility introduces a number of complications to the design of a real-time system, especially around core classifier architectures, resources, and data stream filters. Consider the upstream keyword filters described in Section 2.1 that play a major role in governing the usability of the entire system, for example. Despite their simplicity, Boolean filters offer a number of important practical benefits for the end user, which makes them preferable to more sophisticated data stream filtering methods that rely on supervised learning. Firstly, Boolean(-like) filtering rule definitions and resources from other systems, especially legacy ones, can be incorporated and reused easily. Secondly, most end users understand how to (re)configure and fine-tune them, which makes them easier and faster to debug, verify, maintain, and extend. Thirdly, because their matches are crisp, not probabilistic, Boolean filters are often easier to interpret than probabilistic predictions. Fourthly, they enable the end user to start opinion streams quickly without having to obtain training data for supervised learning, which is critical in the context of low-volume corporate announcements for which only few training examples might be available (either initially or eventually). Lastly, some users' desired keyword filtering criteria change so rapidly that supervised training data compilation activities simply become too cumbersome in practical terms.

There are many similar important practical requirements for the core sentiment analysis architecture. Compositional approaches to sentiment [17,29–32] offer, in general, a number of important benefits over flat classification methods in that (1) they are often relatively robust to ill-formed or ambiguous inputs due to compositional masking effects and basic support for scope phenomena; (2) non-learning-based compositional methods appear to be more resistant to domain dependency effects that can adversely affect flat approaches; (3) their predictions can be interpreted, verified, and debugged more easily and in a more structured manner (as full, exhaustive parse traces can be accessed), which is not the case with flat approaches; (4) their sentiment predictions can be fine-tuned directly to interpret sentiment in some desired manner (eg, stance, point of view) at multiple structural levels or for each individual user, which is, in general, harder to achieve with flat approaches without recourse to multiple models; (5) they can offer a uniform, linguistically sound, and coherent representation across multiple structural levels, again without recourse to multiple models; (6) they can deal with sentiment reversal phenomena in a more structured manner; and (7) their crisp, more deterministic output can, unlike statistical "black box" components, offer extra psychological, procedural, or legal reassurance to the end user that the system can in fact be controlled.

If sentiment (or some other form of) word sense disambiguation (see Section 3.1.1) is attempted, the availability of sufficient training data is likewise a major obstacle for supervised learning approaches to that task. Because there are multiple lexemes that need to be disambiguated, a very large amount of training data would be required collectively, even within a single domain. In this sense, more direct disambiguation mechanisms that target specific lexemes are simply more convenient than those that use supervised learning in practical terms.

Similarly, sentiment confidence estimates (see Section 3.1.3) can be obtained from vanilla probabilities stemming from supervised learning. Note, however, that a predictive probability score does not necessarily indicate how difficult a piece of text is with respect to sentiment ambiguity—unless a specific sentiment ambiguity scoring model has been trained for the said task. Moreover, simple probabilities run the risk of reflecting the distributions in their underlying training data too closely, which can lead to poorer generalization in practical cross-domain and cross-topic use.

Because the ultimate practical goal is to provide real-time feedback for the end user on a continuous basis, long(er)-term maintenance concerns cannot be ignored either. Any classifiers that exploit machine learning can become heavy in this regard as they introduce technical debt in various forms, such as interfaces (at data, component, and system levels), dependencies, feedback loops, changes in the external world, and system-level antipatterns in long-term use [33]. Although more direct non-learning-based approaches require maintenance as well, they tend to be easier and faster to update, verify, and maintain.

5 CONCLUSION

We have described a custom large-scale NLP pipeline that executes fine-grained multilevel compositional sentiment analysis, multidimensional affect analysis, irrealis modality detection, and other analyses that have been optimized to the financial domain. By combining sentiment analysis with other analytical dimensions, one can monitor, quantify, and estimate in real time the downstream ripple effects and chain events of corporate announcements and other related events across multiple data sources. The resultant affective "soft" metrics can provide rich price-sensitive feedback and information to companies and the wider market audience about how a company's announcement is interpreted and viewed in different contexts, what the public mood around it is, and how downstream conversation around it develops.

ACKNOWLEDGMENTS

We thank Simon Guest and David Morgan for their contribution to this chapter.

REFERENCES

[1] D. Bamman, N.A. Smith, Contextualized sarcasm detection on Twitter, in: Proceedings of the Ninth International Conference on Web and Social Media, 2015, pp. 574–577.

[2] F. Barbieri, H. Saggion, Modelling irony in Twitter, in: Proceedings of the Student Research Workshop at the 14th Conference of the European Chapter of the Association for Computational Linguistics, 2014, pp. 56–64.

[3] A. Reyes, P. Rosso, T. Veale, A multidimensional approach for detecting irony in Twitter, Lang. Resour. Eval. 47 (1) (2013) 239–268.

[4] R. Zhang, N. Liu, Recognizing humor on Twitter, in: Proceedings of the 23rd ACM International Conference on Conference on Information and Knowledge Management, 2014, pp. 889–898.

[5] R. Mihalcea, S. Pulman, Characterizing humour: an exploration of features in humorous texts, in: Computational Linguistics and Intelligent Text Processing, 2007 pp. 337–347.

[6] A. Qadir, E. Riloff, Learning emotion indicators from tweets: hashtags, hashtag patterns, and phrases, in: Proceedings of the 2014 Conference on Empirical Methods in Natural Language Processing, 2014, pp. 1203–1209.

[7] K. Gimpel, N. Schneider, B. O'Connor, D. Das, D. Mills, J. Eisenstein, M. Heilman, D. Yogatama, J. Flanigan, N.A. Smith, Part-of-speech tagging for Twitter: annotation, features, and experiments, in: Proceedings of the 49th Annual Meeting of the Association for Computational Linguistics: Human Language Technologies, 2011, pp. 42–47.

[8] J. Nivre, Algorithms for deterministic incremental dependency parsing, Comput. Linguist. 34 (4) (2008) 513–553.

[9] Y. Zhang, S. Clark, Syntactic processing using the generalized perceptron and beam search, Comput. Linguist. 37 (1) (2011) 105–151.

[10] M.-C. de Marneffe, B. MacCartney, C.D. Manning, Generating typed dependency parses from phrase structure parses, in: Proceedings of the Fifth International Conference on Language Resources and Evaluation, 2006, pp. 449–454.

[11] R. Huddleston, G.K. Pullum, The Cambridge Grammar of the English Language, Cambridge University Press, Cambridge, UK, 2002.

[12] G. Qiu, B. Liu, J. Bu, C. Chen, Opinion word expansion and target extraction through double propagation, Comput. Linguist. 37 (1) (2011) 9–27.

[13] B. Liu, Sentiment analysis and opinion mining, Synth. Lect. Hum. Lang. Technol. 5 (1) (2012) 1–167.

[14] B. Liu, Sentiment analysis and subjectivity, in: N. Indurkhya, F.J. Damerau (Eds.), Handbook of Natural Language Processing, second ed., CRC Press, Boca Raton, FL, 2010, pp. 627–666.

[15] B. Pang, L. Lee, Opinion mining and sentiment analysis, Found. Trends Inform. Retr. 2 (1–2) (2008) 1–135.

[16] J. Wiebe, T. Wilson, C. Cardie, Annotating expressions of opinions and emotions in language, Lang. Resour. Eval. 39 (2) (2005) 165–210.

[17] P. Malo, A. Sinha, P. Korhonen, J. Wallenius, P. Takala, Good debt or bad debt: detecting semantic orientations in economic texts, J. Assoc. Inform. Sci. Technol. 65 (4) (2014) 782–796.

[18] K. Moilanen, S. Pulman, Sentiment composition, in: Proceedings of the International Conference RANLP-2007, 2007, pp. 378–382.

[19] K. Moilanen, S. Pulman, Multi-entity sentiment scoring, in: Proceedings of the International Conference RANLP-2009, 2009, pp. 258–263.

[20] J. Ruppenhofer, I. Rehbein, Semantic frames as an anchor representation for sentiment analysis, in: Proceedings of the Third Workshop in Computational Approaches to Subjectivity and Sentiment Analysis, 2012, pp. 104–109.

[21] K. Reschke, P. Anand, Extracting contextual evaluativity, in: Proceedings of the Ninth International Conference on Computational Semantics, 2011, pp. 370–374.

[22] J.L. Tracy, D. Randles, Four models of basic emotions: a review of Ekman and Cordaro, Izard, Levenson, and Panksepp and Watt, Emot. Rev. 3 (4) (2011) 397–405.

[23] K.R. Scherer, What are emotions? And how can they be measured? Soc. Sci. Inform. 44 (4) (2005) 695–729.

[24] R. Morante, C. Sporleder, Modality and negation: an introduction to the special issue, Comput. Linguist. 38 (2) (2012) 223–260.

[25] E. Velldal, L. Øvrelid, J. Read, S. Oepen, Speculation and negation: rules, rankers, and the role of syntax, Comput. Linguist. 38 (2) (2012) 369–410.

[26] M. Ganapathibhotla, B. Liu, Mining opinions in comparative sentences, in: Proceedings of the 22nd International Conference on Computational Linguistics, 2008, pp. 241–248.

[27] N. Jindal, B. Liu, Mining comparative sentences and relations, in: Proceedings of 21st National Conference on Artificial Intelligence, 2006, pp. 1331–1336.

[28] W. Kessler, J. Kuhn, A corpus of comparisons in product reviews, in: Proceedings of the Ninth International Conference on Language Resources and Evaluation, 2014, pp. 2242–2248.

[29] L. Dong, F. Wei, S. Liu, M. Zhou, K. Xu, A statistical parsing framework for sentiment classification, Comput. Linguist. 41 (2) (2015) 293–336.

[30] R. Socher, A. Perelygin, J. Wu, J. Chuang, C.D. Manning, A. Ng, C. Potts, Recursive deep models for semantic compositionality over a sentiment Treebank, in: Proceedings of the 2013 Conference on Empirical Methods in Natural Language Processing, 2013, pp. 1631–1642.

[31] L. Polanyi, A. Zaenen, Contextual valence shifters, in: Exploring Attitude and Affect in Text: Theories and Applications. Papers from the 2004 AAAI Spring Symposium. Technical Report SS-04-07, 2006, pp. 106–111.

[32] T. Wilson, J. Wiebe, P. Hoffmann, Recognizing contextual polarity in phrase-level sentiment analysis, in: Proceedings of the Conference on Human Language Technology and Empirical Methods in Natural Language Processing, 2005, pp. 347–354.

[33] D. Sculley, G. Holt, D. Golovin, E. Davydov, T. Phillips, D. Ebner, V. Chaudhary, M. Young, J.-F. Crespo, D. Dennison, Hidden technical debt in machine learning systems, in: Advances in Neural Information Processing Systems 28, 2015, pp. 2494–2502.

CONCLUSION AND FUTURE DIRECTIONS

16

F.A. Pozzi[a], E. Fersini[b], E. Messina[b], B. Liu[c]

SAS Institute Srl, Milan, Italy[a] University of Milano-Bicocca, Milan, Italy[b] University of Illinois at Chicago, Chicago, IL, United States[c]

After reading this book your feeling is probably that sentiment analysis is highly challenging. And it is. Although the research community has attempted many subproblems and proposed a large number of solutions, none of the subproblems have been completely solved. The past decade has seen significant progress in both research into and applications of sentiment analysis. This is evident from the large number of start-ups and established companies that offer sentiment analysis services. There is a real and huge need in industry for such services because all businesses want to know how consumers perceive their products and services, and those of their competitors (ie, competitive intelligence). In the past, people asked their friends for advice and opinions related to any kind of topic, such as which restaurant is the best one in the city, or who they should vote for in the next elections. Nowadays, consumers want to know the opinions and experiences of other users on the web before purchasing products or services. Governments and private organizations are also showing strong interests in obtaining public opinion about their policies and their public image. These practical needs and the technical challenges will keep the sentiment analysis field vibrant and lively for years to come. Building on what has been done so far, we believe that two research directions are particularly promising.

First, there are many opportunities to design novel machine learning algorithms able to learn from large volumes of textual data and to extract domain-specific knowledge for decision-making purposes. In particular, taking into account that social networks are actually networked environments, the work of incorporating content and relationship information will likely be the core contribution of the next sentiment analysis approaches.

Second, the next generation of sentiment analysis systems should enable us to see the full spectrum of the problem. We believe that a holistic or integrated approach will likely be successful if it will be able to deal with all subproblems at the same time (eg, polarity, irony and sarcasm, opinion spam, and leader) because their interactions can help solve each individual subproblem. We are optimistic that the problem will be solved satisfactorily soon for widespread practical applications. However, we do believe that it is possible to devise effective semiautomated solutions. The key is to fully understand the whole range of issues and pitfalls, cleverly manage them, and determine which portions can be done automatically and which portions need human assistance. In the continuum between the fully manual solution and the fully automated solution, we can push more and more toward automation.

However, much remains to be done also in most of the topics discussed in this book. Linked data technologies are still not widely used by the computational linguistic and natural language processing communities. On the other hand, there is an increasing number of available datasets and an ongoing community effort that supports this approach. Despite these concerns, the increasing popularity of linked data technology and the availability of tools and resources are tremendous incentives for its adoption. Regarding the sentiment analysis community, the World Wide Web Consortium Linked Data Models for Sentiment and Emotion Analysis Community Group provides a suitable forum for fostering the adoption of linked data practices and the generation of interoperable sentiment language resources and services. One of the future directions is the development of business models for sentiment language resources.

Irony and sarcasm detection have been addressed as a text classification task. Salient features such as lexical marks are mainly used to characterize ironic and sarcastic utterances. As figurative language devices, irony and sarcasm need to be studied beyond the scope of the textual content of the utterance. In this regard, both the context in which utterances are expressed and common knowledge could be considered to identify the real intention behind an ironic or sarcastic expression. There are some attempts to take advantage of this kind of information. Besides, it is necessary to consider how affective and emotional content is implicitly embedded in irony and sarcasm. Some work in the literature has already started exploiting affective information by using sentiment and affective lexica. Further investigation is needed to develop approaches that could efficiently identify polarity shift and polarity reversal of ironic and sarcastic content.

Considering that there is a limited amount of research available for the problem of suggestion mining, there are many aspects that remain unexplored. Context-based features have not yet been employed for the classification task in suggestion mining, and the available datasets are still inadequate to train robust classifiers. When bigger datasets are available, deep learning methods could be effectively developed for this task. Finally, from a computational linguistics perspective, the study of suggestions deals with a variety of linguistic phenomena, specially moods and modality. Although there is a considerable amount of linguistic research available on modality, there have been very few investigations on computational approaches for the detection of linguistic moods in text. The focus on suggestion mining would also revive interest in the both semantic and the machine learning approaches toward mood and modality analysis.

Although many algorithms have been proposed to detect fake reviews, there is still a long way to go before we can weed out opinion spamming activities. There are many interesting research directions that have not been or have barely been explored. For example, it would be interesting to compare reviews of the same product across different websites to discover abnormalities; for example, similar reviews (contents or ratings) that are written at the same time, by people with similar user ids, and using the same (similar) IP address. Another important future direction could leverage the language inconsistency. To suit different products and to stress personal experiences, fake reviewers may write something that is inconsistent or against social norms in different reviews. Also, web use abnormality should be studied further. Web servers record almost everything that a person does on a website, which could be valuable for detecting fake reviews.

When addressing opinion leader detection, we should take into account exogenous variables. Even if solutions based on network structure and diffusion models are characterized by a high degree of generality, many recent methods have shifted toward trying to estimate the individual's intrinsic features, by considering the content produced, their observable relations, and their behavior on the net. A potentially promising development would be to correlate the models with external events that might influence the behavior of the individuals, or to use several sources of data to extract information on the same individual (eg, intersocial networks). Analyzing multimedia content in addition to text could also provide a better assessment of an individual's characteristics.

A final concern relates to the modalities of sentiment summarization and visualization. When the results of sentiment analysis tasks need to be presented to an end user, a corresponding level of uncertainty should be taken into account (uncertain results shown as certain may lead to incorrect conclusions). To tackle this problem, it is important to convey the degree of uncertainty to the user as auxiliary information. In this way, users can decide how confident they should be in the conclusions they are drawing from the data. While several techniques for visualizing uncertainty have been proposed in the generic information visualization literature, they have recently been applied to opinion visualization. A common approach to encode uncertainty could be the introduction of error bars to represent the confidence interval. Unfortunately, recent research shows that error bars have many drawbacks from the perceptual perspectives. New techniques such as gradient plots (use transparency in bars to encode uncertainty) and violin plots (use width) could be considered as alternatives to error bars. For text visualization, other visual attributes such as color hue, or saturation of the background, can be used for the encoding of uncertainty. Moreover, opinion visualization needs to deal with the challenges related to the massive amount of data. Unfortunately, most of the visualizations discussed would be inadequate to handle very large amounts of raw opinion data. To tackle such situations, data reduction methods such as filtering and sampling, and aggregation could be considered.

All that said, what made sentiment analysis a trending topic is the changing of the Web from read only to read-write. This evolution created enthusiastic users interacting with each other and sharing information through social networks. Despite the recent and significant progress, sentiment analysis is still finding its own voice as a new interdisciplinary field. Computer scientists, linguists, and social scientists could potentially make major contributions to the field and to society. This is the reason why we have asked them to contribute to this book. Future sentiment analysis systems need broader and deeper common and commonsense knowledge bases. More complete knowledge should be combined with reasoning methods inspired by human thought and grounded on sociological and psychology theories. This will lead to a better understanding of natural language opinions and will efficiently bridge the gap between (unstructured) multimodal information and (structured) machine-processable data. Blending scientific theories of emotions and sentiment with the practical engineering goals of analyzing natural language text could lead to more human-inspired approaches to the design of intelligent opinion-mining systems capable of handling semantic knowledge, detecting sarcasm, making analogies, and learning new affective knowledge to finally detect, perceive, and *feel* emotions.

Author Index

Note: Page numbers followed by *f* indicate figures, *t* indicate tables and *np* indicate footnote.

Subject Index

Note: Page numbers followed by *f* indicate figures and *t* indicate tables.